International Perspectives on Critical English Language Teacher Education

Critical Approaches and Innovations in Language Teacher Education
SERIES EDITOR: Bedrettin Yazan (University of Texas at San Antonio, USA)

The series is dedicated to advancing critical language teacher education research that can transform the dominant practices of language teaching in educational contexts around the world. Language education has become more important than ever, to facilitate the crossing of physical and ideological borders of nation-states, and to meet the needs of increasingly ethnically and linguistically diverse student populations. This series helps inform the preparation of resilient and agentive language teachers with critical social justice orientations. It presents state-of-the-art research to support the formation of teachers who identify as democratic, social agents of formal schooling, and devoted to improving learning experiences of marginalized students. The titles in this series appeal to language teachers, teacher educators, and researchers and can be used as educational materials in graduate and undergraduate studies.

ADVISORY BOARD
Darío Banegas (University of Edinburgh, UK)
Osman Barnawi (Royal Commission Colleges & Institutes, Saudi Arabia)
Yasemin Bayyurt (Bogaziçi University, Turkey)
Ester de Jong (University of Florida, USA)
Andy Xuesong Gao (University of New South Wales, Australia)
Icy Lee (Chinese University of Hong Kong, Hong Kong)
Gloria Park (Indiana University of Pennsylvania, USA)
Ingrid Piller (Macquarie University, New South Wales, Australia)
Richard Smith (University of Warwick, UK)
Zia Tajeddin (Tarbiat Modares University, Iran)

Forthcoming in the series:
Critical Autoethnography in Language Teacher Education, Bedrettin Yazan
Critical Dialogic TESOL Teacher Education: Preparing Future Advocates and Supporters of Multilingual Learners, edited by Fares J. Karam and Amanda Kibler
Language Teacher Education Beyond Borders: Multilingualism, Transculturalism, and Critical Approaches, edited by Fernando Zolin-Vesz, Dario Luis Banegas and Luciana C. de Oliveira
Language Teacher Education, edited by Fernando Zolin-Vesz, Dario Luis Banegas and Luciana C. de Oliveira
Teacher Education for Global Englishes Language Teaching, Denchai Prabjandee
Activism in Language Teaching and Language Teacher Education, edited by Amber N. Warren and Natalia A. Ward

International Perspectives on Critical English Language Teacher Education

Theory and Practice

Edited by Ali Fuad Selvi and Ceren Kocaman

BLOOMSBURY ACADEMIC
LONDON • NEW YORK • OXFORD • NEW DELHI • SYDNEY

BLOOMSBURY ACADEMIC
Bloomsbury Publishing Plc, 50 Bedford Square, London, WC1B 3DP, UK
Bloomsbury Publishing Inc, 1359 Broadway, New York, NY 10018, USA
Bloomsbury Publishing Ireland, 29 Earlsfort Terrace, Dublin 2, D02 AY28, Ireland

BLOOMSBURY, BLOOMSBURY ACADEMIC and the Diana logo are trademarks of
Bloomsbury Publishing Plc

First published in Great Britain 2024
Paperback edition published 2026

Copyright © Ali Fuad Selvi, Ceren Kocaman and Contributors, 2024, 2026

Ali Fuad Selvi, Ceren Kocaman and Contributors have asserted their right under the
Copyright, Designs and Patents Act, 1988, to be identified as Authors of this work.

Series design: Grace Ridge
Cover image © rudchenko and Anastasia Shemetova/iStock

All rights reserved. No part of this publication may be: i) reproduced or transmitted in any form, electronic or mechanical, including photocopying, recording or by means of any information storage or retrieval system without prior permission in writing from the publishers; or ii) used or reproduced in any way for the training, development or operation of artificial intelligence (AI) technologies, including generative AI technologies. The rights holders expressly reserve this publication from the text and data mining exception as per Article 4(3) of the Digital Single Market Directive (EU) 2019/790.

Bloomsbury Publishing Plc does not have any control over, or responsibility for, any third-party websites referred to or in this book. All internet addresses given in this book were correct at the time of going to press. The author and publisher regret any inconvenience caused if addresses have changed or sites have ceased to exist, but can accept no responsibility for any such changes.

A catalogue record for this book is available from the British Library.

Library of Congress Cataloging-in-Publication Data

Names: Selvi, Ali Fuad, editor. | Kocaman, Ceren, editor.
Title: International perspectives on critical English language teacher education : theory and practice / edited by Ali Fuad Selvi and Ceren Kocaman.
Description: London ; New York, NY : Bloomsbury Academic, 2024. | Series: Critical approaches and innovations in language teacher education | Includes bibliographical references and index.
Identifiers: LCCN 2023051005 (print) | LCCN 2023051006 (ebook) | ISBN 9781350400320 (hardback) | ISBN 9781350401938 (paperback) | ISBN 9781350400344 (epub) | ISBN 9781350400337 (ebook)
Subjects: LCSH: English teachers–Training of–Case studies. | English language–Study and teaching–Foreign speakers–Case studies. | Critical pedagogy–Case studies.
Classification: LCC PE1065 .I583 2024 (print) | LCC PE1065 (ebook) | DDC 428.0071–dc23/eng/20240129
LC record available at https://lccn.loc.gov/2023051005
LC ebook record available at https://lccn.loc.gov/2023051006

ISBN: HB: 978-1-3504-0032-0
      PB: 978-1-3504-0193-8
      ePDF: 978-1-3504-0033-7
      eBook: 978-1-3504-0034-4

Series: Critical Approaches and Innovations in Language Teacher Education

Typeset by Integra Software Services Pvt. Ltd.

For product safety related questions contact productsafety@bloomsbury.com.

To find out more about our authors and books visit www.bloomsbury.com
and sign up for our newsletters.

We dedicate this volume to all teachers and teacher educators who embody criticality and work tirelessly and fearlessly to create a more equitable, inclusive, and compassionate world as agents of change, and our families and friends who believed in and supported us throughout this project.

Contents

List of Figures	xii
List of Tables	xiii
Series Editor Foreword	xiv
Foreword	xviii
List of Abbreviations	xx

Part One Introduction

1 Introducing Criticality and Critical English Language Teacher Education: Tensions, Opportunities, and Possibilities *Ali Fuad Selvi and Ceren Kocaman* 3

Part Two Teaching Methods and Methodologies

2 Beyond Language Teaching Methods and Methodologies in Language Teacher Education *Graham Hall* 19
3 Challenging Standard Language Ideology and Promoting Critical Language Awareness in Teacher Education *John Chi and Kellie Rolstad* 27
4 Social Justice Language Teacher Education in Türkiye: Insights from an English as a Foreign Language (EFL) Writing Classroom *Adnan Yılmaz, Deniz Ortaçtepe Hart, and Rabia İrem Durmuş* 33
5 Cultivating a Language Teaching and Social Justice Praxis: Paying Attention to the Tension to Set Intention *Netta Avineri* 41

Part Three Instructional Materials Analysis and Development

6 Pedagogizing Critical Materials Analysis and Development *Yasemin Tezgiden-Cakcak* 51
7 Analyzing Instructional Materials: A Global Englishes Language Teaching (GELT) Activity in a Brazilian Context *Marcia Regina Pawlas Carazzai and Ana Raquel Fialho Ferreira Campos* 59
8 The Affirming Diversity Project: Supporting Teachers Creating and Exchanging Culturally and Linguistically Responsive Materials *Priscila Leal and Perla Barbosa* 65
9 Critical Antiracist Teacher Education: Insights from the Seminar "Racism and the English Language Teaching (ELT) Classroom" *Natalie Güllü* 71

Part Four Classroom Management, Observation, and Practicum

10 A Critical Perspective on Language Classroom Management, Classroom Observation, and the Practicum *David Gerlach* — 79
11 Critically Reflecting on Diversity and Learners' Needs: An Example from Aotearoa New Zealand *Karen Ashton* — 87
12 A Guide for Observing Community, School, and Classroom: Balancing Students' Lives and Language Policies *Alex Alves Egido* — 93
13 Developing Criticality through Professional Development with In-Service Language Teachers *Mareen Lüke* — 99
14 Achieving Social Justice in the English Classroom: Ideas to Introduce Queer Pedagogies to Pre-/In-service Teachers of English *Özge Güney* — 105

Part Five Second Language Assessment

15 Critical Language Teacher Education and Language Assessment *Seyyed-Abdolhamid Mirhosseini* — 113
16 Disrupting Assumptions in English Language Teaching (ELT) Assessment *Laura Loder Buechel* — 121

Part Six Curriculum Development

17 Reimagining Critical Language Teacher Education through Translanguaging and Transknowledging *Sunny Man Chu Lau and Angel M. Y. Lin* — 131
18 A Language-Based Approach to Content Instruction: Critical Reflections on Implementation in a Teaching English to Speakers of Other Languages (TESOL) Methods Course *Hillary Parkhouse, Luciana C. de Oliveira, and Jia Gui* — 141
19 Inquiry-Driven Reflection-in-Action Approach to Promote Culturally Responsive Literacy Practices through Teacher Education Projects *Wing Shuen Lau, Laura Humes Wahied, and Megan Kelley-Petersen* — 147

Part Seven Second Language Development

20 Unsettling Second Language Acquisition Theories through Raciolinguistic, Crip, and Translanguaging Perspectives *Clara Vaz Bauler and Gabriella Licata* — 155
21 Developing a Translanguaging Stance in Teacher Candidates via a Middle School and University-Based Teacher Education Program E-tutoring Partnership *Elizabeth Goulette* — 165

22 Exploring Language, Identity, Power, and Privilege with Secondary-Level EL Teachers: A Critical Language Awareness (CLA) Case Study *Shawna Shapiro* 171
23 Un-teaching Native Speaker Fallacy: A Practical Application and Discussion *Tan Arda Gedik* 179

Part Eight Teaching Young Language Learners

24 Teaching English to Young Learners: Critical, Multilingual, and Decolonial Pedagogies *Mario E. López-Gopar, Verónica Rivera Hernández, and Yesenia Bautista Ortiz* 187
25 Sustainability and Primary Teacher Education in a Swedish Context: From Concept Mapping to Experience Designing *Mai Trang Vu* 195
26 Working against the Monolingual Norms of Teaching English as a Foreign Language (TEFL) at the Primary School Level *Hanna Lämsä-Schmidt* 201

Part Nine Teaching Culture

27 Teaching Culture for Critical Global Citizenship *Britta Freitag-Hild* 209
28 Using Intercultural Virtual Exchange to Promote Critical Pedagogy Practices of English Language Teachers *Laura Torres-Zúñiga and Sibel Söğüt* 217
29 Critical Intercultural Education in Moroccan Teacher Education: Practical Insights for Teacher Candidates *Benachour Saidi and Rania Boustar* 223
30 Immigrant Families and Communities as Agents of Interculturality in Pre-Service Teacher Education *Roxanna Senyshyn* 229

Part Ten Global Englishes

31 Global Englishes: Pluricentricity of Norms, Benchmarks, Functions, and Contexts *Lili Cavalheiro* 239
32 Raising Pre-Service Teachers' Global Englishes Awareness through a Materials Development Project *Michelle Kunkel and Kenny Harsch* 247
33 A *Translingual Project* to Explore Multilingual Identity and Challenge Dominant Language Ideologies *Kristina B. Lewis* 253
34 Building Global Englishes into a Pre-Service Teacher Education Curriculum *Naashia Mohamed* 261

Afterword 267
List of Contributors 270
Index 280

Figures

4.1	The students' mind map on immigration and peacebuilding	35
4.2	The students' posters on immigration and peacebuilding	36
4.3	Cover page of the newsletter	37
16.1	Original task	124
16.2	Adapted task, L. Loder Buechel	125
16.3	Reading circle activity, final product	127
18.1	LACI's six Cs of support for scaffolding content area instruction for multilingual learners	142
20.1	Writing sample from a heritage student moved from introduction to Hispanic literature to Spanish 4 for second language learners	157
20.2	Letter to Tía written by Alexa Lil Borunda White and shared by Sonia Soltero on Twitter on August 20, 2022	160
22.1	Goals for CLA pedagogy	172
22.2	Principles for CLA pedagogy	172
28.1	Virtual exchange diversity and inclusion in our classrooms–tasks and timeline	219
29.1	Illustration of student teachers' product	226
33.1	Page 1 of Brooke's *Translingual Project*	255
33.2	Screenshot of Shweta's *Translingual Project*	256
33.3	Final slide of Jessica's *Translingual Project*	257
33.4	Pages 2 and 4 of Flora's *Translingual Project*	258

Tables

3.1	Overview of activities	31
9.1	Course syllabus	76
12.1	Constituting aspects of a problematizing practice	95
13.1	Overall structure of the program with its activities	100
16.1	Consolidation assignment 2022	126
19.1	U-ACT program core principles	148
19.2	Summary of findings	150
22.1	Overview of CLA fellows program	173
33.1	*Translingual Project* written reflection rubric	260

Series Editor Foreword

Critical Approaches and Innovations in Language Teacher Education

When I was preparing the initial proposal for this book series with Bloomsbury Academic, I was asked to justify why there should be a whole separate book series on critical and innovative language teacher education (LTE). The scholarly conversation on LTE has taken place in venues that have a broader scope and occurs in fields of applied linguistics, TESOL (Teaching English to Speakers of Other Languages), modern language education, or general teacher education. While this interdisciplinarity gives the field of LTE both scope and depth, at times it feels scattered across these various venues of scholarship. Thus, the first aim of this series was to curate and compile volumes centered around the common topic of LTE. The second aim in the series is to highlight the need in our field to focus on critical approaches to innovating LTE due to the ways that language (and therefore, language teaching) is intertwined with cycles of privilege and marginalization and power dynamics among speakers. I feel that this need to bring together scholarship that is critical and simultaneously innovative in nature has been clear to us as members of the research communities who are interested in studying policies, pedagogies, and practices of teacher education. Therefore, the inception of this series was timely.

With the generous support of the contributing authors, editors, editorial board members, and external peer reviewers, what I seek to accomplish with this series is to bring together colleagues from around the world to share their efforts in pedagogy-oriented research in LTE and extend the existing scholarly work further toward the direction of continued criticality and innovation in the interest of social justice. At the same time, practitioners and researchers of LTE can use the publications in this series, partly or fully, as resources in advancing their work.

The two significant constructs undergirding this book series are *criticality* and *innovation*, and their relationship therein. Ideally, *innovation*, or the process of engaging in continuous efforts to create new ways of supporting teachers and teacher educators at all phases of their careers in response to changing dynamics at their institutions and society in general, in LTE should contribute to teachers', teacher educators', researchers', and administrators' increasingly critical approaches to language teaching and learning. What I mean by *criticality* here are the combined efforts to address oppressive language ideologies that inform institutions' and people's stances, decisions, and actions, thus shaping their professional practices as educators writ large. Those language ideologies are never about "language" per se; they are always intertwined with ideologies of culture, nationality, race, ethnicity, gender, sexuality, and ableism, amongst others (see Kubota 2020; Motha 2014; Park 2017).

Very much contextually bound and situated, language ideologies operate invisibly and impact the activities within the scope of LTE at three interlocking layers (see Figure 1): language learning, language teaching, and language teacher education. To parse them out, at one layer, language ideologies influence how we understand the nature, acquisition, and use of language, which subsequently impacts our understanding of the identity positions hierarchically available for language users and learners (Pavlenko and Blackledge 2004). At another layer, we have ideologies that pertain to teaching languages and being language teachers, and the most salient of such ideologies being the monolingual fallacy, the "native" speaker fallacy, and the subtractive fallacy as discussed by Phillipson (2013). As examples, these three fallacies provide dichotomous identity positions for language teachers, reducing the nuance and complexity of teacher identity and essentializing what "good" teachers and teaching practices should be. At a third layer, we encounter ideologies about the formal preparation of language teachers, as well as what it means to become and grow as a language teacher within local educational contexts where economic and cultural globalization are variably accepted or opposed as national educational goals (Hawkins 2011). Those ideologies include the hierarchical positioning of certain academic content as superior to or more important than others based on or aligned with the standards or directives coming from governing bodies that manage the activities of teacher education (e.g., Higher Education Council in Türkiye, State legislative mandates on K-12 curriculum content in the United States). Such hierarchies are typically perpetuated through external high-stakes assessments which operate as gate-keeping mechanisms. Additionally, to reiterate their interconnected nature, ideologies of LTE also encompass the ideologies in circulation around language teaching which therefore also involve the ideologies around language learning and language use. Ideologically laden hierarchies, variably based on the sociopolitical context, define and confine what a language teacher educator is allowed and supposed to be, do, and feel when preparing teachers to work with language learners.

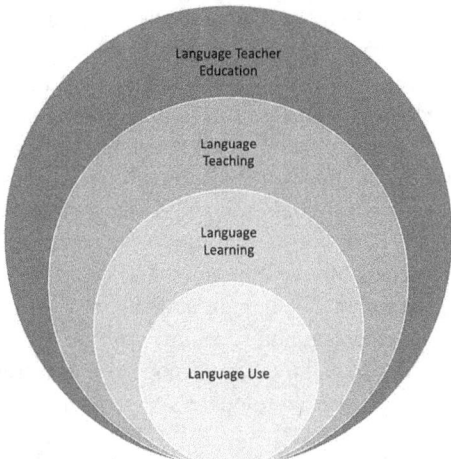

Figure 1 Ideologies in language teacher education.

In the last three decades, critical scholarship in our field (e.g., Canagarajah 2020; Norton and Toohey 2004; Pennycook 1999; Varghese et al. 2016) has called for persistent pushback against dominant language ideologies and the corresponding ways in which institutions and the people ultimately maintain the asymmetrical power relations in society. As the "mission" of LTE is to prepare language teachers (who experience varying degrees of privilege and marginalization) who are going to work with language learners (who also experience varying degrees of privilege and marginalization), LTE practices have strong potential to effect change in society. It is my hope that the scholarly work published in this series will contribute to that change in various educational contexts around the world. I suggest that we, as practitioners and researchers of LTE, keep in mind these two aspects of being critical: first, there are many ways of being critical and acting critically in our contexts and our practices, and identities that inform our criticality are situated at the intersection of personal, professional, and political dimensions of language learning, teaching, and teacher education (Rudolph 2022). Second, being critical requires us to keep critiquing our own criticality by self-reflexively questioning, reconsidering, and innovating our practices to address oppressive forces, uneven power relations, and systemic inequities that impact our efforts as teacher educators (Yazan 2023). Such reflexivity in which we engage and model for our students could also involve endeavors toward developing "political and ideological clarity" (Bartolomé 2004). This clarity includes identifying, problematizing, examining, and reflecting on our orientation vis-à-vis dominant ideologies to better understand the complex ways they operate and we construct our sociopolitically situated identities as language users, learners, teachers, and teacher educators.

Reviewed by peers at multiple stages of the process, this volume, edited by Ali Fuad Selvi and Ceren Kocaman, is another important publication in the book series and will make a great contribution to critical and innovative pedagogies and practices in English language teacher education. The editors bring together practitioners and scholars to share their research-based practices in teacher education classes that support teachers in engaging in critical praxis in the language classroom. They thematically organize the chapters around nine parts, ranging from Teaching Methods to Teaching Young Learners to Language Assessment to Global Englishes and each part is prefaced by theoretical considerations to prepare the reader for the remainder of chapters in that part. Its organization makes it suitable for English language teacher educators to pull the entire book or one part or one chapter to integrate in their course syllabi. As you keep reading this book, you will notice that the contributors from all around the world, as Ali Fuad and Ceren note, "convey criticality as a key quality of English language teachers/teacher educators, and critically oriented practices as a multi-relational, spatiotemporal, and multifaceted endeavor constantly reinventing itself in new ways of being, doing, and becoming with no endpoint" (p. 14). Ryuko Kubota, in her Afterword, also highlights the unique practical orientation of the book which "provide rich perspectives and resources for implementing critical approaches to language education in contextual ways" (p. 268). As a whole, this wonderful collection addresses a wide array of ideologies that impact language learning, use, teaching, and teacher education in various areas of English language education. It will push conversations around criticality toward multiple productive directions with practical applications in the LTE classroom, and captivate the reader from cover to cover with its high-quality content.

References

Bartolomé, L. I. (2004), "Critical Pedagogy and Teacher Education: Racializing Prospective Teachers", *Teacher Education Quarterly*, 31 (1): 97–122.
Canagarajah, A. S. (2020), *Transnational Literacy Autobiographies as Translingual Writing*, New York: Routledge.
Hawkins, M. R. (ed.) (2011), *Social Justice Language Teacher Education (Vol. 84)*, Bristol: Multilingual Matters.
Kubota, R. (2020). "Confronting Epistemological Racism, Decolonizing Scholarly Knowledge: Race and Gender in Applied Linguistics", *Applied Linguistics*, 41 (5): 712–32.
Motha, S. (2014), *Race, Empire, and English Language Teaching: Creating Responsible and Ethical Anti-racist Practice*, New York: Teachers College Press.
Norton, B. and K. Toohey (eds) (2004), *Critical Pedagogies and Language Learning*, Cambridge: Cambridge University Press.
Park, G. (2017), *Narratives of East Asian Women Teachers of English: Where Privilege Meets Marginalization*, Bristol: Multilingual Matters.
Pavlenko, A. and A. Blackledge (eds) (2004), *Negotiation of Identities in Multilingual Contexts*, Multilingual Matters.
Pennycook, A. (1999), "Introduction: Critical Approaches to TESOL", *TESOL Quarterly*, 33 (3): 329–48.
Phillipson, R. (2013), "TESOL Expertise in the Empire of English", *TESOL in Context*, 22 (2): 5–16.
Rudolph, N. (2022), "Narratives and Negotiations of Identity in Japan and Criticality in (English) Language Education: (Dis)Connections and Implications", *TESOL Quarterly*. Advance online. https://doi.org/10.1002/tesq.3150.
Varghese, M., S. Motha, J. Trent, G. Park and J. Reeves (eds) (2016), "Language Teacher Identity in Multilingual Settings", *TESOL Quarterly*, 50 (3): 545–71.
Yazan, B. (2023), "Being a Transnational Language Teacher Educator and Researcher: Borderlands, Ideologies, and Liminal Identities", in M. Gemignani, Y. Hernández-Albújar and J. Sládková (eds), *Migrant Scholars Researching Migration: Reflexivity, Subjectivity, and Biography in Research*, Oxon, New York: Routledge.

Foreword

Language teachers across the world appear to be under intense pressure to deliver learning results. Increasingly, due to neoliberal demands and globally circulated maxims that call for lifelong learning and future readiness, English language teachers in particular are expected to churn out proficient learners (Barnawi 2020) within amazingly short spans of time. Add restraints mediated by standardized curricula, and in the case of the United States, threats by legislators to withdraw public funding lest educational agendas are hijacked by what are deemed woke initiatives, it is not unsurprising that beleaguered teachers find themselves under academic siege. Deskilling teachers and having them deliver scripted instruction is not the solution, however.

Many across the educational spectrum from parents to politicians, principals to practitioners would probably agree that the knowledge base of pre-service and in-service teachers needs to be expanded (Yuan et al. 2022). The million-dollar question then, of course, is what areas of teacher education warrant attention. With respect to English language education, no one would dispute the importance of teaching the "hard" skills of reading, writing, speaking, listening, and grammar; these skills constitute the foundation of language education. But ostensibly "soft" skills such as critical multilingual language awareness (Mirhosseini and De Costa forthcoming; van Gorp and De Costa 2023) are equally crucial. And some would argue even far more valuable, especially in a day and age when both teachers and learners alike need to be aware of potential new threats on the horizon posed by AI, for example.

Now, more than ever, English educators need to center notions of identity, ideology, agency, empathy, and power in their instruction. Hence, as English teachers and teacher educators we enter this delicate dance where we need to balance the teaching of the latter (soft skills) with the former (hard skills). However, instead of seeing both skill sets as binary entities, it is vitally important that criticality be incorporated across the language curriculum and not reside in solitary units or modules of a singular course. For example, what we should be carefully considering is how can criticality be woven into writing instruction, while also taking into account the multimodal nature of learning and teaching. This is best achieved through having teacher engage in praxis, by merging theory with praxis. With praxis as a cornerstone to English language teacher education, this much-needed edited volume offers more than a menu of best practices. Rather, the insightful chapters in this book demonstrate how English educators can fold criticality into and across the ELT curriculum, be it from developing relevant instructional materials and subsequently analyzing these materials to fostering intercultural communication in the classroom. The contributors' commitment to decoloniality, anti-oppression, and educational justice is timely given the multiple biases (e.g., racism, monolingualism, nativism) embedded within ELT.

In sum, possibilities for transformative change within the ELT classroom and beyond abound in this volume, and I hope that you are equally excited and energized about this book as am I.

Peter De Costa
Michigan State University
East Lansing, Michigan
June 2023

References

Barnawi, O. (2020), *TESOL and The Cult of Speed in the Age of Neoliberal Mobility*, London: Routledge.

Mirhosseini, S. A. and P. I. De Costa (eds) (forthcoming), *Critical English Medium Instruction in Higher Education*, Cambridge: Cambridge University Press.

Van Gorp, K. and P. I. De Costa, (eds) (2023), "Developing Critical Multilingual Language Awareness from Pedagogical Stance to Research-Based Practices: Global Perspectives," *Language Awareness*, 32 (4).

Yuan, R., I. Lee and P. I. De Costa (2022), "TESOL Teacher Educators in Higher Education: A Review of Studies from 2010 to 2020", *Language Teaching*, 55 (4): 434–69.

Abbreviations

ACTFL	American Council for the Teaching of Foreign Languages
AIDS	Acquired Immunodeficiency Syndrome
BANA	British, Australasia and North American
BBC	British Broadcasting Corporation
CEET-H	Critical Education for English Teachers in Hesse
CELTE	Critical English Language Teacher Education
CLA	Critical Language Awareness
CLIL	Content and Language Integrated Learning
CLR	Culturally and Linguistically Responsive
COVID-19	Coronavirus Disease
EAL	English as an Additional Language
EFL	English as a Foreign Language
EIL	English as an International Language
EL	English Learner
ELA	English Language Arts
ELF	English as a Lingua Franca
ELL	English Language Learner
ELT	English Language Teaching
ELTE	English Language Teacher Education
ESD	Education for Sustainable Development
ESL	English as a Second Language
ESOL	English to Speakers of Other Languages
GE	Global Englishes
GELT	Global Englishes Language Teaching
ICC	Intercultural Communicative Competence

IELTS	International English Language Testing System
LACI	Language-Based Approach to Content Instruction
LGBTQ+	Lesbian, Gay, Bisexual, Transgender, Queer/Questioning, and more
LTE	Language Teacher Education
MCE	Multicultural Education
ML	Multilingual Learner
NNEST	Non-native English-speaking Teacher
NNS	Non-native Speaker
NS	Native Speaker
PARSNIP	Politics, Alcohol, Religion, Sex, Narcotics, Isms and Pork
SJELT	Social Justice in English Language Teaching
SJLTE	Social Justice in Language Teacher Education
SLA	Second Language Acquisition
TC	Teacher Candidate
TEFL	Teaching English as a Foreign Language
TEIL	Teaching English as an International Language
TEP	Teacher Education Program
TESOL	Teaching English to Speakers of Other Languages
TEYL	Teaching English to Young Learners
TOEFL	Test of English as a Foreign Language
U-ACT	University-Accelerated Certification for Teacher
WE	World Englishes
WWF	World Wildlife Fund

Part One

Introduction

1

Introducing Criticality and Critical English Language Teacher Education: Tensions, Opportunities, and Possibilities

Ali Fuad Selvi and Ceren Kocaman

Introduction

Living today means facing the insurmountable scourge of social, cultural, economic, and environmental issues such as systemic racism, segregation, gun violence, global climate change, wars, (forced) migration, economic recessions, income inequality, access to education, food, housing and healthcare, rampant xenophobia, homo-/bi-/trans-phobia, Islamophobic/anti-Semitic sentiments, ultra-right-wing authoritarianism, and fake news/post-truth politics, just to name a few. Being a teacher today means trying to respond to the pervasive crises that permeate into our lives, identities, classrooms, and practices as a member of the structure that has historically reproduced oppressive power relations, hierarchies, and inequalities. At this seemingly paradoxical yet critical nexus, language (and therefore English Language Teaching [ELT] professionals) has a crucial role as a powerful tool for reflecting on, reifying, dismantling, and constructing discourses around these social inequalities. In response, the notion of "criticality" has emerged as a stance toward discriminatory practices in and beyond the classroom, a theoretical lens and methodological apparatus in making inequalities visible through research as well as a skill set in teacher education and professional development contexts. We find criticality in our field today within various paradigms that facilitate the understanding, problematizing, and transforming of classrooms and research practices—critical pedagogy in ELT (Crookes 2013), queer pedagogy (Paiz 2020), raciolinguistics (Rosa and Flores 2017), critical antiracist pedagogies (Kubota 2021), decolonization/decoloniality as pedagogy (Canagarajah 2023), translanguaging as a decolonizing project (Wei and García 2022), and Global Englishes Language Teaching (GELT, Rose and Galloway 2019). The common denominator of these critical approaches lies in their attempts at promoting more linguistic equity, diversity, and representation, identifying unequal power relations and injustices, problematizing, interrogating, destabilizing, and deconstructing taken-for-granted values, beliefs, practices, and assumptions about language teaching, learning and learners, and finally transforming societies and the language teaching and research practices therein.

Building upon this preamble, we believe and argue that English language teacher education (ELTE), both at pre- and in-service levels, necessitates a critical turn to equip teachers with the knowledge, skills, and attitudes required to become critical agents for change in ELT. Built upon the Freirean notion of critical "praxis," or the symbiotic relationship between "action and reflection upon the world in order to change it" (hooks 1994: 14), as a guiding principle, this volume aims to contribute to the critical turn by showcasing the work that supports ELTE and its transformative mission (Hawkins and Norton 2009; Hawkins 2011). Within the scope of this project, we define critical ELTE as a praxis-oriented approach to the values, beliefs, knowledge base, skills, and identities in teacher education with an ultimate motivation to interrogate and transform the sociocultural and sociopolitical dimension of language teaching and learning. Grounded in Freirean principles of critical pedagogy, this approach has an explicit focus on challenging normative beliefs, power structures, and related practices to make privileged languages and identities visible and seeks to prioritize the voices and experiences of marginalized groups and non-Western and Global South(ern) epistemologies to contribute to the empowerment of those who have been and are still being, othered, marginalized, and erased.

In constructing this project, we purposefully adopted the term "criticality" as a core value, scholarly practice, and conceptual lens in understanding ELTE today and envisioning it for the future. More specifically, we operationalize "criticality" as a dynamic construct affording educators to question, resist against, problematize, and transform values, beliefs, identities, practices, and systems that are often codified into institutionalized systems, exacerbating asymmetrical power relations and enacted in everyday practices in the name of ELT and teacher education. For this reason, criticality is both a recursive process (of being and becoming) and a never-ending goal (of being a critical educator). What lies at the heart of this process is the notion of praxis, which entails not only a commitment to a heightened sense of awareness, referred to as conscientização (Freire 1970), but also a critical and transformative responsiveness to practice at the social, cultural, educational, and political levels.

We also conceptualize this project and the volume in your hands or on your screens as an artifact of imagination of ELTE practices toward envisioning a world in which social justice and pluralism are prioritized and inequities and inequalities are minimized. Therefore, we feel an ethical obligation to elaborate on the key premises guiding our thinking and actions. First, we believe that language is not a neutral tool for communication, but rather a complex sociocultural phenomenon shaped by (often asymmetrical) power relations. It has an indispensable role in constructing, projecting, and negotiating social identities and therefore, reifying and extrapolating social hierarchies. By proxy, language teaching and teacher education cannot be thought of independently from the broader sociopolitical contexts in which they take place. Second, we recognize the critical role, importance, and influence that teachers have on their students' social, linguistic, and cultural identities. Rather than seeing teachers as neutral transmitters of knowledge depositing decontextualized knowledge into their students as objects, critiqued in Freire's (1970) banking model of education, we recognize them as active participants and mediators in the process of meaning-making through dialogue, critical consciousness, and a more democratic relationship. As a corollary, English language teachers must develop a stance, awareness, and skill set to critically examine the values, discourses, and ideologies that underpin language uses, users, functions, and contexts and to challenge and transform narratives that perpetuate social inequalities. In a superdiverse world characterized by the global spread of English as a lingua franca and the increased visibility of diverse ethnolinguistic, gender, and racial identities (among others) in trans-lingual/-national/-cultural encounters, this understanding becomes an exigent issue for English language teachers and teacher educators. Third, we argue that language education (and thereby language teacher education) should always be critical, transformative, and empowering. That is, language teachers play an agentive and indispensable role in creating learning environments conducive to the development of critical stance, consciousness, and skills to question the dominant discourses and to develop their own voices and perspectives. We believe this is an example of language education for social change and transformation. Collectively, critical ELTE represents a transformative approach to LTE that seeks to offer teachers/teacher learners (both at pre- and in-service levels) a critical stance, identity, and skill set to understand, examine, challenge, and transform the sociopolitical dimension of language teaching and learning.

In This Volume: Looking Around

This volume brings together both theoretical contributions and practical ideas for pre- and in-service teacher education and professional development contexts, aiming to critically contribute to teachers' knowledge base on methods and methodologies, materials, classroom management and observations, assessment, language development, and curriculum as well as content and learner-related issues such as teaching culture, linguistic variety, and teaching young learners. To realize our overarching goals in this project and to create spaces of critical praxization, we made the following strategic decisions forming the architecture of this volume:

- a selection of parts that can be readily integrated into many ELTE programs around the world (pre-service) and continuous professional development seminars (in-service),
- individual parts opened with theoretical discussions providing an overview of critical issues on ELT/teacher education and complemented by practical applications chapters offering practical ideas that extend and expand criticality within teacher education programs at pre- and in-service levels,
- brief, concise, accessible, and resourceful texts supported by critical reflections and artifacts (e.g., lesson plans, work samples, and assignment guidelines) whenever possible,
- a diverse collection of contributing authors from various ethnolinguistic backgrounds, geographical contexts, and professional realities showcasing how they approach and reconceptualize ELTE with a critical lens.

Collectively, we conceptualize the current volume as a point of entry or a network of leverage for critical praxis permeating through epistemologies (theoretical ideas and discussions showcased in/generated by the book), humans (teacher educators and teacher learners they work with), systems (programs, courses, modules, and seminars), and practices (enacted by artifacts, projects, assignments, spaces, and discussions). Informed by their contextual dynamics and distilled through their insights and local(ized) practices working closely with teachers/teacher learners in diverse communities, contributors of this volume showcase spaces of engagement, reflection, and resistance against the hegemony that plague various aspects that constitute the knowledge base in ELTE. In the remainder of the chapter, we would like to introduce an overview of individual parts and the contributions therein.

Teaching Methods and Methodologies

Methods and methodologies have traditionally been the backbones of the ELT practice and thereby constitute an omnipresent feature of teacher education programs around the world. Parallel to the growing recognition that language teaching comprises more than decontextualized, universalized and essentialized skills, methods, and techniques, a critical turn in methods/methodologies in LTE is more relevant than ever. **Graham Hall** opens this part with his theoretical considerations chapter by drawing parallels between the move from methods to post-method in the language classroom and from top-down practices in teacher education to the acknowledgment of teachers' own knowledge. He builds a case for why teacher educators should reimagine language teaching methods critically so that there is a stronger focus on teachers as knowledge producers and experts of their local contexts, who can respond to (multilingual) learners' needs. Advancing this mission, **John Chi and Kellie Rolstad**, in their US local teacher education context, engage in humanizing pedagogy and use Critical Language Awareness (CLA) as their critical approach to resist one-size-fits-all teaching methods and instead, explore ways to recognize linguistic variety not only in teacher education contexts but also in the language classroom. Along the same lines, **Adnan Yılmaz, Deniz Ortaçtepe Hart,** and **Rabia İrem Durmuş** showcase how social responsibility projects can be used as a method in the language classroom. In the project they have conducted in Türkiye, pre-service teachers learn how to integrate social justice issues into their instruction, thereby going beyond traditional understandings of methods and methodologies. Finally, **Netta Avineri**, in a US context that prioritizes the exploration of critical topics in relation to pre-service teachers' experiences, perspectives, and goals, shares several activities that strengthen teachers' methodological toolkit by cultivating social justice praxis.

Instructional Materials Analysis and Development

Regardless of context and content, instructional materials play an indispensable role not only as resources supporting pedagogical practices but also as value-laden ideological artifacts constructing a worldview for learners. This prominent realization embodies an ethical and professional responsibility for language educators to critically examine instructional materials as both contexts and tools for reifying categories of identities (e.g., gender, sexuality, class, language, and religion) as well as carrying (often normative) meanings around social injustices, politics, and various forms of racialization/racism. In the opening chapter of this part, **Yasemin Tezgiden-Cakcak** contextualizes the discussion in the epoch of neoliberalism (promoting marketability over the needs/interests of learners) in which teachers' agency, professional expertise, and involvement in decision-making on material selection are ignored, silenced, and limited. She argues that a critical approach to instructional materials is a pressing issue for language teachers who strive to create more inclusive and equitable learning environments for learners. **Marcia Regina Pawlas Carazzai** and **Ana Raquel Fialho Ferreira Campos** showcase how they utilize Global Englishes as a framework to critically examine and resist the linguistic, methodological, and ideological practices in the coursebooks used in the Brazilian context. **Priscila Leal** and **Perla Barbosa** extend this mission by drawing upon The Affirming Diversity Project—a collaborative project in New Mexico and Hawai'i (United States) aiming to foster the design, development, and exchange of effective culturally and linguistically responsive teaching materials for multilingual learners. **Natalie Güllü** complements the discussions in this part by showcasing how a critical antiracist perspective (Kubota 2021) could be used to critically analyze racist knowledge and practices prevalent in society and textbooks in Germany.

Classroom Management, Observation, and Practicum

Managing, observing, and practicing effective instruction are highly valued in teacher education programs but largely based on uncritical methods that fail to adequately prepare teachers for the complex dynamics and realities of diverse classrooms. Effective classroom management is often rooted in behavioristic models prioritizing control, subordinance, compliance, and surveillance. Observation practices often ignore issues of bias, subjectivity, and asymmetrical power relations in the classroom. Practicum experiences fail to provide teacher learners' apprenticeship and their quest to address the challenges of the language classroom as effective educators. In the opening chapter of this part, **David Gerlach** offers unique insights into the strategic use of power as a critical lens in reframing the unequal relationships between teachers and students, teacher educators and teacher candidates, as well as teacher trainers/mentors and trainees/mentees and in promoting the reflective competencies of teachers as part of their identity development. Building on Farrell's (2022) five-stage framework for reflective practice, **Karen Ashton** showcases the role of reflection in supporting teachers' self-observations and classroom management practices for diverse learners in Aotearoa New Zealand. **Alex Alves Egido** describes the details of a reflective guide (consisting of five sections—(i) context, (ii) educational principles, (iii) students' lives and languages, (iv) educator's performance, and (v) social and ethical responsibilities) designed for in-service English language teachers in the context of Brazil as they negotiate macro-level language policies and micro-level language teaching practices on an everyday basis. Drawing from a series of workshops designed as part of a practicum for in-service English language teachers in Germany, **Mareen Lüke** offers criticality as a lens to become aware of, negotiate, and respond to the structural challenges in schools through their teaching practices. **Özge Güney** showcases her work with pre-service English language teachers in Türkiye who were completing their internship at the time, demonstrating how queer pedagogy can support the creation of a safe and inclusive classroom environment for all learners, as well as promoting dialogue and respect.

Second Language Assessment

Ranging from being an essential source of feedback on language learners' development of language proficiency to evaluating program effectiveness, language assessment plays a variety of important roles and functions in ELT. Despite the recognized importance, the field of language assessment is currently under the pressure of the dominance of standardized testing (narrowing the curriculum, teaching to the test, reducing language proficiency to discrete language skills), incompatibility with the sociocultural context of language use (leading to biased and unfair assessment practices exacerbating existing social inequalities), and inability to align language proficiency with complex, dynamic, translingual/transcultural language use (perpetuating standard[ized] language uses, users, functions, contexts, and ideologies). Therefore, a critical approach to language assessment, as a linguistic construct, educational practice, and a frame of reference used to define communicative success, the effectiveness of instruction/instruction, and decision-making, is imperative for all stakeholders in ELT. In the opening theoretical considerations chapter of this part, **Seyyed-Abdolhamid Mirhosseini** offers a forceful critique problematizing language assessment practice, including the assumptions behind psychometric testing, the notion of idealized "native speaker" standards, the sociopolitical dimensions of international tests/testing, and the interplay between language ownership and language assessment. **Laura Loder Buechel** illustrates how she uses a series of tasks as part of an independent-study unit that she developed for pre-service public school English language teachers in Switzerland with a motivation to disrupt and transform their thinking about and planning for assessment.

Curriculum Development

In the most traditional and technical sense, a curriculum is broadly seen as a framework organizing teaching and learning activities and technical specifications therein, such as the scope and sequence of instruction, instructional units/plans, pedagogical resources, and assessment practices. However, each component encapsulates values, beliefs, norms, roles, and attitudes at the individual and societal levels. In this regard, it may be seen as ideological parameters governing the teaching-learning process (as well as teachers and learners) and the role of education in the larger world. Therefore, a critical approach to the curriculum (as well as its development, evaluation, design, and innovation) entails an agentive engagement with and response to curricula, a strategic utilization for transformation or resistance against unequal power relations and normative ways of being and becoming. In their opening chapter, **Sunny Man Chu Lau** and **Angel M. Y. Lin** offer a compelling discussion as to how the recent paradigmatic shifts in applied linguistics, namely, the "trans-" turn (Hawkins and Mori 2018) and the decoloniality-informed onto-epistemological critique of the Anglo/Eurocentric (Kubota 2019) spur criticality by in(forming) teachers' decisions about curricular design, development, and evaluation in ELT. **Hillary Parkhouse, Luciana C. de Oliveira,** and **Jia Gui** showcase how content-area teachers (e.g., mathematics, science, social studies, English language arts, music, and art) in the US context can utilize the language-based approach to content instruction (LACI) (de Oliveira 2016) to design a curriculum that enables multilingual learners to engage in the learning activities and excel both in their respective content area and the English language. **Wing Shuen Lau, Laura Humes Wahied,** and **Megan Kelley-Petersen** describe the details of their capstone project and action research project in the United States as a sustainable example supporting teacher learners' development of culturally responsive literacy practices that support students' critical literacies and various identity work skills.

Second Language Development

Our traditional understandings of language, language uses, users, functions, contexts, and teaching-learning as transnational/transcultural communicative encounters in a superdiverse world have been going through a diverse, dynamic, hybrid, and fluid broadening and reconceptualization in recent years. Bringing the focus on language as lived experiences and taking into account the complex sociopolitical realities that shape our understanding of language learning, who language learners are and what constitutes language learning, to begin with, **Clara Vaz Bauler** and **Gabriella Licata** unsettle SLA theories through raciolinguistic, crip, and translanguaging perspectives. They explore the historical aspects that contribute to the naturalized and habitual ways in which language development is understood, and in their critique, center humanity and socially-oriented stances to languaging and identity. How this unsettling looks in practice is showcased by **Elizabeth Goulette** in an e-tutoring partnership between a middle school and a Liberal Arts university in the United States, where the teacher education course was redesigned to promote a translanguaging stance (Aleksić and García 2022) to the benefit of both the Spanish-speaking eighth graders enrolled in an ESL program and the teacher candidates taking the course. **Shawna Shapiro** presents another US university-school partnership that focuses on CLA in moving beyond traditional conceptualizations of language as consisting of structural and functional knowledge and instead, promoting a deep understanding of how language, identity, power, and privilege intersect. Finally, **Tan Arda Gedik** dismantles the native speaker fallacy in an activity that focuses on highlighting individual differences in L1 acquisition, arguing that native speakers do not uniformly converge on the same grammar.

Teaching Young Language Learners

The widespread belief that criticality is a deep, complex, and highly abstract reasoning skill reserved exclusively for adults is often used as a justification to perceive young learners as not capable of engaging in criticality and embellish teaching with rote memorization, repetitive drills, and isolated language skills. On the other end of the spectrum, a critical orientation means cultivating young learners' natural curiosity and analytical skills as individuals who can interpret and navigate the increasingly complex world around them and question biases/stereotypes, challenge injustices, and embrace diversities therein. Shifting the focus from "how" young learners should be taught to "why," **Mario E. López-Gopar, Verónica Rivera Hernández**, and **Yesenia Bautista Ortiz** introduce the part with a compelling discussion on the proliferation of ELT in public elementary schools under the guise of neoliberal discourses of economic development, which, in turn, prioritizes the teaching and learning of English as an additional language instead of othered Indigenous and/or minoritized languages and epistemologies. **Mai Trang Vu** brings an example of how Education for Sustainable Development (ESD) and drama-based instruction has been incorporated into a TEYL curriculum in a Swedish university to promote experiential learning and critical thinking in the English language classroom. The importance of recognizing young learners' multilingualism and their full linguistic repertoire is the focal point of **Hanna Lämsä-Schmidt**'s contribution from Germany. The teacher candidates in her seminar critically reflect on monolingual ideologies as well as multilingual competence to later plan a microteaching session that integrates a multilingual approach in teaching young learners.

Teaching Culture

Despite the omnipresent popularity of the term "intercultural communication" as an essential skill for language teachers, interculturality is often treated superficially, reduced to individual-level (mis)understanding of cultural differences/conflicts based on nation-state formulations of culture, perpetuating power imbalances and hegemonies, and reducing complexities within and across cultures. Therefore, a critical approach to intercultural communication contextualizes the phenomenon within socioeconomic and political realities both past and present (e.g., globalization, colonialism, power relations), interrogates Western cultural narratives/frameworks as the default option in interactions, and resists any possible cultural hegemony through English as the lingua franca. Recognizing teachers as critical agents with transformative power, **Britta Freitag-Hild** introduces culture pedagogy as a critical and transformative framework affording teachers' conceptualizations, decisions, and organizations of language learning environments conducive to cultural awareness and negotiations of meaning-making through language use. **Laura Torres-Zúñiga** and **Sibel Söğüt** share how they worked with in-service foreign language and content area teachers across Europe in a virtual, collaborative exchange project that aims to promote inclusivity and intercultural competence as integral skills toward being reflective practitioners. Complementing the discussion with insights from an intercultural communication workshop designed for pre-service English language teachers in Morocco, **Benachour Saidi** and **Rania Boustar** highlight the importance of embracing criticality both in developing a self-reflexive positionality in intercultural communication and in constructing a nuanced enactment of culture and interculturality. **Roxanna Senyshyn** exemplifies how a community-based inquiry project grounded in immigrant communities through interpretive and critical stances promotes the nuanced understandings and intercultural developments of pre-service teacher learners in the US context.

Global Englishes

A critical examination of the current policies, discourses, ideologies, narratives, and practices surrounding "traditional" ELT is more imminent than ever (Selvi, Galloway and Rose 2023). For this reason, critically-oriented scholars offered the Global Englishes (GE) framework as a way to celebrate the global linguistic diversity (of uses, users, varieties, functions, and contexts), challenge the "standard" English perpetuating linguistic imperialism, and dismantle dominant ideologies that eradicate linguistic justice, diversity, and inclusivity. In the opening chapter of this part, **Lili Cavalheiro** establishes the connection between the pluricentricity of norms, benchmarks, functions, and contexts and teacher competencies with the ultimate goal of enhancing language learners' mutual understanding and negotiations of the self and the other in transnational/transcultural encounters. **Michelle Kunkel** and **Kenny Harsch** describe their work with pre-service teachers in the US context and how GELT is used as a powerful framework for shaping decisions around their pedagogy, assessment, and instructional materials. Reporting from a similar context, in **Kristina B. Lewis**'s contribution, GE serves as a bridge of reflection and praxization between teacher learners' past histories and future trajectories as language users and teachers navigating within and across various discourse communities, language varieties, and language ideologies. In the closing chapter of this part, **Naashia Mohamed** reports on her undergraduate class in New Zealand and discusses the critical role that the Global Englishes paradigm plays in pre-service language teachers' personal/professional identity negotiations and deliberations as legitimate users/teachers of English.

The Afterword written by **Ryuko Kubota** serves as a concluding reflection extending the conversations and discussions offered throughout the volume and sets the direction for the future of critical ELTE as a fertile and promising line of inquiry. Distilled through her critical insights, experience, and expertise, her discussion recognizes teacher educators as active agents in constructing a better world and attests to the infiniteness of the potential and possibilities of critical ELTE defined as a decolonial, anti-oppressive, and justice-oriented endeavor.

A Critical Self-Reflexive Account: Looking Back, Looking Ahead

As teacher educators who call for criticality in thoughts, words, and deeds, we end the introduction for this volume with our self-reflexive account of our motivations that brought us to this project and takeaways from working with critical practitioners as part of this project. To recap, our overarching goals in this volume were as follows:

- recognizing the potential of teacher education as a space, context, and process of criticality,
- creating a praxization space as a leverage for the enactment of criticality as a stance, identity, and skillset,
- incorporating criticality into the fundamental aspects and practices of the knowledge base of English language teacher educators,
- presenting a myriad of contributions that highlight diverse voices, experiences, and realities of teachers/teacher educators, and
- offering a meaningful contribution for both teacher educators and teacher learners at pre-/in-service levels.

As we conclude this project and begin to contemplate upon new ones, we would like to share our reflections gleaned from this experience:

On How Criticality Manifests Itself in Teacher Education Curricula

- While there is a considerable emphasis, attention, and interest on teacher education at pre- and in-service levels, they often lack an explicit critical focus and orientation. Even though critically-oriented teacher educators and teacher education practices exist, they are often dispersed widely and under different paradigms. Collectively, these understandings served as a justification for the current project and nods to anyone who would like to extend this mission in their own contexts.
- Since our starting point in this project was teachers' knowledge base, we were able to see how critical approaches can take different forms, shapes, and sizes as it relates to the different aspects of this knowledge base and how teacher educators can incorporate criticality at various points of teacher education. This understanding is a testament to the notion of criticality as a continuum (from uncritical to more critical) rather than a juxtaposed binary (critical/uncritical).
- Moving toward a more multidimensional understanding of criticality is particularly important for teacher educators since teacher educators can afford to be agentic and critical to varying degrees in their local contexts and teacher education practices while maintaining a delicate balance among systemic/contextual factors, institutional dynamics, and individual realities. The practical applications showcased in this volume suggest that criticality-oriented innovations may not always require building a new system from scratch and may in fact emerge from fissures in existing teacher education contexts. As such, the volume showcases how teacher educators themselves can resist teacher education curricula by bringing critically-oriented activities to courses commonly found in ELTE programs.

Introducing Criticality and Critical English Language Teacher Education   13

On Where We Find Criticality More and Where Less

- Reflecting on our submission numbers for various parts, we realized that some aspects of the knowledge base of English language teacher educators (e.g., materials analysis and development) are more receptive to critical approaches than others (e.g., language assessment). Readers will find that instructional materials are a common entry point for the introduction of criticality throughout the volume and that reflection plays a key role in bringing critical approaches to seminars, courses, projects, and workshops.
- Throughout the process of bringing this volume together, we have also noticed a number of areas where teacher educators' criticality was especially restrained, namely, in language assessment and curriculum development. Working on this volume leaves us with the question of how teachers and teacher educators can resist more structured and standardized aspects of language teaching, such as assessment and curriculum design. How can critical ELTE address how teacher learners are prepared to navigate curricular constraints and traditional assessment practices? More specifically, how can teacher education programs raise awareness of how to interpret, work with, or resist curricula and the demands that these put on the teachers in their selection of instructional materials, methods, assessment practices, interaction with the parents, requests from the learners, and pressure from institutions?
- This volume has brought together contributions from Brazil, Germany, Morocco, New Zealand, Spain, Sweden, Switzerland, the United States, and Türkiye. Though we see some variety in the contexts represented in this volume, we still don't know how criticality is practiced in other parts of the world.
- In a similar vein, we come across a number of critical approaches more frequently than others. Social justice, critical pedagogy, Global Englishes, culturally-responsive teaching, multilingualism, critical language awareness (CLA), queer pedagogy, diversity, equity and inclusion, critical antiracist pedagogy, asset-based education, and translanguaging are among the approaches that teacher educators in this volume use to approach their teacher education practices critically. Practices with a focus on special educational needs, parental involvement, as well as individual learning differences and disabilities remain a blind spot in the literature, nonexistent in the submissions we received, and therefore undocumented in this volume.

On the Nature of Criticality Represented in the Contributions

- Overall, the practical applications chapters show how teacher educators are moving away from seeing their teacher learners as methods-obsessed, prescriptive, passive technicians to professionals embodying humanizing pedagogy, an identity lens, and a social justice orientation in conceptualizing, imagining, and enacting their (future) teaching practices. In addition, the critically-oriented activities in this volume situate English language learning and teaching practices beyond a set of universally applicable, permanent, fixed, apolitical, ahistorical, and decontextualized skills.

- Many of our contributing authors have worked in teams involving pre-/in-service teachers, which responds to McKinley's (2019) call for teacher-research collaboration. This also contributes to the role, status, and importance of teachers in the publication, dissemination, and integration of research and makes their voices heard.
- In many of the contributions, we see the level of commitment teacher educators put into (1) conceptualizing the activities, (2) implementing them, (3) establishing group dynamics to create safe spaces, and perhaps different from traditional LTE practices, and (4) maintaining communication and dialogue with pre-/in-service teachers (oftentimes in the form of individual engagement/feedback/conference/reflection with course participants). This commitment is a testament to the engaged and relational nature of critical ELTE.
- Teachers' identity work emerges frequently as a powerful and valuable lens in the chapters throughout the volume. Therefore, in concluding this part, we feel obliged to emphasize the connection between identity, agency, and criticality to foster the development of a professional stance, an identity, and a comprehensive skill set. Building upon this premise, the contributions in our edited volume could be seen as nuanced ways of teachers and teacher educators taking agentic action to disrupt ideologies, mainstream ELT practices, unquestioned and taken for granted beliefs about language learning and teaching.

In closing, this edited volume leaves you and the broader ELTE community with hopes, possibilities, and inspiration. We hope that the project has managed to convey criticality as a key quality of English language teachers/teacher educators, and critically-oriented practices as a multi-relational, spatiotemporal, and multifaceted endeavor constantly reinventing itself in new ways of being, doing, and becoming with no endpoint. The contributions throughout the volume will hopefully ignite your passion for transformative pedagogy or serve as a catalyst in reaffirming the power of criticality in your beliefs, values, identities, and practices undergirding ELT and teacher education. We appreciate contributing teacher educators/teacher learners for their pivotal role and agentive willingness to transform ELTE by challenging the status quo, disrupting normative and oppressive ideologies, and creating inclusive learning environments. They played a key role in conveying the message that criticality is not just an intimidating theoretical construct but a contextualized embodied practice that can empower teacher learners and language learners to become agents of change striving for a more inclusive, equitable, and compassionate world.

References

Aleksić, G. and O. García (2022), "Language beyond Flags: Teachers' Misunderstanding of Translanguaging in Preschools", *International Journal of Bilingual Education and Bilingualism*: 1–14. doi:10.1080/13670050.2022.2085029.

Canagarajah, S. (2023), "Decolonization as Pedagogy: A Praxis of Becoming in ELT". *ELT Journal*: 283–93. doi:10.1093/elt/ccad017.

Crookes, G. (2013), *Critical ELT in Action: Foundations, Promises, Praxis*, New York: Routledge.
de Oliveira, L. C. (2016), "A Language-Based Approach to Content Instruction (LACI) for English Language Learners: Examples from Two Elementary Teachers", *International Multilingual Research Journal*, 10 (3): 217–31.
Farrell, T. S. C. (2022), *Reflective Practice in Language Teaching*, Cambridge: Cambridge University Press.
Freire, P. (1970), *Pedagogy of the Oppressed*, New York: The Continuum.
Hawkins, M. and B. Norton (2009), "Critical Language Teacher Education", in A. Burns and J. C. Richards (eds), *Cambridge Guide to Second Language Teacher Education*, 30–9, New York: Cambridge University Press.
Hawkins, M. R. (ed.) (2011), *Social Justice Language Teacher Education*, Bristol: Multilingual Matters.
Hawkins, M. R. and J. Mori (2018), "Considering 'Trans-' perspectives in Language Theories and Practices", *Applied Linguistics*, 39 (1): 1–8. doi:10.1093/applin/amx056.
hooks, b. (1994), *Teaching to Transgress: Education as the Practice of Freedom*, New York: Routledge.
Kubota, R. (2019), "Confronting Epistemological Racism, Decolonizing Scholarly Knowledge: Race and Gender in Applied Linguistics", *Applied Linguistics*, 41 (5): 712–32. doi:10.1093/applin/amz033.
Kubota, R. (2021), "Critical Antiracist Pedagogy in ELT", *ELT Journal*, 75 (3): 237–46. doi:10.1093/elt/ccab015.
McKinley, J. (2019), "Evolving the TESOL Teaching–Research Nexus", *TESOL Quarterly*, 53 (3): 875–84. doi:10.1002/tesq.509.
Paiz, J. M. (2020), *Queering the English Language Classroom: A Practical Guide for Teachers*, Sheffield: Equinox Publishing.
Rosa, J. and N. Flores (2017), "Unsettling Language and Race: Toward a Raciolinguistic Perspective", *Language in Society*, 46 (5): 621–47. doi:10.1017/S0047404517000562.
Rose, H. and N. Galloway, N. (2019), *Global Englishes for Language Teaching*, Cambridge: Cambridge University Press. doi:10.1017/9781316678343.
Selvi, A. F., N. Galloway and H. Rose (2023), *Teaching English as an International Language*. Cambridge: Cambridge University Press.
Wei, L. and O. García (2022), "Not a First Language but One Repertoire: Translanguaging as a Decolonizing Project", *RELC Journal*, 53 (2): 313–24. doi:10.1177/00336882221092841.

Part Two

Teaching Methods and Methodologies

2

Beyond Language Teaching Methods and Methodologies in Language Teacher Education

Graham Hall

Introduction

Language teacher education (LTE) lies at the confluence of "teaching in theory" and "teaching in practice." Many LTE programs seek to draw on theoretical or academic knowledge to develop "the specialized kind of knowledge that teachers use to actually teach" (Johnson 2016: 125), albeit in differing ways and to different extents in differing contexts. Meanwhile, language teaching methods, "theories translated into classroom applications" (Hinkel 2005: 631), occupy a similar position at the interface of practice and theory. It is unsurprising, therefore, that discussion of methods and methodologies has long been a feature of LTE programs.

And yet, the idea that language teaching theory can be straightforwardly "translated" into practical classroom applications and activities has been significantly problematized since the early 1990s; similarly, the concept of method, the relevance of particular methods to many contexts and classrooms, and even the idea that such methods actually exist in the real world that lies beyond the pages of the methodological literature have been widely critiqued. Claims that methods are "dead" (Allwright 1991) have underpinned suggestions that language teaching has entered a "Postmethod" era (Kumaravadivelu 2003; 2006; 2012), whilst Postmethod thinking itself overlaps with more explicitly "critical" perspectives which explore and expose inequitable power relationships both within language teaching and across wider society, seeking transformation and, ultimately, social justice. From a critical perspective, the concept of method and the promulgation of methods across the field generally favor academics (who are often male) over language teachers (who are often female), valuing theoretical interests and forms of knowledge over more the practical, local, and contextualized knowledge that teachers have about classroom life and activities, and thus often favoring "Western" approaches and interests over non-Western practices (Crookes 2013; Pennycook 1989).

Thus, as Postmethod thinking and, to a lesser extent, critical perspectives have increasingly taken hold in language teaching over the last thirty years, it is necessary to rethink and/or re-evaluate the position of language teaching methods as a key focus of many LTE programs, asking how LTE might look "beyond" methods and methodologies. This chapter seeks to explore this question by tracing two related developments in language teaching and LTE. It first outlines how thinking about "method" and methods has changed, from "traditional" understandings to the emergence of more recent Postmethod and critical perspectives from the 1990s onwards. The discussion then reflects on the ways in which thinking about LTE itself has developed over the same period, similarly moving from top-down prescriptions for practice to an acknowledgment of the value of teachers' own contextually-based understandings and knowledge in their professional development. The chapter brings these developments together by drawing parallels with the emergence of criticality and critical perspectives within the field, looking at the implications of this for critical LTE.

Key Issues

Method and Methods: Central Concepts and "Traditional" Perspectives

Many accounts suggest that, for much of the twentieth century, teacher educators "sought to solve the problems of language teaching by focusing exclusively on teaching method" (Stern 1983: 452—emphasis in original; see also Kumaravadivelu 2006; 2012; Richards and Rodgers 2014). Traditionally defined as "a theory of language teaching … which has resulted from practical and theoretical discussions in a given historical context" Stern (1983: 452–3), all methods "assume[d] there is a single set of principles [which] propose a single set of precepts for teacher and learner classroom behaviour, and assert that if these principles are faithfully followed, they will result in learning for all" (Nunan 1991: 30).[1] Consequently, language teaching until the 1990s has often been conceptualized as a sequence of methods—broadly speaking, from grammar-translation to the direct method in the early part of the twentieth century, through to the Audiolingual Approach in the 1950s, on, via a 1970s era of "Humanistic" approaches, to Communicative Language Teaching and subsequently Task-based Teaching in the 1980s, and so forth. However, this idea, of a sequence of identifiable methods dominating identifiable time-limited periods, has been strongly critiqued in recent years, as we shall now see.

Competing Narratives and Emerging Critiques

Originally, the sequence of methods outlined above was accounted for via a progressive narrative which suggested that each method in the series was "succeeded by a better one until we reach the present" (Pennycook 1989: 597). From this perspective, the role of LTE was to inculcate teachers into learning to teach "correctly" through the specific method which dominated the field at that particular time. Looked at critically, this approach to methods sees a flow of ideas from theorists to teachers, the favoring of decontextualized academic knowledge over practitioners' locally embedded understandings of how to teach effectively, and the "de-skilling" of teachers who become merely "technicians" implementing the ideas of others (Pennycook 1989); in effect, the imposition of method becomes a form of "control" (Allwright and Hanks 2009).

More contemporary perspectives, however, argue that the development of methods has been cyclical and context-dependent, that we can find commonalities between what happens in language classrooms now and what has happened throughout history (suggested by, for example, Kelly's 1969 review of 2,500 years of language teaching), and that "no method is inherently superior to another; instead some methods are more appropriate than others in a particular context" (Adamson 2004: 605). This critique of the progressive narrative instead sees methods as products of their times, in which "different approaches emerged in response to changing geopolitical circumstances and social attitudes and values, as well as to shifts in fashion in linguistics" (Cook 2003: 30). From this standpoint for example, grammar-translation was appropriate to an era when languages were often learned by relatively few, often as an intellectual pursuit or to read literature in its original languages rather than for communicative purposes; audiolingualism can be linked to the 1950s emergence of behavioral psychology, structuralism in linguistics, and a focus on oral drills which had developed in the teaching of languages to US servicemen following the Second World War; and Communicative Language Teaching emerged in an era of mass travel where the ability to communicate, usually in English, was increasingly seen as a key skill for workers around the world (Hall 2016).

Yet despite their contrasts, both these narratives of methods share the key perspective that a succession of methods can be identified and labeled across "bounded periods of history" (Hunter and Smith 2012: 430). Pennycook (1989) points out, however, that accounts of methods (e.g., Larsen-Freeman and Anderson 2011; Richards and Rodgers 2014) differ in the number of methods they present, the terminology used, their sequencing over time, and their conceptual coherence. Furthermore, "there is little evidence that methods ever reflected classroom reality" (602). Hunter and Smith (2012) thus argue that a "mythology" has developed around methods which "packages up" complex and contested classroom practices in simplistic and stereotypical ways. For example, far from disappearing in the early twentieth century, grammar-translation continues today in many contexts; audiolingual approaches had a limited global reach, even in the 1950s.

The acknowledgment that there is "no best method" for teaching languages (Prabhu 1990), and even that methods themselves are, in practical terms, "mythological" has significantly shifted the ways in which developments in language teaching are perceived and, with it, the possibilities for methodological discussion in LTE. With a "shift to localization" (Howatt with Widdowson 2004: 369), there is recognition that, rather than searching for universal solutions to the dilemmas of language teaching, local conditions, learner diversity, and teacher agency must be acknowledged (Larsen-Freeman and Anderson 2011). For LTE, therefore, the discussion of methods potentially offers a range of empowering options for teachers who are transformed into engaged decision-makers within their own classrooms. From this perspective, teachers need to be aware of the range of pedagogical possibilities available in order to make informed choices as they seek to meet the needs of their learners. Discussion of methods can be a prompt for deeper reflection as to what underpins their classroom practices, and can broaden teachers' range of teaching techniques (Larsen-Freeman and Anderson 2011). Developing knowledge of methods via LTE is thus seen as a potential source of teacher empowerment as they develop their own principled and eclectic pedagogy (we will return to the evident connection between "teacher empowerment" and ideas around social transformation, justice and critical perspectives on LTE toward the end of the chapter).

From Method to Postmethod?

Beyond this idea of methods as a source for teachers' "principled methodological eclecticism," a more fundamental rejection of "method" can be found in the Postmethod thinking of the 1990s onward. Postmethod pedagogy, suggest its proponents, moves beyond concerns which might be associated with "method" (such as teaching practices, materials, curriculum, and assessment) to also consider the range of historical, political, and sociocultural experiences that influence language teaching in any particular context. In effect, therefore, the influence of methods and methods-driven teaching, which emerged from and reflect the assumptions and cultural norms of dominant British, Australasia, and North American (i.e., BANA) contexts (Holliday 1994) is challenged as local pedagogic and contextual knowledge and perspectives guide pedagogy.

Consequently, teaching results from bottom-up rather than top-down processes, in which teacher autonomy, self-observation, self-analysis, and self-evaluation shape and reshape classroom pedagogy (Kumaravadivelu 2003). Teachers may take ideas from existing methods, but are not constrained by them. For Kumaravadivelu (2012: 12–14), Postmethod pedagogy draws on three key principles: particularity (i.e., sensitivity to the local individual and institutional, and social and cultural, contexts of teaching and learning); practicality (i.e., teachers develop and put into practice their own theories, based on their contextual knowledge; thus, the superiority of academic theorists over practitioners is broken); and possibility (i.e., the sociopolitical consciousness of teachers and learners is developed so they can "form and transform their personal and social identity").

Like "principled eclecticism," therefore, the "principled pragmatism" of Postmethod envisions an enhanced role for teachers in which they have the power and freedom to make methodological decisions based on their local knowledge and expertise. Clearly, however, most teachers around the world are not completely free to decide how they teach—they are constrained by school and ministry policies, by learner (and, often, parent) expectations, by end-of-course evaluations, and, more generally, by social conventions (Crookes 2003). And yet bringing Postmethod thinking, and ideas around Particularity, Practicality, and Possibility, into LTE can create space for more critical approaches to language teacher education. Before looking at these possibilities, however, the chapter will first trace how LTE itself has, like ideas around method, developed from largely top-down approaches aiming to transmit "expert knowledge" to bottom-up, "located" perspectives which value teachers' perspectives, again creating discursive space for more critical LTE.

The Emergence of "Located" Language Teacher Education

Unsurprisingly, LTE has developed in differing ways in different contexts. In the UK, for example, there was no requirement, until 1973, for language graduates working in state schools to hold an additional teaching qualification; in Germany, meanwhile, language teachers had undertaken a compulsory year's practical training since the late 1800s (McClelland 2018). Yet as both these examples indicate in contrasting ways, language teaching was generally seen as "a practical activity" until the mid-twentieth century, and although relatively short training courses existed in many contexts, much LTE focused on "providing teaching materials and guidance on their use in the classroom" (Howatt with Widdowson 2004: 237).

In the post-1945 period, however, LTE became more widespread; it also often became more academically oriented. For example, responsibility for LTE moved from schools to universities in the United States (Labaree 2004, in Johnson 2016), whilst LTE programs, particularly those at university level, often focused on specialized knowledge about language and language learning derived from Applied Linguistics which emerged as an academic discipline in the 1960s. This was based on the view that teachers' classroom pedagogy would improve if they had knowledge of theory and research. Thus, as Johnson (2016: 121–2) suggests:

> Teachers were considered to be "doers" rather than "thinkers", and the doing of teaching was conceptualized as a set of instructional behaviours that, if carried out systematically and efficiently, would ultimately lead to greater gains in student learning, regardless of institutional and/or social context.

The approach to LTE in this period is, therefore, clearly intertwined with the traditional conception of method which we have already seen, i.e., the transmission of universal principles, devised by "experts" and "handed down" for teachers to subsequently implement (Clarke 1994; Hall 2019).

Subsequently, however, thinking about LTE changed in ways which again parallel developments around method. The 1990s recognition that there are few, if any, global certainties in language teaching, the reevaluation of the role of context, and the re-valuing of teachers' own experiences and knowledge led to less emphasis on providing teachers with "top-down solutions" and more focus on teachers' own theories, hypotheses, and critical reflections on teaching. From this perspective, the role of LTE was, and is, no longer to provide one-size-fits-all, method-oriented theories to teachers; rather it is to create opportunities for teachers' own methodological or Postmethod thinking and practices to emerge (Hall 2019). This provides "space" for critical English language teacher education, which could focus on, for example, how classroom management might be made more democratic; how needs analysis can take on the actual life concerns of learners, rather than preassigned curricula; and how language itself embeds ideological perspectives, and so forth.

Implications and Conclusions

As the discussion above indicates, a major element in the reconsideration of both method and methods in language teaching, and of LTE, has been the acknowledgment of power and hierarchical relationships within the field, the recognition of the locally constituted nature of language teaching practices, and, consequently, a desire to challenge and change a status quo of the top-down transmission of agendas, assumptions and cultural norms, usually from the Global North to the Global South. Similarly, the goal of critical approaches to education is to challenge apparently "natural" constructs such as "rationality" and "neutrality," instead recognizing "the subjective, the social and the partisan nature of reality" and the ways in which "our ideas, interactions ... learning practices, and so forth are shaped by and within social relationships that systematically advantage some people over others" (Hawkins and Norton 2009: 31). Thus, although much of the literature around Postmethod does not tend to explicitly align itself with critical approaches to language teaching and to critical LTE, there are evident connections.

Language teacher education which provides opportunities for teachers to develop pedagogies that are particular and practical and which seek to explore and expand what is possible (i.e., build upon the three key principles of Postmethod) in effect creates a site for "praxis"—from a critical perspective, when theorizing and practice come together to create action for further social and political change (Hawkins and Norton 2009). Such actions can be focused on the profession of language teaching itself, addressing how language teachers can work and develop in ways and with goals which are appropriate to their own contexts, and thus rebalancing the relationships between theorists and practitioners, academic and practical knowledge, and such like. This may be through the operationalization of the "microstrategies" of Postmethod teaching, which include, for example, ensuring the social relevance of pedagogy by embedding within it the complex social and critical concerns of the local environment, and raising cultural consciousness, explicitly recognizing and addressing the implications of the learners' ethnic heritage, class, ages, and gender both within and beyond the classroom (Kumaravadivelu 2003).

And praxis can see the focus of LTE itself go beyond language teaching methods and methodologies as traditionally conceptualized (in other words, as outlined in the early stages of this chapter) to find space to engage critically with a broader range of issues which are of immediate concern in particular contexts. Often overlooked by the relatively constrained, method-oriented curricula of many LTE programs, these might include gender and sexuality, standard language ideology and language varieties, race and ethnicity, and other issues with implications for social justice both within the classroom and in wider society.

However, given its locally constituted, bottom-up, and thus almost inevitably varied nature, how might such critical LTE be brought to a more central location within the field? How might accounts be shared, in order to avoid critical LTE becoming a marginal concern, overlooked within the traditional hierarchies of language teaching and pedagogical knowledge? Smith (2015) calls for bottom-up accounts of practice which challenge methods-based perspectives, whilst Braine's (2005) edited collection gives voice to teachers from a range of countries as they examine their own priorities, perspectives and practices, and illuminate the complex political, social, and economic relationships which affect classroom pedagogy. Such a rebalancing the literature of LTE, to provide space for language teachers' and teacher educators' accounts of praxis which others can learn from and be inspired by, is one way of supporting the turn in a more critical direction of language teacher education as it continues to move beyond language teaching methods and methodologies.

Note

1   In contrast to these understandings of "method", "methodology" is "a general word to describe classroom practices ... irrespective of the particular method that a teacher is using"—it is "the how of teaching" (Thornbury 2006: 131 and 2011: 185), or, as Kumaravadivelu (2006: 84) puts it, "Method [refers to] established methods constructed by experts in the field ... Methodology [is] what practising teachers actually do in the classroom to achieve their stated or unstated teaching objectives."

References

Adamson, B. (2004), "Fashions in Language Teaching Methodology", in A. Davies and C. Elder (eds), *The Handbook of Applied Linguistics*, 604-22, London: Blackwell.
Allwright, D. (1991), "The Death of the Method", *CRILE Working Paper No. 10*, Lancaster: Lancaster University.
Allwright, D. and J. Hanks (2009), *The Developing Language Learner: An Introduction to Exploratory Practice*, Basingstoke: Palgrave Macmillan.
Braine, G. (ed.) (2005), *Teaching English to the World: History, Curriculum and Practice*, Mahwah, NJ: Lawrence Erlbaum Associates.
Clarke, M. (1994), "The Dysfunctions of the Theory/Practice Discourse", *TESOL Qu*, 28 (1): 9-26.
Cook, G. (2003), *Applied Linguistics*, Oxford: Oxford University Press.
Crookes, G. (2003), *A Practicum in TESOL: Professional Development through Teaching Practice*, Cambridge: Cambridge University Press.
Crookes, G. (2013), *Critical ELT in Action: Foundations, Promises, Praxis*, New York: Routledge.
Hall, G. (2016), "Method, Methods and Methodology: Historical Trends and Current Debates", in G. Hall (ed.), *The Routledge Handbook of English language Teaching*, 209-23, London: Routledge.
Hall, G. (2019), "Locating Methods in ELT Education: Perspectives and Possibilities", in S. Walsh and S. Mann (eds), *The Routledge Handbook of English Language Teacher Education*, 285-98, London: Routledge.
Hawkins, M. and B. Norton (2009), "Critical Language Teacher Education", in A. Burns and J. Richards (eds), *Cambridge Guide to Second Language Teacher Education*, 30-9, Cambridge: Cambridge University Press.
Hinkel, E. (2005), "Introduction", in E. Hinkel (ed.), *Handbook of Research in Second Language Teaching and Learning*, 631-4, Mahwah, NJ: Lawrence Erlbaum.
Holliday, A. (1994), *Appropriate Methodology and Social Context*, Cambridge: Cambridge University Press.

Howatt, A. and Widdowson, H. (2004), *A History of English Language Teaching*, 2nd edn, Oxford: Oxford University Press.

Hunter, D. and R. Smith (2012), "Unpackaging the Past: 'CLT' through ELTJ Keywords", *ELT Journal*, 66 (4): 430–9.

Johnson, K. E. (2016), "Language Teacher Education", in G. Hall (ed.), *The Routledge Handbook of English Language Teaching*, 121–44, London: Routledge.

Kelly, L. (1969), *25 Centuries of Language Teaching*, Massachusetts: Newbury House.

Kumaravadivelu, B. (2003), *Beyond Methods: Macrostrategies for Language Teaching*, New Haven, CT: Yale University Press.

Kumaravadivelu, B. (2006), *Understanding Language Teaching: From Method to Postmethod*, Mahwah, NJ: Routledge.

Kumaravadivelu, B. (2012), *Language Teacher Education for a Global Society*, London: Routledge.

Labaree, D. (2004), *The Trouble with Education Schools*, New Haven, CT: Yale University Press.

Larsen-Freeman, D. and M. Anderson (2011), *Techniques and Principles in Language Teaching*, 3rd edn, Oxford: Oxford University Press.

McClelland, N. (2018), *Teaching and Learning Foreign Languages*, London: Routledge.

Nunan, D. (1991), *Language Teaching Methodology*, New York: Prentice Hall.

Pennycook, A. (1989), "The Concept of Method, Interested Knowledge, and the Politics of Language Teaching", *TESOL Quarterly*, 23 (4): 589–618.

Prabhu, N. S. (1990), "There Is No Best Method—Why?", *TESOL Quarterly*, 24 (2): 161–76.

Richards, J. and T. Rodgers (2014), *Approaches and Methods in Language Teaching*, 3rd edn, Oxford: Oxford University Press.

Smith, R. (2015), "Review of Teacher Research in Language Teaching: A Critical Analysis by S. Borg", *ELT Journal*, 69 (2): 205–8.

Thornbury, S. (2006), *An A-Z of ELT*, Oxford: Macmillan.

Thornbury, S. (2011), "Language Teaching Methodology", in J. Simpson (ed.), *The Routledge Handbook of Applied Linguistics*, 185–99, London: Routledge.

Suggested Readings

- Crookes, G. (2013), *Critical ELT in Action: Foundations, Promises, Praxis*, New York: Routledge.
- Kumaravadivelu, B. (2012), *Language Teacher Education for a Global Society*, London: Routledge.
- Pennycook, A. (1989), "The Concept of Method, Interested Knowledge, and the Politics of Language Teaching", *TESOL Quarterly*, 23 (4): 589–618.

3

Challenging Standard Language Ideology and Promoting Critical Language Awareness in Teacher Education

John Chi and Kellie Rolstad

Background

Language education imposes standard language varieties at the expense of other varieties, typically without any critique of the impact of standard language ideology (SLI)—"a bias toward an abstracted, idealized, homogenous spoken language which is imposed and maintained by dominant bloc institutions" (Lippi-Green 2012: 67). While scholars debate discrete language teaching methods, students—especially heritage language learners—are often shamed for a nonstandard linguistic variety they may bring to class. This "methods fetish" (Bartolomé 1994) behind language teacher education only further dehumanizes individual students while reifying SLI. Critical pedagogy examines the role of education in perpetuating inequities, "largely reject[ing] assimilation as an educational objective" (Leeman 2005: 35). More specifically, critical language awareness (CLA) interrogates how language and power operate, challenges assumed language ideologies and structures, and guides teachers in transforming language education (Fairclough 1992). In short, CLA goes beyond the discrete language teaching methodologies and aims to promote broader humanizing pedagogy.

In this chapter, we engage in humanizing pedagogy (Freire 1970) by de-centering one-size-fits-all discrete language teaching methods, and instead, we suggest centering CLA in language teacher education as a remedy for deficit-oriented "methods," which typically focus only on teaching standard language varieties. This includes pre-service teachers reflecting on their own biases from a sociolinguistic perspective as we challenge them to implement anti-bias education in their own classrooms. We introduce activities that engage pre-service teachers in critical analysis of language learning curriculum, of teacher beliefs about language, and the prevalence of indiscriminate language correction.

Our Teacher Education Context

Both authors are teacher educators at a large public university in the Mid-Atlantic region of the United States, in an area where many families speak languages or dialects other than "mainstream American English." The pre-service teachers—largely middle-class, white females—have little or no background in linguistics and take our language variation course in the final year of their undergraduate teacher preparation program, while interning at public elementary schools. This course helps them think explicitly and critically about the nature of language and its role in the classroom, described in the syllabus as follows:

> Explores dimensions of language variation across a wide range of social, economic, regional, and ethnic groups, and issues in multilingualism. The study of language variation is used to help teacher candidates examine their assumptions about language differences, and to think critically about how language variation can be used as a resource to promote learning in school contexts. The course is designed to make teachers more aware of language differences and multilingualism as preparation for working with [state]'s diverse students.
>
> (Rolstad and Chi 2022)

While the course was developed for pre-service teachers in elementary education, the content has been adapted for our university's secondary teacher education program and can be incorporated into world and heritage language teacher education programs as well. Through various activities, discussions, and projects, we engage our pre-service teachers in challenging their SLIs and promoting CLA in their own teaching.

Description of the Practice

Each week, our pre-service teachers work on two readings or media content and participate in an online discussion board, where they reflect on the content and have meaningful dialogues with their classmates. In weekly class meetings, we deepen these discussions, gradually developing ways to recognize SLIs in themselves and others as they develop philosophies on teaching, language, diversity, and linguistic justice. We do this by providing explicit examples of language prejudice (e.g., videos, news clips), having students engage in thoughtful discussion circles, and sharing personal experiences of language shaming. Below, we detail four major assignments and how they encourage pre-service teachers to adopt critical perspectives on language and education (see Table 3.1 in Appendix for full description).

In the first assignment, My Language Heritage, pre-service teachers consult family members to explore their own language heritage, with a brief description through text or visuals in an online discussion board. Later in the course, pre-service teachers revisit their initial statements both to reflect on instances of SLI in their original writing and to highlight their development of CLA. This assignment helps pre-service teachers look inward—at their own language experiences—to deepen their understanding of linguistic diversity, as well as examine their own biases toward standard language. In turn, pre-service teachers can use this knowledge to better understand the heterogeneity of their students' language histories and utilize these funds of knowledge in their teaching practice. See Appendix Part A, for details.

In the second assignment, pre-service teachers serve as Discussion Leaders each week to facilitate conversations with their peers on the assigned topics, based on the primary textbook (Reaser et al. 2017) and supplementary readings. Each group leads a one-hour discussion in alternating weeks, where they summarize the readings, provide related media content, create an interactive activity, and develop thoughtful questions to engage their peer audience. They connect the content to language-related interactions they experience in their internships. This activity exemplifies dismantling teacher-centeredness in our own teacher education classroom, allowing pre-service teachers to experience a student-centered classroom. By demonstrating this, pre-service teachers can then take this approach into their own teaching practices to center their students' experiences in the language classroom. See Appendix, Part B, for details.

In the third assignment, pre-service teachers participate in Conversational Inquiry by playing "language detectives" (Monahan 2003). Each pre-service teacher records a thirty-minute conversation that they would normally have in their daily life, and then transcribes a three-minute segment to analyze. In class, they share feedback on their discoveries. Next, they write a 400-word analysis of their transcription, and then they record presentations about their analysis and findings to share in an online discussion board. This assignment allows pre-service teachers to personally examine authentic language use, complicating their assumptions about so-called academic or formal language. In turn, this helps them understand their own linguistic patterns and idiosyncrasies, thus giving them a new perspective on language varieties and styles, and how language can be taught communicatively. See Appendix, Part C, for details.

In the fourth assignment, pre-service teachers work in small groups to create a Multilingual Story, where they creatively write a children's storybook that encompasses two or more languages or language varieties. They should consult with a multilingual or multidialectal speaker who is proficient in their chosen languages/varieties. This activity guides pre-service teachers in resisting monoglossic language ideologies and promoting an asset-based perspective of multilingualism, translanguaging, and codeswitching. Having a heteroglossic language ideology allows pre-service teachers to consider how to utilize their students' multilingual capabilities as assets to the class when designing lessons. While all these assignments can be modified for any setting, the storybook project is particularly enjoyable and adaptable for children. See Appendix, Part D, for details.

Critical Reflections: Potentials and Challenges

We must reiterate that CLA is not a discrete teaching method that can be "achieved." Rather, it is a continually growing sociolinguistic awareness of how language functions in education and society at large. When pre-service language teachers study "how to teach language" in a teacher education program, they should incorporate CLA to engage with their students' linguistic varieties in ways that empower—rather than disparage—them. This goes beyond the one-size-fits-all teaching "methods fetish" (Bartolomé 1994) that we normally see in teacher education programs. When pre-service teachers eventually enter their own classrooms, they should take CLA into perspective when engaging students, designing lessons, and creating a humanizing classroom environment. As teacher educators, we need to be aware of how we foster CLA in our pre-service teachers and find opportunities to engage them in hands-on applications.

The activities we provided are examples of ways to promote CLA in language teacher education and can be easily adapted. In a study investigating the effectiveness of this course, Shi and Rolstad (2020) found that their pre-service teachers progressively displayed discursive changes in developing CLA in their written self-reflections. The primary purpose of this course is to plant the seeds that will lead to our pre-service teachers' CLA development and eventually to resisting SLI, all while fostering advocacy for their multilingual students. While the "growth" in the previously mentioned study suggests a positive change in pre-service teachers' discursive practices, it is nonetheless only a starting point for them to engage in critical language pedagogy. Readers should be mindful that our course is only a semester long, while the development of CLA occurs over a long period of time. Thus, the biggest challenge that we have encountered is the limitation of time. To address this, we suggest that language teacher education programs incorporate CLA throughout the program, allowing the seeds to cultivate throughout their years of coursework. We also suggest that language teacher educators who focus on promoting CLA in their teacher education programs share resources with each other (e.g., Godley, Reaser, and Moore 2015).

One final insight: We may think of the path toward CLA as linear, ranging from traditional approaches—eradication or expansion—toward more contemporary approaches—appreciation, appropriateness-based, critical—to language variation (see Beaudrie 2015). However, in our experience working with pre-service teachers, this path is rarely linear. One factor that influences their fluctuating ideologies is their experiences outside of our class—in other courses, in their internships, with school supervisors—which often conflict with the content and critical philosophies of this course. At times early in the semester, pre-service teachers may begin to think critically about their language ideologies, but then at a later point, they may step back and suggest that standard language use and suppression of minoritized varieties may give their students the "right tools to be successful." While our goal is to encourage them to think critically, we should mention that the development of CLA ebbs and flows, and that our pre-service teachers' language ideologies may waver from time to time. We have witnessed this in our course over the years, and it is something that language teacher educators should recognize as part of the undulating process of becoming (Freire 1970; Salazar 2013) a wholesome teacher and human.

References

Bartolomé, L. (1994), "Beyond the Methods Fetish: Toward a Humanizing Pedagogy", *Harvard Educational Review*, 64: 173–95.
Beaudrie, S. M. (2015), "Approaches to Language Variation: Goals and Objectives of the Spanish Heritage Language Syllabus", *Heritage Language Journal*, 12 (1): 1–21.
Fairclough, N. (ed.) (1992), *Critical Language Awareness*, 1st edn, London: Longman.
Freire, P. (1970), *Pedagogy of the Oppressed*, New York: Continuum.
Godley, A. J., J. Reaser and K. G. Moore (2015), "Pre-service English Language Arts Teachers' Development of Critical Language Awareness for Teaching", *Linguistics and Education*, 32: 41–54.

Leeman, J. (2005), "Engaging Critical Pedagogy: Spanish for Native Speakers", *Foreign Language Annals*, 38 (1): 35–45.

Lippi-Green, R. (2012), *English with an Accent: Language, Ideology, and Discrimination in the United States*, New York: Routledge.

Monahan, M. B. (2003), "'On the Lookout for Language': Children as Language Detectives", *Language Arts*, 80 (3): 206–14.

Reaser, J., C. T. Adger, W. Wolfram and D. Christian (2017), *Dialects at School: Educating Linguistically Diverse Students*, New York: Routledge.

Rolstad, K. and J. Chi (2022), *Language Variation and Multilingualism in Elementary Classrooms* [Syllabus], University of Maryland.

Salazar, M. D. C. (2013), "A Humanizing Pedagogy: Reinventing the Principle and Practice of Education as a Journey toward Liberation", *Review of Research in Education*, 37 (1): 121–48.

Shi, L. and K. Rolstad (2020), "'A Good Start': A New Approach to Gauging Preservice Teachers' Critical Language Awareness", *Journal of Language, Identity & Education*, 21 (6): 408–22.

Appendix

Table 3.1 Overview of activities (Rolstad and Chi 2022)

Assignment	Description	Goal(s)
A. My Language Heritage	Pre-service teachers share in an online discussion board about their language heritage: • What dialects or languages were spoken at home as a child? • What were your parents' or grandparents' experiences? • What were your experiences in learning another dialect or language? • Do you ever switch between languages or styles? Can you provide examples or an explanation of why you do this?	• Allows pre-service teachers to reflect on their personal languages at the start of the semester, prior to course content • Provides pre-service teachers with a starting point to reflect back on at the end of the semester • Gives pre-service teachers opportunities to share their background, and their funds of knowledge with the instructor and classmates
B. Leading Discussion/ Readings Facilitation	Pre-service teachers work together in small groups to lead weekly discussions based on the assigned readings/content: • Summary of the readings • A media component (e.g., YouTube) • A creative activity to engage audience • Several key discussion questions to promote critical thinking of readings • Implications or recommendations for the classroom	• Provides pre-service teachers with opportunities to lead important discussions related to language variation and multilingualism • Allows for creativity as a group in designing a reading facilitation • Highlights what pre-service teachers think is or is not important from the readings, as it relates to their internship experiences • De-centers the instructor's role in the teacher education classroom and centers the pre-service teachers' experiences

Assignment	Description	Goal(s)
C. Conversational Inquiry: Transcription & Description	1) Transcription: Pre-service teachers will record and transcribe a normal conversation in their daily life • Record at least thirty minutes of a regular conversation you are in • Transcribe a short segment (approximately three minutes) • Choose a two-page section of that segment to submit and share 2) Description: Pre-service teachers will write a 400-word description (analysis) • Why did you select this segment to transcribe and analyze? • What did you find linguistically (e.g., phonological, semantic, syntactic) interesting about the segment? • Was there anything discursively (e.g., turn-taking, discourse markers) interesting about the segment? • What are your conclusions or implications of your findings?	• Gives pre-service teachers hands-on practice in playing language detectives (Monahan 2003), an activity they can share with their own students, with adaptations • Engages pre-service teachers in ethnographic data collection and provides them with (socio-)linguistic analytic abilities, based on readings and videos • Helps pre-service teachers understand the myth of "standard" and/or "academic" language and the complexities of language use • Illuminates the variability between users of the supposedly same language or language variety
D. Multilingual Story Creation	Pre-service teachers work together in small groups to co-create a children's storybook using translanguaging/codeswitching between 2+ languages/varieties • Create an 8–12-page children's book using a mixture of languages/varieties • Be creative and include visuals • Follow the grammar of codeswitching in the two languages/varieties (check with a proficient bilingual to make sure it makes sense)	• Allows pre-service teachers to be creative with their classmates and create a storybook that represents multilingual and multicultural perspectives • Provides pre-service teachers insight into how translanguaging or codeswitching works (that it is not simply random) • Gives bilingual pre-service teachers a chance to see their multiple, complex identities play out in story creation • Highlights pre-service teachers' diverse language backgrounds in an asset-based, heteroglossic language perspective

4

Social Justice Language Teacher Education in Türkiye: Insights from an English as a Foreign Language (EFL) Writing Classroom

Adnan Yılmaz, Deniz Ortaçtepe Hart, and Rabia İrem Durmuş

Background

English language teacher education has historically been confined to "content" delivery through prescribed methodologies (Wright 2015: 19), resulting in limited attention to the impact of social, cultural, and political ideologies on language use and the existing power dynamics in the classroom (Hawkins 2011). The field has recently taken a social justice turn to integrate issues such as race, ethnicity, social class, gender, and sexuality into language classrooms (Hastings and Jacob 2016; Hawkins 2011; Nieto 2010; Ortaçtepe Hart 2023; Ortaçtepe Hart and Martel 2020). This shift aims to equip teachers with the skills, knowledge, and dispositions to address the existing inequities and injustices across and beyond systems of schooling (Zeichner 2011). By providing a space for discussions on peace, conflict, environment, migration, and human rights, social justice language education seeks to disrupt existing hierarchies, encourage learners' critical thinking, and lead to educational and social transformation at large (Freire 1970; Glynn, Wesely and Wassell 2014; Hastings and Jacob 2016; Nieto 2010).

While language teaching for social justice has started to gain prominence in the United States and the UK, English as a foreign language contexts such as Türkiye have a long way to go when it comes to integrating social justice issues into language curriculum. Critical and social justice-based pedagogies have only recently gained traction and visibility in Türkiye, with limited research (Akayoğlu, Üzüm and Yazan 2022; Balbay 2019; Zorba 2020) and professional events such as the Symposium on Social Justice in English language teaching (ELT) that was held at Sinop University, first in 2019 and then in 2022. Given the imminent need for transformative, inclusive, and equitable pedagogies in Türkiye, this paper, by drawing on the first two authors' Social Justice in ELT project carried out in Türkiye between 2018 and 2022 with pre-service English language teachers, aims to provide immediate takeaways on social justice language teacher education (SJLTE).

Description of the Practice: Social Justice in ELT (SJELT) Project

Social Justice in ELT (SJELT) Project, which Deniz and Adnan coordinated and İrem participated in as a pre-service teacher, aimed to develop pre-service English language teachers' capacity to integrate social justice issues in their classes and, as a result, to address the inequalities in their educational contexts as well as the larger communities. The project aimed to transcend traditional language teacher education methodology as described by Wright (2015) and to equip language teachers with knowledge, skills, and dispositions to become transformative intellectuals (Giroux 2018) through incorporating issues around equity and justice in their teaching (Hastings and Jacob 2016; Hawkins 2011).

The project began with an in-person introductory seminar on social justice language education at four different universities in Türkiye: Trabzon University, Sakarya University, Kocaeli University, and Ondokuz Mayis University. This seminar was organized specifically for the fourth-year pre-service English language teachers for the following reasons. All fourth-year students in ELT programs in Türkiye enroll in a Teaching Practice course which allows them opportunities to observe and teach in different educational contexts under the supervision of a mentor teacher. Therefore, this group had immediate access to language learners and could easily implement a social responsibility project (SRP) in their placement schools. Following the introductory seminars, nine pre-service English language teachers (seven female and two male identifying) were selected as the project participants. These pre-service teachers then received four webinars on environmental education and sustainability, gender equality, LGBTQ+ inclusive pedagogies, and peacebuilding and immigration. Freire's (1970) critical pedagogy informed the training and the nature of the interactions between the project coordinators and participants. In addition to critical pedagogy, the webinars also drew from feminist pedagogy (Enns and Forrest 2005), queer pedagogy (Mayo and Rodriguez 2019), critical race theory (Ladson-Billings 1999), and frameworks of environmental justice (Gilio-Whitaker 2019).

During each webinar, the pre-service teachers were encouraged to (re)construct their identities as not authorities in their classroom but as active learners, explorers, and facilitators who, along with language learners, engage in a critical reflection of issues around power in both educational contexts and the larger society. For instance, during the webinar on gender equality, the pre-service teachers participated in a group activity using the picturebook "The Paper Bag Princess"—a storybook in which gender roles are reversed (i.e., a princess rescues the prince from a dragon). In Zoom breakout rooms, they read the story and discussed topics such as the plot, gender roles, and societal comparisons of these gender roles using a Google Forms link. Each group then chose a speaker to share their discussion notes with the whole class while their Google Forms responses were displayed on the screen.

After each webinar, the pre-service teachers reflected on the discussed themes and shared their reflections on their own blogs on the project website (www.socialjusticeinelt.com). For example, they analyzed environmental education and sustainability in an English textbook used in their placement school and shared their analysis on their blogs. In another task, they interviewed an LGBTQ+ member in their local community and shared the interviews on their blogs with permission and by protecting their interviewee's identity. Additionally, they designed lesson plans on the discussed themes and received feedback from the project coordinators. To design their own lesson plans, they were provided topics and sample lesson plans which included content, language, and social justice objectives (Glynn et al 2014; Ortaçtepe Hart 2023).

The SJELT project encouraged pre-service English language teachers to become transformative intellectuals through social action. After the webinars, they carried out their own small-scale SRPs in their placement schools. Through these SRPs, the project coordinators aimed to help pre-service teachers build bridges between their educational contexts, lived experiences, and community; develop critical consciousness in their learners/target audience; and lead to social transformation at large (Harven and Gordon-Biddle 2016). The next section will discuss İrem's SRP and present a critical reflection on the affordances and challenges of SJLTE within the Turkish context.

İrem's Social Responsibility Project: Social Justice in the Writing Classroom

İrem's SRP with five tenth-grade students at a high school in Türkiye, aimed to (a) raise awareness within the high school community regarding gender equality and bullying, environmental education and sustainability, and peacebuilding and immigration, and (b) develop students' writing skills in opinion, cause-and-effect, and argumentative essays. She encouraged her students to adopt an activist approach while developing their understanding of social justice issues and writing skills.

İrem's nine-week SRP started with a general introduction to social justice and continued with students' discussions, mind maps, and posters on the themes mentioned above (see Figures 4.1 and 4.2).

Figure 4.1 The students' mind map on immigration and peacebuilding.

Figure 4.2 The students' posters on immigration and peacebuilding.

After these activities, İrem moved onto the writing phase using a process writing approach (Listyani 2018). The students pursued four major steps while writing their essays: (1) writing an initial draft, (2) receiving feedback from their peers on the initial draft, (3) revising the initial draft and sharing the second draft with İrem for feedback, and (4) revising the second draft and submitting the final draft. Following this writing cycle, students' essays and posters were published in a newsletter (see Figure 4.3) called "Juster Together," which was distributed to neighboring schools and cafés for a wider social impact. While distributing this newsletter, students engaged in informal conversations with different people (e.g., café managers,

Figure 4.3 Cover page of the newsletter.

teachers, students) and received positive feedback and support for their efforts to be involved in such a project and raise awareness on social justice issues. İrem's project, in that sense, went beyond the traditional language learning and teaching methods by building a bridge between the classroom and the broader social context, with emphasis on social justice issues.

Critical Reflections: Potentials and Challenges

İrem, who was a pre-service English language teacher at that time, perceived this project as a milestone in cultivating an alternative and novel perspective of language education. In Türkiye, language teaching and learning has traditionally been circumscribed to the acquisition of basic language skills (e.g., vocabulary, grammar, and reading), and as a pre-service language teacher, İrem was largely required to focus on developing her knowledge and capabilities of prescribed methodologies to teach these in her classrooms. Through this project, İrem started to view the language classroom as a potential space to integrate social justice issues and raise her students' awareness on these issues through critical, transformative approaches and methods. She felt empowered to take action for social and educational change as her project helped her high schoolers not only develop their knowledge and awareness regarding various social justice issues but also promote a sense of achievement, agency and advocacy through their multimodal products like the posters and the newsletter. Engaging learners in tasks that would produce authentic, creative, and multimodal products is only one of the ways in which İrem's project transcended traditional language teaching and learning methods and promoted student-centered, activism-based approaches into classroom teaching. İrem believed that this project was taboo-breaking since it included not only more commonly taught issues in the language classrooms (e.g., environmental education) but also the less commonly mentioned ones such as gender equality, immigration, and peacebuilding—topics still considered "sensitive" and "controversial" in Türkiye. İrem's participants, despite their eagerness to fight injustices, were sometimes reluctant to share their ideas especially during the early weeks; felt vulnerability and discomfort when they shared their ideas. Vulnerability and discomfort within social justice teacher education can, however, be interpreted as a sign of learning, unlearning, and relearning (Ortaçtepe Hart 2023).

As the project coordinators, we believe that SJLTE disrupts the traditional language teacher education methodology and offers potential for social and educational transformation at local and global levels. Particularly empowering language teachers as transformative intellectuals through small-scale SRPs during their training as pre-service teachers, SJLTE develops teachers' awareness of equity and justice and encourages them to act as agents of social and educational change. Resonating with İrem about the potential challenges (e.g., backlash from the administrators or parents) and criticizing the restrictive understanding and practices of traditional language teacher education methodology, we believe that SJLTE can help pre-service language teachers understand the hidden curriculum of any educational program and institution and work against dismantling the power relations between teachers and learners and within the larger societies. SRPs within SJLTE, therefore, play an essential role in terms of connecting pre-service language teachers with the local community and challenging the larger oppressive institutions in their societies.

References

Akayoğlu, S., B. Üzüm and B. Yazan (2022), "Supporting Teachers' Engagement in Pedagogies of Social justice (STEPS): Collaborative Project between Five Universities in Turkey and the USA", *Focus on ELT Journal*, 4 (1): 7–27.

Aydınlı, J. and D. Ortaçtepe (2018), "Selected Research in Applied Linguistics and English Language Teaching in Turkey: 2010–2016", *Language Teaching*, 51 (2): 210–45.

Balbay, S. (2019), "Enhancing Critical Awareness through Socratic Pedagogy", *Eurasian Journal of Applied Linguistics*, 5 (3): 515–36.

Enns, C. Z. and L. M. Forrest (2005), "Toward Defining and Integrating Multicultural and Feminist Pedagogies", in C. Z. Enns and A. L. Sinacore (eds), *Teaching and Social Justice: Integrating Multicultural and Feminist Pedagogies in the Classroom*, 2–24, Washington, DC: American Psychological Association.

Freire, P. (1970), *Pedagogy of the Oppressed*, London: Penguin Random House.

Gilio-Whitaker, D. (2019), *As Long as Grass Grows: The Indigenous Fight for Environmental Justice from Colonization to Standing Rock*, Boston: Beacon Press.

Giroux, H. A. (2018), "Teachers as Transformative Intellectuals", in E. B. Hilty (ed.), *Thinking about Schools: A Foundation of Education Reader*, 183–9, New York: Routledge.

Glynn, C., P. Wesely and B. Wassell (2014), *Words and Actions: Teaching Languages through the Lens of Social Justice*, Alexandria, VA: ACTFL.

Harven, A. M. and K. A. Gordon-Biddle (2016), "Critical Literacy and Multicultural Literature: Pedagogical Strategies for the Everyday Classroom", in R. Papa, D. M. Eadens and D. W. Eadens (eds), *Social Justice Instruction: Empowerment on the Chalkboard*, 161–70, Cham, Heidelberg, New York, Dordrecht, London: Springer.

Hastings, C. and L. Jacob (eds) (2016), *Social Justice in English Language Teaching*, Alexandria, VA: TESOL Press.

Hawkins, M. R. (ed.) (2011), *Social Justice Language Teacher Education*, New York: Multilingual Matters.

Ladson-Billings, G. (1999), "Just What Is Critical Race Theory and What's It Doing in a Nice Field like Education?", in L. Parker, D. Deyhle and S. Villenas (eds), *Race Is … Race Isn't: Critical Race Theory and Qualitative Studies in Education*, 7–30, New York: Routledge.

Listyani, L. (2018), "Promoting Academic Writing Students' Skills through 'Process Writing' Strategy", *Advances in Language and Literary Studies*, 9 (4): 173–9.

Mayo, C. and N. M. Rodriguez (eds) (2019), *Queer Pedagogies: Theory, Praxis, Politics*, Switzerland: Springer.

Nieto, S. (2010), *Language, Culture, and Teaching: Critical Perspectives*, New York: Routledge.

Ortaçtepe Hart, D. (2023), *Social Justice and the Language Classroom: Reflection, Action, and Transformation*, Edinburgh: Edinburgh University Press.

Ortaçtepe Hart, D. and J. Martel (2020), "Introducing the Special Issue on Exploring the Transformative Potential of Language Instruction for Social Justice", *TESOL Journal*, 11 (4).

Wright, J. (2015), "Take Action: Social Justice in ELT", *The English Connection*, 19 (4): 19–20.

Zeichner, K. (2011), "Teacher Education for Social Justice", in M. R. Hawkins (ed.), *Social Justice Language Teacher Education*, 7–22, New York: Multilingual Matters.

Zorba, M. G. (2020), "Personal and Professional Readiness of In-service Teachers of English for Culturally Responsive Teaching", *Eurasian Journal of Educational Research*, 88: 41–66.

5

Cultivating a Language Teaching and Social Justice Praxis: Paying Attention to the Tension to Set Intention

Netta Avineri

Background

In recent years, critical applied linguists (see Motha 2020) and language teacher educators (Hawkins 2011; Varghese 2016) have been focusing more explicitly on issues of social change and social justice, highlighting that justice is relational and aspirational (Avineri and Martinez 2021). Some practical resources have been developed that focus on the integration of social issues into our pedagogical practices (see Glynn, Wesely and Wassell 2018). I teach at the Middlebury Institute of International Studies at Monterey (MIIS), a US graduate professional school with teacher candidates (TCs) from around the world. This chapter focuses on two critical language teacher education courses ("Introduction to Sociolinguistics" and "Language Teaching for Social Justice"), where we explore historical and contemporary topics (e.g., intersectionality, power, language and race, language and gender, privilege and oppression) in relation to TCs' experiences, perspectives, teaching contexts, and goals.

This chapter highlights approaches to cultivating a language teaching and social justice praxis (Freire 1972) that integrates theory and reflection for action. I will share several activities aligned with the dialogic pedagogical practice of "paying attention to the tension to set intention". In my critical reflection on this practice, I have identified three key pedagogical tensions: structure vs. agency, proactive vs. responsive approaches, and building community vs. building knowledge. The examples I share in this chapter demonstrate how centering the role of tension can meaningfully deepen TCs' critical knowledge, skills, and dispositions in the service of social justice.

Description of the Practice

TCs at MIIS are increasingly interested in exploring language and social justice in relation to their pedagogy. I have found that centering the role of tension at multiple scales (macro, meso, micro, and "me-cro"/individual) has been especially impactful in their coursework.

In this process, TCs gradually learn how to mindfully pay attention to tensions, navigate complex dialogues, and work with others to build toward something new. This section highlights specific activities during which TCs practice 'pay attention to the tension to set intention' in meaningful ways. We highlight a "language for social justice" orientation that integrates noticing the world as it is, critically examining the structures that have created present-day realities, and collectively building toward a new world—what is, what has been, and what could be (Avineri and Baquedano-López 2024).

In the Introduction to Sociolinguistics and Language Teaching for Social Justice courses, the TCs and I spend time creating Community Agreements in response to the prompt "What will make this a meaningful learning environment for you?". This discussion involves tension, as we are just beginning to build trust and open communication with one another. For blended synchronous courses this also involves co-creating Zoom chat guidelines to ensure everyone respectfully engages with the course content and with one another. This 'pay attention to the tension to set intention' activity provides a proactive structure alongside responsive agency, as we return regularly to the community agreements to gauge their relevance and impact for the classroom community.

TCs also reflect meaningfully upon their own identities and intersectionalities (e.g., race, gender, class, nationality), exploring their subjectivities and relationships to one another, the content, and to their own students. They then take this a step further by considering their positionalities (social identities in relation to their language teaching context) and their commitments to particular social issues (see Avineri and Baquedano-López 2024). They also consider situations in which their positionality means they can act in solidarity with a group or issue for which they are advocating (even when it is a group or an issue they do not have personal experience with). This critical practice highlights a key tension in language and social justice advocacy and provides the TCs with tools for acknowledging and navigating these tensions in their language classroom spaces.

We also explore tensions involved in their engagement with terms, authors, and texts. Based on readings on language, education, and social justice, TCs in the Language Teaching for Social Justice course collectively build a glossary of key terms for their developing praxis (e.g., intersectionality, equity, language ideologies). They are encouraged to explore tensions around the key terms they would teach their language learners and how they might explain/exemplify the terms for different levels and teaching contexts. Midway through the Introduction to Sociolinguistics course, we have in-depth metacognitive discussions about their reading responses, highlighting their "default" modes of posting about the readings and also challenging them to engage differently with the readings and with one another. They review their earlier reading responses, categorizing those into: 1. Clarifying (e.g., a term, an example, a concept), 2. Deepening: specific to the reading (topic/issue/context), 3. Exploring: about related areas (topic/issue/context), or 4. Applying: pedagogical applications. This categorization and reflection process allows TCs to consider their academic and professional socialization and experiment with a different type of reading response for future postings. We highlight the tensions involved in issues of "audience" (Avineri 2020). They are encouraged to move away from simply writing *about* the readings and instead imagine writing their responses to the authors of those readings. This process can encourage a deeper engagement with the course material, by humanizing the scholars whose work they are reading.

In the Introduction to Sociolinguistics course, we explore the tensions involved in observation and narrative methodologies, through a Linguistic Landscapes activity (observation and documentation of language use in public contexts) and a Language Learner Interviews project (semi-structured interviews with learners of the language they plan to teach/are teaching, then displayed in a visual format). They dialogue about the tensions of observing one's surroundings and engaging with personal stories of language learning, especially as these relate to their own subjectivities. They share themes and findings in a visual format, affording sustained explorations around the topic of "audience" and multimodality for awareness-raising and social change. They bring these threads together through their final Pedagogical Philosophies & Practices Project (see Appendix for guidelines), integrating the various course themes and crystallizing how critical tensions, complexity, and dialogue can inform their approach to language education moving forward. Encouraged to write this project as a letter to their future selves, they engage in a unique student agency-focused approach to sharing about their learning and aspirations. It is heartening to read how these philosophies and practices coalesce with their visions of a new world.

In the Language Teaching for Social Justice course, global language teaching and social justice case studies (see Hastings and Jacob 2016) provide meaningful opportunities for exploring tensions, complexity, and dilemmas involved in the "what," "how," and "why" of diverse social justice-oriented pedagogical approaches. "What" refers to topics, content, and language foci; "How" refers to creation of spaces and navigating of dynamics. We explore the role of ethics in decision-making and whether/how to teach empathy in a language classroom. Reading about these case studies complements TCs' own case studies, examples, and anecdotes, deepened in their Critical Reflections. By sharing their perspectives and stories, they recognize the importance of narrative (including storytelling and "storylistening") in fostering a language education and social justice praxis.

Within the Language Teaching for Social Justice course we also discuss the relevant language education and social justice lesson planning components for different audiences (e.g., themselves, their MA professors, possible substitute teachers) and how TCs can shape the lesson plans accordingly (e.g., including course goals, essential questions, learning objectives, activities, assessments, backup plans). They have multiple opportunities for brainstorming and feedback during class and in asynchronous discussion board activities. We discuss critical incidents (Avineri 2017) and "hot moments" (Glynn, Wesely and Wassell 2018) in language courses focused on social justice, to highlight the complexity and tensions involved in this work. In pairs, TCs review one another's lesson plans and in Google Docs "comments" provide feedback—words of encouragement, points of clarification, and possible "critical incidents" that may occur during the lesson. The TCs revise their lesson plans (see Appendix for guidelines) to proactively plan for and address these issues and engage in in-depth reflection about the different phases of this exercise. This multi-step approach to lesson conceptualization, planning, feedback, and revision is a relevant framework for critical language teacher education since it highlights the central roles of dialogue, complexity, audience, and tension.

The last activity highlighting the role of tension in the Language Teaching for Social Justice course is a language and social justice advocacy plan (see Appendix for guidelines), which highlights questions around a language teacher's possible impact and at what scale(s). TCs are encouraged to identify a topic of interest to them, based on a combination of their positionalities, commitments, lesson plan topics, and teaching contexts (e.g., "standard" and "non-standard" language varieties, students with learning differences in the language classroom, racial equity). This phase broadens the scope beyond classrooms and institutions to wider issues of social concern, moving from "language for language" to a "language for social justice" orientation. "Audience coalescence" is central to language-based advocacy work since it integrates a range of perspectives and modes of communication to mobilize for social change (Avineri and Perley 2018). Tensions around the role of audience are important to consider, as students explore how to frame one's message for those with a range of perspectives. The TCs create group "advocacy plans" for an issue they identify, integrating discussion of audience, multimodality, awareness-raising, and action. These activities also recognize individual language teachers' agency in broader social systems, which can be a productive outcome of tension—both empowering and critically important.

Critical Reflections: Potentials and Challenges

Tension has been central in cultivating my own language education and social justice praxis, in particular the tensions between humility and expertise, participation and observation, and inquiry and action (Avineri 2019). I have found it essential for TCs to notice, engage with, and set goals based on the tensions (Britzman 2012) they are experiencing in the development of their praxis. The activities and assignments shared here provide TCs with opportunities to share about themselves, their experiences, and their contexts (e.g., Linguistic Landscapes, Language Learner Interviews, Sociolinguistics Teaching Philosophy and Practices, Lesson Planning, Advocacy Plan). The tension of objectivity vs. subjectivity comes up frequently in terms of TCs' questions about bias, their positions as teachers, and how to cultivate meaningful conversations with their own students. These courses create generative spaces where the TCs learn about themselves and one another as educators (past, present, and future). They creatively bring together research, course topics, class discussions, and their personal experiences to a deeper understanding of the role of language in social justice.

The tensions that I personally experience when teaching these courses center around three main areas: prioritizing structure vs. agency, being proactive vs. responsive, and building community vs. focusing on content knowledge. I have found that by centering the role of tension, each moment in these courses becomes an opportunity for meta-level dialogue, modeling, and reflection. Through my experience in these courses, it has become clear that co-creating critical language education classrooms that integrate dialogue, tensions, and complexity can provide TCs with essential approaches for their future language teaching contexts. In this ever-changing world it is imperative for us to shape our relationships and pedagogies in innovative ways to collectively build toward a more just world.

References

Avineri, N. (2017), *Research Methods for Language Teaching: Inquiry, Process, and Synthesis*, Basingstoke, UK: Palgrave Macmillan.

Avineri, N. (2019), "'Nested Interculturality': Dispositions and Practices for Navigating Tensions in Immersion Experiences", in D. Martin and E. Smolcic (eds), *Redefining Teaching Competence through Immersive Programs*, 37–64, Cham: Palgrave Macmillan.

Avineri, N. (2020), "Audience (and Audience Design)", in J. Stanlaw (ed.), *The International Encyclopedia of Linguistic Anthropology*, 1–5, Wiley: Blackwell Publishers.

Avineri, N. and D. C. Martinez (2021), "Applied Linguists Cultivating Relationships for Justice: An Aspirational Call to Action", *Applied Linguistics*, 42 (6): 1043–54.

Avineri, N. and P. Baquedano—López (2004), *An Introduction to Language and Social Justice: What Is, What Has Been, and What Could Be*, New York: Routledge Publishers.

Avineri, N. and B. C. Perley (2018), "Mascots, Name Calling, and Racial Slurs", in N. Avineri, L. Graham, E. Johnson, R. C. Riner and J. D. Rosa (eds), *Language and Social Justice in Practice*, 1st edn, 147–56, New York: Routledge.

Britzman, D. P. (2012), *Practice Makes Practice: A Critical Study of Learning to Teach*, New York: SUNY Press.

Freire, P. (1972), *Pedagogy of the Oppressed*, London, UK: Penguin Books.

Glynn, C., P. Wesely and B. Wassell (2018), *Words and Actions: Teaching Languages through the Lens of Social Justice*, 2nd edn, Alexandria, VA: The American Council on the Teaching of Foreign Languages.

Hastings, C. and L. Jacob (2016), *Social Justice in English Language Teaching*, Alexandria, VA: TESOL Press.

Hawkins, M. (2011), *Social Justice Language Teacher Education*, Bristol: Multilingual Matters.

Motha, S. (2020), "Is an Antiracist and Decolonizing Applied Linguistics Possible?", *Annual Review of Applied Linguistics*, 40: 128–33.

Varghese, M. M. (2016), "Language Teacher Educator Identity and Language Teacher Identity: Towards a Social Justice Perspective", in G. Barkhuizen (ed.), *Reflections on Language Teacher Identity Research*, 51–6, New York: Routledge.

Appendix

Introduction to Sociolinguistics Teaching Philosophy & Practice Project

The Sociolinguistics Teaching Philosophy & Practice Project is an opportunity for you to crystallize your belief systems in relation to your pedagogical practice.

For this project you will engage in the following steps.
1. Identify 5–6 key sources/resources relevant to specific sociolinguistic aspects of your language teaching (2 in-class sources + outside book chapters, articles, blog posts, podcasts) (integrated in your write-up of #2–5 below)
2. Create a sociolinguistic teaching philosophy that identifies your core beliefs about language teaching (max. 1 page)

3. Share 3–4 specific practices you will engage in as a sociolinguistically sensitive language teacher (based on the sources/resources you identified above) (max. 1 page)
4. Pinpoint 2–3 tensions that arise when you consider taking these approaches as well as how you might address those tensions (max. 1 page)
5. Specify what sociolinguistics topics you still want to explore and how you might explore these topics in the future (1–2 paragraphs)

You will then write a letter to your future self as a language teacher OR to a fellow teacher/administrator with the information listed above.

Language Teaching for Social Justice Lesson Plan Assignment

You will create a social justice in language education lesson plan for your (target) language context, integrating everything we have learned throughout the semester.

The Lesson Plan will include the following ten components:
1. Basic Information about Context
    a. Lesson context at various scales (nation, region, local community, university, private company, Spanish as a Foreign Language)
    b. Level, age, and number of students
    c. Their sociocultural and sociolinguistic background(s)
    d. Students' learning goals
2. What has been covered in class already, what will be covered after this lesson
3. Lesson Objectives (SWBATs, or "students will be able to"): include language objectives & social justice objectives
4. Teaching Objectives
5. Topic (social justice), Language Skills (speaking, listening, reading, writing; oracy & literacy; receptive & productive; form, meaning, & use), Specific Vocabulary
6. Timetable
7. Procedures/Tasks/Activities (e.g., Pre, During, Post; Engage, Study, Activate; Into, Through, Beyond)
8. 2–3 Relevant Resources that connect language and social justice objectives (e.g., websites, videos)
9. Corrective Feedback, Assessment, Differentiation (considering social justice goals)
10. Anticipated problems/issues and how you might address them

2–3 Paragraph Rationale for your approach:
1. Demonstrate an understanding of both the how and the what of social justice in relation to language education
2. Identify at least 3 of our glossary terms that are relevant for your lesson plan and describe how they are relevant
3. Discuss your positionalities and your commitments in relation to the lesson plan's focus and/or approach

4. Where are 2–3 possible "hot moments" and how you would proactively plan for these & also responsively address them?
5. Identify 1–2 tensions that arise as you plan this lesson. How might you address them?

Language Teaching for Social Justice Advocacy Plan Assignment

In small groups you will create an advocacy plan for a topic/group of students relevant to language education for social justice. Your advocacy plan should demonstrate an understanding of both the how and the what of social justice in relation to language education. Note also that advocacy includes both awareness-raising and a call to action.

Your advocacy plan will include the following ten components:
1. What type of advocacy do you plan to engage in? Self-advocacy, individual advocacy, or systems advocacy? https://cedwvu.org/resources/types-of-advocacy/
2. What social issue will you focus on? What is your operationalized definition of this social issue?
3. What are your positionalities and commitments in relation to this social issue?
4. What is feasible social change at the scales you can impact (e.g., me-cro, micro, meso, macro)?
5. Who are your key audiences? What do they already know? How do they engage with information?
6. What are your goals for this advocacy plan? What do you want to communicate? How will you do so?
7. What resources do you need to attain your goals? What information do you want to share with these audiences? What is your call to action?
8. What is your timeline?
9. What tensions might arise during this advocacy work? How might you address these?
10. How will you know if you have attained your goals?

Part Three

Instructional Materials Analysis and Development

6

Pedagogizing Critical Materials Analysis and Development

Yasemin Tezgiden-Cakcak

Introduction

Language education under neoliberal globalization has been marked by pre-packaged, teacher-proof, commercial materials (Gray 2013; McGrath 2013) and characterized as "an era of textbook-defined practice" (Akbari 2008: 647). While the textbook has become "the curriculum" (Masuhara 2011) shaping the way languages are learned, taught, and practiced, the teacher has become a passive technician responsible for teaching it (Kumaravadivelu 2003). In this regime of "edu-businesses" (Ball 2012), planners (i.e., curriculum developers, materials producers) are separated from executors (i.e., teachers and administrators) (Apple 1995). While material writers and publishers exert great control over what gets selected, promoted, and legitimized (Ball 2012; Gray 2013), teachers are divorced from curriculum development processes and become deskilled (Apple 1995).

Teacher autonomy is further restricted by undemocratic administrative practices where teachers are not involved in decision-making practices, and thus dehumanized. Teachers are often stripped off their agency and not allowed to select their coursebooks. The decision is made among available commercial coursebooks on their behalf by a superior power (e.g., ministries of education or school administrations) and imposed upon them in a top-down fashion. Without preparation in their teacher education programs, teachers may not have the confidence or competence to take part in course design and/or material selection, either, and may readily accept to rely on "experts" telling them what to do (Apple and Jungck 1990). Due to their lack of professional competence, they may see materials as indispensable for learning to teach (Richards 1998). They may also attach so much unjustified value and authority to textbooks (reification), they feel obliged to use them slavishly (McGrath 2013; Richards 1998). Intensification of workload (Apple and Jungck 1990) could be another reason for teachers' overdependence on coursebooks. Under heavy teaching loads with limited resources and income, they may have restricted time available for themselves and for professional development and become pleased to follow the book.

Despite the existence of various factors curtailing teacher and learner autonomy in terms of material development, selection, and use, it is still possible to resist, deconstruct, or challenge "the authority" of the coursebooks (Canagarajah 1999; Graves 2019; Thornbury 2013). The emergence of the Dogme movement as a reaction against the hegemony of coursebooks and the attention it drew showcase the existence of counter-hegemonic acts among language educators (Thornbury 2013). Teachers may very well adapt, supplement, or abandon textbooks. They may critically analyze their content and "turn the materials on their head" with their students (Littlejohn and Windeatt 1988, as cited in Thornbury 2013: 221). They may also generate critical materials from scratch. Yet, for teachers and learners to take a more active role in material analysis and development, it is necessary for them to be ready to take the challenge (McGrath 2013) even under difficult conditions. Although this might be easily said than done, it could actually be probable if teachers are supported by critical teacher education programs (Tezgiden-Cakcak 2019a). With critical English language teacher education (ELTE), teachers could (re)gain critical consciousness, develop competence and confidence to use their agency to select, adapt, develop, and use critical materials with the participation of their students (Crookes 2013), develop resilience to struggle with the challenges along the process, and co-build a professional community to support their decisions.

Drawing its theoretical lens from critical pedagogy, this chapter aims to direct attention to teacher education's crucial role in supporting and empowering teachers in claiming their rights to become involved in course design, material analysis, and development. This chapter also provides a blueprint for pedagogizing critical language material analysis and development in teaching and teacher education.

Current Issues

No matter how dominant textbook use is in language education, instructional materials in language learning/teaching are not restricted to coursebooks. Materials could be anything that facilitate the learning of a target language such as coursebooks, songs, dictionaries, mobile phone applications, games, and realia (Tomlinson and Masuhara 2018). This broad range of tools used in language education is distinguished on the basis of institutions which produce them (commercial publishers, Ministries, or large institutions), for what use and purpose they are prepared (real-life use or pedagogic purpose, General English or English for Specific Purposes), for which audience they are produced (global, national, local, or glocal), what variety of English they use (English as a Native Language, Global Englishes, English as a lingua franca), by whom they are generated (textbook writers, teachers, or learners), which medium they use (print or digital), for which end they are written (commercial or non-commercial) and for which markets they are produced (globally marketed or versioned) (Buchanan and Norton 2022; Cogo 2022; Gray 2013; McGrath 2013). Although these distinctions might just appear to be analytical, they may in fact have a lasting impact on the design, selection, and implementation of materials.

Contrary to mainstream educational views, instructional language materials are not prepared and implemented solely taking into account pedagogic and/or linguistic considerations. Nor are they produced and/or consumed in a vacuum isolated from the politic-economic or sociocultural realities of the glocal context. Selection of language, knowledge, and images in the textbooks are never neutral or disinterested; they serve the interests of dominant groups and reproduce existing power relations with regard to class, gender, sexuality, race, ethnicity, citizenship, language, ability, etc. Materials are not only curriculum artifacts used to facilitate language learning, but they are also cultural and ideological artifacts, which legitimize particular uses of language along with a certain body of knowledge and culture (Gray 2013). Language teaching materials reveal cultural and ideological messages about "proper" ways of being, living, consuming, and languaging through pictures, stories, and dialogues (Block 2018; Gray 2012; Pennycook 2010).

Materials are developed and utilized in a complex web of relations (McGrath 2013) and often serve contradictory interests (i.e., pedagogic, commercial, ideological, and ethical) (Gray 2013). For instance, a commercially produced Anglo-American-based global ELT textbook could prioritize maximizing profit for mass consumption and not touch upon so-called "sensitive" political issues or include LGBTQ+ individuals not to offend conservative markets (Gray 2013). As a matter of fact, global ELT coursebooks depict a sanitized world free of problems avoiding PARSNIP (politics, alcohol, religion, sex, narcotics, isms, and pork) to appeal to a larger population (Gray 2002). In a similar vein, global coursebooks legitimize neoliberal ideologies and promote an individualistic, competitive, and consumption-oriented middle-class lifestyle erasing working-class characters and issues (Gray and Block 2014). In a recent work, Bori (2022) argued neoliberal ideologies infiltrate in language coursebooks and normalize neoliberal entrepreneurship and consumer culture. On the other hand, national ELT coursebooks, such as those published by the Ministry of Education in Türkiye, might prioritize home culture and national values over global ones (Özcan 2019). While teacher-produced materials address pedagogic purposes much better in line with particular learner needs, they might reproduce dominant gender and sexuality norms in the society (Selvi and Kocaman 2021).

Implications for Teaching and Teacher Education

For language teachers to see materials not only as educational tools, but also as cultural, ideological, and commercial artifacts and to imagine using their agency to take critical action, critical ELTE is necessary. It aims to educate teachers as transformative intellectuals (Giroux 1983), who raise critical consciousness in and out of the class to create a democratic, just, and equitable society. Critical language teacher education programs do not only provide pre-service and in-service teachers with technical knowledge, but aim to foster their critical reflection and transformative action situating educational issues in a broader political, economic, social, and cultural context (Hawkins and Norton 2009). Teacher candidates and/or practicing teachers are invited to critically analyze their own values, beliefs, thoughts, and emotions to unlearn some of their taken-for-granted views. They are also encouraged to take critical action by problematizing current daily issues in teachers' and students' lives and/or working as allies with the marginalized students for inclusion. Instructional materials might work as a gateway for critical teachers and learners to (de-/re-)construct the explicit and/or implicit messages conveyed in them.

Here I will theorize my own critical teacher education practice to facilitate critical materials analysis, development, and use among language teachers. As a teacher-educator working at a pre-service ELTE program in central Türkiye, I strive to incorporate critical reflection and action (praxis) in my teacher education practices. In my materials evaluation and development course, I aim to help student teachers develop their skills, imagination, and confidence to produce and use critical materials. To this end, I provide student teachers with theoretical background on critical pedagogy and critical materials analysis, and engage student teachers in collective hands-on work in a dialogic, democratic classroom atmosphere. My pedagogic experiment enabled student teachers to problematize language, visuals, and content in their textbooks and to introduce critical materials after graduation (Tezgiden-Cakcak 2019a, b). Theorizing my pedagogy, I argue that language teacher education for critical material analysis and development should incorporate three components in a respective order:

A Dialogic Democratic Classroom Atmosphere as a Professional Community

Dialogue, inclusion, respect, trust, and democratic participation are indispensable elements in critical education along with humility, love, and hope (Freire 1970). Without having a humble attitude to learn with and from student teachers, teacher educators cannot open space to become teachers and learners at the same time. Loving and respecting student teachers and believing in their agentive potential are essential without which you cannot assign intellectually challenging tasks requiring research, collaboration, imagination, critical, and creative thinking skills. Building a sincere dialogic relationship with student teachers based on trust is necessary to work collectively in generating critical language teaching materials. Another crucial dimension in critical praxis is having an "educated hope" (Giroux 2022: 26) for transformation to take place. Teacher educators, pre-service and in-service teachers should believe in the "possibility" of their critical materials to create change in themselves, their students, and the larger community.

Theoretical Background Knowledge of Critical Pedagogy and Critical Materials Analysis

Student teachers need to understand how mainstream education and critical education differ in defining the purpose of education: the former socializing students to become "good" workers, consumers, and citizens without causing any trouble for the maintenance of the system, the latter helping students to understand the reasons behind their financial, political, social, cultural, and psychological troubles and to take action to change them. Introductory readings in critical pedagogy are useful (e.g., Freire 1970; Kincheloe 2008) for student teachers to get a basic understanding of the main concepts of critical education. Student teachers also need to see how these basic principles translate into critical language materials analysis. Rashidi and Safari's (2011) framework, which applies main principles of critical pedagogy to language materials design, helps student teachers make the necessary connections. In this framework, researchers divide five factors of materials design (program, content, pedagogical, teacher, and learner factors) into subgroups and come up with eleven principles (e.g., Principle 1—ELT materials should develop learners' communicative competence and raise critical consciousness) for materials design. After gaining a general theoretical perspective, student teachers form groups to facilitate discussion on critical language materials analysis studies from the global and local context (e.g., Arıkan 2005, 2008; Gray 2012, 2013; Gray and Block 2014; Selvi and Kocaman 2021). These readings and discussions enable student teachers to broaden their critical lens in materials analysis.

Collaborative Hands-On Work for Critical Materials Analysis, Development, and Use

Having gained a theoretical understanding of critical education and materials analysis, student teachers are ready to experiment with critical materials analysis, development, and use. First, they form groups and investigate global, glocal, or national coursebooks, as in the critical research studies they read. Collaboratively, they write research papers, give poster presentations, and share their findings with their classmates. Such hands-on work sharpens their research skills and deepens their understanding of critical analysis.

After their mini-scale research study on language teaching materials as cultural and ideological artifacts, student teachers work together to face a new challenge: they produce their own sample critical language teaching units focusing on a specific theme (e.g., class, gender, race, linguistic diversity, multiculturalism, ability, citizenship, etc.). Student teachers may feel a bit overwhelmed in imagining critical language teaching materials not having encountered such materials before. They might also feel challenged in producing materials from page design to language tasks. Although it may take time to activate their creativity, they usually show their full creative potential when encouraged by teacher educators (Tezgiden-Cakcak 2019a).

Another concern student teachers may have is the plausibility of the implementation of such materials in real life given the realities of test-oriented traditional schooling systems under the rising authoritarian, neoliberal regimes around the world. Although they may be right considering the risks using such materials might entail in certain contexts, we need to show them it is important to imagine designing such tasks in the first place. After analyzing the dynamics of their teaching context, they might also experiment with some of their critical materials. Once student teachers see the impact of their critical materials on engaging language learners and developing critical consciousness, they usually have a hard time using mainstream materials as they are.

Conclusion

Despite heavy constraints on teachers' work, autonomy, critical, and creative action, it might be possible for language teachers to engage in critical language materials analysis, development, and use with their students if encouraged by critical teacher educators. In this way, teachers might find it easier to read what is legitimized in language materials. They may use this interpretation to supplement their coursebooks with critical ideas and/or tasks. They may also engage in a similar critical materials analysis, design, and use processes with their students, as suggested for teacher education above. First, they could create a dialogic, democratic, and safe classroom space. Even if they are forced to follow a certain textbook, they could use a problem-posing pedagogy and invite students to raise questions on the content, design, and use of materials they have in hand. They could also include students in choosing and/or constructing new materials.

Hegemony of the textbook industry notwithstanding, teachers, teacher educators, and learners may open space for critical praxis if they empower themselves and support one another. Only would such solidarity enable transformation of the "textbook-defined practice" (Akbari 2008: 647) for an inclusive, participatory, and critical education. When teachers feel competent and confident to take part in critical educational practices, they may not only change their classroom pedagogy, they may also take action to challenge institutional practices leading the way to a deep-rooted change. After all, creating an equitable, just, and democratic education/society is a never-ending process and we are all in the process of becoming as "unfinished beings" (Freire 1970: 84).

References

Akbari, R. (2008), "Postmethod Discourse and Practice", *TESOL Quarterly*, 42 (4): 641–52.

Apple, M. W. (1995), *Education and Power*, 2nd edn, New York: Routledge.

Apple, M. W. and S. Jungck (1990), "You Don't Have to Be a Teacher to Teach This Unit!: Teaching, Technology, and Gender in the Classroom", *American Educational Research Journal*, 27 (2): 227–51.

Arıkan, A. (2005), "Age, Gender and Social Class in ELT Coursebooks: A Critical Study", *Hacettepe Üniversitesi Eğitim Fakültesi Dergisi*, 28: 29–38.

Arıkan, A. (2008), "Topics of Reading Passages in ELT Coursebooks: What Do Our Students Really Read?", *The Reading Matrix*, 8 (2): 1–16.

Ball, S. J. (2012), *Global Education Inc: Policy Networks and Edu-business*, New York: Routledge.

Block, D. (2018), *Political Economy and Sociolinguistics: Neoliberalism, Inequality and Social Class*, New York: Bloomsbury Publishing.

Bori, P. (2022), "Representation in Coursebooks: A Critical Perspective", in J. Norton and H. Buchanan (eds), *The Routledge Handbook of Materials Development for Language Teaching*, 123–35, New York: Routledge.

Buchanan, H. and J. Norton (2022), "Versioning Coursebooks", in J. Norton and H. Buchanan (eds), *The Routledge Handbook of Materials Development for Language Teaching*, 307–20, New York: Routledge.

Canagarajah, A. S. (1999), *Resisting Linguistic Imperialism in English Teaching*, Oxford: Oxford University Press.
Cogo, A. (2022), "From Global English to Global Englishes: Questioning Current Approaches to ELT Materials", in J. Norton and H. Buchanan (eds), *The Routledge Handbook of Materials Development for Language Teaching*, 93–108, New York: Routledge.
Crookes, G. V. (2013), *Critical ELT in Action: Foundations, Promises, Praxis*, New York: Routledge.
Freire, P. (1970), *Pedagogy of the Oppressed 30th Anniversary Edition*, New York: Continuum.
Giroux, H. (1983), *Theory and Resistance in Education towards a Pedagogy for the Opposition*, New York: Bergin & Garvey Publishers.
Giroux, H. (2022), "An Interview with Henry A. Giroux: Cultural Studies and Pandemic Pedagogy", in F. Mızıkacı and E. Ata (eds), *Critical Pedagogy and the Covid-19 Pandemic*, 15–28, New York: Bloomsbury.
Graves, K. (2019), "Survey Review: Recent Books on Language Materials Development and Analysis", *ELT Journal*, 73 (3): 337–54.
Gray, J. (2002), "The Global Coursebook in English Language Teaching", in D. Block and D. Cameron (eds), *Globalization and Language Teaching*, 161–77, London: Routledge.
Gray, J. (2012), "Neoliberalism, Celebrity and 'Aspirational Content' in English Language Teaching Textbooks for the Global Market", in D. Block, J. Gray and M. Holborow (eds), *Neoliberalism and Applied Linguistics*, 91–118, London: Routledge.
Gray, J. (2013), *Critical Perspectives on Language Teaching Materials*, New York: Palgrave Macmillan.
Gray, J. and D. Block (2014), "All Middle Class Now? Evolving Representations of the Working Class in the Neoliberal Era: The Case of ELT Textbooks", in N. Harwood (ed.), *English Language Teaching Textbooks Content, Consumption, Production*, 45–71, Hampshire: Palgrave Macmillan.
Hawkins, M. and B. Norton (2009), "Critical Language Teacher Education", in A. Burns and J. Richards (eds), *The Cambridge Guide to Second Language Teacher Education*, 30–9, Cambridge: Cambridge University Press.
Kincheloe, J. K. (2008), *Critical Pedagogy*, 2nd edn, New York: Peter Lang Publishing.
Kumaravadivelu, B. (2003), *Beyond Methods Macrostrategies for Language Teaching*, New Haven, CT: Yale University Press.
Masuhara, H. (2011), "What Do Teachers Really Want from Coursebooks?", in B. Tomlinson (ed.), *Materials Development in Language Teaching*, 2nd edn, 236–66, Cambridge: Cambridge University Press.
McGrath, I. (2013), *Teaching Materials and the Roles of EFL/ESL Teachers: Practice and Theory*, London: Bloomsbury Academic.
Özcan, E. N. (2019), *The Analysis of Global Values in ELT Coursebooks Published by the Ministry of National Education for 2018-2019 Academic Years*. Unpublished master's thesis. Uludağ University.
Pennycook, A. (2010), "Critical and Alternative Directions in Applied Linguistics", *Australian Review of Applied Linguistics*, 33 (2): 16.1–16.16.
Rashidi, N. and F. Safari (2011), "A Model for EFL Materials Development within the Framework of Critical Pedagogy (CP)", *English Language Teaching*, 4 (2): 250–9.
Richards, J. (1998), "Textbooks: Help or Hindrance?", in *Beyond Training*, 125–40, Cambridge: Cambridge University Press.

Selvi, A. F. and C. Kocaman (2021), "(Mis-/Under-) Representations of Gender and Sexuality in Locally-Produced ELT Materials", *Journal of Language, Identity & Education*, 20 (2): 118–33.

Tezgiden-Cakcak, Y. (2019a), *Moving beyond Technicism in English Language Teacher Education*, A case study from Turkey. Lanham, MD: Lexington Books.

Tezgiden-Cakcak, Y. (March 12, 2019b), "Critical Awareness in a Materials Analysis and Development Course", *AAAL 2019*, Atlanta, GA: Atlanta.

Thornbury, S. (2013), "Resisting Coursebooks", in J. Gray (ed.), *Critical Perspectives on Language Teaching Materials*, 204–23, London: Palgrave Macmillan.

Tomlinson, B. and H. Masuhara (2018), *The Complete Guide to Materials Development for Language Learning*, London: Wiley.

Analyzing Instructional Materials: A Global Englishes Language Teaching (GELT) Activity in a Brazilian Context

Marcia Regina Pawlas Carazzai and Ana Raquel Fialho Ferreira Campos

Background

Textbooks are a major influence on the way language is taught and perceived by students (Matsuda 2012), and it is a crucial field for critical reflection in language teacher education. Teacher learners will have contact with a variety of textbooks professionally, and it is profitable that they become aware of the premises that inform the textbooks used so that they can adapt or expand the material. Despite the global use of English, it is widely noticed in textbooks the presence of hegemonic varieties and stereotypical cultural aspects that ignore the dynamic variety and plurality students will meet (Lopriore and Vettorel 2018; Siqueira 2020). The majority of coursebooks for English instruction have been anesthetized politically and socially with the goal of being harmless for an international audience (Akbari 2008). Hence, critically analyzing textbooks is an important intellectual exercise for teacher learners, enabling them for their professional tasks and future choices.

In this chapter, we describe an activity that critically examines coursebooks and can be conducted with pre- and in-service English language teachers. Since we work as teacher educators in Brazil, we take our context into consideration as an example. Our goal was to guide teacher learners into noticing how these coursebooks are linguistically, methodologically, and ideologically conceived, discussing if there is a place for Global Englishes Language Teaching (GELT) practice (Rose and Galloway 2019; Cavalheiro in this volume). We also wanted to tackle positive outcomes of handling in class a material that considers students' local culture and their identities, contrasting with an international textbook that will hardly foster a similar approach.

We conducted the activity described here with a group of seven Brazilian teacher learners; all of them were speakers of Portuguese as a first language. These teacher learners were enrolled in an English language and literature undergraduate program, in which they have modules focusing on the four skills to develop their proficiency, as well as teaching methodology. Both of us taught the same group and we decided to plan and conduct the activity together so that the entire group could reflect more critically on the adoption and use of English language coursebooks.

Description of the Practice

The activity consisted of critically examining two coursebooks for teaching English widely used in Brazil. One of the coursebooks is called "Way to English for Brazilian learners—6° ano" (year 6) (Franco and Tavares 2019), it is from a series written by Brazilian authors and for Brazilian students, and it is frequently used in basic compulsory education as it is part of the National Textbook Program. The other coursebook is called "Touchstone—level 1" (McCarthy et al. 2014), which is an international textbook commonly adopted in language centers in Brazil. The choice was based on analyzing contrasting materials, one with a local (Brazilian in this case) perspective and another with a more international approach, besides the fact that both books are comparable in terms of proficiency level (beginners).

We decided to analyze one unit from each textbook and chose two that shared a common language structure and presented thought-provoking content. For "Way to English for Brazilian learners—6° ano," we chose unit 8, entitled "Let's go to school" (Franco and Tavares 2019: 42–54); while for "Touchstone—Level 1" we chose unit 4, entitled "Everyday life" (McCarthy et al. 2014: 33–42). Besides the popularity of these two materials in Brazil, our choice was based on the level of the books and on the contents of the units, so that in both cases the units focus on everyday events, using the simple present tense. In both textbooks, units have about ten pages with exercises, pictures, and illustrations, and include activities that cover the four skills centered in the main theme and grammar point of the units. The major difference is that "Touchstone—Level 1" has an obvious Anglo-American orientation, while "Way to English for Brazilian learners—6° ano" is more aligned with a GELT perspective.

Before leading the activity, we went over the theoretical background of GELT to recollect the premises and call teacher learners' attention to the most important aspects of the status of English. Since teacher learners were already familiar with some readings about global English conducted in a previous course (Jordão 2004; Kachru 1985; for example), we mostly revised this content with them to start. After this theoretical overview with the teacher learners, we used the adapted GELT framework for textbook evaluation (Rose and Galloway 2019) to guide the analysis of the materials and conducted it in three steps:

1. Teacher learners were divided into four pairs and received a copy of both units of the coursebooks.
2. Each pair was instructed to analyze both units based on the four questions suggested by Rose and Galloway (2019: 141): (1) What models/norms of English are used in the book and audio materials? (2) Who are the target interlocutors in the materials? (3) How is ownership/culture depicted in the materials? (4) What linguistic orientation is promoted in the book?

3. Each pair presented their findings to the class while the others could make questions and comments.

In the beginning of the discussion, teacher learners tended to talk less than we expected. In order to help them, we decided to ask teacher learners specific questions about the materials, such as questions regarding the images and the varieties of English and nationalities. This made the teacher learners' participation increase, and they started making connections to their personal experiences.

After comparing the units from both textbooks, teacher learners concluded that the locally produced material (Franco and Tavares 2019) was a better option since it takes into consideration teacher learners' and students' local culture and their identities, which contrasts with the international textbook.

Critical Reflections: Potentials and Challenges

Based on the outcomes we had in class with our teacher learners, we can say that activities with textbooks evoke teacher learners' personal experiences. While browsing the pages and handling the material, teacher learners made comments about their own experiences learning English at language centers or in basic compulsory education.

Moreover, teacher learners noticed that the international material (Touchstone 1) took the native speaker norm as reference for pronunciation and language ownership. For example, the audios use American English (McCarthy et al. 2014: 38), there are references to American cities (2014: 39), and the reading section states "In the lifetime of an average American" (2014: 40). This observation led us to critically reflect on the current status of English and how limited connections like those do not benefit students. We also tackled the work with minimal pairs inside an English classroom and the need to critically look at pronunciation exercises, guiding the class into noticing the role of environment and context, reinforcing that communication happens beyond words.

At the end of the task, one of the teacher learners explained that while doing the analysis, she realized how taking her students and their culture into consideration was a crucial part of textbook choice. Another teacher learner also commented that in the future they might be in the position of choosing textbooks to be adopted at work and an activity like this has critically prepared them for a better look at textbooks.

The main challenges of this activity were related to the teacher learners' lack of familiarity with coursebook analysis, especially based on Rose and Galloway's (2019) GELT perspective. We understand this happened mainly because most teacher learners in our group still did not have experience with teaching, and thus they were not aware of how to analyze, use, and adapt coursebooks. One possible solution for this would be making Rose and Galloway's (2019) text available to teacher learners in advance, to familiarize them with this specific content. During the task, we noticed that although we explained that teacher learners should indicate the pages or exercises that supported their analysis, they began the discussion with superficial and overall comments, which led us to ask them about the page and activity that reflected that opinion. Thus, it would be profitable to better guide teacher learners into the analysis by giving teacher learners a handout in which they could write the pages of the unit and the exercises that mirrored the point being discussed.

It would also be helpful to show teacher learners some examples of analysis of other materials before they start their work, so they could visualize with more details how the investigation could be done. One possibility would be discussing the work of Siqueira (2020), who analyzed a few English textbooks approved by the National Textbook Program (PNLD) for local public high schools.

Also, we asked teacher learners to work in pairs since we had a small group and this has helped them to discuss and share their views; besides the fact that material analysis is often a task performed in small team/groups. However, working in trios or in groups of four could be more profitable, as there would be more points of view which would culminate in a more diverse discussion.

With reference to replicating this activity in other contexts, a potential challenge might be the lack of locally produced coursebooks for the teaching of English, which in our case was a book written by Brazilians and for Brazilians. In this case, different coursebooks produced internationally can be compared to identify which one is more aligned with the local culture and what possible adaptations to approximate the material to a GELT perspective are.

As a result, this activity can provide opportunities to discuss how the EFL orientation endorses practices that are disengaged from social, historical, cultural, and political matters, ingrained in a native speakerism perspective (Siqueira 2020). It can also serve as an inspiration for teacher learners to adapt the international materials available or even to produce their own materials, including aspects related to their students' culture and identity.

References

Akbari, R. (2008), "Transforming Lives: Introducing Critical Pedagogy into ELT Classrooms", *ELT Journal*, 62 (3): 276–83.

Franco, C. P. and K. C. A. Tavares (2019), *Way to English for Brazilian Learners—6º ano*, São Paulo: Editora Ática.

Jordão, C. M. (2004), "A língua inglesa como commodity: Direito ou obrigação de todos?", in J. Romanowsky, P. Martins and S. Junqueira (eds), *Conhecimento local e conhecimento universal*, 287–96, Curitiba: Champagnat.

Kachru, B. B. (1985), "Standards, Codification, and Sociolinguistic Realism: The English Language in the Outer Circle", in R. Quirk and H. Widdowson (eds), *English in the World: Teaching and Learning the Language and the Literature*, 11–30, Cambridge: Cambridge University Press.

Lopriore, L. and P. Vettorel (2018). "Perspectives in WE—and ELF-Informed ELT Materials in Teacher Education", in N. Sifakis and N. Tsantila (eds), *English as a Lingua Franca for EFL contexts*, 97–116, Bristol: Multilingual Matters.

Matsuda, A. (2012), *Principles and Practices of Teaching English as an International Language*, Bristol: Multilingual Matters.

McCarthy, M., J. McCarten and H. Sandiford (2014), *Touchstone—Level 1*, Cambridge: Cambridge University Press.

Rose, H. and N. Galloway (2019), "Global Englishes and Language Teaching Materials", in H. Rose and N. Galloway (eds), *Global Englishes for Language Teaching*, 134–61, Cambridge: Cambridge University Press.

Siqueira, S. (2020). "ELT Materials for Basic Education in Brazil: Is There Room for an ELF-Aware Practice?", *Estudos Linguísticos e Literários*, 65 (1): 118–46.

8

The Affirming Diversity Project: Supporting Teachers Creating and Exchanging Culturally and Linguistically Responsive Materials

Priscila Leal and Perla Barbosa

Background

Language teaching is not exclusive to second or foreign language teachers—"teaching language belongs to all teachers" (Westerlund and de Oliveira 2016), including K-12 content teachers. As critical applied linguists in K-12 teacher education programs (TEPs), it is our goal to prepare all teachers, regardless of grade or subject, to be effective culturally and linguistically responsive (CLR) teachers of language. This chapter describes *The Affirming Diversity Project* (the Project), a collaborative activity that invites all teachers to design, develop, and exchange CLR teaching materials.

Our teachers represent diverse social, cultural, and linguistic backgrounds. When we first implemented the Project, twenty of the twenty-two teacher learners[1] in Priscila's class at the University of Hawai'i at Mānoa (UHM), US, were pursuing an elementary education major.[2] Ten grew up speaking only English at home, seven were bilingual in English and French, Japanese, Korean, or Spanish, and three spoke Cantonese and Mandarin or Japanese as their first languages. The forty-nine teacher learners in Perla's class at New Mexico State University (NMSU), US, were pursuing either elementary or secondary education majors with a bilingual or Teachers of English to Speakers of Other Languages (TESOL) endorsement. Most of them were of Hispanic origin representing both English-only speakers and Spanish-English bilinguals.

In 2019, 10.4 percent of K-12 public school students in the United States were multilingual learners (MLs)[3] compared to 9.9 percent in Hawai'i and 16.5 percent in New Mexico (National Center for Education Statistics 2022). The growing number of MLs in schools in the United States has led TEPs across the country to increase their efforts in preparing teachers to teach in ways that incorporate students' diverse cultural and linguistic backgrounds.

Multicultural Education[4] (MCE) is one such way. MCE seeks to create equitable education for all students by changing policies and practices "that devalue the identities of some students while overvaluing others" (Nieto 2010: 270). Those whose identities are devalued include MLs whose home language is "associated with low prestige and limited power—especially if they do not speak English well, or speak it with an accent" (Nieto 2010: 114). Despite the increased efforts in preparing teachers to teach MLs, these have focused mainly on the cultural aspect, not giving adequate attention to the linguistic element (Lucas and Villegas 2010). One, however, is intrinsically connected to the other (Moran 2011) and teachers must explicitly incorporate both CLR approaches to implement MCE successfully. A linguistically responsive teaching approach, as suggested by Lucas and Villegas (2013), puts language and linguistic diversity front and center. It proposes that all teachers must have certain sociolinguistic orientations, second language acquisition knowledge, and pedagogical skills to teach MLs well (for a list of CLR teaching principles, see Appendix A[5]).

Two of the most common questions we hear from teacher learners when introduced to MCE are:

1. How can I help MLs know that their cultural and linguistic knowledges matter?
2. Where can I find CLR teaching materials to support my MLs?

While there has been an increase in ready-to-use CLR teaching materials available in the last few years, there is still much to be done—especially within the context of language teacher education. We address this need by implementing the Project where teacher learners collaboratively design and develop ready-to-use[6] CLR teaching materials that nurture, perpetuate, and foster the cultural and linguistic diversity of their respective classroom contexts. The Project is grounded in Nieto's (2010) framework of an MCE that moves beyond tolerating and accepting differences to understanding, respecting, and affirming them—hence its title. While respect "implies admiration and high esteem for diversity" (255), the premise of affirmation "begins with the assumption that the many differences that students and their families represent are embraced and accepted as legitimate vehicles for learning" (257).

Description of the Practice

The Project design and implementation were inspired by a Project-Based Learning (PBL) framework (Blumenfeld et al. 1991), and it was divided into three phases (further described below). We had three main goals for implementing the Project. First, we desired for our teacher learners not only to learn *about* MCE but also *through* MCE. Being that collaboration is an essential aspect of MCE as it promotes a safe space for dialogical encounters and facilitates different negotiations and knowledge co-creation (Banks 2016), we designed the Project so that it would be a collaborative effort between the teacher learners.

Second, we wished to expose our teacher learners to different perspectives and experiences, discuss their thinking, and ultimately learn from one another. Therefore, we expanded the Project's collaboration aspect beyond our individual classrooms to include each other's. Accordingly, we co-designed and co-taught several lectures on the principles of CLR teaching and structured the Project to culminate in a mini conference.

Third, we wanted our teacher learners to rethink how to leverage their respective MLs' cultural and linguistic repertoire. Thus, the Project invited teacher learners across both institutions to design, develop, and exchange ready-to-use CLR teaching materials that reflected, perpetuated, and fostered the cultural and linguistic diversity of their individual classroom contexts.

To meet these goals each phase built upon the previous one (see Appendix B). In the first phase, design and development of materials, teacher learners came together in self-selected groups and submitted a material proposal (for a sample, see Appendix C) outlining Larmer's (2018) components as described above. To lay the Project's theoretical framework, teacher learners engaged with selected pages of Nieto (2010) before completing the proposal. In the proposal, they were asked to form a driving question based specifically on the needs of the MLs in their respective contexts. Good driving questions are engaging, challenging, open-ended, and linked to learning goals and require participants to gain the intended knowledge, build the skills, and think critically to be able to answer it (Larmer 2018). An example of an actual driving question is, "How can I help math teachers reshape their lessons to connect culturally with their students?" Teacher learners were further asked to relate their driving questions to one or more CLR teaching principles, develop a CLR teaching material or resource as the public product, identify a group (other than MLs) that could also benefit from these materials (e.g., caregivers, other teachers, the larger community, etc.), and justify their choices with direct references to Nieto (2010). We reviewed and provided feedback for all proposals and each group had the opportunity to revise their proposal to better reflect their driving question and to rethink their public product. Upon our approval, teacher learners then started to develop the actual public product (i.e., teaching material).

In the second phase, the asynchronous mini-conference, groups from both institutions presented their public products with a pre-recorded, fifteen-minute-long presentation. In these presentations, they introduced the main elements of their proposal, explained the teaching material development process, demonstrated how to use it, and shared images and links to the actual public product. All eighteen presentations, images, and links are publicly available on the Project's YouTube Channel (https://bit.ly/theaffirmingdiversityproject). After watching different presentations, teacher learners were asked to engage with each other authentically and meaningfully by asking material-related questions, sharing ways in which they could apply the teaching material to their own context, and offering feedback.

In the third and final phase, reflection, teacher learners reflected on the connection between the public products they engaged with and Nieto's (2010) call for cultural and linguistic solidarity in education. Teacher learners also identified the CLR teaching principles related to their respective public products, and shared feedback and/or suggestions about the Project. They were provided with prompts (see Appendix B) to guide their reflective process, and with a variety of modes and media to choose from to re/present their thinking (e.g., composing a piece of writing, recording an audio explanation, creating an illustration, combining drawing and text, among others).

Critical Reflections: Potentials and Challenges

Materials are an important part of the language classroom, yet access to ready-to-use CLR materials is scarce. We recognized this as an opportunity for our teacher learners to collaboratively design and develop authentic materials not only with real-world applications, but also that, as previously stated, nurture, perpetuate, and foster the cultural and linguistic diversity of their respective classrooms. While material development was our entry point to introducing our teacher learners to MCE and the principles of CLR teaching, it was through our collaboration that we were able to integrate and model the very CLR teaching principles we introduced to our teacher learners.

Although all our teacher learners were already somewhat familiar with a culturally responsive framework and easily connected their public products to its principles, for most of them, this was their first time contemplating a linguistically responsive framework during their TEP. Many had difficulty identifying linguistically responsive principles in their public products. As we prepare to implement the Project again in the future, we plan to emphasize the linguistically responsive framework and make it more prominent in the design and development phase.

As you adopt and adapt the Project, remember it can be implemented in several ways. While we opted for an asynchronous mini-conference (due to the Covid-19 pandemic restrictions and the time difference between our institutions' geographic locations), other forums such as virtual or in-person Gallery Walks and short publications in local TESOL organizations' newsletters can also create spaces for exchanging materials.

While it may not be feasible for some teacher educators to collaborate with other institutions, we highly encourage those to retain the collaborative element of the Project. Teacher educators facing these circumstances can look for opportunities for collaboration between teacher learners within their own institutions. If it is not possible to collaborate within one's own institution, teacher learners from the same class or cohort can still collaborate and exchange materials. There is value in thinking with others, being exposed to different experiences, and exchanging resources. It can open new ways of applying these resources to the different ethnic, linguistic, and geographic contexts each teacher learner finds themselves.

We hope that all teacher learners who participate in this Project, both past and future, will remember not only *what* they learn about MCE, but also *how* they feel as they learn through MCE and that this experience infuses them with the desire to continue designing and exchanging CLR teaching materials.

Notes

1   We use the term "teacher learner" to reflect the variety of teacher certification statuses and experience of those enrolled in our courses and our position that all teachers, regardless of certification status or experience, are learners. We deliberately avoid the terms "teacher candidate" and "student teacher" due to the lack of uniformity in their usage. For example, NSMU uses "student teacher" to refer to those who have completed all course requirements but field experience/practicum; UHM uses "teacher candidate."

2   The other two teacher learners were majoring in French and Hawaiian Studies.
3   We use the term MLs to highlight these individuals' linguistic resources rather than to use the English language as the measuring stick.
4   This broad term includes different perspectives of MCE such as Culturally Responsive, Culturally Relevant, Culturally Sustaining, Critical Pedagogy, Teaching for Social Justice, among others.
5   All appendices are publicly available at https://bit.ly/lealbarbosa2023.
6   We highly discourage our teacher learners from the unexamined use of ready-to-use materials for there is an increased risk of disregarding certain cultural and linguistic aspects MLs bring to the classrooms (Bartolomé 1994; La Luz Reyes 1992). Instead, when contemplating the adoption of ready-to-use materials, we encourage them to consider their unique classroom and adapt such materials to reflect their respective contexts.

References

Banks, J. A. (2016), *Cultural Diversity and Education: Foundations, Curriculum, and Teaching*, 6th edn, New York: Routledge.

Bartolomé, L. I. (1994), "Beyond the Methods Fetish: Toward a Humanizing Pedagogy", *Harvard Educational Review*, 64 (2): 173–95.

Blumenfeld, P. C., E. Soloway, R. W. Marx, J. S. Krajcik, M. Guzdial and A. Palincsar (1991), "Motivating Project-Based Learning: Sustaining the Doing, Supporting the Learning", *Educational Psychologist*, 26 (3–4): 369–98.

Larmer, J. (2018), Getting Started with Project-Based: Quick Reference Guide. Available online: https://shop.ascd.org/PersonifyEbusiness/Store/Product-Details/productId/204079018 (accessed November 1, 2022).

Lucas, T. and A. M. Villegas (2010), "The Missing Piece in Teacher Education: The Preparation of Linguistically Responsive Teachers", *National Society for the Study of Education*, 109 (2): 297–318.

Lucas, T. and A. M. Villegas (2013), "Preparing Linguistically Responsive Teachers: Laying the Foundation in Preservice Teacher Education", *Theory into Practice*, 52 (2): 98–109.

Moran, P. R. (2011), *Teaching Culture: Perspectives in Practice*, Boston: Heinle, Cengage Learning.

National Center for Education Statistics (2022), "English Learners in Public Schools: Condition of Education, U.S. Department of Education", *Institute of Education Sciences*. Available online: https://nces.ed.gov/programs/coe/indicator/cgf (accessed February 13, 2022).

Nieto, S. (2010), *Language, Culture, and Teaching Critical Perspectives*, 2nd edn, New York: Routledge.

Paris, D. (2012), "Culturally Sustaining Pedagogy: A Needed Change in Stance, Terminology, and Practice", *Educational Researcher*, 41 (3): 93–7.

Reyes, M. D. (1992), "Challenging Venerable Assumptions: Literacy instruction for Linguistically Different Students", *Harvard Educational Review*, 62 (4): 427–46.

The Affirming Diversity Project (2022), [Videos]. Available online: https://bit.ly/theaffirmingdiversityproject (accessed March 22, 2022).

Westerlund, R. and L. de Oliveira (2016), "Much More Than a Reclassification Issue: ELLs In K-12: A Response to Keeping Long-Term English Learners from Getting Stuck", Reclaiming The Language for Social Justice, February 2. Available online: https://reclaimingthelanguage.wordpress.com/2016/02/02/much-more-than-a-reclassification-issue-ells-in-k- (accessed February 13, 2023).

Critical Antiracist Teacher Education: Insights from the Seminar "Racism and the English Language Teaching (ELT) Classroom"

Natalie Güllü

Background

The course "Racism and the ELT Classroom," parts of which will be presented in this paper, aims to encourage teacher candidates to adopt a critical antiracist perspective (Kubota 2021) on English language teaching (ELT). It provides theoretical input on the history and mechanisms of racism as well as its impacts on school in general and on ELT in particular. For this purpose, a critical textbook analysis is conducted.

I conducted the seminar at a university in North Rhine-Westphalia, Germany, implemented in the department of ELT, where I also work on critical antiracist language teacher education in my dissertation project. The thirty teacher candidates (bachelor and master) came from different profiles such as primary, secondary I, and secondary II school types, thus the group was heterogeneous, especially in terms of prior knowledge. Some had hardly considered racism; others were educated through their studies or personal interest. Few were negatively affected by racism. The majority was white (and female)—just like me, the instructor—which corresponds to the current population of teachers in Germany (Pasternak 2019).

In the broadest sense, the criticality of the endeavor is grounded in a critical stance toward social power relations. Education should contribute to initiating processes of social change and to breaking down institutional and structural constraints that have grown historically and grant privileges to some while oppressing others (Bartolomé 2008). In-class discussions revealed racism to be a matter of concern for all participants, as it also has an impact on ELT in German schools, even though this institution claims to reduce or even prevent racism through educational processes (Coşkun 2019). One of the main aims of ELT is to create intercultural learning opportunities, which can lead to the (re)production of racist narratives when approached from a white perspective (Güllü and Gerlach 2023), which curricula and textbooks predominantly hold. Therefore, the role of the teacher is significant in that they run the risk of using ELT materials without a critical antiracist lens. The seminar activity takes up on this issue by training participants to recognize racism in instructional materials and explore ways of dealing with it constructively.

Description of the Practice

In the seminar, we defined racism as a "social construct" (Hall 1989: 913) that is learned, reproduced, and passed on in the course of (in)formal socialization. Racist knowledge (Terkessidis 2010) is not innate, nonetheless highly prevalent in society and ELT textbooks in German classrooms. These cover, for instance, the UK, the United States, and Australia as topics including aspects of these countries' colonial pasts, but in a glossed over and abbreviated way. In addition, racist language is reproduced at various points. Black, Indigenous, and People of Color are portrayed as the other while white people become the invisible norm (Bönkost 2020). Thus they perpetuate racism through underlying assumptions they transport and shape the learners' perception both unnoticed and in the long term (Jeismann 1982). A closer look at textbooks shows the cross-section of a society's widespread views and provides a representative insight into current educational practices (Sikorová and Bagoly-Simó 2021). As a traditional educational medium, they "are a kind of autobiography of states and nations [and] account for the interpretation of the past that a society wants to convey to future generations" (Mendoza et al. 2021: 24). For critical textbook analysis, the book pages or units should be analyzed as a whole, in context and in relation to one another, for they are understood as a "composite medium [that] is more than an additive collection of discontinuous and continuous text elements" (Bagoly-Simó 2021: 134).

Textbooks are not used to the same extent in all lessons by all teachers, but ELT particularly is considered a textbook-defined practice (Akbari 2008). This underlines the necessity of a critical antiracist material analysis with teacher candidates, which we conducted in the fifth session. Prior to that critical antiracism in ELT was introduced. The teacher candidates and the teacher educator reflect their positionality and agreed on a sensitive, respectful interaction during class. Theoretical input was provided (definitions, history, forms of racism). White defensiveness (Stone-Sabali 2022) and the discourse in post-national socialist Germany are thematized. Teacher candidates recognized the need to look at social interactions closely and to reflect on their (white) perspectives. Thus, they manufactured a critical antiracist lens.

For the fifth session ("Critical Antiracist Textbook Analysis," see Table 9.1 in the Appendix) I selected English textbooks for year 8 from the university library, published between 2008 and 2018. These mainly thematize the United States, including Indigenous peoples' lives, migration, and the Civil Rights Movement. One week in advance, the participants were asked to analyze a textbook page of their choice drawing on the knowledge gained in previous sessions. They were provided with five problem-posing steps according to Crookes (2013) as support for structuring the analysis:

1. Describe what you see; name the relevant items or passages in the material.
2. Define the problem; why do you think this could be relevant in the context of racism?
3. Apply the problem to your life: tell how you feel about it; you may refer to your profession or your (school) experience.
4. Discuss the social/economic reasons: tell why there is a problem.
5. Ask what you can do about it; how can you as a teacher deal with this constructively?

Participants prepared at home and presented their findings orally in class on a voluntary basis. The relevant pages were projected on the wall for others to see, follow the argumentation, and join the discussion. First, participants were hesitant to present so I used encouraging phrases, such as:

- Is there something that struck you as odd? We can brainstorm what this might have to do with racism.
- You don't have to provide a complete analysis including theory. We can do this together.
- If you feel more comfortable doing so, you can switch to German at any time.
- Instead of giving answers, you may ask questions.
- Is there anything familiar from previous sessions that might give us a clue as to what is relevant to the analysis here?

One or two hands were raised, and then a lively discussion started. The teacher candidates helped each other to connect results with the theoretical framework. About a third of the group initiated textbook analysis, another third entered the conversation. Overall, I estimate the engagement in session 5 to be higher than that in the previous ones. The participants were able to successfully uncover implicit racism and showed skills in interpreting textbooks as a composite medium. For instance, the participants detected a homogenization of Indigenous peoples in the textbooks. Their struggles are broadly outlined, but not related to causes. The genocide and the role of white supremacy are not mentioned. The settlement of a land we today know as the United States is addressed, but in a way that has little to do with the historical events. It is not problematized or linked to present-day continuities of oppression and violence. In the course of the discussion, the white gaze that is pervasive in this representation is thematized. We asked ourselves critically who is marked as the other here and made an object of learning (the Indigenous population as the cultural other). From the temporal and geographical distance, we found that the learner in the German classroom is invited to discover history from the perspective of the oppressor. Whiteness remains unmarked.

In the last part of the session, we then discussed what to do with our findings. The group has considered options for reducing the reproduction of racism in ELT:

1. Not use these textbooks and remove them. Write to publishers and inform them.
2. Use the textbook but contextualize the materials. Enrich them with additional materials to foster multi-perspectivity. Address racist narratives.

3. Use textbooks when racism is the subject of the lesson and teach learners to examine them as data with a critical antiracist lens, just like we did today.

Critical Reflections: Potentials and Challenges

This activity is one example for how racism as a global phenomenon can be approached locally. My observation was that the analysis of currently used materials makes the issue tangible for teacher candidates and highlighted its importance for critical antiracist EFL teaching. They reported that the abovementioned theoretical input helped to uncover implicit racism and demonstrate its omnipresence. They said to be more aware of implicit racism in their environment and see the difficulty to confront and deconstruct it, even in a supposedly open society. In the course of the following semester, some approached me to ask for advice on how to call out racism in their personal and professional lives as the frequency of racist incidents they observed increased. In this sense, I have achieved my overall goal of giving the participants a first push in the direction of becoming an antiracist.

The teacher candidates stated that they intended to be more critical of teaching materials from now on for they gradually elaborated which profound consequences (e.g., reinforcement of racist narratives, misinformation about historical events) the use of materials can have when not contextualized and analyzed from critical (antiracist) perspective. I assume that a critical antiracist textbook analysis has the potential of making power structures in ELT visible. Through the examples, participants learn how ideologies shape education and how social relations of dominance are upheld in the practices of the school system. At best, they are motivated to engage with theory about other forms of discrimination such as sexism, classism, or ableism. Teachers should systematically address these phenomena in class. I imagine that once the mechanisms of one of these have been grasped and their ubiquity has been recognized, the individual begins to reflect their privileges. Sensitized to notice other forms of discrimination, at least some will put the dismantling of these on their agenda.

That being said, it was challenging to design and conduct this seminar, as it came with responsibilities. Flexibility is necessary in order to react sensitively to the unexpected, such as responses shaped by white guilt/defensiveness. I tried to make the topic accessible to a heterogeneous group in a space where the power relations addressed are at play. As a white teacher educator, I am still in a process of learning and deconstructing internalized racisms, years after this journey has started. I do not aim at becoming non-racist. Instead, I actively position myself as antiracist and try to keep being critical, understanding myself as co-learner. I tell upfront that white privilege has put me in the position of teaching and researching in academia, which is a recurring dilemma for me. Coming back to the activity, I realized that the ultimate challenge arises from the consequence of our material analysis: How can we as critical teachers deal with it constructively? How can we transform teaching in a sustainable way? Which challenges await us and which resources are available for networking, support, and reflection? And how do we do this knowing that we are operating in an environment, in which racism is structural, epistemic, and an everyday practice?

References

Akbari, R. (2008), "Postmethod Discourse and Practice", *TESOL Quarterly*, 42 (4): 641–52.
Bagoly-Simó, P. (2021), "Doing Research on Geography Textbooks. An Overview of Methods, Samples, and Topics in International and German Journals (1960–2020)", in P. Bagoly-Simó and Z. Sikorová (eds), *Textbooks and Educational Media: Perspectives from Subject Education: Proceedings of the 13th IARTEM Conference 2015*, 134–46, Basel: Springer International Publishing.
Bartolomé, L. I. (2008), "Beyond the Fog of Ideology", in L. I. Bartolomé (ed.), *Ideologies in Education. Unmasking the Trap of Teacher Neutrality*, IX–XXIX, New York: Peter Lang.
Bönkost, J. (2020), "Konstruktion des Rassesdiskurses in Englisch-Schulbüchern", in K. Fereidooni and N. Simon (eds), *Rassismuskritische Fachdidaktiken. Theoretische Reflexionen und fachdidaktische Entwürfe rassismuskritischer Unterrichtsplanung*, 19–47, Wiesbaden: Springer VS.
Coşkun, M. (2019), "Schulen mit Rassismus und zu wenig Courage, es zuzugeben", in Deutsches Institut für Menschenrechte (eds), *Maßstab Menschenrechte. Bildungspraxis zu den Themen Flucht, Asyl und rassistische Diskriminierung*, 55, Berlin: Deutsches Institut für Menschenrechte.
Crookes, G. V. (2013), *Critical ELT in Action: Foundations, Promises, Praxis*, Abingdon: Routledge.
Güllü, N. and D. Gerlach (2023), "White Gaze und der fremdsprachendidaktische Kanon. Wie Rassismuskritik (trotzdem) zum Gegenstand von Fremdsprachenunterricht werden kann", *PFLB—PraxisForschungLehrer*innenBildung*, 5 (2): 23–9.
Hall, S. (1989), "Rassismus als ideologischer Diskurs", *Das Argument: Zeitschrift für Philosophie und Sozialwissenschaften*, 31 (6): 913–21.
Jeismann, K. (1982), "Einleitung", in K. Jeismann and H. Schissler (eds), *Englische und deutsche Geschichte in den Schulbüchern beider Länder: Wahrnehmungsmuster und Urteilsstrukturen in Darstellungen zur neueren Geschichte*, 7–10, Braunschweig: Georg-Eckert-Institut Schulbuchforschung.
Kubota, R. (2021), "Critical Antiracist Pedagogy in ELT", *ELT Journal*, 75 (3): 237–46.
Mendoza, M. Á. G., L. F. D. Gómez and M. V. A. Piedrahita (2021), "Colombia's Social and Political Conflict in Primary School Textbooks on Social Sciences: Narrative and Historical Representation (2003–2013)", in P. Bagoly-Simó and Z. Sikorová (eds), *Textbooks and Educational Media: Perspectives from Subject Education: Proceedings of the 13th IARTEM Conference 2015*, 23–34, Basel: Springer International Publishing.
Pasternak, P. (2019), "Gute Lehre, gutes Studium in der Lehrer_innenbildung—was ist das?", in L. Brockerhoff and A. Keller (eds), *Lust oder Frust? Qualität von Lehre und Studium auf dem Prüfstand*, 31–42, Bielefeld: wbv.
Sikorová, Z. and P. Bagoly-Simó (2021), "Textbook as a Medium: Impulses from Media Studies for Research on Teaching Materials and Textbooks in Educational Sciences", in P. Bagoly-Simó and Z. Sikorová (eds), *Textbooks and Educational Media: Perspectives from Subject Education: Proceedings of the 13th IARTEM Conference 2015*, 1–22, Basel: Springer International Publishing.
Stone-Sabali, S. (2022), "Who Is the White Antiracist Student? An Exploratory Investigation of Individual Characteristics", *Journal of Diversity in Higher Education*. Available online: https://psycnet.apa.org/fulltext/2022-61898-001.pdf?auth_token=ed071fe6f0d52487c8e35a9c2014db1df2ee56cf (accessed June 1, 2023).
Terkessidis, M. (2010), *Interkultur*, Berlin: Suhrkamp.

Appendix

Table 9.1 Course syllabus

	Syllabus
1	Introduction
2	Theoretical Foundations I
3	Theoretical Foundations II
4	Racism at School and at Home
5	**Critical Antiracist Textbook Analysis**
6	Teaching about Culture, and Culturalism
7	Linguicism and the ELT Classroom
8	Approaches to Antiracist Education
9	Teaching Poetry
10	Teaching Literature
11	Teaching Films
12	Teaching Non-Fiction
13	Racism and Language Awareness
14	Anti-Fatness
15	Revision and Reflection

Part Four

Classroom Management, Observation, and Practicum

10

A Critical Perspective on Language Classroom Management, Classroom Observation, and the Practicum

David Gerlach

Introduction

In 2019, Steve Walsh and Steve Mann (2019) edited *The Routledge Handbook of English Language Teacher Education* in which John Gray (2019) began his article on "Critical language teacher education?" by explaining that it was the editors who made him use a question mark at the end of the chapter title to make that "particular kind of language teacher education appear literally questionable" (2019: 68). The only other contribution to that volume with a question mark is the one that deals with the (actual) question as to whether classroom management is an "art, craft or science" (Buchanan and Timmis 2019), which I thought was a rather interesting fact during my own literature review for this chapter about these very concepts. Although the idea of critical language teacher education (CLTE) has benefited from a growing awareness in the field, it has not yet (or so it seems) had a substantial influence on the parts of teacher education that this section is supposed to focus on, i.e., classroom management. There still seems to be a general neglect of critical concepts or, for instance, an integration of identity development in teacher education programs. This contribution, therefore, argues against common, unreflected standardized conceptualizations of classroom management as well as classroom observations and also aims to provide a theoretical basis for rethinking the role of teacher educators and their (power) relationships with student teachers in in-service or practical phases of language teacher education.

Current Issues

The issues that I try to identify and summarize in the following are based, on the one hand, on my own experience comparing German, Scandinavian, and US American contexts of language teacher education. On the other hand, I will integrate and refer to sources that have, based on similar (ethnographically informed) observations and additional empirical analyses, written about these issues and challenges. The following paragraphs should, however, by no means be considered exhaustive in trying to deliver a complete picture of what CLTE might need to address and (re)consider in the areas of classroom management, classroom observation, and gaining practical experiences.

Classroom Management

In a very traditional sense, classroom management has—and maybe still is—a rather technical aspect of teaching, focusing on handling groups of learners and, especially for novice teachers, surviving in a sea of interactions and interests. Many introductions to classroom management view these interests in most cases not as those of the teacher, but those of the learner. Yet they are equally the teacher's interest as well, as they want to support "the ability of a teacher to manage students and the environment to make the most of the opportunities for learning and practicing language" (Lewis 2002: 47). This is a complex and substantial task that is unfairly often denigrated as "little more than a 'bag of tricks'" (Buchanan and Timmis 2019: 333).

The goal of classroom management, as Lewis (2002) thus frames it, is not to educate in a pedagogical sense but rather to make learning (or rather: teaching) possible, to offer opportunities to learn. If one then interprets classroom management in the technical or even behaviorist sense, one might fall victim to (only) teaching to lesson goals or "teaching to the test," and thus, not really "teaching" as the conditions necessary for students to learn are ignored. Moving away from this might be considered, by itself, a first step toward a critical approach: You then might consider classroom management which looks at the needs of different learners. Then classroom management becomes a more pedagogical endeavor, although not yet in the sense of critical pedagogy (Freire 1974; Giroux 1983). The latter would necessitate a teaching and learning situation that is fueled by the empowerment of learners and meaningful consideration of their interests and identities, discussing with learners such things as the classroom layout and setup or equity-based pedagogies. This, however, also implies that the teacher needs to have a positive relationship with learners, which is, especially during the process of initial language teacher education and in short periods of internships, very challenging.

Observations

While classroom management focuses on the macro- and micro-management of the teaching environment, classroom observations are supposed to provide insights into teaching, learning, and interaction processes. Yet, although they might make action visible, and sometimes even illuminate aspects of the classroom environment hidden to the teacher, we need to consider that observable action might not provide an insight into what teachers and learners actually (want to) do or (do not) know. It is important to acknowledge this mismatch between performance and the actors' objectives or their competence, as is the difference between action and explicit knowledge on the one hand and implicit knowledge on the other hand. Explicit knowledge is the one that teachers use to explain (to teach) and learners to explain what they understood or which they show in a classroom product or task. On the other hand, implicit knowledge, which is often considered to be the knowledge that crucially guides our actions (Polanyi 1966), is not directly observable. However, it may be reconstructed through observation. For episodes of action to be reconstructable and, therefore, understandable for purposes of language teacher education, clear observation criteria and a group of observers or interpreters for the data provided through the observation are necessary. Only then might one be able to reconstruct from actions, intentions, and therefore learn something about the implicit knowledge of the teacher and learners from their behavior and their interactions. This reconstruction and deconstruction of lesson discourse can then be used as an opportunity to design lesson ideas that engage learners (and teachers) in critical interaction and critical discourse, e.g. within a broader context of disrupting the multi-faceted power imbalance within a language classroom.

Another important aspect in observation phases is that it is hard to grasp learner identity. The identities of learners in a classroom are multifaceted and multilayered; and it is relevant to explore them in order, for example, to find out whether learners will actually be interested in the lesson topic and, thus, be motivated. Fostering (or at least addressing) learner identity has become one of the most important goals of language teaching in light of the seminal work of Bonny Norton (2013). Likewise, in CLTE, the identity (or identities) of the teachers are an important factor as well (Barkhuizen 2017; De Costa and Norton 2017). Identity determines, for instance, whether or not a pedagogical goal or theory becomes personally meaningful and thus serves as a guiding principle of one's own teaching practice. An example: Language teacher education courses might emphasize the need to address learners so-called special educational needs through, for example, differentiation. If, however, the student teacher's belief system and identity, and their implicit knowledge, are not fully convinced of the idea that inclusion is worthwhile pursuing, any CLTE intervention probably will not have a lasting effect on the future teacher's independent practice.

Despite all of these potential challenges regarding their efficacy in addressing what teachers implicitly know or believe, observations provide a starting point for reflection and professional development. The observations might take place in the form of peer observation, in which student teachers observe each other and subsequently engage in peer feedback and reflections. Classroom observations that include a teacher educator can create power imbalances if the teacher educators supervise or assess student teachers based on their performance during an observation.

Practicum

The practicum as part of teacher education aims at providing pre-service teachers with "hands-on" experience (Cirocki, Madyarov and Baecher 2019; Gebhard 2009). They are often excited to—finally—observe and try out methods and approaches "in real life," but are frequently quickly disappointed or demoralized because the approaches they acquired in their theoretical preparation do not work as expected and cannot easily be implemented. This is the supposed gap between theory and practice that grapples with the need to illustrate the relevance of theoretical knowledge for the reality of the classroom. However, this infamous gap is a mischaracterization: It is not a real gap because there is nothing to "bridge." These two forms of knowledge—theory and practice—cannot be transformed into one another. They exist independently from each other and need to be reconfigured anew each and every time and in each and every context (Clarke 1994). The traditional conceptualization of the pre-service teacher practicum, based on the presence of a mythical gap, focuses on providing the teaching candidates with recipes to use in class, thus giving them the opportunity to "survive" the complexity of classroom practice. A more modern approach would—in addition to such survival recipes—foster reflection regarding why the lesson plan, based on the theoretical concepts and models, did not work out as intended.

Teacher learning in a practicum is not only learning about different types of knowledge based on classroom observation and trial lessons. It is also meta-reflection with peers, teachers, and teacher educators about the implications of one's observations and experiences (e.g., Bailey 2006). In many cases, practicing teachers become mentors of novice teachers or pre-service teachers and help them navigate through the first teaching experience, providing emotional support (Ngyuen 2017). The teacher educator who supports pre-service teachers' learning as they gain experiential knowledge during that phase is another important variable. Teacher educators are crucially important because they formally guide and mentor the candidates through that process. At the same time, there is also a hierarchical relationship between the pre-service teacher and the teacher educator or mentors in terms of knowledge and power, especially in some contexts where teacher educators also give students grades for practicum performances that denote success or failure. Both the mentor and the teacher educator, therefore, might exhibit a position of power which needs to be transparent, reflected upon, and maybe even transformed, provided that CLTE is part of the goal of the practicum learning experience.

Another important trend in the last twenty years, when it comes to the implementation of concepts or evaluating one's own teaching impact, has been action research. Teachers develop a research design around their own classroom intervention (e.g., a reading intervention) and assess learner's performance (e.g., through assessing reading speed or reading comprehension). The theory is that a better understanding of one's own teaching will develop through this integration of research and teaching. Yet, it is important to remember that, again, the results and reflection of this process are closely connected to explicit teaching knowledge, which is important, but which may not have a direct connection to one's relevant beliefs and implicit knowledge. However, it is still relevant for developing a sound foundation of teaching knowledge, and it might be enhanced with a critical perspective that looks at the personal and individual use of power in certain classroom interactions.

Implications for Teaching and Teacher Education

CLTE does not only want to create "transformative intellectuals" who help learners develop a critical awareness for social change (e.g., Crookes 2009; Gray 2019). It often encompasses an anti-neoliberal agenda that aims to address the dangers of politically neutral teaching materials and overly standards-oriented educational practice in which teachers are taught to follow curricular requirements without regard for humanistic facets of teaching (for a fundamental critique of neoliberal language education tendencies, see Block and Gray 2016). In such a setting, pedagogical relationships and individual opinions do not matter, only language skills do. Given the danger that the bigger concepts of this article—classroom management, observation, and the practicum—can be easily constructed as standards-oriented reservoirs of knowledge and teacher education, I would like to propose three principles (or foci) that, once integrated, might help overcome these problematic tendencies.

Focus on Reflection

Reflection and reflective practice have had broad recognition in language teacher education due to the comprehensive work of, for example, Farrell (2015). What he has emphasized in his more recent publications is the need to develop an individual teaching philosophy, which emerges through a reflection process and a process of professional growth that is probably very closely linked to one's own language teacher identity. One might argue that teachers should become aware of the inner motivations that make them a language teacher. This seems both relevant and challenging, because of the increasing recognition of the importance of teachers' beliefs and implicit knowledge, paired with a growing understanding that we might not even be able to reflect on what we do because we are ourselves incapable of explaining or fully comprehending our actions. One way of addressing this dilemma might be through what I call "implicit reflection," the goal of which is to make implicit knowledge explicable or tangible (Gerlach 2021). An essential element in this process is the involvement of another person, for example, a mentor or a teacher educator, who is able to elicit implicit beliefs and interpret narrations about teachers' own practice and experiences (e.g., in the practicum). Only by helping pre-service teachers verbalize what they think they know, believe, and do might it be possible for these mentors to reconstruct the underlying convictions of emerging teachers. This implicit reflection, externalizing one's beliefs about a certain aspect of language teaching (be it regarding language skills, culture, or critical topics—to name but a few) might be considered a first step toward criticality, i.e., raising one's own critical awareness of certain issues in the language classroom.

In a practicum session which focuses on classroom management, for instance, it might be fruitful to encourage pre-service teachers to narrate their experiences, not solely for the purpose of finding out what strategies they employed, but rather to determine what power structures were established through this process of managing the learner group (one of the first empirically documented examples of novice language teachers humanizing classroom management: Tigert et al. 2022). The externalization of (hidden) power relationships might be critical for developing a productive teacher-learner relationship fairly early in the process of becoming a teacher.

Focus on Teacher Educator and Pre-Service Teacher Relationship for Democratizing and Humanizing Practice

Given that to implement the concept of "implicit reflection" one actually needs a teacher educator or mentor to determine what is implicitly guiding the novice teacher's actions, the relationship between teacher educator and student teacher is, within the context of institutionalized teacher education, extremely vital and fragile at the same time. In my own research, I was able to extrapolate from data examining the practice of language teacher educators that there needs to be a certain "fit" between the implicit orientations of both the teacher educators and the trainee teachers when it comes to establishing a relationship that is supposed to lead to professionalization (Gerlach 2020). For that "fit" to be established, though, both sides need to share insights into their own belief systems, contexts, and presuppositions of what they expect from each other—despite the hierarchical relationship between the two. One starting point for such a conversation about language classrooms and power relationships in teacher education (between pre-service teachers and teacher educators; see above) might be the concept of language teacher identity.

Focus on Language Teacher Identity

If becoming a language teacher is understood as a biographical process, which starts even before primary school, and which eventually entails having cultural experiences abroad and participating in exchange programs and teacher preparation courses, etc., developing an awareness of one's language teacher identity becomes a trajectory for professionalization. Identity development helps language teachers reflect on and become aware of their own principles of teaching, which can be used to sharpen their perspectives on classroom management and make their classroom observations productive. Critical identity work, however, goes one step beyond this: It forces future professionals to take a stance (whatever the outcome) toward a certain, i.e., critical and important, societal topic. If this is the goal, there is an obvious need to design courses around the idea of identity development, since merely integrating instances of reflection is unlikely to make a difference in a course that focuses primarily or exclusively on skills or standards. A more community-driven approach to language teacher education, in which pre-service as well as in-service teachers are encouraged to acknowledge their biographical experiences and expertise, and share their opinions as well as their thoughts about their own teaching practice, needs to be implemented more thoroughly and with a critical lens.

References

Abednia, A. (2012), "Teachers' Professional Identity: Contributions of a Critical EFL Teacher Education Course in Iran", *Teaching and Teacher Education*, 28 (5): 706–17.

Bailey, K. M. (2006), *Language Teacher Supervision: A Case-Based Approach*, Cambridge: Cambridge University Press.

Barkhuizen, G. (ed.) (2017), *Reflections on Language Teacher Identity Research*, New York: Routledge.

Block, D. and J. Gray (2016), "'Just Go Away and Do It and You Get Marks': The Degradation of Language Teaching in Neoliberal Times", *Journal of Multilingual and Multicultural Development*, 37 (5): 481–94.

Buchanan, H. and I. Timmis (2019), "Classroom Management: Art, Craft or Science?", in S. Walsh and S. Mann (eds), *The Routledge Handbook of English Language Teacher Education*, 319–34, Abingdon, Oxon/New York: Routledge.

Cirocki, A., I. Madyarov and L. Baecher (2019), *Current Perspectives on the TESOL Practicum*, Cham: Springer.

Clarke, M. A. (1994), "The Dysfunctions of the Theory/Practice Discourse", *TESOL Quarterly*, 28 (1): 9–26.

Crookes, G. (2009), *Values, Philosophies, and Beliefs in TESOL: Making a Statement*, Cambridge: Cambridge University Press.

De Costa, P. I. and B. Norton (2017), "Introduction: Identity, Transdisciplinarity, and the Good Language Teacher", *The Modern Language Journal*, 101: 3–14.

Farrell, T. S. C. (2015), *Promoting Teacher Reflection in Second Language Education: A Framework for TESOL Professionals*, New York: Routledge.

Freire, P. (1974), *Pedagogy of the Oppressed*, New York: Seabury.

Gebhard, J. G. (2009), "The Practicum", in A. Burns and J. C. Richards (eds), *The Cambridge Guide to Second Language Teacher Education*, 250–8, New York: Cambridge University Press.

Gerlach, D. (2020), *Zur Professionalität der Professionalisierenden: Was machen Lehrerbildner*innen im fremdsprachendidaktischen Vorbereitungsdienst? [What do teacher educators do in language teacher education?]*, Tübingen: Narr.

Gerlach, D. (2021), "Making Knowledge Work: Fostering Implicit Reflection in a Digital Era of Language Teacher Education", *Language Education and Multilingualism*, 3: 39–51.

Giroux, H. (1983), *Theory and Resistance in Education: A Pedagogy for the Opposition*, South Hadley, MA: Bergin & Garvey.

Gray, J. (2019), "Critical Language Teacher Education?", in S. Walsh and S. Mann (eds), *The Routledge Handbook of English Language Teacher Education*, 68–81, Abingdon, Oxon/New York: Routledge.

Lewis, M. (2002), "Classroom Management", in J. C. Richards and W. A. Renandya (eds), *Methodology in Language Teaching: An Anthology of Current Practice*, 40–8, Cambridge: Cambridge University Press.

Nguyen, H. (2017), *Models of Mentoring in Language Teacher Education*, Cham: Springer.

Norton, B. (2013), *Identity and Language Learning: Extending the Conversation*, Bristol: Multilingual Matters. https://doi.org/10.21832/9781783090563

Pennycook, A. (2004), "Critical Moments in a TESOL Praxicum", in B. Norton and K. Toohey (eds), *Critical Pedagogies and Language Learning*, 327–45, Cambridge: Cambridge University Press.

Polanyi, M. (1966), *The Tacit Dimension*, Chicago: University of Chicago Press.

Sardabi, N., R. Biria and A. A. Golestan (2018), "Reshaping Teacher Professional Identity through Critical Pedagogy-Informed Teacher Education", *International Journal of Instruction*, 11 (3): 617–34.

Tigert, J. M., M. M. Peercy, D. Fredricks and T. Kidwell (2022), "Humanizing Classroom Management as a Core Practice for Teachers of Multilingual Students", *TESOL Quarterly*, 56 (4): 1087–111.

Varghese, M., B. Morgan, B. Johnston and K. Johnson (2005), "Theorizing Language Teacher Identity: Three Perspectives and Beyond", *Journal of Language, Identity, and Education*, 4: 21–44.

Walsh, S., and S. Mann (eds) (2019), *The Routledge Handbook of English Language Teacher Education*, New York: Routledge.

Yazan, B. (2019), "Toward Identity-Oriented Teacher Education: Critical Autoethnographic Narrative", *TESOL Journal*, 10 (1): 1–15.

Suggested Readings and External Links

- Pennycook, A. (2004), "Critical Moments in a TESOL Praxicum", in B. Norton and K. Toohey (eds), *Critical Pedagogies and Language Learning*, 327–45, Cambridge: Cambridge University Press.
  → A reflective narrative about the chances of integrating critical perspectives in practice-oriented phases of language teacher education.

- Walsh, S., and S. Mann, (eds) (2019), *The Routledge Handbook of English Language Teacher Education*, New York: Routledge.
  → A comprehensive selection of state-of-the-art articles on language teacher education and its different facets. Worth looking at through a CLTE lens.

11

Critically Reflecting on Diversity and Learners' Needs: An Example from Aotearoa New Zealand

Karen Ashton

Background

The critical education practice described in this chapter comes from the postgraduate course Advanced TESOL for Diverse Learners and Contexts, which forms part of Massey University's Master of Applied Linguistics (TESOL) in Aotearoa New Zealand. This qualification is designed for experienced teachers seeking further professional development to enhance their teaching practice and classroom decision-making. Teachers may be based in Aotearoa New Zealand or anywhere around the globe, with most opting to take the qualification part-time and online alongside their existing teaching roles. A diverse range of teaching roles are common, e.g., working with migrant and refugee students in classrooms where English is the medium of instruction, adult migrant and refugee learners, international students at higher or tertiary education institutions where English is the medium of instruction, or in international settings where English is taught as a second or foreign language.

Advanced TESOL for Diverse Learners and Contexts takes a postmethods approach (Kumaravadivelu 2003), with no single method of language teaching prioritized. The course is designed to support English language educators to critically reflect on issues relating to diversity and equity within their teaching contexts, the specific needs of their learners, and effective classroom management approaches and strategies to respond to these needs (de Jong et al. 2013; Nguyen and Dang 2020). Students bring with them "a multitude of differences," e.g., age, gender, ethnicity, interests, language proficiency, learning goals, linguistic and cultural background, motivation, sexuality, etc. (Krish et al. 2010: 1), and one course aim, in line with policy objectives in Aotearoa New Zealand, is to support teachers in examining their classroom practice to enhance equity and to ensure the success of every learner (Alton-Lee 2005; Education Council 2017).

According to the literature, critical reflection can support teachers in becoming more effective teachers as they examine their own teaching beliefs and classroom management practices and observe what is happening in their classrooms, and then use this as a basis for making informed decisions to provide students with more effective learning opportunities (Farrell 2022). This aligns well with recommended practice in Aotearoa New Zealand where teachers are expected to critically "reflect on the effectiveness of [their] practice in an ongoing way" (Education Council 2017: 18).

Farrell's (2007) three levels of critical reflection are embedded in the course design: reflection-in-action (reflection and response during teaching), reflection-on-action (retrospectively looking back on practice and analyzing why something has arisen), and reflection-for-action (reflection on and planning for what might happen in future teaching). These critical practices are drawn primarily from the practice stage of Farrell's (2022) framework for reflective practice which encompasses the following five stages: philosophy (the factors that shape a teacher's teaching philosophy, e.g., background, knowledge, and experience); principles (a teacher's beliefs and assumptions about language teaching and learning); theory (theory of language teaching practice); practice (exploring and examining what a teacher does in the classroom); and beyond practice (exploring issues outside the classroom that impact a teacher's practice).

Description of the Practice

Two assignment tasks are examined to illustrate the role reflection plays in supporting teachers to make new observations about their teaching and classroom management for diverse learners.

Assignment 1

Assignment 1 is an awareness raising task where teachers critically reflect on diversity within their classrooms. A course learning guide written by the lecturer summarizing the literature on diversity, key readings (e.g., Alton-Lee 2005; Krish et al. 2010; Liu and Nelson 2017; Nguyen and Dang 2020), a wider reference list on different aspects of diversity, and guided videos from the lecturer talking through the material and assignment requirements are provided via an online learning platform.

Assignment 1 requires teachers to first consider and outline the types of diversity they encounter in one of their classes and to briefly describe how each aspect impacts their planning and classroom management. To support this work, teachers are strongly encouraged to actively engage in the online professional learning community (online synchronous teaching sessions and asynchronous online forums) facilitated by the lecturer. As an example, teachers are invited to informally present an overview of their teaching context (country, city, rural/urban, type of institution), types of diversity typically encountered, and any examples or critical incidents from their teaching practice to further illustrate aspects of diversity and the impacts on their planning and classroom management. Following this, other teachers are invited to ask questions and to make comparisons with their own context and practice. Online discussions are always respectful and typically very rich with teachers genuinely interested in each other's practices. This task supports teachers in obtaining a distanced perspective from which to observe and critically reflect on their own classroom management. For example, through this task, one teacher in a private language school became more aware of the uniqueness of her teaching context where learners within a single class can vary in age from fifteen to sixty, and how she finds it difficult to manage group work and to choose topics that cater for this variation in age and life experience.

Following this, teachers research two or three aspects of diversity in more detail, and critically reflect on their classroom management practices in relation to these (reflection-on-action). Reflective questions to guide this process include: for the aspect, e.g. age, proficiency, etc., and class chosen, what variation exists and how does this manifest in the classroom? Do you consider the aspect in your planning and classroom management? If so, provide examples of how you go about this and what you do; What are the main challenges for you as a teacher? Throughout try to provide examples about specific learners (anonymized) and incidents from your teaching. A wider reference list on different aspects of diversity is provided and online forums allow teachers and the lecturer to discuss ideas and suggest additional resources. To complete the assignment, teachers reflect on their key learning, on the challenges and benefits of teaching diverse learners, and establish "next steps" to improve their future classroom management for diverse learners (reflection-for-action). Each teacher produces a written report comprising their findings and learning from the above steps.

Assignment 2

This assignment operates as a mini action research project where teachers carry out a needs analysis with a small group of their learners, before creating and implementing a plan for addressing one or more arising need. The goal is to scaffold teachers through "data-led reflective practice" as they collect concrete data, work with their own learners, and focus critical observations and reflections "so they can make more insightful analysis and gain a fuller sense of their own teaching" (Farrell 2022: 6). The discussion below focuses on the first part of the assignment task, the needs analysis.

Teachers are provided with a range of resources including a course learning guide written by the course lecturer summarizing the literature on needs analysis (e.g., what needs analysis is, needs analysis approaches and tools), key readings (e.g., Altschuld and Watkins 2014; Dudley-Evans and St John 1998; Hall 2016), as well as guided videos from the lecturer on the material and assignment requirements. Online synchronous teaching sessions and forum discussions are particularly important as teachers engage in a process of reflection-for-action as they discuss the following questions with the lecturer and each other: Which learners would you most like to learn more about and why? In thinking about this, consider diverse learners in your class and any areas of diversity you would like to learn more about; Which needs analysis approach(es) are most suitable for learning more about these learners, and why? Consider your teaching context, learners, and course purpose.

After completing the needs analysis, the following questions are designed to support teachers engage in a process of reflection-on-action: What did you learn about your learners' needs? Remember to highlight any diversity of results. What did you learn that you didn't already know? Did you learn what you thought you would? If not, comment more fully on this and consider why this was. Looking at the results of the needs analysis, is there anything additional you would have liked to have learnt to support your teaching of these diverse learners?

The final component of the assignment requires teachers to critically reflect on their broader learning and to establish next steps to support them in their future planning and classroom management for diverse learners (reflection-for-action): Would you use the needs analysis approach again? Why/why not? What might you do differently next time? How will what you have learnt impact your future planning and approach to classroom management to support these learners? Each teacher produces a written report comprising the results and reflections from the above steps.

Critical Reflections: Potentials and Challenges

Assignment 1 supports teachers in making new observations about their learners and approaches to classroom management as they become more aware of the diversity that exists in their classes. The following quote from Liu and Nelson (2017: 4) appears to particularly speak to teachers: "While instructors should cultivate a sensitivity to learners' cultures, they must be vigilant in their commitment to seeing individuals as more than representatives of these cultures." For some teachers this has led to a deeper understanding of the importance of treating learners as individuals, rather than assuming them to have characteristics stereotypical of the group.

One experienced teacher stated that she valued the opportunity to reflect on diversity as this was not something that she had ever previously considered. Through this reflective practice, she observed that she had been teaching for the majority group in her classroom, males from a particular ethnic group. On reflection, she felt that she could easily adapt her planning and approach to classroom management to ensure that all learners were considered.

Through critically reflecting on learners' needs, assignment 2 supports teachers in making new observations, and in questioning their own assumptions about their learners and teaching practice. For example, one teacher was surprised that her teenage learners were able to self- and peer-assess, while another found that counter to her expectations her young learners were able to articulate their reasons for learning English. One teacher thought she was applying best practice but found that her learners did not like activities requiring peer interaction in mixed-gender groups. On reflection, she attributed this to the cultural background of her learners and planned to have more variety in her approach to grouping in the future.

Overall, the most positive aspect of these activities is that they provide teachers with a safe space for critically observing and reflecting on their practice. As one teacher commented, although she had been in her current role for over six years, she had never undertaken a needs analysis before. This was common; most teachers were simply too busy in their day-to-day practice to pause, observe, and reflect on their classroom management at this level.

One challenge is when teachers work in environments not supportive of reflective practice. For example, one teacher worked in a traditional context where decisions about pedagogy and curriculum were top-down. Reflective practice was not supported, and diversity and equity were not acknowledged or considered important. Teacher educators need to be aware of potential gaps between recommended best practice and what is possible for a teacher within their context. They also need to carefully consider how to support teachers when they find themselves in a position where the reflective practices align with their own values but sit uncomfortably within their current teaching role, management structure or context.

References

Alton-Lee, A. (2005), *Using Best Evidence Synthesis to Assist in Making a Bigger Difference for Diverse Learners*, Wellington: Ministry of Education.

Altschuld, J. W. and R. Watkins (2014), "A Primer on Needs Assessment: More Than 40 Years of Research and Practice", *New Directions for Evaluation*, 144: 5–18.

de Jong, E., C. Harper and M. Coady (2013), "Enhanced Knowledge and Skills for Elementary Mainstream Teachers of English Language Learners", *Theory into Practice*, 52 (2): 89–97.

Dudley-Evans, T. and M. J. St John (1998), "Needs Analysis and Evaluation", in T. Dudley-Evans and M. J. St John (eds), *Developments in English for Specific Purposes: A Multi-disciplinary Approach*, 121–44, Cambridge: Cambridge University Press.

Education Council (2017), "Our Code our Standards: Code of Professional Responsibility and Standards for the Teaching Profession". Available online https://teachingcouncil.nz/resource-centre/our-code-our-standards/ (accessed December 10, 2022).

Farrell, T. S. C. (2007), *Reflective Language Teaching: From Research to Practice*, London: Continuum.

Farrell, T. S. C. (2022), *Reflective Practice in Language Teaching*, Cambridge: Cambridge University Press.

Hall, N. (2016), "What You Need to Include in an ELL Needs Assessment". Available online http://blog.tesol.org/what-you-need-to-include-in-an-ell-needs-assessment (accessed February 15, 2023).

Krish, P., S. Hussin and N. Sivapuniam (2010), "Learner Diversity among ESL Learners in the Online Forum", *Procedia—Social and Behavioral Sciences*, 7: 92–6.

Kumaravadivelu, B. (2003), *Beyond Methods: Macrostrategies for Language Teaching*, New Haven, CT: Yale University Press.

Liu, D. and R. Nelson (2017), "Diversity in the Classroom", in J. I. Liontas (ed.), *The TESOL Encyclopedia of English Language Teaching*, 1–6, New Jersey: John Wiley & Sons.

Nguyen, C. D. and T. C. T. Dang (2020), "Second Language Teacher Education in Response to Local Needs: Preservice Teachers of English Learning to Teach Diverse Learners in Communities", *TESOL Quarterly*, 54 (2): 404–35.

12

A Guide for Observing Community, School, and Classroom: Balancing Students' Lives and Language Policies

Alex Alves Egido

Background

The core argument of this writing is that any language policy will be unfruitful if teachers do not reflect and be critical about who their students are and what constitutes their school communities. In that sense, a guide is proposed for in-service teachers working in the Brazilian context (and possibly other contexts around the globe) on how to cope with top-down language policies while also involving language learners. In other words, the guide may be implemented and discussed in teacher education/professional development contexts. Ultimately, it relates to this book's section, i.e., classroom management/observation, as such teachers can use this guide to observe their own teaching contexts and students. Also, the guide may be adopted by a peer to observe one teacher's class.

It is important to mention, though, that such a guide is not supposed to be read and adopted as a save-the-world approach—which would be inconsistent with the critical perspective that supports this writing. It needs to be taken, then, as one among many other tools available for language teachers who often struggle to better understand their students and contexts, when implementing language policies.

In Brazil, language policies have been proposed, questioned, revised, and expanded for decades; it is, indeed, an endless cycle (Brossi 2022). Every time a new one is proposed, regardless of how strong its innovative tone is, language teachers—myself included for most of the times—feel the same pressure to absorb as much as possible from it, sometimes, because of the promise that it will guarantee an effective[1] language education (Egido, Tonelli, and De Costa forthcoming). What most of these propositions seem to disconsider, though, is the learner; not as someone who is biologically capable to adapt to a given classroom environment or to a certain teaching style, but as someone who has feelings, lived experiences, own opinions, and assumptions about the language that either hinders or enhances the learning (Mello 2013; Tanaca 2017).

Regarding the aimed audience of the proposed guide, it is in-service English language teachers. However, there is also room for adoption of the guide in pre-service teacher development courses, specifically on disciplines focusing on practicum and on language policies. On that note, the guide I later present was piloted with one group of pre-service English language teachers from a public university in the Midwest of Brazil. The teachers' reflections are briefly indicated on the critical reflection.

As far as the theoretical foundations of the guide are concerned, there are two central concepts orienting the guide's proposal. One of them relates to the three models of change, as discussed by Kennedy (2013). The first model, named mechanistic, refers to national, large-scale, and external projects that are top-down. It disconsiders the local, diverse contexts where the projects will ultimately be implemented; it has a central control. The second one, which is the opposite of the prior, is called individual. In this case, the projects are created and implemented in specific classrooms, spaces, and seen as small-scale. As they are locally controlled and context-sensitive, it is quite difficult to be implemented in other various contexts, although equally local. These projects are seen as bottom-up. A middle-ground model of change is labeled as ecological, as it considers both what is proposed from the macro institutions (e.g., federal and state language education policies) and what is, in facto, implemented in language classrooms (e.g., teachers' interpretations of the language policies and how such interpretations orient their classroom performance).

I argue that we, as English language educators, need to create more ecological experiences. One way to do so is by teachers critically reflecting about their students' backgrounds and contexts while implementing language policies they are expected to by governments and school boards. In that sense, teachers may benefit from classroom observation using the proposed guide to better comprehend their highly complex teaching contexts. Then, the need for such a reflection is oriented by Pennycook's (2001; 2004) work; it leads to the second key concept discussed.

The second concept concerns the perspective of critical adopted here. Pennycook (2001) argues that there are three approaches to critical work, namely: critical thinking, which is based on a humanism theoretical base; emancipatory modernism, led by the critical theory; and problematizing practice, which comes from the poststructuralism. Below, it is presented a summary of the third approach, according to Tílio's reading of Pennycook's proposal (2004).

According to Tílio's (2017) understanding (see Table 12.1), the main purpose of a problematizing practice is to engage with difference. The politics sustaining this practice comes from feminism, postcolonialism, queer theory, etc. Complementarily, the theoretical framework orienting this perspective is mostly post-Westernism and anarcho-particularism. The analytical focus is on discursive mapping, resistance and appropriation, and engagement with difference. Despite its strong constituting aspects, Tílio (2017) also addresses the weak features, which, in his view, are the possible relativism, unrealism, and discourse overvaluation.

In this writing, English language education is taken as an ongoing, never-ending problematizing practice. Such a view opens the room for a constant reflection about teachers' own practice, which is the goal of the guide presented in the following section. For instance, by adopting this practice teachers can question the myth of

Table 12.1 Constituting aspects of a problematizing practice

Aspects	
Purposes	Engagement with difference
Politics	Feminism, postcolonialism, queer theory, etc.
Theoretical framework	Post-Westernism, anarcho-particularism
Analytical focus	Discursive mapping, resistance and appropriation, engagement with difference
Weak features	Possible relativism, unrealism, and discourse overvaluation

Source: Adapted from Tílio (2017: 21).

the native speaker. In practical terms, the guide is supposed to support teachers on getting to know their students and contexts; in this example, related to the myth of the native speaker. They can problematize how such a myth constructs a certain profile of English speaker, one that is white skin-color, either American or British, middle class, well-educated, and cultured. Questioning this myth, teachers create the room for students from marginalized communities all over the world to see themselves as legitimate English speakers. By questioning this discourse, it is aimed at, ultimately, deconstructing oppressive institutional and language structures and promoting a more humane, critical, reflective, and inclusive English language education and, hopefully, a more just society. Based on this example, the guide contributes to classroom observation and, by doing so, to identify situations, beliefs, or instances that deserve to be problematized.

Description of the Practice

The guide fits the Classroom Management, Observation & Practicum section of this book as it represents as a peer-observation protocol or questions for use with "critical friends" that aims at assisting in-service English language teachers to get to know their students and contexts before implementing any language policy, which will need to be adapted to the specific educational setting. Also, this guide values the ecological model, as proposed by Kennedy (2013), as it orients teachers on the practical level before implementing any language policy conceived on the macro level. The guide is organized in five main sections, namely: (i) context, (ii) educational principles, (iii) students' lives and languages, (iv) educator's performance, and (v) social and ethical responsibilities. On the first section, teachers are invited to answer questions regarding the community where the school is located in terms of its social, historical, and linguistic aspects (i.e., questions, a, b, and c). On the second one, they are introduced to reflective questions concerning the principles that the school values. On the third one, teachers are presented with questions related to students' social, identity, and linguistic aspects. On the fourth one, they are invited to reflect upon their professional performance in the classroom; that is, what they do as language educators. The fifth section aims at relating all the previous ones. The main questions here will be: What actions have you enacted to observe the language policies and institutional principles and, at the same time, respect students' social, identity, and linguistic traits? As a critical educator, how have you been answering to the social and ethical responsibilities you see your profession poses to you, even though you need to observe language policies and regulations? Here it is:

1. Context
    a. What historical events have been milestones to the community where the school is located?
    b. How is the community's development understood by governmental agencies?
    c. What considerations can be made regarding the quality of life of the citizens of that community and maybe are not captured by the governmental agencies' understanding of development?
    d. What can be depicted about the community's linguistic repertoires?

2. Educational Principles
    e. What are the language policies that orient the language education in the school?
    f. What can you infer that is valued as a good language education in the school? Think about it from the perspective of the principal, parents, students, and other teachers.
    g. What is—or seem to be—the school's mantra?
    h. How often are students assessed? What tools are adopted? What is—or seem to be—the goal of the assessments?

3. Students' Lives And Languages
    i. In what moments can students freely interact with each other and their teachers?
    j. How would you describe students' language use (both native and foreign)? Consider, for example, the influence of social class, gender, race, and communicative purpose. Take into consideration both inside and outside classroom interactions.
    k. In what sense do students' linguistic repertoires relate to the language policies institutionally proposed and or enforced?

4. Educator's Performance
    l. How much do your students participate in the decision-making process of (i) what is taught, (ii) the material that is used, (iii) the language practices that are enacted, and (iv) the assessment that is carried out?
    m. What aspects of students' social, economic, linguistic, artistic, historical lives are considered when preparing the classes?
    n. Is there any social issue being addressed at all? Which one? How was it selected? Examples of social issues are, but not limited to, gender, social class, ethnicity, race, language.

o. During the class, what opinions are often mostly valued? Whose opinions? Examples of opinions valued are, but not limited to, the ones based on cultural, historical, scientific, religious, personal, collective arguments. Whose opinions may include, for instance, teachers', education policies', principals' and or school managements', students' or society's.

5. Social And Ethical Responsibilities
   p. How have you incorporated the institutionally proposed language policies in the classes you teach?
   q. What are some of the evident adaptations you have needed to do in order to consider the students' social, economic, linguistic, artistic, historical lives?
   r. How have students responded to the materials taken to the classes?
   s. What are your social and ethical responsibilities to the students and to the institution?

Critical Reflections: Potentials and Challenges

I invite the reader/English language teacher to adopt the problematizing practice previously discussed and improve and expand this guide. As any teaching context is unique, so should it be the guide's use. In that sense, the reader is invited to submit additional questions to the guide here (https://forms.gle/5eMiX5tQ34qhrbwe7). Whenever it is possible, an updated version of the guide will be made available for English language teachers. In sum, I am hopeful that by experimenting this guide English language teachers may realize (even more) how nuanced the language education is and how complex and distinct students are. More than a singular answer, I expect that this guide be used as a question-provocative tool for and by teachers; it will happen, though, by observing the classroom, which can happen with the assistance of a peer. By doing so, English language teachers may get closer to an enactment of the ecological model, as proposed by Kennedy (2013). Such a model as here taken as the teachers' attitude toward contextually implementing and adapting language policies to their specific teaching contexts, that is, seen the top-down policies as always incomplete and in need of a contextual touch. When this guide was once adopted in a teacher development course with pre-service and in-service language educators in Brazil, they expressed both the in-depth of such questions—which is crucial for this work—but also a slight impression that adopting the guide may create some extra work for the teacher.

Acknowledgments

I am deeply thankful to Dr. Giuliana Brossi (UEG) for adopting and reflecting about an earlier version of the guide with her pre-service and in-service language teachers. Their feedback was of the utmost importance to the version that is here presented. Any discrepancies that the reader may find on it are still my sole responsibility.

Note

1 The term can mean different things to different individuals and organizations.

References

Brossi, G. C. (2022), *Movimentos dialógicos de realização de políticas locais em ação no ensino de inglês com crianças na escola pública*, Londrina: EDUEL.

Egido, A. A., J. R. A. Tonelli and P. I. De Costa (Forthcoming), Rolling out the Red Carpet: A Critique of Neoliberal Motivations Orienting the Promotion of Public Bilingual Schools to Young Learners in Brazil.

Kennedy, C. (2013), "Models of Change and Innovation", in K. Hyland and L. Wong (eds), *Innovation and change in English Language Education*, 13–27, New York: Routledge.

Mello, M. G. B. (2013), Ensino de inglês nos anos iniciais do ensino fundamental um estudo de política pública no município de Rolândia, PR. [Master Thesis, State University of Londrina]. ProQuest Dissertations & Theses Global.

Pennycook, A. (2001), *Critical Applied Linguistics: A Critical Introduction*, New York: Routledge.

Pennycook, A. (2004), "Critical Applied Linguistics", in A. Davies and C. Elder (eds), *The Handbook of Applied Linguistics*, 784–807, New York: Blackwell Publishing.

Tanaca, J. J. C. (2017), *Aprendizagem expansiva em espaços híbridos de formação continuada de professoras de Inglês para crianças no Projeto Londrina Global*, Londrina: EDUEL.

Tílio, R. (2017), "Ensino crítico de língua: afinal, o que é ensinar criticamente?", in D. M. Jesus and F. C. Zolin-Vesz (eds), *Perspectivas críticas no ensino de línguas: novos sentidos para a escola*, 19–31, Campinas: Pontes.

13

Developing Criticality through Professional Development with In-Service Language Teachers

Mareen Lüke

Background

Particularly in Germany, there is a lack of research on critical approaches in ELT, which is why it must urgently be researched (e.g., Gerlach 2020). To integrate critical approaches, English language teachers must be critically educated for raising their critical awareness about social injustice and initiating identity development (e.g., Gerlach and Fasching-Varner 2020). Being critical is understood as the ability to identify and transform power relations and discrimination in language teaching cooperatively with students and people being affected (Hawkins and Norton 2009). Due to a growing transmission orientation excluding students' needs and critical practices in language teaching, a (too narrow) focus on students' performances as well as neoliberal tendencies in education, there is a need for critical English language teacher education (CELTE) in Germany (e.g., Akbari 2008). I will present insights from a program conducted as a workshop with a practicum for in-service English language teachers in Germany. Connected to the section "Classroom Management, Observation and Practicum," the workshop includes lesson planning activities and reflective tasks on critical teaching used in a short practicum in the form of an action research project, which will be foregrounded in this contribution. These activities can be adapted for other practicum courses, in which material development and lesson planning take place.

To become aware of the practical challenges for critical teaching in German secondary schools, the workshop was designed for in-service teachers. These teachers are very experienced and, thus, aware of structural challenges in schools, such as teaching for tests or grading performances, when aiming at implementing critical teaching. Twelve English teachers from Hesse, Germany, participated in the program Critical Education for English Teachers in Hesse (CEET-H). I conducted CEET-H for seven months (from May to November 2021) at the Philipps-University of Marburg. The sessions took place once a month for four hours partly at university and partly online due to restrictions during the Covid-19-pandemic. CEET-H is embedded in the context of my Ph.D project on CELTE in Germany.

Description of the Practice

The workshop is based on principles of CELTE according to Gerlach and Lüke (2023) putting the enhancement of criticality (Banegas and Villacañas de Castro 2016) and context-orientation (Gerlach and Fasching-Varner 2020) at its center while framing all activities by dialogical practice and cooperation (Fairley 2020). These principles can then be practiced by activities, such as exploring teaching practice, lesson planning, reflective tasks, and material development (see Table 13.1).

The activities, reflective tasks and lesson planning, will be described in more detail with a focus on the overall aims of raising critical awareness about injustice in language teaching and initiating identity development toward a more autonomous and critical professional identity.

Reflective Tasks

Reflective tasks include questions for teachers' self-reflection and reflective questions on (un)critical material. With reflective tasks for self-reflection, teachers should observe and question their roles in the classrooms, which can also be done in other practicums. Reflective questions on materials should enhance critical teaching practice by becoming aware of discriminatory practices within teaching materials. For reflective questions on materials, I first gave a brief introduction on categories (e.g., sexism, racism, or classism) and forms of discrimination (e.g., individual, ideological, or discursive forms) to then look at discriminatory tasks that were gathered by the

Table 13.1 The overall structure of the program with its activities. (relevant activities for this chapter are highlighted in bold)

Meeting	Activities
(1)	• **Reflective tasks about social injustice in language teaching**
	• Input on critical approaches to language teaching
(2)	• **Critical analysis of teaching materials with regard to discriminatory practices**
	• **Critical material development**
(3)	• Planning an action research project
	• **Lesson planning**
	Conducting action research project
(4)	• Presenting and discussing the results of the action research project
(5)	• Introduction to collegial case advice
(6)	• Collegial case advice
	• Evaluation and feedback

teachers and myself, e.g., an authentic, coursebook task on slavery in which students had to take over the position of a slave holder, gather arguments for slavery, and write a dialog between a slave and his/her owner.

The teachers discussed the following reflective tasks in small groups:
- Discuss the following questions:
  - In how far do these exercises reveal discrimination?
  - Should one use such materials for teaching? Why? Why not?
- Be prepared to present the results of your discussion to the other participants.

After the presentation and discussion in larger groups, the teachers completed a written reflection to raise awareness of their own roles and their possibilities for action. These reflective questions should enhance teachers' observation of their teaching practices, which might (re)produce discrimination. With this, teachers also gather practical ideas for classroom management and later practice with a critical agenda.

These were the reflective guiding questions (Fäcke et al. 2017: 89):
- To what extent do I, as a teacher, have a social responsibility to reduce social inequality and discrimination?
- How do power and influence manifest themselves in one's teaching discourse?
- How can power structures, social injustice, and discrimination be addressed in the classroom and, if necessary, changed, for example, by setting tasks?
- Are there approaches that allow power structures, social injustice, and discrimination to be reduced in a targeted manner in the classroom?

Finally, the teachers discussed their results in groups and presented and discussed their ideas within the entire group afterward.

Lesson Planning

The lesson planning activities were embedded in action research projects conducted in meetings 3 and 4 (see Table 13.1). The lesson planning aims at applying principles for critical teaching and using newly developed materials (Crookes 2009: 184). In the following practicum in the form of an action research project, teachers should observe their newly planned lessons with focus on criticality. With help of guided lesson planning, teachers acquire new techniques of classroom management, reducing power structures between learners and teachers as well as supporting cooperation and dialogue among the learners and, thus, enhance context-sensitivity and criticality in ELT. Before planning lessons cooperatively, the participants were paired with a colleague, found a research question concerning critical teaching they would like to address in their lesson, and found instruments (e.g., questionnaires or videography) for answering the question. Then, the following guiding questions adapted from Glynn et al. (2014: 119–23) were given to the teachers for critically adapting existing curricula topics:

- Is there a story behind the topic that reveals past or present inequalities?
- Are there accepted opinions about the topic that can be challenged?
- Is this a topic that people (of a different or different socioeconomic status/class, ethnicity, residence status, or ability) might see differently?
- What do students want to learn and how can these topics be meaningfully addressed in a socially just and critical way?
- Are there points of overlap between the objectives for critical English instruction and the objectives of the curricula? To what extent can these objectives be related?

Teachers were presented possible topics (e.g., climate change, gender, youth, or racism), which can be adapted in a critical way. The teachers planned their lessons and presented their work to the plenary to receive feedback. After implementing the feedback to revise the lesson plans, teachers conducted and observed the lessons in a simulation with the group of the workshop. In this simulation, one of the teachers in each group conducted the lesson in the practicum. The other teachers observed the lesson with the research question in mind (e.g., how do learners cooperate) and collected data (e.g., through videography) to answer their question. They documented problems of classroom management occurring during the practicum.

Critical Reflections: Potentials and Challenges

As a teacher educator, I think that the practical orientation of the workshop and the described activities are very helpful as the participants were able to apply the theoretical input on critical teaching directly to their classrooms. We were able to give each other advice on problems occurring during teaching, which can be very helpful for adapting teaching practice during a practicum through observation and feedback by other colleagues. The reflective tasks also led to more awareness about existing discrimination in the language classroom. Many participants were surprised by subliminal discrimination in common language teaching materials and their inability to identify such discrimination prior to participating in CEET-H. This awareness was supported by observing existing teaching practice and, then, changing this practice for the practicum in the form of action research projects. I observed during the group sessions that some teachers found it difficult to share their intimate reflections as this corresponded to an admittance of inadvertent contribution to discriminatory practices. This can be linked to processes of identity development because the participants reflected on their roles reproducing discrimination and began to change their identity toward a more transformative one by questioning and adapting discriminatory teaching practice. For future workshops, I would adapt the activity so that teachers only needed to share their reflections in small groups and voluntarily in the larger group. Probably because of voluntary participation, nobody in the groups showed resistance toward the workshop and critical approaches.

Regarding the teachers, their reflections are based on informal feedback and discussion occurring during the workshop or at the end of each workshop session. The participants appreciated the workshop as an opportunity to consciously take time to reflect on their teaching materials and practices. They regarded the workshop as a safe space existing outside their school contexts. Teachers could share reflections on their own role in critical teaching and could openly discuss the experienced challenges of critical teaching in school. Focusing on the challenges of activities during the workshop, the teachers described pressure to fulfill curricular guidelines, which to them contradicts critical teaching. They named time constraints due to exams as a hurdle for reflecting on and transforming teaching materials, cooperatively planning lessons and, finally, reflecting on one's own role as an English teacher. These challenges show that teachers willing to practice critical teaching must be highly committed to their job to plan and reflect on lessons critically. Despite these challenges, the workshop made me aware of the potential of cooperative planning and teaching and the misbelief that critical teaching would need much time. One can rely on existing materials and simply add more questions for discussion.

There is a great potential of workshops for critical teaching for in-service English teachers because they can be made aware of existing discrimination. Although they need commitment for participating in this workshop for seven months, I think that the length of the workshop seems necessary for initiating reflection about teaching. In the long run, schools could systematically enhance workshop participation by providing extra time for it. As an outlook, digital working and collaboration should be encouraged among teachers, as it is worthwhile to work in asynchronous formats or remotely on designs for critical teaching.

References

Akbari, R. (2008), "Transforming Lives: Introducing Critical Pedagogy into ELT Classrooms", *ELT Journal*, 62 (3): 276–83.

Banegas, D. L. and Villacañas de Castro, L. S. (2016), "Criticality", *ELT Journal*, 70 (4): 455–7.

Crookes, G. (2009), *Values, Philosophies, and Beliefs in TESOL: Making a Statement*, Cambridge: Cambridge University Press.

Fäcke, A., J. Plikat and B. Tesch (2017), "Perspektiven der Lehrerinnen und Lehrer", in A. Grünwald (ed.), *Praxismaterial: Politische Bildung im Spanischunterricht: Didaktische Grundlagen, Methoden, Materialien*, 87–9, Seelze: Kallmeyer.

Fairley, M. J. (2020), "Conceptualizing Language Teacher Education Centered on Language Teacher Identity Development: A Competencies based Approach and Practical Applications", *TESOL Journal*, 78 (3): 1–28.

Gerlach, D. (2020), "Einführung in eine Kritische Fremdsprachendidaktik", in D. Gerlach (ed.), *Kritische Fremdsprachendidaktik: Grundlagen, Ziele, Beispiele*, 7–32, Tübingen: Narr Francke Attempto.

Gerlach, D. and K. Fasching-Varner (2020), "Grundüberlegungen zu einer kritischen Fremdsprachenlehrer*innenbildung", in D. Gerlach (ed.), *Kritische Fremdsprachendidaktik: Grundlagen, Ziele, Beispiele*, 217–34, Tübingen: Narr Francke Attempto.

Gerlach, D. and M. Lüke (2023), "Integrating Critical Approaches into Language Teacher Education", in C. Ludwig and T. Summer (eds), *Routledge Research in Language Education. Taboos and Controversial Issues in Foreign Language Education: Critical*

Language Pedagogy in Theory, Research and Practice, 40–9, London and New York: Routledge.

Glynn, C., P. M. Wesely, B. A. Wassell and T. A. Osborn (2014), *Words and Actions: Teaching Languages through the Lens of Social Justice*, n.n.: American Council on the Teaching of Foreign Languages.

Hawkins, M. and B. Norton (2009), "Critical Language Teacher Education", in A. Burns and J. C. Richards (eds), *Cambridge Guide to Second Language Teacher Education*, 30–9, New York: Cambridge University Press.

14

Achieving Social Justice in the English Classroom: Ideas to Introduce Queer Pedagogies to Pre-/In-service Teachers of English

Özge Güney

Background

Adopting a queer-informed approach to language teaching entails incorporating LGBTQ+ issues in classroom discourse in culturally relevant ways to provide a safe classroom environment for the learners of diverse sociosexual backgrounds to express their identities (Nelson 2009). Research has pointed out the lack of and thereafter the need for queer-inclusive teacher education programs. Without proper training on the relevance of queer pedagogies, teachers of English may fail to acknowledge LGBTQ+ individuals in their classroom instruction, sometimes reinforcing homophobia either consciously or unconsciously.

To address classroom management issues related to sexual identity, this section presents a brief account of five class sessions where I, as a guest researcher, introduced queer pedagogies to undergraduate pre-service teachers at English Language Teaching (ELT) programs of three Turkish universities. Each pre-service teacher attended one class session only. The pre-service teachers were all seniors also doing their internship at diverse state/private schools as trainee teachers. I had no previous contact with the pre-service teachers and was introduced to them by the faculty in their programs.

In the Türkiye context, the particular need for queer-informed teacher education originates from the conservative setting of the country (as is the case in certain Asian and Middle Eastern contexts), where discussions of sexuality are considered a taboo and avoided at every walk of life including schools and other academic settings (Gelbal and Duyan 2016). Simply avoiding LGBTQ+-related discussions in the classroom may cause several classroom management issues for teachers: (i) learners may express homophobic ideas during in-class activities causing tensions, (ii) LGBTQ+ learners may face micro-aggression and bullying from peers, and (iii) learners may initiate conversations of sexual identity when discussing topics such as family, relations, and celebrities, which may catch teachers off guard if they are not informed about how to handle these issues. Thus, this chapter aims to give teachers and teacher educators some practical ideas to deal with the challenges related to sexuality issues.

Description of the Practice

Each class session started with a discussion about the relevance of queer pedagogies for the language classroom because some teachers may have the misconception that queer issues do not fall within the scope of language teaching (Nelson 1993). Hence, I introduced different guidelines from reliable and renowned institutions toward achieving a fair classroom environment for LGBTQ+ learners. For example, in Teaching Respect for All: Implementation Guide, the United Nations Educational, Scientific and Cultural Organization (UNESCO 2014) includes sexual orientation among different facets of identity to be respected in the classroom and recognizes any negative attitude toward different sexual orientations as a form of discrimination.

Afterwards, I showed pre-service teachers a slide with the screenshots of academic research on LGBTQ+ in the English classroom in diverse countries. This snapshot of literature enabled pre-service teachers to realize that queer-inclusive teaching and homophobia are legitimately discussed within the ELT framework even if such topics may not be addressed in their respective ELT programs as revealed by pre-service teachers themselves (Güney 2018; 2022). A brief review of queer literature also helped pre-service teachers to understand that many topics discussed in the English classroom such as family, relationships, marriage, leisure time activities, diseases (AIDS) have references to sexual and gender identity, thus push LGBTQ+ learners to talk about their private life and personal ideas. Gaining this awareness is important for teachers because unless they acknowledge sexual identity issues are an inherent part of the English classroom, they will be neither prepared nor willing to deal with related classroom management issues.

Having presented some background information on the relevance of sexuality issues in ELT, I wanted to initiate discussions on the Turkish educational context. Hence, I showed pre-service teachers an award-winning documentary that narrates the struggles of a transgender individual who lives in Türkiye (Akşahin 2014). Choosing a local resource is particularly important because sexuality and homophobia are conditioned by local cultures, traditions, and religions among other sociocultural variables (Ó'Móchain 2006; Richardson 2008). After pre-service teachers watched the documentary, they had whole-class discussions guided by the following questions (adjusted from Nelson 2009) on the Türkiye context:

(i) In Türkiye, which sexual identities seem natural or acceptable? Which do not? How can you tell? How is this different in another country? How is it similar?
(ii) Why do people sometimes want to be able to identify others as straight, gay, or bisexual? When is it important to know this about someone? When is it not important at all?
(iii) What difficulties do LGBTQ+ identified students/ teachers have in their education life in Türkiye? How is this different in another country? How is it similar?

For most of the pre-service teachers, it was the first time they talked about queer issues within the ELT context. Many of them were supportive of queer-informed teaching and appreciated the discussions triggered by the above questions. The pre-service teachers acknowledged that LGBTQ+ learners are bullied in Türkiye and have to hide their identity due to the social and political oppression. Such realization is fundamental to successful classroom management because if teachers do not recognize the existence of the issue and what contributes to it in the local context, they will not consider fighting against homophobia or bullying in their future classrooms.

Pre-service teachers also talked about the issues faced by the LGBTQ+ students and teachers that they know, referencing their stories and experiences in a supportive manner. At this moment, I showed pre-service teachers a brief video of an English language learner who suddenly makes a homophobic comment about a gay celebrity as his peers talk about their favorite celebrities in the English classroom. Then, I asked pre-service teachers how they would respond if one of their students made a homophobic comment in their future classroom. With this activity, I wanted them to realize that even if teachers do not initiate conversations on sexuality in their classroom instruction, learners may bring up LGBTQ+ topics, and teachers will inevitably need to deal with the situation. Pre-service teachers came up with a variety of ideas for this question such as asking the student to elaborate on the reasons for the homophobic attitude, talking with the student in private to inquire about the reasons and ways of fixing the situation, designing a speaking or a reading class about the improvement of social justice, and guiding the student through school counselors.

One efficient way to deal with homophobia in the classroom is to take preventive measures. Homophobia might appear with other social justice issues such as racism and gender bias. The best way to prevent any bias and hate speech is to address them all on the first day of school before they emerge (Wadell, Frei, and Martin 2012). The teacher may simply lay out the rules that no hate speech will be tolerated and put up a poster that reads "Respect All!" or "We welcome all races, nationalities, genders, sexual orientations, religions, and (dis)abilities." However, fighting against homophobia is not a one-time activity as it requires a progressive teaching philosophy that penetrates overall teaching practices. Consistency is the key in classroom management, so it would help to incorporate queer-inclusive materials in the classroom instruction to remain persistent across the semester. For example, in a grammar class, teachers may talk about how the pronoun *they* refers to nonbinary individuals in English. Teachers could be more flexible with tasks and activities that do not limit students with heteronormative roles. Hence, instead of writing a dialogue between a husband and a wife, students may simply be asked to form their own families (Dumas 2008).

At the end of the sessions, to give pre-service teachers more concrete ideas about how to adopt a queer inclusive discourse in the English classroom, I showed them sample instructional materials that include queer identities and issues. If time permits, teacher educators could also ask pre-service teachers to design their own queer-informed materials. Since queer issues and individuals are not typically represented in the heteronormative instructional materials (Selvi and Kocaman 2021), teachers need to be more inclusive in the materials they prepare to fight homophobia. Incorporating LGBTQ+ issues in their discourse and classroom instruction consistently helps to maintain a peaceful classroom environment as making such sensitivity an inherent part of the instruction will remind learners to be mindful and respectful toward marginalized identities and may even prevent homophobia from emerging.

Critical Reflections: Potentials and Challenges

The sessions overall went smoothly, and pre-service teachers stated that they were informed and gained a different perspective about inclusive teaching. However, there were some pre-service teachers who remained silent throughout the sessions, and few teachers said there was not enough time in the English classroom to cover all the social justice issues. One pre-service teacher said that he would ignore homophobia. At this point, teacher educators might once again remind pre-service teachers that avoiding social justice issues in the classroom is not going to make them disappear as English classes relate to real-life issues including sexuality by nature, and issues of homophobia may deteriorate throughout the semester if not handled immediately. There may always be teachers who do not want to be involved in any kind of controversy, especially in communities where discussions of sexuality are rare. This is exactly why it is crucial for teacher education programs to teach pre-service teachers the relevance of and the need for creating a safe classroom environment for all where learners can interact respectfully even if they do not agree with each other.

As is also revealed by the pre-service teachers themselves, faculty at teacher education programs need to teach pre-service teachers how to incorporate queer issues in the language classroom in a meaningful and structured way because pre-service teachers need guidance as novice teachers. Queer-inclusive pedagogies could easily become a topic of discussion in courses related to classroom management, methods/approaches, or material development in teacher education programs. Pre-service teachers should be taught to promote social justice starting on the first day of school and maintain a queer-inclusive discourse throughout the semester as consistency is crucial in classroom management.

Teacher educators could also invite guest speakers who specialize in the field or self-identified LGBTQ+ students and/or teachers or show pre-service teachers films featuring queer individuals so that teachers can discuss sexuality issues and homophobia in a culturally appropriate way. Teachers touch the lives of students forever, and it is the responsibility of teacher education programs to raise sensitive and fair teachers who appreciate diversity in their classroom. Successful classroom management entails engaging all the learners in classroom activities meaningfully and comfortably irrespective of their sociosexual background as marginalized individuals make up the culture and society we live in and exist in actual classrooms, albeit sometimes in secret (Dumas 2008; Vandrick 1997).

References

Akşahin, V. (Director) (2014), Hala [Paternal aunt] [Video File]. YouTube. Available at https://www.youtube.com/watch?v=B7bTAWrd9f0.

Dumas, J. (2008), "The ESL Classroom and the Queerly Shifting Sands of Learner Identity", *TESL Canada Journal*, 26 (1): 1–10.

Gelbal, S. and V. Duyan (2006), "Attitudes of University Students toward Lesbians and Gay Men in Turkey", *Sex Roles*, 55: 573–9. doi:10.1007/s11199-006-9112-1.

Güney, Ö. (2018), "Queering Teacher Education Programs: Perceptions of Pre-service EFL Teachers towards Queer Issues", MA diss., College of Education, Bilkent University, Ankara.

Güney, Ö. (2022), "Pre-service Teachers Discussing Queer-inclusive Pedagogies in Turkish EFL classrooms", In C. E. Poteau and C. A. Winkle (eds), *Advocacy for Social and Linguistic Justice in TESOL Nurturing Inclusivity, Equity, and Social Responsibility in English Language Teaching*, 166–82, New York: Routledge. doi:10.4324/9781003202356.

Nelson, C. D. (1993), "Heterosexism in ESL: Examining Our Attitudes", *TESOL Quarterly*, 27 (1): 143–50.

Nelson, C. D. (2009), *Sexual Identities in English Language Education: Classroom Conversations*, New York: Routledge.

Ó'Móchain, R. (2006), "Discussing Gender and Sexuality in a Context-Appropriate Way: Queer Narratives in an EFL College Classroom in Japan", *Journal of Language, Identity and Education*, 5 (1): 51–66. doi:10.1207/s15327701jlie0501_4.

Richardson, E. M. (2008), "Using a Film to Challenge Heteronormativity: South African Teachers 'Get Real' in Working with LGB Youth", *Journal of LGBT Youth*, 5 (2): 63–72.

Selvi, A. F. and C. Kocaman (2021), "(Mis-/Under-)Representations of Gender and Sexuality in Locally Produced ELT Materials", *Journal of Language, Identity and Education*, 20 (2). doi:10.1080/15348458.2020.1726757.

UNESCO (2014), Teaching Respect for All: Implementation Guide, UNESDOC Digital Library. Available online: http://unesdoc.unesco.org/images/0022/002279/227983E.pdf.

Vandrick, S. (1997), "The Role of Hidden Identities in the Postsecondary ESL Classroom", *TESOL Quarterly*, 31 (1): 153–7.

Wadell, E., K. Frei and S. Martin (2012), "Professional Development through Inquiry: Addressing Sexual Identity in TESOL", *The CATESOL Journal*, 23 (1): 99–109.

Part Five

Second Language Assessment

15

Critical Language Teacher Education and Language Assessment

Seyyed-Abdolhamid Mirhosseini

Introduction

Critical language teacher education (CLTE) may be explored in terms of critical perspectives of various interconnected elements such as methodology, curriculum, and materials, as well as dynamics like intercultural communication, language development, and online teaching. Language assessment is an aspect of language education that influences and is influenced by almost all of these elements and dynamics. Examining some theoretical considerations about this aspect of CLTE, in this chapter, first I briefly discuss how language assessment can be viewed in the context of language teacher education (LTE) and language teachers' involvements. More specifically, this discussion considers the idea of teachers' language assessment literacy in the wider landscape of CLTE. Then, the chapter presents four focal topics of critical assessment ideas in LTE: problematizing psychometric measurement mentalities; questioning the so-called native speaker norms; examining the politics of international tests; and understanding assessment for language ownership. From a perspective other than the one suggested by expertise in the technicalities of language testing and assessment, the chapter is hoped to offer critical insights not primarily influenced by those technicalities.

Current Issues

Language assessment has been considered a challenging part of what language teachers do and an important aspect of LTE for a long time (Davies 2008; Freeman, Orzulak, and Morrisey 2009). This has been particularly reflected in extensive discussions and research on language assessment literacy, "generally viewed as a repertoire of competences, knowledge of using assessment methods, and applying suitable tools in an appropriate time that enables an individual to understand, assess, construct language tests, and analyze test data" (Coombe, Vafadar, and Mohebbi 2020: 2). Language assessment literacy has been discussed in terms of a wide range of components variously considered as skills, knowledge, and principles (Davis 2008; Fulcher 2012; Hidri 2021; Inbar-Lourie 2017; Taylor 2009). In relation to the topic of this chapter within the context of this book, it is notable that this concept is by some accounts viewed "in conjunction with the development of a critical understanding about the roles and functions of assessment within society" (O'Loughlin 2013: 363).

This social aspect of language assessment literacy is obviously connected with some developments in language assessment that lean toward critical orientations (Lynch 2001; Mirhosseini and De Costa 2020; Shohamy 2017; 2022). Within the wider landscape of critical applied linguistics (Pennycook 2021), such views consider language testing as "both a product and an agent of cultural, social, political, educational and ideological agendas that shape the lives of individual participants, teachers and learners" (Shohamy 1998: 332). Culture is, therefore, occasionally included among the many components and elements of language assessment literacy (Vogt, Tsagari, and Spanoudis 2020). As an example, Sun and Zhang (2022: 9) specifically consider "[h]aving cultural awareness and sensitivity when writing test items" as one factor in their investigation of the status of teachers' language assessment literacy. Nonetheless, sociocultural concerns seem to be still overshadowed by measurement issues. For instance, two recent reviews, although mentioning critical and localized views, emphasize that measures should be developed to assess language assessment literacy "scientifically" (Gan and Lan 2022: 519) and that assessment literacy "is related to educational measurement and influenced by current paradigms in this field" (Coombe, Vafadar, and Mohebbi 2020: 11).

Stepping beyond testing technicalities and measurement mentalities that may propagate a banking conception of education, critical attitudes can be more seriously included in language teachers' preparation and their actual assessment practices. McNamara and Roever (2006: 255) "stress the importance of a well-rounded training for language testers that goes beyond applied psychometrics" and advocate "a critical view of testing and social consequences." Nurturing such critical attitudes about language assessment (further specified in the four considerations in the next section) can be conveniently accommodated in CLTE (Gray 2019; Hawkins and Norton 2009), which similarly resides within the wider realm of critical applied linguistics (Pennycook 2021). Hawkins and Norton (2009: 36) specify "critical awareness," "critical self-reflection," and "critical pedagogical relations" as "central heuristics in critical language teacher education." Such heuristics have informed the small stream of scholarship in the field that explore how critical attitudes can enrich understandings of various aspects of language teachers' roles (e.g., Cross 2010; Kubanyiova 2020; Mambu 2022; Mirhosseini and Bayat, 2023; Nuske 2015), which can significantly include engaging with language assessment. The next section offers further insights and examples of what may specifically be problematized in language assessment from critical perspectives.

Implications for Teacher Education

A concern for language teachers' critical understanding of language assessment can be an important part of preservice teacher preparation processes and in-service support offered by teacher educators as well as teachers' ongoing learning and unlearning about their own language teaching praxis. Such critical understandings and attitudes may be embedded in fundamental perceptions of the nature of language, learning, and teaching. In the rest of this chapter, I specifically discuss four major foci of critical language assessment awareness that can be created in CLTE.

Measurementism

Setting out from a basic premise of critical language assessment which "assumes that the act of testing is not neutral" (Shohamy 1998: 332), perhaps the primary aspect of assessment that teachers can be invited to revisit in CLTE is the very idea of psychometrics. Measurement may appear to be a taken-for-granted universal essence of assessment, but it is actually an ideological construct rooted in certain epistemological standpoints. Measurementism—that is, the dominant mentalities that favor educational measurement—tends to foster positivist scientific conceptions of knowledge (Mirhosseini 2017), which can foreground quantification at the expense of understanding learning processes (Gipps 1994). Measurement may be "difficult to argue against because it has the allure of impartiality" (Kress 2011: 43), but educational measurement and possible sediments of measurementist tendencies even in alternative assessment approaches can create some of the most deeply rooted obstacles on the way of adopting critical assessment perspectives by language teachers.

The positivist epistemological underpinnings of measurementism (such as quantification and decontextualization) are in clear contrast with social constructivist foundations of critical perspectives. However, measurement technicalities are so normalized as an indispensable aspect of assessment that even critical language assessment may fail to question them, as it tends to focus on test use and the constructs of what is assessed rather than the epistemological construction of assessment procedures. For instance, while advocating critical views, McNamara and Roever (2006: 255) emphasize that "We are in no way advocating the abandonment of training in psychometrics." This is ironic given the epistemological incongruence of critical and positivist perspectives underlying psychometrics. In another recent manifestation of this incongruence, instruments have been developed to "measure" critical language assessment literacy (Tajeddin, Khatib, and Mahdavi 2022). Even alternatives such as portfolio assessment, dynamic assessment, formative assessment, self-assessment, etc., might be interpreted by different people based on different extents of deep residing measurementist mentalities. Therefore, CLTE needs to challenge strict quantification tendencies or at least create an awareness for teachers about hinderances that psychometrics and measurement can make on the path of humanizing pedagogy.

Native-speakerism

A second critical consideration of language assessment that should be part of CLTE is about how language assessment mechanisms at different levels may foster and be fostered by the so-called native speaker norms (Holliday 2005). Although native-speakerist ideals are argued to be imagined discursive constructs rather than real entities (Holliday 2021), these very constructs can be set as criteria of good contents, methodology, and achievements in language education. Along with the possible influence on defining ideal teachers, teaching and learning materials, and teaching methods, native-speakerism may significantly influence expectations about the learning goals and assessment criteria of different language abilities. In the context of English language education, teachers' awareness of debates around World Englishes, English as a Lingua Franca, and English as an International Language in relation to language assessment can be an important part of a critical encounter with native-speakerism (e.g., Davies 2009; Jenkins 2006; Jenkins and Leung 2017; Shohamy 2019) (although there are reservations about these perspectives as briefly discussed in the final section below). "The crucial issue here is how achievement is defined" (McNamara 2012: 199). It can be defined based on an image of the standard language of idealized native speakers or in reference to the actual use of English in its various contexts of use by a diversity of people around the world (Cheng, Im, and Jabeen 2021; Doecke and Mirhosseini 2023).

International Testing

High-stakes international proficiency tests are manifestations of measurementist and native-speakerist views of language assessment to varying extents, but they can go beyond that by the sheer magnitude of their influence as image-building and gatekeeping instruments. In addition to administrative and economic issues of large-scale international proficiency tests (Alsagoafi 2018; Pearson 2019), they have been problematized for various consequences in terms of problems of fairness and their influence (washback) on teaching and learning practices as well as questions of power, dominance, and social justice (Khan 2009; Pearson 2019; Pilcher and Richards 2017). The tests have also been critically examined for their "carrier content" that can discursively reproduce certain ideas and worldviews, especially when they are used as teaching materials by language teachers around the world (Noori and Mirhosseini 2021).

Templer (2004) specifically counted on teachers in his discussion of concerns about "testing industry that require critical examination" (197) and argued that "Imperative now is advocacy to get this entire regimen and its abuses more centrally onto the sounding boards … An initiative can begin locally, at your own institution, bottom-up, articulated by teachers from an array of disciplines" (211). Therefore, CLTE should be able to offer critical perspectives in this regard, significantly confronting the naïve perception that the aim of language learning is simply gaining a certain score at an international proficiency test. In other words, teachers should be invited to consider that, as I have argued elsewhere, needing a certain test score to satisfy gatekeepers is one thing and believing that scores indicate the real knowledge of language is another: "If the latter notion prevails, the dominance of gatekeepers over educational practices may fortify obscured utilitarian images of language" (Mirhosseini 2015: 939).

Language Ownership

As discussed in the section on native-speakerism above, an important concern in English language assessment is the kind of English that is set as the criterion. Critical discussions of English language assessment have raised the question of "what English" or "whose English" (e.g., Cheng, Im, and Jabeen 2021; Pilcher and Richards 2017; Templer 2004). The perspectives of World Englishes, English as a Lingua Franca, and English as an International Language have already challenged the illusive standard native English in teaching and assessment, but CLTE may need to go beyond these perspectives, as they tend to focus on surface-level variations of pronunciation, lexis, and syntax. Various aspects of language teachers' activities, including their assessment praxis, can aim to cultivate an attitude in learners that helps them own the language that they learn and appropriate it for their diverse ways of meaning-making within their lifeworld (Doecke and Mirhosseini 2023). "Real proficiency is when you are able to take possession of the language, turn it to your advantage, and make it real for you" (Widdowson 1994: 384).

With an awareness of insights about the dominance of psychometrics and measurement, imagined native standards, and international high-stakes testing, teachers can adopt critical assessment perspectives and practices to encourage language ownership by center-staging learners and their own languages and cultures (Doecke and Mirhosseini 2023; Shohamy 2007). Assessment processes can be conceptualized as critical endeavors that facilitate challenging those dominant trends, and critical language teachers can appreciate and support language learners' processes of meaning-making within their own diverse cultural contexts and in their own ways. For example, the carrier contents of tests can always be a topic for critical reflection in terms of how they include or exclude local cultures of language learners (Noori and Mirhosseini 2021). Constantly seeking alternative assessment approaches, localizing language assessment practices, and understanding issues of society, ideology, and identity can enhance the role of language assessment to a socially relevant and responsible act that can contribute to language teaching and learning, educational endeavors in general, and even broader goals of social life beyond education. CLTE can provide the environment for nurturing intellectual capacities for understanding such conceptions of critical language assessment and generating the passion and courage to put them into action.

References

Alsagoafi, A. (2018), "IELTS Economic Washback: A Case Study on English Major Students at King Faisal University in Al-Hasa, Saudi Arabia", *Language Testing in Asia*, 8 (1): 1–13. doi:10.1186/s40468-018-0058-3.

Cheng, L., G.-H. Im and R. Jabeen (2021), "Whose English(es) Are We Assessing and by Whom?", in B. Lanteigne, C. Coombe. and J. D. Brown (eds), *Challenges in Language Testing around the World: Insights for Language Test Users*, 169–79, Cham: Springer.

Coombe, C., H. Vafadar and H. Mohebbi (2020), "Language Assessment Literacy: What Do We Need to Learn, Unlearn, and Relearn?", *Language Testing in Asia*, 10 (3): 1–16. doi:10.1186/s40468-020-00101-6.

Cross, R. (2010), "Language Teaching as Sociocultural Activity: Rethinking Language Teacher Practice", *The Modern Language Journal*, 94 (3): 434–52. doi:10.1111/j.1540-4781.2010.01058.x.

Davies, A. (2008), "Textbook Trends in Teaching Language Testing", *Language Testing*, 25 (3): 327–47. doi:10.1177/0265532208090156.

Davies, A. (2009), "Assessing World Englishes", *Annual Review of Applied Linguistics*, 29: 80–9. doi:10.1017/S0267190509090072.

Doecke, B. and S. A. Mirhosseini (2023), "Multiple Englishes: Multiple Ways of Being in the World (A Conversational Inquiry)", *English in Education*, 57 (2): 76–90. doi:10.1080/04250494.2023.2189910.

Freeman, D., M. Orzulak and G. Morrisey (2009), "Assessment in Second Language Teacher Education", in A. Burns and J. C. Richards (eds). *Second Language Teacher Education*, 77–90, Cambridge: Cambridge University Press.

Fulcher, G. (2012), "Assessment Literacy for the Language Classroom", *Language Assessment Quarterly*, 9 (2): 113–32. doi:10.1080/15434303.2011.642041.

Gan, L. and R. Lam (2022), "A Review on Language Assessment Literacy: Trends, Foci and Contributions", *Language Assessment Quarterly*, 19 (5): 503–25. doi:10.1080/15434303.2022.2128802.

Gipps, C. V. (1994), *Beyond Testing: Towards a Theory of Educational Assessment*, London: The Falmer Press.

Gray, J. (2019), "Critical Language Teacher Education?," in S. Walsh and S. Mann (eds). *The Routledge Handbook of English Language Teacher Education*, 68–81, Abingdon, Oxon/New York: Routledge.

Hawkins, M. and B. Norton (2009), "Critical Language Teacher Education", in A. Burns and J. C. Richards (eds). *Cambridge Guide to Second Language Teacher Education*, 30–9, New York: Cambridge University Press.

Hidri, S. (ed.) (2021), *Perspectives on Language Assessment Literacy: Challenges for Improved Student Learning*, London: Routledge.

Holliday, A. (2005), *The Struggle to Teach English as an International Language*, Oxford: Oxford University Press.

Holliday, A. (2021), "Linguaculture, Cultural Travel, Native-speakerism and Small Culture Formation on the Go: Working Up from Instances", in R. Rubdy, R. Tupas and M. Saraceni (eds), *Bloomsbury World Englishes (Volume II: Ideologies)*, 101–13, London: Bloomsbury.

Inbar-Lourie, O. (2017), "Language Assessment Literacy", in E. Shohamy, I. G. Or, and S. May (eds), *Language Testing and Assessment*, 3rd edn, 257–70, Cham: Springer.

Jenkins, J. (2006), "The Spread of EIL: A Testing Time for Testers", *ELT Journal*, 60 (1): 42–50. doi:10.1093/elt/cci080.

Jenkins, J. and C. Leung (2017), "Assessing English as a Lingua Franca", in E. Shohamy, I. Or and S. May (eds), *Encyclopedia of Language and Education (Volume 7: Language Testing and Assessment)*, 103–18, Cham: Springer.

Jenkins, J. and C. Leung (2017), "Assessing English as a Lingua Franca", *Language Testing and Assessment*, 7: 103–17.

Khan, S. Z. (2009), "Imperialism of International Tests: An EIL Perspective", in F. Sharifian (ed.), *English as an International Language: Perspectives and Pedagogical Issues*, 190–205, Clevedon: Multilingual Matters.

Kress, T. M. (2011), *Critical Praxis Research: Breathing New Life into Research Methods for Teachers*, Dordrecht: Springer.
Kubanyiova, M. (2020), "Language Teacher Education in the Age of Ambiguity: Educating Responsive Meaning Makers in the World", *Language Teaching Research*, 24 (1): 49–59. doi:10.1177/1362168818777533.
Lynch, B. K. (2001), "Rethinking Assessment from a Critical Perspective", *Language Testing*, 18 (4): 351–72. doi:10.1177/026553220101800403.
Mambu, J. E. (2022), "Co-constructing a Critical ELT Curriculum: A Case Study in an Indonesian-Based English Language Teacher Education Program", *TESOL Journal*, 13 (3), e667. doi:10.1002/tesj.667.
McNamara, T. (2012), "English as a Lingua Franca: The Challenge for Language Testing", *Journal of English as a Lingua Franca*, 1 (1): 199–202. doi:10.1515/jelf-2012-0013.
McNamara, T. and C. Roever (2006), *Language Testing: The Social Dimension*, Malden: Blackwell.
Mirhosseini, S. A. (2015), "Resisting Magic Waves: Ideologies of 'English Language Teaching' in Iranian Newspaper Advertisements", *Discourse: Studies in the Cultural Politics of Education*, 36 (6): 932–47. doi:10.1080/01596306.2014.918462.
Mirhosseini, S. A. (2017), "Scientism as a Linchpin of Oppressing Isms in Language Education Research", in D. J. Rivers and K. Zotzmann (eds), *Isms in Language Education: Oppression, Intersectionality and Emancipation*, 185–202, Berlin: Mouton De Gruyter.
Mirhosseini, S.-A. and G. Bayat (2023), "Probing the Sociocultural Relevance of TESOL in Three Stories of Becoming an English Teacher", *TESOL J*, 57: 1463–89.
Mirhosseini, S. A. and P. De Costa (eds) (2020), *The Sociopolitics of English Language Testing*, London: Bloomsbury.
Noori, M. and S. A. Mirhosseini (2021), "Testing Language, but What?: Examining the Carrier Content of IELTS Preparation Materials from a Critical Perspective", *Language Assessment Quarterly*, 18 (4): 382–97. doi:10.1080/15434303.2021.1883618.
Nuske, K. (2015), "Transformation and Stasis: Two Case Studies of Critical Teacher Education in TESOL", *Critical Inquiry in Language Studies*, 12 (4): 283–312, doi:10.1080/15427587.2015.1096734.
O'Loughlin, K. (2013), "Developing the Assessment Literacy of University Proficiency Test Users", *Language Testing*, 30 (3): 363–80. doi:10.1177%2F0265532213480336.
Pearson, W. S. (2019), "Critical Perspectives on the IELTS Test", *ELT Journal*, 73 (2): 197–206. doi:10.1093/elt/ccz006.
Pennycook, A. (2021), *Critical Applied Linguistics: A Critical Reintroduction*, 2nd edn, London: Routledge.
Pilcher, N. and K. Richards (2017), "Challenging the Power Invested in the International English Language Testing System (IELTS): Why Determining 'English' Preparedness Needs to Be Undertaken within the Subject Context", *Power and Education*, 9 (1): 3–17. doi:10.1177/1757743817691995.
Shohamy, E. (1998), "Critical Language Testing and Beyond", *Studies in Educational Evaluation*, 24 (4): 331–45. doi:10.1016/S0191-491X(98)00020-0.
Shohamy, E. (2007), "The Power of Language Tests, the Power of the English Language and the Role of ELT", in J. Cummins and C. Davison (eds), *International Handbook of English Language Teaching*, 521–31, Dordrecht: Springer.
Shohamy, E. (2017), "Critical Language Testing", in E. Shohamy, I. G. Or and S. May (eds), *Language Testing and Assessment*, 3rd edn, 441–54, Cham: Springer.

Shohamy, E. (2019), "Critical Language Testing and English Lingua Franca: How Can One Help the Other?", in K. Murata (ed.). *English-Medium Instruction from an English as a Lingua Franca Perspective: Exploring the Higher Education Context*, 271–85, London: Routledge.

Shohamy, E. (2022), "Critical Language Testing, Multilingualism and Social Justice", *TESOL Quarterly*, 56 (4): 1445–57. doi:10.1002/tesq.3185.

Sun, H. and J. Zhang (2022), "Assessment Literacy of College EFL Teachers in China: Status Quo and Mediating Factors", *Studies in Educational Evaluation*, 74: 101157. doi:10.1016/j.stueduc.2022.101157.

Tajeddin, Z., M. Khatib and M. Mahdavi (2022), "Critical Language Assessment Literacy of EFL Teachers: Scale Construction and Validation", *Language Testing*, 39 (4): 649–78. doi:10.1177/02655322211057040.

Taylor, L. (2009), "Developing Assessment Literacy", *Annual Review of Applied Linguistics*, 29: 21–36. doi:10.1017/S0267190509090035.

Templer, B. (2004), "High-Stakes Testing at High Fees: Notes and Queries on the International English Proficiency Assessment Market", *Journal for Critical Education Policy Studies*, 2 (1): 189–226. http://www.jceps.com/archives/414.

Vogt, K., D. Tsagari and G. Spanoudis (2020), "What Do Teachers Think They Want? A Comparative Study of In-Service Language Teachers" *Beliefs on LAL Training Needs'*, *Language Assessment Quarterly*, 17 (4): 386–409. doi:10.1080/15434303.2020.1781128.

Widdowson, H. G. (1994), "The Ownership of English", *TESOL Quarterly*, 28 (2): 377–89. doi:10.2307/3587438.

Suggested Readings and External Links

- Gipps, C. V. (1994), *Beyond Testing: Towards a Theory of Educational Assessment*, London: The Falmer Press.
- Mirhosseini, S. A. and P. De Costa (eds) (2020), *The Sociopolitics of English Language Testing*, London: Bloomsbury.
- Shohamy, E. (2007), "The Power of Language Tests, the Power of the English Language and the Role of ELT" in J. Cummins and C. Davison (eds), *International Handbook of English Language Teaching*, 521–31, Dordrecht: Springer.
- Shohamy, E. (2022), "Critical Language Testing, Multilingualism and Social Justice", *TESOL Quarterly*, 56 (4): 1445–57.
- Templer, B. (2004), "High-Stakes Testing at High Fees: Notes and Queries on the International English Proficiency Assessment Market", *Journal for Critical Education Policy Studies*, 2 (1): 189–226.

16

Disrupting Assumptions in English Language Teaching (ELT) Assessment

Laura Loder Buechel

Background

At the Zurich University of Teacher Education in Switzerland, pre-service public school English language teachers have been taught in much the same way for the past twenty years—too much emphasis on mechanical acts (especially in the field of assessment), and little emphasis on critical stances and skills to question the content and materials they are expected to work with in public schools. Though perhaps not quite a banking model of education or an invasive, prescriptive pedagogy as Freire (2005) discusses, it is not really the libertarian model he may have promoted. Perhaps we have not, as teacher educators, promoted creative or critical acts (Freire 1994) enough, but still focus too much on mechanical acts.

This is why an independent study unit entitled "Disrupting Assumptions in ELT" has been added to the regular, traditional content mandatory for graduation[1]. The aim is to get educators to think more deeply about what they think they "know"; not to provide recipes for teaching, but help them to challenge what they think they know and what we think we are teaching them. The general assumptions and disruptive thoughts stem from a range of resources and experiences that have been deemed problematic in the practice. For instance:

- Do coursebooks and curricula really provide good guidelines and ensure a given level upon completion—or not?
- Do mandatory coursebooks promote the humanistic values that the curricular tenets suppose—or not?
- Should English language learning start with easy contexts and language and be made more complex later—or not?
- Learners need scaffolding—or do we help our learners too much or in the wrong ways?
- And most importantly, even though assessment should be ongoing, there is summative and formative which should be strictly separated—or should it not?

The world of assessment is messy. Rethinking assessment is thus essential as pre-service teachers, and even teachers in the field, often do not dare stray from their experienced assessment practices (Tsagari and Vogt 2017) despite there being much known about alternative practices. During their own certification process, teachers experience many assessment practices including standardized tests (e.g., the Cambridge exams), projects, small weekly quizzes, test redos, and portfolio development. These practices offer a range of examples that could theoretically be transferred to a future teacher's own public school practices. Yet in terms of ELT in Switzerland, there are quite a few assessment-related issues (Buechel and Lichtenauer 2019) that remain pervasive:

- Teachers are over-dependent on coursebook suggestions and uncritically use pre-fabricated end-of unit tests that do not always include the best item-types (e.g., true/false/not in the text are common but not necessarily good item-types due to the idea that we actually want to teach learners to infer [Van Blerkom 2017]).
- The extensive use of vocabulary-translation testing is a major source of motivating learners but is problematic (Buechel 2022).
- Smaller, regular quizzes or larger, open projects are better for learning (Dunlosky et al. 2013) but are not frequently used.
- Though the report cards are said to be competency-based, they are actually domain-based. Teachers give grades in reading, writing, speaking, and listening (which are difficult to separate), but not on learner attainment of more specific A2 or B1 aims.
- Teachers put points on tests and quizzes and rarely think about why they do this or alternatives (see the Gurus section on https://padlet.com/laura_buechel/assessment for more).
- Teachers often believe that one tool (e.g., a test) can only be used for one purpose (e.g., for summative assessment) as opposed to myriad purposes (e.g., an end-of-unit test can be used as a "diagnostic" or "placement" test at the start of a unit).
- Some of the material presented in local coursebooks is misogynistic or biased (e.g., there are generic Native People presenting their totems) and thus the language aims need to be separated from the context, the context changed or not given to learners, and thus both presented and assessed differently (Massler et al. 2014).

A more critical approach is necessary and thus is the aim of this newer content which addresses the issues above but also other more general points on assessment such as what performance at a given CEFR level looks like, what the role of accuracy is in a world where English is a lingua franca, the role of informal learning, the role of criteria versus norm-referenced assessment and more. Select syllabi and materials from various courses have been made available to the reader at https://padlet.com/laura_buechel/assessment.

Description of the Practice

Over the years, students have done myriad assignments related to disrupting their thinking about and planning for assessment. Four elements that have been especially well-received are presented here.

Using Tests for Learning

Input on using tests for learning includes comparing standardized tests to those in local coursebooks, analyzing test item-types and a short workshop with ideas that include

- Using end-of-unit tests as diagnostic or placement tests and then setting up stations or more open instructional settings based on results;
- Letting learners take the test alone, then the same test with a partner, and then, a week later, the same test alone again;
- Letting learners re-take a test after having "done" something (defined by themselves or the teacher);
- Having learners create the test items themselves;
- Allowing learners to decide when they want to take the test;
- Setting the highest grade a learner can receive to "5" ("6" is the highest in Switzerland) and "6" is for other performances, but not tests;
- Using exam-wrappers;
- Making learners write, for each item they got wrong, WHY it was wrong (as compared to simply correcting the test) and then having them re-take the test;
- Not putting points on tests.

Pre-service teachers are asked to respond to the presentation by either making quiz questions, adding ideas, or ranking the ideas from their most to least favorites. Though presented rather traditionally, this content gets students talking and is frequently referred to thereafter.

Rethinking Textbook Tasks

The second much-appreciated element has been to have pre-service teachers take an end-of-unit task from local coursebooks and rework it based on "better" assessment principles or create a new, creative performance assessment. They are to include a rubric and think about a definition of "task" whereby there are reasons for listening that can be assessed and where accuracy and other subskills play a role. Figures 16.1 and 16.2 show an original task and an adapted one and a Life Hacks example is found on the author's padlet. Here the aim is to learn about different types of rubrics (single-point, holistic, analytic, hyper), to think about if these hinder learner creativity or not and to consider how a task and rubric can be adapted to a particular grade or level and which criteria belong to English and which to other subjects (e.g., Art) or soft skills.

124 *International Perspectives on Critical English Language Teacher Education*

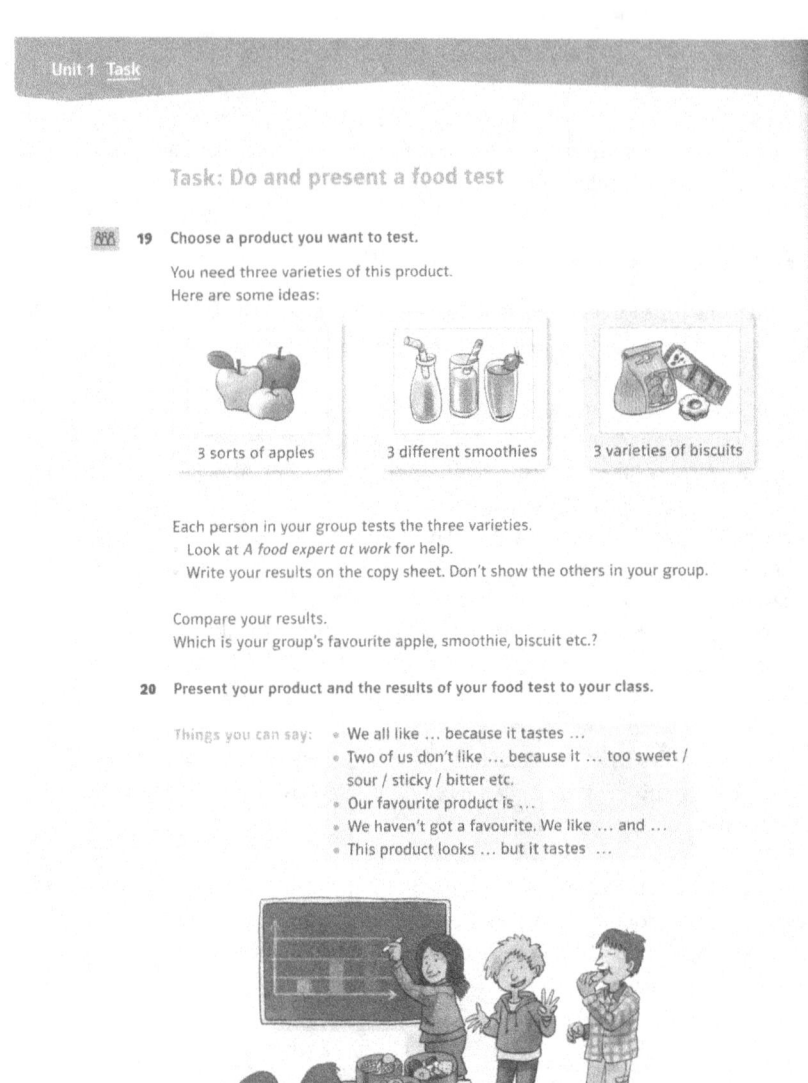

Figure 16.1 Original task. Image taken from Coursebook by Klett und Balmer AG.

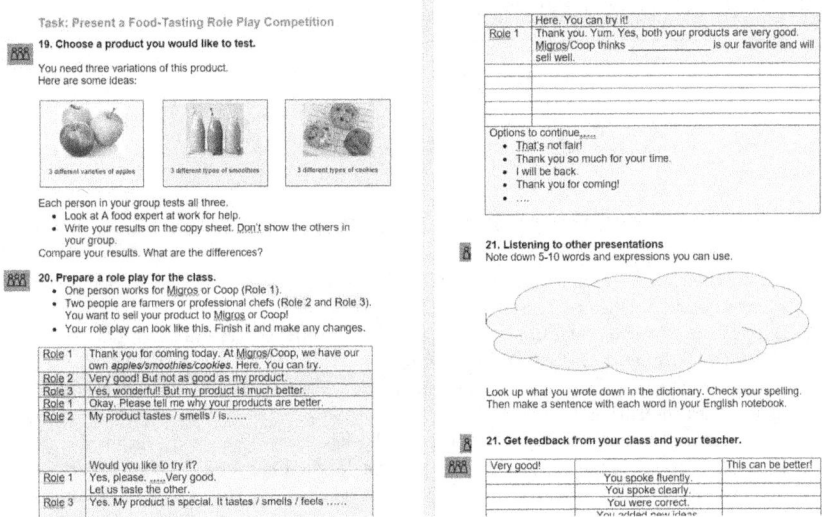

Figure 16.2 Adapted task, L. Loder Buechel.

Comprehensive Task

The third appreciated task asks pre-service teachers to apply concepts to a coursebook unit. Table 16.1 describes what they must do with drafting and peer-feedback involved in the process.

The success criteria in Table 16.1 have been provided by the lecturer, but specific formal criteria are developed in class as a participatory/democratic exercise in developing shared expectations and accountability as well as with a motivation to encourage pre-service teachers to think about readability. No page limit is set because creativity should not be hindered nor are examples of work from previous years shown because the task changes frequently and independent thinking should be promoted. This task is integrated throughout the semester and bridges more academic readings and input with the practical application.

Reading Circle Presentations

Throughout the semester, small groups work with various texts and books on assessment in different ways that should be transferrable to their future work as primary school teachers (e.g., they give a one-minute speech on a favorite chapter, create a word cloud on a topic and do an exercise with it; see https://padlet.com/laura_buechel/assessment for a list of books used). The final Reading Circle activity is for them to create a product (Figure 16.3) that summarizes highlights of the discussions and findings from all of the Reading Circles and gives a ten-minute interactive presentation. The idea behind this is to get students to think about more creative ways of getting their own learners to work with books (cereal box book reports, interactive posters) and give and assess presentations.

Table 16.1 Consolidation assignment 2022

Rethink and Redevelop

Choose a unit from the local coursebooks you are expected to work with. Go through the units before so you know what the aims were. Create a document that includes the following sections:

1. Your general grading policy—What balance of quizzes/observations/tests/projects is a good rule of thumb for your philosophy of education?
2. The unit in general—what parts would you use for formative, summative, assessment of/for/as learning, etc. and how?
3. Quizzes and Classroom Assessment Techniques—What little quizzes and classroom assessment techniques (5–10 minutes each) could you create for this unit? Develop an example for a lesson starter and a lesson ender (two examples). Describe, for each example, what you are measuring.
4. Observations—Imagine you are a fly on the wall during a more open activity during this unit. What activity would you observe? Why? What do you think you'd be able to observe? Which of these observations might be useful for the report cards? How would you record these observations?
5. Performance assessments—What project or product could be created from this unit? Create a rubric for it! Explain how you would use this rubric with your learners.
6. Tests—Look at the provided unit test. How would you use it? Do you have any criticism of it? Suggest changes. Think about the aims of this test. How else might you assess the same aims in a different, more authentic, way?
7. Recording information—how will you record learner performance from the tests, quizzes, CATs, observations, in a standards or competence-based way when one measure (e.g., a test) covers several standards? Provide an example of an online gradebook or other system you would use and list some of the categories you might include.
8. Concluding thoughts—Is there anything else assessment-related you'd like to add?

Success Criteria

- Points 1–6 are included and reflect the content and input from this course.
- Your English is at a C1 level (has been peer edited).
- You provide feedback to two other students' work.
- Formal criteria as worked out in class (e.g., length, formatting, etc.).

Critical Reflections: Potentials and Challenges

The content has been an eye-opener as pre-service teachers confront their own histories—many had never even questioned practices they experienced though every single one has had a negative experience with an assessment policy or practice. These negative experiences provide much fuel to the assessment fire and grounds for discussion. The occasional positive experience (such as conferencing about grades) is thus even more well-received and helps to challenge assumptions. The products created are called up again when student teachers become teachers (as contact with ex-students will attest). The time taken in teacher education to concretely work with what pre-service teachers will most likely see in the local schools (coursebooks do not

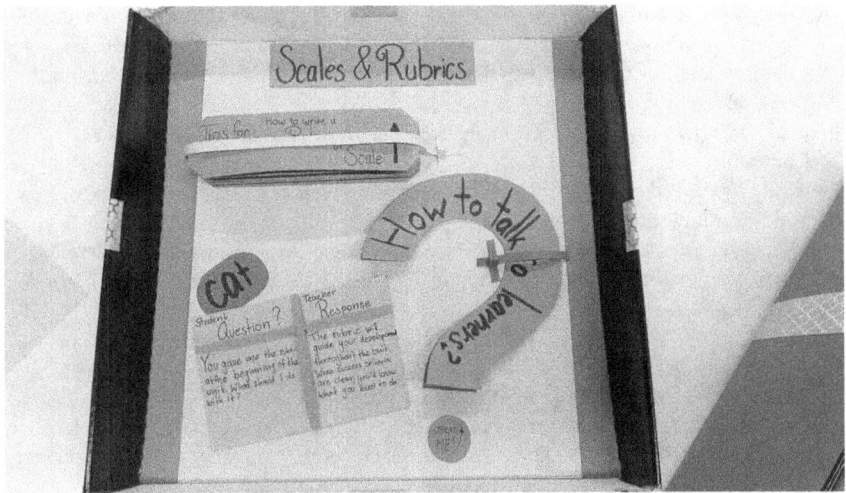

Figure 16.3 Reading circle activity, final product.

change quickly) is extremely valuable as teachers in the field often say they do not have time, agency, or motivation to rethink their practices.

What is often difficult is the realization that course book writers don't always do it better than teachers themselves and fieldwork in the schools does not often allow pre-service teachers to try out new ideas. Furthermore, getting pre-service teachers to work at a meta-level can be trying (they like to use materials without asking "which subskills they could assess" or "why the data from an exit card means that they should actually change the next lesson"), but is important. All in all, integrating these activities has proven to bring in a critical approach to both materials and practice and also the system as a whole.

Note

1   Per 2024, these materials will be Open Access and available on the ILIAS learning platform through www.phzh.ch.

References

Arnet-Clark, I., S. Schmid and G. Ritter (2019), *Young World 2 Activity Book*, Baar: Klett und Balmer.

Buechel, L. (2022), "But I Know the Word in English, Just Not in German! The Unfairness of Vocabulary-Translation Testing and Lists", *European Journal of English Language Teaching*, 7 (1): 59–69.

Buechel, L and K. Lichtenauer (2019), "Grading and Gathering Evidence in Swiss Elementary and Lower Secondary School English Language Classrooms", in P. Mickan and I. Wallace (eds), *The Routledge Handbook of Language Education Curriculum Design*, 222–37, London: Routledge.

Dunlosky, J., K. Rawson, E. Marsh, N. Mitchel and D. Willingham (2013), "Improving Students' Learning with Effective Learning Techniques: Promising Directions from Cognitive and Educational Psychology", *Psychological Science in the Public Interest*, 14 (1): 4–58.
Freire, P. (1994), *Pedagogy of Hope: Reliving Pedagogy of the Oppressed*, New York: Continuum.
Freire, P. (2005), *Pedagogy of the Oppressed (30th Anniversary ed.)*, trans. M. Ramos, New York: Continuum.
Massler, U., D. Stotz and C. Queisser (2014), "Assessment Instruments for Primary CLIL: The Conceptualisation and Evaluation of Test Tasks", *The Language Learning Journal*, 42 (2): 137–50.
Tsagari, D. and K. Vogt (2017), "Assessment Literacy of Foreign Language Teachers Around Europe: Research, Challenges and Future Prospects", *Papers in Language Testing and Assessment*, 6 (1): 41–63.
Van Blerkom, M. (2017), *Measurement and Statistics for Teachers*, London: Routledge.
White, K. (2017), *Softening the Edges: Assessment Practices That Honor K-12 Teachers and Learners*, Bloomington: Solution Tree Press.

Part Six

Curriculum Development

17

Reimagining Critical Language Teacher Education through Translanguaging and Transknowledging

Sunny Man Chu Lau and Angel M. Y. Lin

Introduction

Drawing on critical applied linguistics (Pennycook 2001), critical language teacher education (CLTE) aims to cultivate teachers' critical perspectives toward how English is perceived, taught, and used to provide or deny access to certain knowledge and more powerful positions in school and society. Its goal is to prepare teachers to engage language education in ways that ensure equitable educational opportunities for intersectionally marginalized social groups. Latest developments in the field of applied linguistics, second language acquisition (SLA), and bilingual education characterized as the "trans-" turn (Hawkins and Mori 2018) challenge fixed boundaries and static notions of language, communication, and learners. The movement has prompted drastic shifts in our understanding and practice of language and education, particularly disrupting the Anglo/Eurocentric onto-epistemological basis on which the disciplines have been founded (Kubota 2019). In this chapter, we focus on the English language and teachers who work with learners of English as a subject and/or in content areas. We first elaborate on the current developments related to the "trans-" turn and its associated interest in adopting decoloniality-informed onto-epistemologies to interrogate Anglo/Eurocentric and anthropocentric traditions underlying the field. We then discuss how these paradigmatic shifts invite curricular innovations in CLTE in order for teachers to embody and enact criticality in their choices and decisions about curricular design, development, and evaluation.

Current Issues

The notion of "trans-" is gaining momentum in the field of applied linguistics, with a marked uptick in research and practice related to translanguaging (García and Li Wei 2014), translanguaging and trans-semiotizing (Lin 2019), translingual practice (Canagarajah 2013), among others. Destabilizing language boundaries, the "trans-" movement disrupts the often taken-for-granted notions of language, communication, learner agency, as well as their underlying onto-epistemologies. Below we explain how these changing understandings of language and communication impact CLTE and curricular development.

From Language to Trans/languaging

Many language and literacy scholars have come to adopt a multilingual and multimodal view of language (Block 2014), positing that human communication is seldom confined to one language nor only the verbal mode. Individuals in multilingual contexts often shuttle between languages to negotiate meaning and perform communication acts, whether through code-switching, translating, language brokering, or interpreting (Canagarajah 2013). Besides, speakers often draw on a combination of linguistic and other semiotic resources to communicate, including paralinguistic elements such as gestures, head movements, tone, and pitch of voice, as well as other nonverbal, visual, auditory, and artifactual resources (Li Wei 2018). In this sense, language and communication are multimodal and embodied, entailing neural, affective, and sociocultural engagements with other co-acting agents (including human and nonhuman bodies, objects, space, and technological enhancements) across time and space (Pennycook and Otsuji 2014; Thibault 2017). Under this view, language is trans/languaging, not a static object to be learned and owned but rather ongoing, dynamic processes of assembling multiple semiotic features—linguistic, bodily, cognitive, affective, and material—to instantiate communicative acts across time and space (Lin and Lo 2017). This invites new perspectives toward the language curriculum—rather than teaching a language in isolation, teachers need to rethink how other languages, whether in the community or the curriculum, can be strategically mobilized to foster students' meta-linguistic and cultural awareness for greater conceptual coherence and knowledge construction (Piccardo 2013). Further, as language is always enacted in an ensemble of multiple semiotic resources, the curricular focus needs to shift to learners' situated language use in multilingual, multimodal, and multisensory ways. Language engagements in expressive arts, whether music, dance, movements, video making, etc., allow for multiple opportunities of trans/languaging and trans-semiotizing for alternative knowing, thinking, feeling, communicating, and identity negotiations (Lau 2020).

From Individual Language Learners to Intra-acting Participants

Considering how language is trans/languaging with individuals entangled with/in a wider semiotic landscape, the notion of individuals as autonomous agents is also brought into question. Humans, rather than being the central actors of communication, are "co-participants" (Lemke and Lin 2022) with other human and nonhuman mediums, whether linguistic, musical, spatial, material, or technological. Each medium has its own histories and unique affordances and constraints, and human participants are caught up with these co-acting mediums, things, and bodies that are all shaping the unfolding of the flow of communication. Borrowing the anthropologist Tim Ingold's (2020) concept of "going along together" (41), Lemke and Lin argue for the importance to focus on the "in-between-ness" of beings and things, to examine how they go along together as flows and processes in/through which conversations and communication unfold.

Lemke and Lin's notion of translanguaging as dynamic flows resonates with the non-anthropocentric way of re/thinking humanity and human activities proposed by posthumanist and new-materialist scholars (Barad 2007). New materialism and posthumanism seek to reposition humans as one among other living and nonliving actants. Under this lens, knowledge and agency are understood as "emerging from the relations between various elements" (Ravindran and Ilieva 2021: 113), rather than residing within the individual. Barad calls this "intra-action" (as opposed to interaction) to underscore that agency emerges from the relational networks of experiences, embodied responses, memories, and thought processes. These anti-anthropocentric views are not new to Indigenous onto-epistemologies which, however, have long been ignored and dismissed as irrelevant to language and literacy education (see next section for more).

Taken together, language learning is trans/languaging and is becoming, as new meanings, thinking and feelings arise through the intra-activity of entangled human and nonhuman participants (Toohey and Smythe 2022). This complicated view calls for curricular innovations that allow for emergent curriculum that responds to learners' evolving understanding and questions. Rather than closing down unexpected moments or fissures from a planned curriculum, teachers need to attend to those moments and reposition themselves as co-participants in the learning process with their students and strive to support their whole-body experiences and engagement (Kuby 2018).

From Euro/Anglocentric and Anthropocentric Onto-epistemologies to Ecologies of Knowledges

The "trans-" movement brings together competing language practices and knowledges to transgress and problematize received wisdom and language boundaries and hierarchies (Li Wei and García 2022) steeped in colonial histories of nation building and governance (Flores and Rosa 2023). Colonization discourses of modernity and capitalism have imposed global patterns of power relations along racial/ethnic lines, naturalizing dominance of White, Eurocentric culture, knowledge, and languages (Quijano 2000). Individuals with a colonial mindset, or as Flores and Rosa (2015) call the White listening and reading subjects, pass racialized judgment onto minoritized language learners/speakers, positioning them as language-deficient or inferior, or even languageless (Rosa 2016). Combating race-based ideologies and practices (i.e., raciolinguistics) is to not only call out but also dismantle the abyssal line that arbitrarily separates language practices as pure/impure or standard/nonstandard dichotomies (García et al. 2021), reclaiming all language varieties, registers, and other "non-academic" semiotic resources as legitimate, relevant, and pertinent to meaningful learning. In other words, it aims to recover the subjugated and obliterated languages and knowledge bases of the colonized people for "social and cognitive justice in education" (Li Wei and García 2022: 312).

Indigenous and Southern perspectives have traditionally been dismissed and erased from language and education through various forms of colonization. They both share similar linguistic and epistemic ecologies that are largely based on land and people who are part of, not superior to, the ecological world (Daniels et al. 2021; de Sousa Santos 2018). Heugh (2021) argues that multilingualism and multilinguality have for centuries been the norm for Africa, the Américas, Asia, and Australasia. Multilingual communities, particularly among border and frontier communities, including Indigenous peoples, have learned to work with different language groups and care for each other's words and thoughts in order to survive sociopolitical and environmental precarities. In this sense, translanguaging is not merely about fluid and dynamic use of languages but also about the learning to cross linguistic and epistemic borders and to translate for "reciprocal exchanges of knowledge" or transknowledging (Heugh 2021). A key curricular innovation is hence to decolonize the curriculum, not only examining the compounding issues of language, race, class, gender, and sexuality, but also to integrate Indigenous and Southern perspectives in CLTE to decentralize Anglo/Eurocentric and anthropocentric worldviews. Translanguaging can be used as a tool for transknowledging to learn about and critically reflect on alternative ways of understanding and relating ethically to the world.

Implications for Teaching and Teacher Education

The changing visions of language and its onto-epistemology beg urgent reconfigurations of CLTE for equity and eco-social justice purposes. Teachers need to be engaged with these new understandings to inform and reform their curriculum, pedagogy, and assessment methods. First, teachers need to be exposed to not only Anglo/Eurocentric scholarships but also Indigenous and Southern perspectives to challenge colonial idealization of accent- and error-free monolingual competence and to re/discover dismissed and erased knowledges that inform what language learning means within the wider multilingual ecologies. Engaging teachers with literature on Southern multilingualism (e.g., Heugh et al. 2017) can help illuminate the long-standing practice of bi/multilingual instruction and mediation (using code-mixing, code-switching, and translating) across education systems in Africa or Asia that disrupts the postcolonial monolingual European models of teaching and learning. Teachers can also gain insight into how assessment can be revamped to support students' use of their wider multilingual repertoire for more equitable learning and grading purposes (see Makgamatha et al. 2013 on their multilingual design of math assessment tasks in Afrikaans, English, and isiXhosa).

Further, CLTE has traditionally taken the form of awareness-raising in supporting teachers' critical understanding of language and power (Hawkins and Norton 2009). While critical awareness is still key in CLTE, recent insights from translanguaging as multilingual, multimodal, and multisensory processes remind us that any learning, including teacher education, is "embodied, emplaced, and ensembled" (Lin 2019: 8). Direct instruction through telling and showing in CLTE classroom, while important, is reportedly insufficient for sustainable change and embodiment of critical dispositions (Vasquez, Janks, and Comber 2019). CLTE programs need to create spaces for teachers to think, feel, and experience learning in multilingual, multicultural, embodied ways, so that they can also do the same with their own students. For example, engaging teachers in critical reflections of their own lived trans/languaging experience can support understanding of communicative repertoires in holistic ways beyond a mere monolingual, logocentric vision of language. Arts-based language portraits or biographies (e.g., Lau 2016), for instance, allow teachers to use multimodal means to map and trace their complex entanglements of multiple linguistic/semiotic resources and critically explore how particular time/space interactions and power relationships have shaped their language "aspirations, desires and memories" (Busch 2021: 202). These activities can similarly be used in both teacher education and K-12 programs.

Critical scholars (Janks 2020; Vasquez, Janks and Comber 2019) are also urging for more embodied and action-orientated approach to CLTE, engaging teachers in reading the word/world while also taking actions to gain first-hand experiences in critical social practices so that they would actively seek out spaces to engage their learners in such practices. The idea is to live the curriculum (Leland and Murtadha 2011) for which their teacher educators advocate. In other words, curricula at both teacher education and classroom levels need to engage students in multiple, alternative ways of knowing, feeling, thinking, and acting to facilitate the development and embodiment of critical stance and enactment. López and colleagues' study (2020) in Oaxaca, Mexico, for example, engage their prospective elementary ESL teachers in a critical ethnographic action research project before their praxicum (i.e., praxis in practicum) to understand the children's interests, strengths, and concerns, based on which, they then worked in teams to develop a critical theme-based unit for learning English. One team addressed the malnutrition problem in the community by exploring with the children healthy food options in their local communities (versus fast/junk food). While learning the related English grammar and vocabulary, the children also used a hybrid of languages and borrow words (English, Spanish, and Mixe) to construct meaning and represent their learning in multimodal and multisensory ways. In the process, both the children and teacher candidates also came to problematize their internalized sense of inferiority about their indigenous languages and identities. Importantly, the student teachers, having enacted the curriculum, developed a stronger sense of self-efficacy in adapting an inquiry-based curriculum according to students' emergent learning, rather than following it blindly.

Another example of living the curriculum is Sterzuk's (2020) study in Saskatchewan, Canada, in which she engaged her predominantly White, English monolingual preservice teachers in some embodied, immersive experiences such as volunteering in a local ESL classroom, conducting linguistic landscaping of their neighborhoods, and creating a family language profile in which they reflected on their own cultural and linguistic locations in relation to the peoples who live in those spaces, including migrants and Indigenous peoples. These multimodal and multisensory experiences created multiple opportunities for critical reflections and discussions of language policies and practices that are rooted in colonial histories and its continual oppressions of other Indigenous and immigrant languages (see Chung and Chung Arsenault 2023, for similar arts-based "landguaging" reflection activities). This holistic and immersive approach to CLTE allows multilingual, multimodal, and embodied ways of understanding and experiencing ideas that support deeper critical reflections of privilege and colonial complicity.

The examples above illustrate some translingual, multimodal, multisensory embodied learning possibilities for CLTE and K-12 programs, with an integrated focus on knowing, feeling, living, and reflecting on what translanguaging and transknowledging mean, inside and outside of classrooms. An expanded and distributed view of language and education prompts us to attend to other co-participants (beings, objects, buildings, nature) in the learning environment and how we might "go along together" for co-learning and to challenge inequitable power structures for more desirable sociospatial relationships. Land-centered approaches also allow teachers to develop local teaching materials to better meet the specific contexts. It is of primordial importance that teachers learn to become inquirers and researchers with their learners (Van Viegen and Lau 2022); not technicians nor consumers but rather producers of pedagogical knowledge and material as a way to decolonize the curriculum and teaching practice (Kumaravadivelu 2016). Importantly, teacher educators also need to shift understanding of what CLTE engenders, not as a close-ended process with grand-scale changes, but rather as dynamic, open, and unfolding processes with multiple, and even unpredictable, possibilities. As Toohey and Smythe (2022:31) aptly wrote:

> Seeing the goal of teacher education not as the development of master teachers but as vulnerable engagement with learners, in considering questions, problems, developing new questions and experimenting with possible (and temporary) solutions, may be a way we can move EAL [English as an additional language] teacher education forward.

This emergentist and process-oriented approach to CLTE removes its grandiose claims for social justice but encourages more sustained, ongoing efforts in critical reflective praxis in local contexts.

References

Barad, Karen (2007), *Meeting the Universe Halfway: Quantum Physics and the Entanglement of Matter and Meaning*, Durham: Duke University Press.

Block, David (2014), "Moving beyond 'Lingualism': Multilingual Embodiment and Multimodality in SLA", in S. May (ed.), *The Multilingual Turn: Implications for SLA, TESOL and Bilingual Education*, 54–77, New York: Routledge.

Busch, Brigitta (2021), "The Body Image: Taking an Evaluative Stance Towards Semiotic Resources", *International Journal of Multilingualism*, 18 (2): 190–205. doi: 10.1080/14790718.2021.1898618.

Canagarajah, A. Suresh (2013), *Translingual Practice: Global Englishes and Cosmopolitan Relations*, London: Routledge.

Chung, Rhonda and W. Chung Arsenault (2023), "'Landguaging' the L2 Classroom: Inclusive Pedagogies and Land-Sensitive Curriculum through Teacher Reflection Art", *Concordia University Working Papers in Applied Linguistics*, 7, 29–54. http://doe.concordia.ca/copal/documents/7_Chung_ChungArsenault.pdf.

Daniels, Belinda, Andrea Sterzuk, Peter Turner, William Richard Cook, Dorothy Thunder and Randy Morin (2021), "ē-ka-pimohteyāhk nīkānehk ōte nīkān: nēhiyawēwin (Cree language) Revitalization and Indigenous Knowledge (Re)generation", in Kathleen Heugh, Christopher Stroud, Kerry Taylor-Leech and Peter I. De Costa (eds), *A Sociolinguistics of the South*, 199–213, New York: Routledge.

de Sousa Santos, Boaventura (2018), *The End of the Cognitive Empire: The Coming of Age of Epistemologies of the South*, Durham: Duke University Press.

Flores, Nelson and Jonathan Rosa (2015), "Undoing Appropriateness: Raciolinguistic Ideologies and Language Diversity in Education", *Harvard Educational Review*, 85 (2): 149–71.

Flores, Nelson and Jonathan Rosa (2023), "Undoing Competence: Coloniality, Homogeneity, and the Overrepresentation of Whiteness in Applied Linguistics", *Language Learning*. doi:10.1111/lang.12528.

García, Ofelia and Li Wei (2014), *Translanguaging: Language, Bilingualism and Education*, London: Palgrave Macmillan.

García, Ofelia, Nelson Flores, Kate Seltzer, Li Wei, Ricardo Otheguy and Jonathan Rosa (2021), "Rejecting Abyssal Thinking in the Language and Education of Racialized Bilinguals: A Manifesto", *Critical Inquiry in Language Studies*, 18 (3): 203–28. doi: 10.1080/15427587.2021.1935957.

Hawkins, Margaret R and Junko Mori (2018), "Considering 'Trans-' Perspectives in Language Theories and Practices", *Applied Linguistics*, 39 (1): 1–8. doi: 10.1093/applin/amx056.

Hawkins, M. and B. Norton (2009), "Critical Language Teacher Education", in A. Burns and J. Richards (eds), *Cambridge Guide to Second Language Teacher Education*, 30–9, Cambridge: Cambridge University Press.

Heugh, Kathleen (2021), "Southern Multilingualisms, Translanguaging and Transknowledging in Inclusive and Sustainable Education", in P. Harding-Esch and H. Coleman (eds), *Language and the Sustainable Development Goals: Selected Proceedings of the 12th Language and Development Conference Dakar, Senegal, 2017*, 37–47, London: British Council.

Heugh, Kathleen, Cas Prinsloo, Matthews Makgamatha, Gerda Diedericks and Lolita Winnaar (2017), "Multilingualism(s) and System-Wide Assessment: A Southern Perspective", *Language and Education*, 31 (3): 197–216. doi: 10.1080/09500782.2016.1261894.

Ingold, Tim (2020), *Correspondences*, Medford, MA: Polity.

Janks, Hilary (2020), "Critical Literacy in Action: Difference as a Force for Positive Change", *Journal of Adolescent & Adult Literacy*, 63 (5): 569–72. doi: 10.1002/jaal.1035.

Kubota, Ryuko (2019), "Confronting Epistemological Racism, Decolonizing Scholarly Knowledge: Race and Gender in Applied Linguistics", *Applied Linguistics*, 41 (5): 712–32. doi: 10.1093/applin/amz033.

Kuby, Candace R. (2018), "Rhizomes and Intra-Activity with Materials: Ways of Disrupting and Reimagining Early Literacy Research, Teaching, and Learning", in JeanneMarie Iorio and Will Parnell (eds), *Meaning Making in Early Childhood Research: Pedagogies and the Personal*, 146–65, London: Routledge.

Kumaravadivelu, B. (2016), "The Decolonial Option in English Teaching: Can the Subaltern Act?", *TESOL Quarterly*, 50 (1): 66–85.

Lau, S. M. C. (2016), "Language, Identity, and Emotionality: Exploring the Potential of Language Portraits in Preparing Teachers for Diverse Learners", *The New Educator*, 12 (2): 147–70, doi: 10.1080/1547688X.2015.1062583.

Lau, S. M. C. (2020), "Translanguaging as Transmediation: Embodied Critical Literacy Engagements in a French-English Bilingual Classroom", *Australian Journal of Applied Linguistics*, 3 (1): 42–59. doi: 10.29140/ajal.v3n1.299.

Leland, Christine and Khaula Murtadha (2011), "Cultural Discourse on the Frontline: Preparing and Retaining Urban Teachers", *Urban Education*, 46 (5): 895–912.

Lemke, Jay L. and Angel M. Y. Lin (2022), "Translanguaging and Flows: Towards an Alternative Conceptual Model", *Educational Linguistics*, 1 (1): 134–51. doi:10.1515/eduling-2022-0001.

Lin, A. M. Y. (2019), "Theories of Trans/Languaging and Trans-semiotizing: Implications for Content-Based Education Classrooms", *International Journal of Bilingual Education and Bilingualism*, 22 (1): 5–16. doi: 10.1080/13670050.2018.1515175.

Lin, A. M. Y. and Yuen Yi Lo (2017), "Trans/Languaging and the Triadic Dialogue in Content and Language Integrated Learning (CLIL) Classrooms", *Language and Education*, 31 (1): 26–45.

López-Gopar, Mario E., William M. Sughrua, Lorena Córdova-Hernández, Beatriz Patricia López Torres, Elvira Ruiz Aldaz and Victor Vásquez Morales (2020), "A Critical Thematic Unit in a Teaching Praxicum: Health Issues and Plurilingualism in the 'English' Classroom", in S. M. C. Lau and S Van Viegen(eds), *Plurilingual Pedagogies: Critical and Creative Endeavors for Equitable Language in Education*, New York: Springer International.

Makgamatha, Matthews M., Kathleen Heugh, Cas H. Prinsloo and Lolita Winnaar (2013), "Equitable Language Practices in Large-Scale Assessment: Possibilities and Limitations in South Africa", *Southern African Linguistics and Applied Language Studies*, 31 (2): 251–69. doi:10.2989/16073614.2013.816021.

Pennycook, Alastair (2001), *Critical Applied Linguistics: A Critical Introduction*, New York: Routledge.

Pennycook, Alastair and Emi Otsuji (2014), "Metrolingual Multitasking and Spatial Repertoires: 'Pizza mo Two Minutes Coming'", *Journal of Sociolinguistics*, 18 (2): 161–84. doi:10.1111/josl.12079.

Piccardo, Enrica (2013), "Plurilingualism and Curriculum Design: Toward a Synergic Vision", *TESOL Quarterly*, 47 (3): 600–14.

Quijano, Aníbal (2000), "Coloniality of Power and Eurocentrism in Latin America", *International Sociology*, 15 (2): 215–32. doi:10.1177/0268580900015002005.

Ravindran, Aisha and Roumiana Ilieva (2021), "Pedagogies in the Act: Movements of Teacher-Becomings in Second Language Education", *The Canadian Modern Language Review*, 77 (4): 410–26. doi:10.3138/cmlr-2020-0106.

Rosa, Jonathan Daniel (2016), "Standardization, Racialization, Languagelessness: Raciolinguistic Ideologies across Communicative Contexts", *Journal of Linguistic Anthropology*, 26 (2): 162–83.

Sterzuk, Andrea (2020), "Building Language Teacher Awareness of Colonial Histories and Imperialistic Oppression through the Linguistic Landscape", in D. Malinowski, H.H. Maxim and S. Dubreil (eds), *Language Teaching in the Linguistic Landscape*, 145–62, New York: Springer.

Thibault, Pual J. (2017), "The Reflexivity of Human Languaging and Nigel Love's Two Orders of Language", *Language Sciences*, 61: 74–85.
Toohey, Kelleen and Suzanne Smythe (2022), "A Different Difference in Teacher Education: Posthuman and Decolonizing Perspectives", *Language and Education*, 36 (2): 122–36. doi:10.1080/09500782.2021.1980002.
Van Viegen, S. and S. M. C. Lau (2022), "Becoming Critical Sociolinguists in TESOL through Translanguaging and Embodied Practice", *TESL Canada*, 38 (2): 199–213. doi:10.18806/tesl.v38i2.1361.
Vasquez, Vivian Maria, Hilary Janks and Barbara Comber (2019), "Critical Literacy as a Way of Being and Doing", *Language Arts*, 96 (5): 300–311.
Wei, Li (2018), "Translanguaging as a Practical Theory of Language", *Applied Linguistics*, 39 (1): 9–30.
Wei, Li and Ofelia García (2022), "Not a First Language but One Repertoire: Translanguaging as a Decolonizing Project", *RELC Journal*, 53 (2): 313–24. doi: 10.1177/00336882221092841.

Suggested Readings and External Links

- Heugh, K., C. Stroud, K. Taylor-Leech and P. I. De Costa (eds) (2021), *A Sociolinguistics of the South*, 1st edn, New York: Routledge. doi:10.4324/9781315208916.
- Lemke, Jay L. and Angel M. Y. Lin (2022), "Translanguaging and Flows: Towards an Alternative Conceptual Model", *Educational Linguistics*, 1 (1): 134–51. doi:10.1515/eduling-2022-0001.
- Lau, S. M. C., Z. Tian and A. M. Y. Lin (2022), "Critical Literacy and Additional Language Learning: An Expansive View of Translanguaging for Change-Enhancing Possibilities", in J. Z. Pandya, R. A. Mora, J. Alford, N. A. Golden and R. S. de Roock (eds), *The Handbook of Critical Literacies*, 381–90, New York: Routledge.
- Wei, Li and O. García (2022), "Not a First Language but One Repertoire: Translanguaging as a Decolonizing Project", *RELC Journal*, 53 (2): 313–24. doi: 10.1177/00336882221092841.
- Toohey, K. and Suzanne Smythe (2022), "A Different Difference in Teacher Education: Posthuman and Decolonizing Perspectives", *Language and Education*, 36 (2): 122–36. doi: 10.1080/09500782.2021.1980002.

18

A Language-Based Approach to Content Instruction: Critical Reflections on Implementation in a Teaching English to Speakers of Other Languages (TESOL) Methods Course

Hillary Parkhouse, Luciana C. de Oliveira, and Jia Gui

Background

Like many educator preparation programs across the United States, the one in which we currently teach (at Virginia Commonwealth University) has recently expanded instruction in TESOL beyond those planning to become ESOL teachers. Due to a dramatic increase in the number of multilingual learners (MLs) in our region, all teacher candidates, regardless of their content area specialization, must take a three-credit course called Methods for Teaching Multilingual Learners. This course is designed to help content area teachers (e.g., mathematics, science, social studies, English language arts, music, art) ensure that MLs are able to fully engage and succeed in the learning activities while they are also developing proficiency in the English language. To help our teacher candidates design curriculum that accomplishes this, we use an approach called the language-based approach to content instruction, or LACI (de Oliveira 2016: 218; 2020; 2023: 4; de Oliveira, Braxton and Gui 2021: 1–2).

LACI focuses on language and content learning simultaneously as inseparable components of teaching MLs in the content area classroom. Similar to content and language integrated learning (CLIL) approaches used in Europe and many other parts of the world, LACI is a way to integrate content and language; however, it was designed for a context where English is the majority language not a foreign language. The scaffolding support provided in LACI could also be implemented in various contexts, including those that use CLIL.

LACI is designed around six Cs of support for scaffolding instruction for MLs: connection, culture, code-breaking, challenge, community and collaboration, and classroom interactions (see Figure 18.1). In the lesson planning process, the Cs are attended to separately; however, during instruction they overlap and interconnect.

The six Cs of support represent a critical approach as the model develops MLs' awareness of language as social practice and uses asset-based approaches to affirm

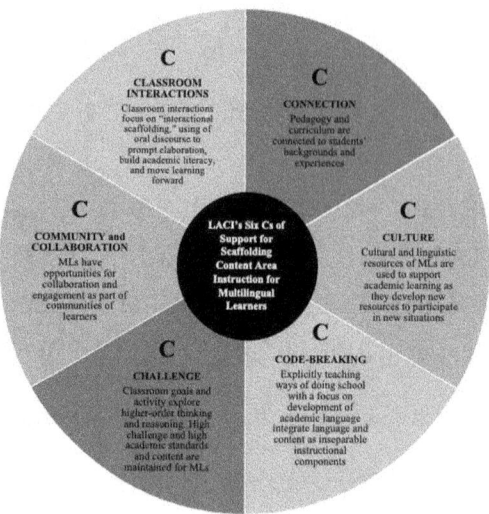

Figure 18.1 LACI's six Cs of support for scaffolding content area instruction for multilingual learners (de Oliveira 2023: 15).

MLs' identities, experiences, backgrounds, and funds of knowledge. For example, the C of culture positions students' cultures and languages as central to their academic success and to classroom activities, replacing deficit-oriented views with asset-based approaches (de Oliveira 2020; Moll et al. 1992: 132–41; Valenzuela 1999: 3–30). Relatedly, the C of connection involves teachers connecting the content, language, and tasks to MLs' prior knowledge, experiences, and interests (Cochran-Smith 2004: 70–2; Villegas and Lucas 2002: 20–32).

The C of code-breaking involves explicitly teaching ways of doing school, including disciplinary, linguistic, and cultural codes of content learning (Fang 2006: 491–520; Schleppegrell 2001: 431–59; 2004: 3–19). Code-breaking supports the development of academic language—or the language used for schooling purposes—as emerging from the same repertoire as everyday language used for communicative purposes (Schleppegrell 2013: 47–60).

The C of challenge counteracts the tendency for teachers to hold lower expectations of their MLs' abilities and to overlook opportunities for MLs to practice higher-order reasoning (Athanases 2012: 18–22; Hammond 2009: 56–76). The implementation of high challenge needs to happen with parallel use of strategies that provide necessary and targeted high levels of support and to be interwoven with explicit and systematic teaching of language (Hammond 2009: 56–76).

Relatedly, the C of classroom interactions considers what teachers can do to scaffold these challenging demands and to fully engage MLs in teacher–student interactions. Teachers can elicit more from MLs if they know which interactional scaffolding moves encourage MLs to say more and do more with language (see de Oliveira, Jones and Smith 2023, for interactional scaffolding moves to support MLs).

Finally, the C of community and collaboration refers to joint productive activity in which students co-construct knowledge (Lave and Wenger 1991: 91–4) in communities of learners co-created with teachers in their classrooms (Nieto 2000: 12–3). This allows students to recognize the nature of knowledge as socially constructed and ultimately enhance their skills in social critique.

Description of Practice

Because our course is taught asynchronously online, we introduce LACI to teacher candidates through a fifteen-minute video made by the instructors (link to video: https://youtu.be/Hmq-AcdV1gA). In the video, the instructor provides examples of the LACI's six Cs of support for scaffolding and shows how the LACI framework can be applied to the teaching of various content area disciplines. After learning LACI's six Cs of support, candidates read Many Ways to Build a Model: Content-Based ESL Instruction Models and Approaches in K-12 (Reynolds and O'Loughlin 2019: 101–28), Implementing LACI in the Classroom (de Oliveira 2023: 198–228), and The LACI Six Cs of Support and Teaching and Learning Cycle (de Oliveira 2023: 13–62).

We use two approaches to assess candidates' understanding of the LACI model. First, candidates meet via video conferencing in small groups to respond to four questions. The first asks them to identify the Cs of support in a segment of classroom discourse. The remaining questions ask them to reflect on which Cs they think might be challenging to implement, and which they anticipate focusing on in their own teaching.

Toward the end of the term, we ask candidates to design one sixty-minute lesson plan for a class of MLs in their subject area and grade level using the LACI model (see lesson plan template at https://secureservercdn.net/166.62.112.107/ugm.885.myftpupload.com/wp-content/uploads/2020/11/laci_lesson_plan.pdf). Candidates then video themselves teaching an eight-minute portion of their LACI lesson with their choice of audiences. Instructors provide feedback on candidates' comprehensibility, the LACI principles, and teaching skills. In the next section, we describe patterns we have noticed in which Cs have appeared to be more and less challenging to embed in these lessons.

Critical Reflections: Potentials and Challenges

Our teacher candidates generally have minimal trouble with the connection, culture, and collaboration and community Cs. They develop lesson plans that offer multiple opportunities for students to collaborate with one another in a community of practice. Their lesson plans also typically build on students' prior academic learning and personal experiences, in part because this is a component of effective instruction taught in their other courses.

The C of culture is often one that is present, but could be improved, in the lesson plans. In particular, candidates often overlook opportunities to incorporate translanguaging pedagogies at multiple points throughout the class. For example, one student (majoring in English education) created a lesson plan to teach poetry. Although she incorporated the C of culture through opening the class with a discussion of students' knowledge of poetry in their first languages, she did not encourage students to use translanguaging in the construction of their own poems. The instructions to students did not specify that their poems had to be entirely in English. However, without explicitly telling students they could translanguage, the candidate missed an opportunity to help students (both multilingual and monolingual) recognize the value of multilingualism for expressing a greater range of ideas and sentiments than can be expressed in a monolingual poem.

Some candidates from the course state that it is hard to include the C of culture in classes, such as earth science or physical science, because these do not allow for a culturally related conversation. Here we prompt teachers to consider how they can allow students to draw on their cultural and linguistic resources to make meaning of science concepts. For example, during a lesson on lunar cycles, teachers can ask students what role the moon plays in folk tales or stories from their cultures. Reflecting on that background knowledge might allow students to recognize how the moon's changes have been observed and incorporated into stories across the world.

Other candidates express concern about the potential for mischaracterizing a student's culture when trying to leverage cultural knowledge for deeper learning. This is a teachable moment for prompting the candidates to think about how they can allow students to characterize their own cultures. We also discuss how culture should be thought of as fluid and dynamic sets of practices that continually evolve, rather than a fixed set of traditions that can necessarily be ascribed to a particular group (Paris 2012: 93–7). This may help prevent teachers from oversimplifying or essentializing cultures and cultural practices.

Finally, we have noticed that teacher candidates sometimes incorporate the C of challenge in their lesson plans to a lesser degree than they could. They often include learning activities that will be challenging in the linguistic sense, such as introducing new vocabulary and asking students to construct sentences in English using these new terms. However, candidates sometimes fail to think about challenging students from a broader, cognitive sense, such as having students not just recall and apply new concepts in English, but also engage in evaluation and critique. For example, one US history lesson plan on the Homestead Acts asked students to discuss the risks homesteaders faced in moving west, which are not difficult to imagine (natural disasters like tornadoes, dangerous wildlife, running out of food). Additional higher-order questions the teacher could have asked include: "What dangers did the Homestead Act present to the native Americans already living in those lands? Was the U.S. government justified in giving those lands away to homesteaders?" These are the kinds of questions that not only give students opportunities to consider multiple perspectives on complex issues, but also reveal how history can be a much richer and more fascinating subject than many students come to believe after memorizing historical facts and dates for multiple choice exams. We have found that teachers can sometimes focus so much on MLs' comprehension and expression that they neglect to cultivate their skills in synthesis, analysis, and judgment.

The curriculum in various subject areas (e.g., math, science, social studies) is enhanced when teachers embed language-based approaches to content instruction through the LACI 6 C's of support. Candidates are able to improve their curriculum in these ways after receiving modeling and feedback from the instructor. Thus our recommendations for other teacher educators interested in using LACI are to provide a model of a well-designed LACI lesson and to allow candidates to submit rough drafts of their lesson plans for instructor feedback. The hope is that, once they have graduated and are independently creating lessons, they will have formed a habit of thinking about culture, connection, code-breaking, and the other Cs every time they design lessons for their students.

References

Athanases, S. (2012), "Maintaining High Challenge and High Support for Diverse Learners", *Leadership*, 42 (1): 18–36.

Cochran-Smith, M. (2004), *Walking the Road: Race, Diversity, and Social Justice in Teacher Education*, New York: Teachers College Press.

de Jong, E. J., C. A. Harper and M.R. Coady (2013), "Enhanced Knowledge and Skills for Elementary Mainstream Teachers of English Language Learners", *Theory into Practice*, 52 (2): 89–97.

de Oliveira, L. C. (2016), "A Language-Based Approach to Content Instruction (LACI) for English Language Learners: Examples from Two Elementary Teachers", *International Multilingual Research Journal*, 10 (3): 217–31.

de Oliveira, L.C. (2020), "Planning and Application Using a Language-Based Approach to Content Instruction (LACI) in Multilingual Classrooms", *MinneTESOL Journal*, 36 (2). Retrieved from https://minnetesoljournal.org/journal-archive/mtj-2020-2/planning-and-application-using-a-language-based-approach-to-content-instruction-laci-in-multilingual-classrooms/.

de Oliveira, L.C. (2023), *Supporting Multilingual Learners' Academic Language Development: A Language-Based Approach to Content Instruction*, New York: Routledge.

de Oliveira, L. C., D. Braxton and J. Gui. (2021), "Planning for Instruction Using a Language-Based Approach to Content Instruction for Multilingual Learners", *Journal of English Learner Education*, 13 (1): 12–29. Retrieved from https://stars.library.ucf.edu/jele/vol13/iss1/2.

de Oliveira, L.C., L. Jones and S.L. Smith. (2023), "Interactional Scaffolding in a First-Grade Classroom through the Teaching–Learning Cycle", *International Journal of Bilingual Education and Bilingualism*, 26 (3): 270–88. DOI: 10.1080/13670050.2020.1798867.

Fang, Z.H. (2006), "The Language Demands of Science Reading in Middle School", *International Journal of Science Education*, 28 (5): 491–520.

Hammond, J. (2006), "High Challenge, High Support: Integrating Language and Content Instruction for Diverse Learners in an English Literature Classroom", *Journal of English for Academic Purposes*, 5 (4): 269–83.

Hammond, J. (2009), "High Challenge, High Support Programmes with English as a Second Language Learners: A Teacher-Researcher Collaboration", in J. Miller, A. Kostogriz and M. Gearon (eds), *Culturally and Linguistically Diverse Classrooms*, 56–76, Clevedon: Multilingual Matters.

Lave, J. and E. Wenger (1991), *Situated Learning: Legitimate Peripheral Participation*, Cambridge: Cambridge University Press.

Moll, L. C., C. Amanti, D. Neff and N Gonzalez (1992), "Funds of Knowledge for Teaching: Using a Qualitative Approach to Connect Homes and Classrooms", *Theory into Practice*, 31 (2): 132–41.
Moore, J. and M. Schleppegrell (2014), "Using a Functional Linguistics Metalanguage to Support Academic Language Development in the English Language Arts", *Linguistics and Education*, 26: 92–105.
Nieto, S. (2000), *Affirming Diversity: The Sociopolitical Context of Multicultural Education*, 3rd edn, New York: Longman.
Paris, D. (2012), "Culturally Sustaining Pedagogy: A Needed Change in Stance, Terminology, and Practice", *Educational Researcher*, 41 (3): 93–7.
Reynolds, K. M. and J.B. O'Loughlin (2019), "Many Ways to Build a Model: Content-Based ESL Instruction Models and Approaches in K-12", in L.C. de Oliveira (ed.), *The Handbook of TESOL in K-12*, 101–28, Hoboken: John Wiley & Sons.
Schleppegrell, M.J. (2001), "Linguistic Features of the Language of Schooling", *Linguistics and Education*, 12 (4): 431–59.
Schleppegrell, M.J. (2004), *The Language of Schooling: A Functional Linguistics Perspective*, Mahwah: Routledge.
Schleppegrell, M.J. (2013), "Systemic Functional Linguistics", in M. Handford and P. G. James (eds), *The Routledge handbook of Discourse Analysis*, 47–60, London: Routledge.
Valenzuela, A. (1999), *Subtractive Schooling: U.S.-Mexican Youth and the Politics of Caring*, Albany: State University of New York Press.
Villegas, A. M. and L. Tamara (2002), "Preparing Culturally Responsive Teachers: Rethinking the Curriculum", *Journal of Teacher Education*, 53 (1): 20–32.

19

Inquiry-Driven Reflection-in-Action Approach to Promote Culturally Responsive Literacy Practices through Teacher Education Projects

Wing Shuen Lau, Laura Humes Wahied, and Megan Kelley-Petersen

Background

With a focus on standards-based literacy instruction in the United States, students from diverse backgrounds are rarely invited to sustain their family's cultural assets and linguistic strengths in mainstream English-only curricula. "As transformative intellectuals, teachers can take an active role in reshaping curriculum and pedagogy for diverse learners through their own research-based actions … " (Liu and Ball 2019: 92). Teacher education, then, represents a key way in which educators can cultivate their teacher agency to push for educational justice by encouraging, supporting, and training teachers to use criticality to take responsibility and action within the walls of their own classrooms.

The University-Accelerated Certification for Teacher (U-ACT) program is an alternative route graduate-level teacher preparation program at the University of Washington, Seattle, in the United States, that works to center criticality as a mindset and practice for teachers (UW College of Education 2022). Enrolled teacher candidates (TCs) teach full-time in Washington schools, earning a state teaching certificate in the first year and a Master's in Teaching degree in the second year. The U-ACT program uses a set of Core Principles as a vision and framework for ambitious teaching (see Table 19.1).

In the final course of the program, TCs complete a capstone project, focused on an aspect of educational equity, over ten weeks. With support from the course instructor (Megan Kelley-Petersen, one of the authors), TCs meet weekly in collaborative groups to workshop their developing projects, bringing their individual work to the collective to deepen their own understanding and learning. This chapter will present key learning activities for TCs during the capstone project, as well as an action research project that emerged from the U-ACT course. This project examined a curricular intervention that a TC (Laura Wahied, one of the authors) designed to investigate how culturally responsive literacy practices support students' critical literacy and identity work skills.

Table 19.1 U-ACT program core principles

Core principle	Description of ambitious teaching
Position Students as Competent Sense-makers	• Have the pedagogical know-how to learn about students' prior knowledge, assess, and build on that knowledge. • Believe that all kids are capable of engaging with and understanding high-level content.
Know Students	• Know students across facets, including, but not limited to, academic assessment, understanding child development, building relationships with children, families, and communities. • Have practices that support them to continually learn about their students.
Engage Students in Rigorous Content	• Focus student learning on developing knowledge of content that requires them to engage in intellectually rich and challenging ways.
Challenge Inequities	• Given the current context of schooling and the inequitable access to opportunities and outcomes, ambitious teaching demands that teachers identify and interrupt patterns of inequity and bias. Such patterns limit access to rigorous content and learning for individuals and groups of students.

Description of the Practice: Overview of Equity Oriented Capstone Project

The Capstone Project in the course begins with TCs generating their own inquiry question and drafting a project proposal. In workshops, TCs engage in protocoled discussions to analyze inquiry questions to consider what is meaningful and manageable in their teaching contexts. Ensuring that TCs have complete autonomy for determining their inquiry question is a key part of the instructional design. TCs bring rich cultural and lived experiences from their personal identities and constantly learn each day alongside their students. Their expertise is valued as they design their own project, deeply reflecting on their own questions and ideas.

The inquiry question Laura selected was motivated by the opportunity she identified to bridge learning outcomes related to critical literacy and identity work in a multicultural, multilingual classroom setting. Her classroom included students from a wide range of racial, cultural, linguistic, and religious backgrounds in a predominantly working-class community, who rarely saw their identities reflected in the existing curriculum. The U-ACT core principles and literature around culturally responsive pedagogies (e.g., Muhammad 2020), culturally relevant pedagogy (e.g., Ladson-Billings 1995), and culturally sustaining practices (e.g., McCarty and Lee 2014) provided a conceptual framework for this project. Through collaborating with other

TCs, Laura identified key cultural and linguistic assets in her classroom to incorporate into the action research design.

Next, TCs work to develop a conceptual framework for their capstone project. They review relevant resources to design their project so they can answer their inquiry question. TCs workshop their conceptual framing with peers to consider others' perspectives and questions to help them finalize their framework as they continue their process.

Through this process, Laura designed a month-long unit where students learned explicitly about identities through the context of literacy activities. In a pre-survey, students were asked to describe their own identity and to name characters in books who held identities that were similar and different to theirs. They also created an initial portrait representing their identities. Next, the class explored identity through interactive reading and discussion (Fountas and Pinnell 2019) to contextualize important vocabulary relating to identity such as race, language, traditions, and so on. Laura chose realistic fiction to provide a relatable context for learning about identity that could offer students windows (new perspectives) and mirrors (reflections) into the lived experiences of characters holding a wide range of identities. Finally, students engaged in an activity to refine their identity portraits (i.e., with new understandings of race, language, traditions, religion, gender, etc.), and they completed a post-survey the questions in the pre-survey.

TCs next begin collecting and analyzing data. Each data set looks different based on the inquiry question and methods used. TCs bring their data to collaboratively analyze the data set with peers, looking for patterns and themes. Through collaborative discussions, Laura developed a data analysis protocol that included surveys both before and after the unit, coding of observational data taken during class discussions, and analysis of student-generated materials, such as identity portraits.

TCs continue to analyze their data on their own, coming to the next sessions with drafted findings and conclusions. They discuss findings in a workshop setting, seeking feedback and insights gained from their data. Through this, Laura noticed that students' thinking about identity in relation to themselves and the books they read deepened and evolved over the course of the project. After completing the unit, student expanded their understanding of identity beyond character and personality traits. They were able to recognize and connect a wider range of personal, social, and cultural identities that not only apply to themselves but also to characters they encounter in their readings (see Table 19.2). Students not only developed a deeper sense of self, but also gained literacy skills, such as the ability to engage with characters, connect with realistic stories, and learn about the wider world.

In the final stage of the course, TCs collaborate to determine how to tell the story of their project by writing a research brief and creating a presentation. When TCs present, they receive feedback from peers and instructors. This becomes another start for them in a cycle of inquiry and creates an opportunity for a celebration of TCs' learning.

Table 19.2 Summary of findings

Objective	Pre-survey	Post-survey
Students name specific personal and social identities they hold when asked about their identities.	16% of students	100% of students
Students can compare and contrast their identities to characters in books they have read.	17% of students	88% of students

Negotiations of Curriculum for Future Practices

Through presenting her project to instructors and peers, Laura was able to convey the significance of her project and to lay out for continued action. While mainstream literacy curricula used in public elementary schools in the United States rarely contain learning objectives related to identity, Laura saw immediate benefits to providing students with a multicultural classroom library and equipping them with the skills to undertake identity work to engage more deeply with the characters in the stories they read and each other. When identity work was embedded within literacy objectives, it opened up space to reimagine the traditional role that students assume in the mainstream literacy curricula, positioning students as powerful sense-makers. Additionally, having the experience of engaging in action research in a collaborative teacher education setting motivates Laura to continue to implement critical literacy practices in her classroom.

Critical Reflections: Potentials and Challenges

Designing and implementing reflective action research liberates TCs from merely adopting conventionally teacher-centered curriculum. The reflection-in-action approach to literacy instruction opens doors for innovative approaches that validate cultural and linguistic diversity, thereby empowering TCs to deepen their understanding of the community they work with and to model practices for literacy instruction.

Being an elementary teacher in practice, Laura sees how school systems reflect the issues and injustices occurring across society as a whole, but also holds the strong belief that action research can play a key role in righting these injustices in the pursuit of liberation and freedom. Action research is significant because it can provide a blueprint for continued action beyond the scope of a teacher education program. Equipping TCs with the skills to conduct action research is an important way to promote teacher agency, particularly in this time when technocratic approaches are increasingly touted as 'solutions' to educational inequities. Action research provides clear imperatives for the inclusion of critical practices that center students' identities in the learning process.

Megan, a teacher educator with specialized areas in teaching, learning and curriculum, frames courses and leads action research projects in hopes that TCs build a habit of asking questions centered around equity. She continues to reflect on how to guide TCs to constantly question and learn from their own practice when so much of their work is impacted and monitored by the "structures" inside of the school system. With the reflective approach, TCs genuinely wonder how they can learn with and from their instruction and see themselves as professionals who always want to learn more because asking critical questions is a part of their professional identity. Criticality is a key part of that process.

Wing Shuen Lau, whose research work has focused on instruction for multilingual learners, expects effective teacher education practices to extend far beyond meeting school-based standards or other forms of standardized assessment. For TCs with little research experience, designing and making meaning out of their data could be daunting. The in-class discussions with peers from a variety of subject areas and teaching experiences throughout the capstone project can offer ample opportunities of intellectual stimulation. These interactions enable TCs to interpret the evidence gathered from their instruction and to bridge gaps between research, theory, and practice to challenge inequitable access.

Through this collaborative work, we rethink how the teacher education curriculum could be designed to empower TCs to translate the theories they learned from the courses into their literacy instruction in daily classrooms to advance asset-based pedagogies (e.g., racial literacy, Rolón-Dow, Flynn, and Mead 2021; culturally and historically literacy, Muhammad 2020). Teacher-led, classroom-based action research increases opportunities for TCs and to promote sustained efforts to affirm students' funds of knowledge. When adopted along with well-planned pedagogical training and sufficient reflection opportunities, this inquiry-driven approach empowers TCs and educators to make equity-oriented decisions informed by evidence-based analysis.

References

Fountas, I. and G. S. Pinnell (2019). "What Is Interactive Read-Aloud?", *Fountas & Pinnell Literacy*, January 25. Available online: https://fpblog.fountasandpinnell.com/what-is-interactive-read-aloud (accessed January 29, 2023).

Ladson-Billings, G. (1995), "Toward a Theory of Culturally Relevant Pedagogy", *American Educational Research Journal*, 32 (3): 465–91.

Liu, K. and A. F. Ball (2019), "Critical Reflection and Generativity: Toward a Framework of Transformative Teacher Education for Diverse Learners", *Review of Research in Education*, 43: 68–105.

McCarty, T and T. Lee (2014), "Critical Culturally Sustaining/Revitalizing Pedagogy and Indigenous Education Sovereignty", *Harvard Educational Review*, 84 (1): 101–24.

Muhammad, G. (2020), *Cultivating Genius: An Equity Framework for Culturally and Historically Responsive Literacy*, New York: Scholastic Teaching Resources.

Rolón-Dow, R., J. E. Flynn and H. Mead (2020), "Racial Literacy Theory into Practice: Teacher Candidates' Responses", *International Journal of Qualitative Studies in Education*, 34 (7): 663–79.

UW College of Education (2022), "U-ACT: UW Accelerated Certification for Teachers". Available online: https://education.uw.edu/programs/teacher/u-act (accessed January 29, 2023).

Part Seven

Second Language Development

Unsettling Second Language Acquisition Theories through Raciolinguistic, Crip, and Translanguaging Perspectives

Clara Vaz Bauler and Gabriella Licata

Introduction

One of the biggest challenges we face in language teacher education is to unsettle existing harmful beliefs about what it means to learn a language, who is a language learner, and when language learning is happening. Popular beliefs about language learning are shaped and sustained collectively and systemically by hegemonic ideologies that privilege standard language, purism, and monolingualism as normalized defaults. Without deep awareness and reflexivity about the ways these ideologies undergird the status quo of language teaching, language teacher education programs continue to perpetuate the very ideas that need to be resisted and disrupted, resulting in teachers perceiving students and their language production as in need of remediation.

Unfortunately, mainstream second language acquisition (SLA) theories often serve to reinforce and perpetuate these same harmful ideologies. Take for example the "input" and "output" hypothesis popularly used to explain the "acquisition" process. In this perspective, communication and interaction are conceived as the computer-like, neutral process of exchange or transmission of information from one mind to another (Firth and Wagner 1997), rendering language learning as an individual accomplishment that has been disembodied from community (Block 2014; Firth and Wagner 2007; Henner and Robinson 2023). The consequences of adopting such theories are to avoid human complexity, social problems that include linguistic discrimination, racism, and linguistic variability altogether. After all, many would say, these themes do not belong to the language classroom as they are deemed "too political," an epistemology that ignores language as lived experiences.

A critical approach to language learning is grounded in the possibility of social change by making transparent as well as by deconstructing some of these naturalized and habitual ways of perceiving the world and people. In doing *conscientização* (Freire 1996; Pennycook 2021), or becoming critically aware that the social world is not a given, but it is ongoingly reconstructed and rearranged by all people, a critical perspective can turn the once familiar into the unfamiliar, convert the learned into the unlearned, pushing us to think and act in new ways. This chapter aims at discussing and critically reflecting on the ways SLA has been positioned vis-à-vis the humanity of language and the act of languaging. We will explore the history of the field focusing on what has been and what can be, particularly using raciolinguistic, translanguaging, and crip perspectives to resist mainstream, dominant concepts and ideologies. In doing so, we aim at centering humanity in more critical and socially oriented stances to languaging and identity.

Current Issues

The fictitious borders that name, delineate, and *limit* language are ideologically incepted to homogenize identity through nationalization, belonging, and the idealized hearer–speaker. A tool of unabashed colonialism, these ideologies allow for codified languages to maintain distinct and "superior" identity that becomes a target of mastery for those learning language in the classroom. This process of language and cultural subordination is conceptualized through coloniality of power (Quijano 2000), which describes how colonial linguistic legacies persist in modern societies. The subjugation of people via language oppression results in widespread linguistic discrimination and linguistic genocide (Skutnabb-Kangas 2012) across lands where the ruling colonial languages are imperialistically enforced.

Standard language ideologies serve as a present-day remnant of the Eurocentric language planning during colonization. As such, standard language ideologies are enforced institutionally in ways that exclude those whose primary or home language is not the hegemonic standard. Likewise, those who learn the hegemonic language as a "second" or "foreign" language are frequently categorized as limited proficient as opposed to active language users or multilingual individuals in their own right (Canagarajah 1999). The expectation that students produce standardized language as demonstrated "mastery" of language ignores the dynamic capabilities of language production. Take, for instance, the rejection of a student's admittance to an Introduction to Hispanic Literature course based on one diagnostic assessment (see Figure 20.1). A Latinx student whose home language is Spanish was deemed not ready for the class by the instructor. This course normally follows the language sequence of Spanish levels 1–4 for second language students or the two-class sequence for heritage language students.

The instructor claimed that the "student doesn't have good comprehension and does not write well … maybe they speak good enough [Spanish] for a heritage speaker, but not for a literature course." By indicating that a *heritage* language student cannot communicate sufficiently in a literature course, the teacher made heritage synonymous with unacademic, which is a form of dehumanization. The rejection of this student in large part demonstrates how language separateness underpins notions of the idealized languager and frames the marginalized student's linguistic and intellectual capabilities as inferior, resulting in racialized symbolic violence that reiterates linguistic hierarchization and inequitable access to education.

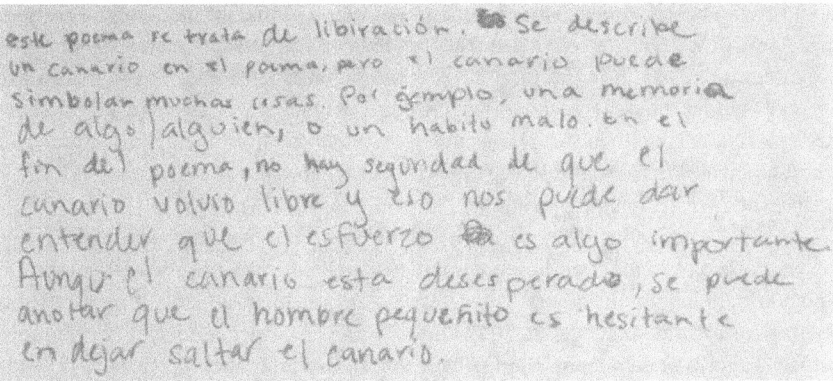

Figure 20.1 Writing sample from a heritage student moved from introduction to Hispanic literature to Spanish 4 for second language learners (see ALT Text for translation).

These ideologies of "appropriate" language expression have permeated SLA theory, elevating the idealized speaker–hearer as a monolingual, white, able-bodied subject as the model of communicative competence (Flores and Rosa 2022; Namboodiripad and Henner 2022). Since the 1990s, there has been a push against the idealized, monolingual native speaker model and the implications of this ideology for language education. Firth and Wagner (1997) dispute the seemingly "neutral" concepts of *interlanguage*, *native speaker*, and *non-native speaker*, which, in their view, promote an overly technical model of interaction that (1) essentializes and dichotomizes social identities between native and non-native speakers, disregarding the complexities involved in identity negotiation and re-creation; (2) reduces learners to the status of "subjects," not agents in their own learning processes and practices; (3) prioritizes a narrow view of language as an ideal system of universal and essentialized grammatical rules, as opposed to viewing language as action constantly subject to change, re-creation, and transformation; and (4) limits learning to a mental process of acquisition of grammatical rules, not considering the situated and sociohistorical dimensions of learning as social and cognitive practice.

Returning to Figure 20.1, this student did not abide by the stringent "academic" requirements of "literary analysis," and this was excluded from the course, despite the lack of consensus as to what "academic" registers even entail (Martínez and Mejía 2020). These varieties, once divorced from communities, are disembodied as a means to transform them into "inputs" and "outputs" that are measurable and easily assessed according to fictitiously drawn parameters in line with conventions of categorizing dynamic entities into monoliths. As a result, language learning is conceived as a constant and universal unidirectional process. Resultantly, this epistemological footing of language learning has the tendency to find problem sources, rather than achievements and interactional success in dynamic and innovative language practices (Firth and Wagner 2007).

Absent from the 1990s critique against the native speaker model was the need to highlight the co-construction of language, race, and ability in shaping societal perspectives about stigmatized language practices that do not look, sound, or feel "normal" (Flores and Rosa 2015; 2022). Raciolinguistic theory provides a critical approach through which we can examine language and race/ethnicity as co-constructed, meaning that language forms can index different meanings that are dependent on how those linguistic practices are uptaken. A raciolinguistic perspective shifts the focus from the linguistic practices of the language learner to the perceiving practices of those in power, such as teachers, as well as their epistemological positions (Flores and Rosa 2015).

Analyses of raciolinguistic ideologies in the classroom demonstrate how language serves as a proxy for longstanding systems of racism, ethnicity, misogyny, transphobia, and homophobia, among others. It also reveals ways Blackness is blatantly omitted from mainstream world languages and TESOL curricula and teacher education programs, which is a form of dehumanization (Austin 2022). Raciolinguistic perspectives (Flores and Rosa 2015) have the potential to inform similar conversations in various parts of the world, displaying the living legacy of colonialism in coloniality of power (Quijano 2000) that rely on language separateness to flourish, allowing for discrimination to be interweaved and normalized into social orders and systems. A raciolinguistic perspective (Flores and Rosa 2015) helps us challenge the ways artificial dichotomies, such as "standard" and "nonstandard," are perpetuated in language learning contexts.

A reliance on standardized language and monolingual ideologies to define what constitutes "appropriate" language has resulted in the marginalization of dynamic uses of languaging via a rejection of individual's full linguistic and intellectual capabilities. Henner and Robinson (2023) bring a crip perspective by drawing attention to ways disabled students whose sounds, abilities, and looks are racialized and marginalized are forced to communicate according to white, standardized norms that are not reflective or affirming of their culture, disability, or linguistic backgrounds. Ideals of native-like proficiency or ability have historically placed disabled as well as nonconforming ways of knowing at the margins by ignoring, pathologizing, or seeking to correct bodyminds whose language practices are deemed as disordered from the perspective of ideologies of whiteness (Gerald 2022; Henner and Robinson 2023). This also includes stigmatization of bodies that are deemed not fully human due to their fatness and gender identities. A crip perspective advocates for dismantling deficit and disorder in language education to welcome and affirm the infinite potential of the bodymind in all individuals' languaging practices and identities (Henner and Robinson 2023). Through a crip perspective, we are all invited to center disabled voices by rejecting the very notion of normal while defying pathologizing views that wrongly frame the perceived "non-nativeness," "accented," and/or "crippled" language practices of traditionally marginalized students as deficient.

Implications for Teaching and Teacher Education

Without thoughtful and intentional reflection and design aimed at disrupting raciolinguistic ideologies and ableism, teachers might end up following routines, adopting materials, and implementing practices and policies that perpetuate potentially harmful language ideologies and unjust disciplinary actions that can exclude individual students' voices, bodies, and active participation. How do we aim at centering humanity in more critical and socially-oriented stances to languaging and identity? How do we engage in *conscientização* or deep awareness about harmful ideologies that frame language teaching and learning practices?

Once pre-service teachers have a thorough understanding of the connections between systems, language, and power, they can begin to explore a translanguaging stance (García et al. 2017) in the classroom and beyond. Translanguaging is a stance about what it means to learn, teach, and embody languaging. The trans means transcending artificial linguistic boundaries; languaging encompasses a process of knowledge construction (García and Wei 2014). Learning and languaging are at the same time construction and transformation of knowledge, which is always socially negotiated, mediated, and open ended.

Particularly students who have been positioned as inferior in racial, cultural, and linguistic terms due to historical processes of colonization and domination need to be supported while also being afforded spaces where their ways of knowing, their dynamic, complex, and hybridized languaging practices, and their socioemotional development and identities are leveraged, affirmed, and welcomed (García et al. 2017). Students in particular whose language practices have been marginalized and inferiorized have their dynamic, hybridized, and creative uses of language rendered invisible or excluded (Canagarajah 2023). The only knowledge that counts is the one realized and modeled after white, monolingual, standardized ideals of "pure" and "uniform" academic language registers (Flores 2020).

In her sociolinguistic perspectives in education, Clara has been engaging pre-service teachers in attempting to shift the focus away from monolingual corrective practices to naturalizing multilingualism and multimodality; that is, tapping into students' whole linguistic and semiotic repertoires. One assignment consists of asking pre-service teachers to examine a sample student writing (Figure 20.2) adopting a raciolinguistic and translanguaging perspective. After reading multiple sources, pre-service teachers discuss and reflect about the prompt: What do we see, hear, feel outside the white gaze? They use a sense chart to help them take notes. They then reflect about their analysis of student writing, posting a reflection about what they used to think and what they think now about shifting their perspective from the writer, speaker, signer (the student) to the hearer, reader, seer (that is, YOU, as a teacher) as well as implications for teaching. As an online discussion, they also comment on each other's analyses.

Pre-service teachers' reflections reveal previously held raciolinguistic ideologies while making visible their journeys in starting to "see, feel, hear" through raciolinguistic and translanguaging perspectives (see the Appendix for an example of three pre-service teachers' reflections). Initially, pre-service teachers expressed that the child's letter looked messy, unorganized, or aimlessly switching from one language to the other. However, upon examining the letter from a raciolinguistic and translanguaging perspective, reflections started to demonstrate a rejection of the more typical practices of corrective feedback that disembody language while dehumanizing the learners. The reflections indicated a potential shift from perceiving what would be considered "errors" in the language practices of racialized children to considering children's translanguaging as creative meaning-making resources.

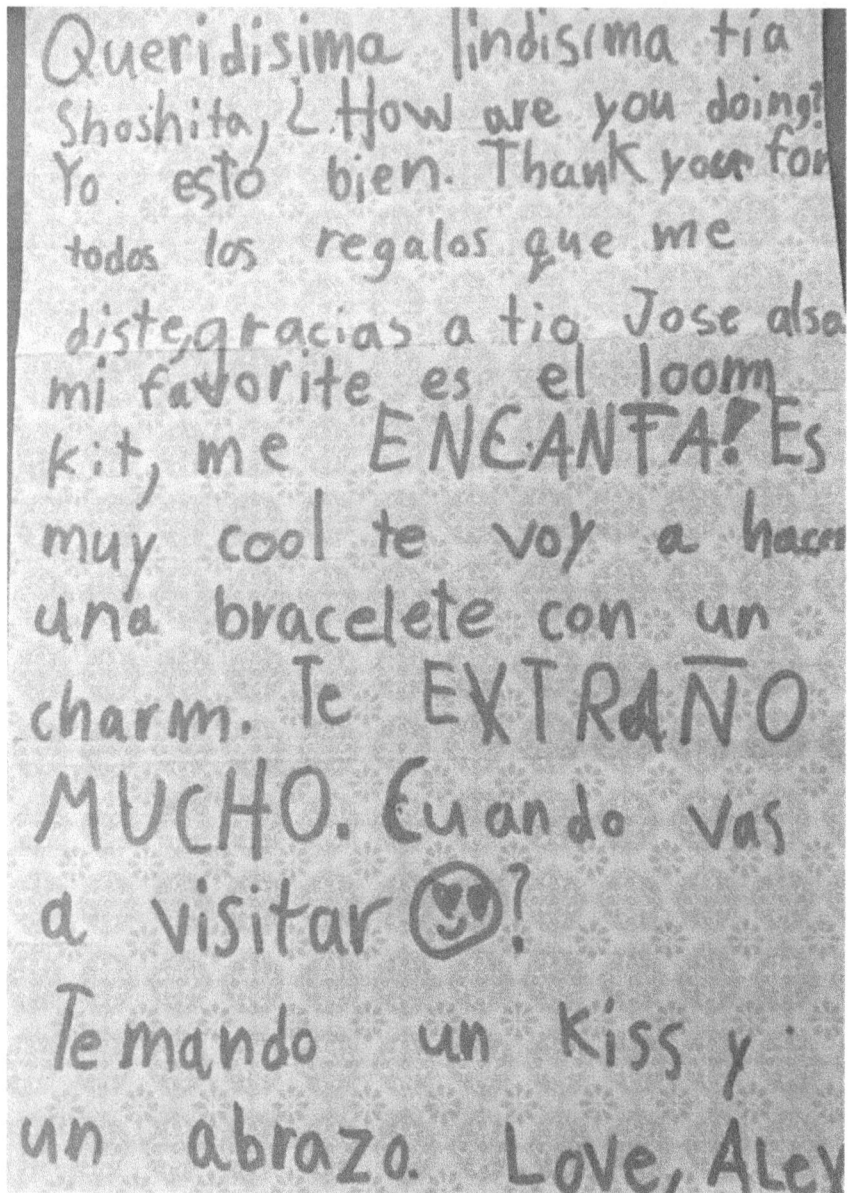

Figure 20.2 Letter to Tía written by Alexa Lil Borunda White and shared by Sonia Soltero on Twitter on August 20, 2022.

In spite of the importance of potential shifts in analytical activities such as these, reflective practices should not end with such an assignment. *Conscientização* is a recursive process. Ideologies are deeply ingrained and sustained through repetitive messages, experiences as well as systems and routines we engage in education. For example, translanguaging is not simply about whether the teacher should or not allow students to use their first language in the classroom (Wei and García 2022). Adopting a translanguaging stance is about creating environments that affirm and leverage multilingual ways of being, knowing, and doing. Aligned with a raciolinguistic and crip perspective, all teachers are invited to resist the harmful ideologies that frame the language practices of racialized students as deficient (Ascenzi-Moreno and Seltzer 2021). This can only be meaningfully done if pre-service teachers have the opportunity to explore their emerging translanguaging stances during fieldwork and student teaching. These practices promote interrogation of harmful ideologies and allow us to reflect on the often-ableist, racist, and deficit-oriented tacit underpinnings of mainstream SLA theory.

Translanguaging is a political, theoretical, and pedagogical stance which resists any form of language policing or monolingual end goals. A raciolinguistic and crip perspective helps us understand that schools can be the sites for both linguistic oppression and linguistic liberation. Schooling practices often force students into monolithic categories, resulting in the dehumanization and erasure of their dynamic identities, cultures, language practices, and knowledge experience. So, how can the critical language educator counteract the status quo? First, it is crucial to keep challenging the very notion that learning the standardized version of the target language and native mastery should be the end goal of language teaching and learning. As critical language educators, we will keep fighting, even when we find our efforts thwarted by systemic barriers. But how can our own reflection and practice be reimagined in spite of oppression? Finding community and embracing a liberating stance through raciolinguistic, crip and translanguaging perspectives are paramount to unsettling harmful ideologies that are rooted in invented language and culture boundaries. Without community and liberation, there is no transformation.

References

Ascenzi-Moreno, L. and K. Seltzer (2021), "Always at the Bottom: Ideologies in Assessment of Emergent Bilinguals", *Journal of Literacy Research*, 53 (4): 468–90. doi:10.1177/1086296X211052255.

Austin, T. (2022), "Linguistic Imperialism: Countering Anti Black Racism in World Language Teacher Preparation", *Journal for Multicultural Education*, 16 (3): 246–58. doi:10.1108/JME-12-2021-0234.

Block, D. (2014), *Social Class in Applied Linguistics*, London: Routledge.

Canagarajah, S. (1999), *Resisting Linguistic Imperialism in English Language Teaching*, Oxford: Oxford University Press.

Canagarajah, S. (2023), "A Decolonial Crip Linguistics", *Applied Linguistics*, 44 (1): 1–21. doi:10.1093/applin/amac042.

Firth, A. and J. Wagner (1997), "On Discourse, Communication, and (Some) Fundamental Concepts in SLA Research", *The Modern Language Journal*, 81 (3): 285–300. doi:10.1111/j.1540-4781.1997.tb05480.x.

Firth, A. and J. Wagner (2007), "Second/Foreign Language Learning as a Social Accomplishment: Elaborations on a Reconceptualized SLA", *The Modern Language Journal*, 91 (1): 800–19. doi:10.1111/j.1540-4781.2007.00670.x.

Flores, N. (2020), "From Academic Language to Language Architecture: Challenging Raciolinguistic Ideologies in Research and Practice", *Theory into Practice*, 59 (1): 22–31. doi:10.1080/00405841.2019.1665411.

Flores, N. and J. Rosa (2015), "Undoing Appropriateness: Raciolinguistic Ideologies and Language Diversity in Education", *Harvard Educational Review*, 85 (2): 149–71. doi:10.17763/0017-8055.85.2.149.

Flores, N. and J. Rosa (2022), "Undoing Competence: Coloniality, Homogeneity, and the Overrepresentation of Whiteness in Applied Linguistics", Language Learning. doi:10.1111/lang.12528.

Freire, P. (1996), *Pedagogia da Autonomia: Saberes Necessários à Prática Educativa*, Rio de Janeiro: Paz e Terra.

García, O. and L. Wei (2014), "Language, Bilingualism and Education", in O. García and L. Wei (eds), *Translanguaging: Language, Bilingualism and Education*, 46–62, London: Palgrave Pivot.

García, O., S. I. Johnson and K. Seltzer (2017), *The Translanguaging Classroom: Leveraging Student Bilingualism for Learning*, Philadelphia: Caslon.

Gerald, J. P. B. (2022), *Antisocial Language Teaching: English and the Pervasive Pathology of Whiteness*, Bristol: Multilingual Matters.

Henner, J. and O. Robinson (2023), "Unsettling Languages, Unruly Bodyminds: A Crip Linguistics Manifesto", *Journal of Critical Study of Communication and Disability*, 1 (1): 11–21. doi:10.48516/jcscd_2023vol1iss1.4.

Martínez, R. A. and A. F. Mejía (2020), "Looking Closely and Listening Carefully: A Sociocultural Approach to Understanding the Complexity of Latina/o/x Students' Everyday Language", *Theory into Practice*, 59 (1): 53–63. doi:10.1080/00405841.2019.1665414.

Namboodiripad, S. and J. Henner (2022), "Rejecting Competence: Essentialist Constructs Reproduce Ableism and White Supremacy in Linguistic Theory", PsyArXiv. doi:10.31234/osf.io/fc8sv.

Pennycook, A. (2021), *Critical Applied Linguistics: A Critical Re-introduction*, London: Routledge.

Quijano, A. (2000), "Coloniality of Power and Eurocentrism in Latin America", *International Sociology*, 15 (2): 215–32. doi:10.1177/0268580900015002005.

Skutnabb Kangas, T. (2012), "Linguicism", The Encyclopedia of Applied Linguistics, 1–6.

Wei, L. and O. García (2022), "Not a First Language but One Repertoire: Translanguaging as a Decolonizing Project", *RELC Journal*, 53 (2): 313–24. doi:10.1177/00336882221092841.

Suggested Readings and External Links

- CUNY-NYSIEB Translanguaging Guides
  A comprehensive website of translanguaging resources produced by teachers in the United States
  https://www.cuny-nysieb.org/translanguaging-resources/translanguaging-guides/
- Critical Conversations
  A series of conversations that elevate and affirm Blackness and Black ways of being and knowing in world languages and English Language Teaching
  https://youtu.be/KKVGbCU5VXE?si=oXKzROJGOch6Vg0m

- Crónicas de una clase de español en EEUU
  Critical reflections and resources written by a secondary Spanish as a world and heritage language teacher
  https://abelardo-almazan1910.medium.com/cr%C3%B3nicas-de-una-clase-de-espa%C3%B1ol-en-ee-uu-elles-muxes-latinx-y-las-identidades-9daa6657d7f3
- How to Write Inclusive Materials
  Ideas and materials that include multiple perspectives and voices, especially focusing on the LGBTQ community's ways of being and knowing
  https://eltteacher2writer.co.uk/our-books/how-to-write-inclusive-materials/

Positionality Statements

Gabriella is Italian-American and grew up in a multilingual household. She considers herself a heritage languager of Italian and Genoese. Gabriella is a former secondary Spanish teacher and was trained to view Latinx students as possessing deficits and needing to develop "full bilingualism," though she now supports and appreciates dynamic multilingualism and languaging in the classroom and beyond. A sociolinguist, Gabriella openly critiques the ways in which languages are framed and examined as separate cognitive systems that conveniently pave the way for deficit perspectives in both folk ideologies and empirical study.

Clara is a Jewish-Brazilian-American individual, mother, and educator. She was born in the United States and grew up in Rio de Janeiro, Brazil. This plurality has created multiple paths for her to engage in identity construction through languaging in her life. As a mother, she tries to disrupt the cycle of assimilation and standardization in teaching and learning with her children. As a teacher educator, she resists the ways raciolinguistic ideologies systemically stigmatize, sort, and discriminate against students simply for being themselves.

21

Developing a Translanguaging Stance in Teacher Candidates via a Middle School and University-Based Teacher Education Program E-tutoring Partnership

Elizabeth Goulette

Background

The concept of a target language is a restrictive language practice that is widely accepted in the US education system as being optimal for learning. For example, on its website, the American Council for the Teaching of Foreign Languages (ACTFL) adopts this monolingual ideology, recommending, "that learning take place through the target language for 90 % or more of classroom time except in immersion program models where the target language is used exclusively." This position manifests itself in the fact that classroom-based second language learning is typically done in isolation from the first language, even though this position does not reflect the realities of second language use in the home or community. As Torpsten (2018: 106) acknowledged, "multilingual speakers do not keep their languages apart as they operate in multilingual and multicultural environments." Still, in most US schools, language learners are required to exclusively use the target language in the classroom (Faltis 2020), and they are sometimes penalized by teachers for using their first language in this setting. Likewise, most tutoring programs mirror this monolingual ideology supported by ACTFL as a best practice, so they are typically designed to focus on developing language skills in isolation. However, this design is based upon the outmoded conception that bilinguals possess two separate linguistic systems. A critical perspective recognizes that bilinguals can "translanguage" or use their unitary linguistic repertoire (Wei and García 2022) to make meaning. Translanguaging is a critical approach to language learning because it disrupts traditional ideologies of language separation.

Description of the Practice

This chapter highlights the way that I redesigned a university-based teacher education course to develop a translanguaging stance (Aleksić and García 2022) in a group of teacher candidates by demonstrating its potential for language learning. The middle school and university-based teacher education program partnership mutually benefited the language development of Spanish-speaking eighth graders enrolled in an English as a Second Language (ESL) program and teacher candidates at a small, private, Liberal Arts university who were studying Spanish. The partnership arose from a conversation between a middle school ESL teacher and me during an academic conference. The ESL teacher mentioned that her school lacked paraprofessionals to assist ESL students who were struggling academically. Coincidentally, I was in the process of redesigning WL 4900 for the upcoming semester. WL 4900 Language Immersion Service-Learning has the following objectives. At the conclusion of the course, students will be able to

1. examine aspects of second language learning, including the acquisition of sociolinguistic competency, the acquisition of fluency, and the development of speaking and writing skills.
2. apply and integrate the communicative strategies learned throughout the program in interpersonal interactions with the community.
3. assess how cultural awareness and proficiency in a second language may be utilized through service to the community.
4. articulate, in the target language, the meaning of a language service-learning experience in terms of their professional growth and civic participation.

Four female teacher candidates were enrolled in WL 4900; two were White, one identified as Latina and spoke Spanish at home, and one was African American.

The ESL teacher identified ten Spanish-speaking eighth graders who needed additional academic support. She recommended students who were struggling academically due to truancy or misunderstanding content presented in English. The middle school students were Latinx (two males and eight females) with familial ties to Mexico, Puerto Rico, and the Dominican Republic. Some were newcomers to the United States, and others had been in US schools for a few years. I first obtained approval from each school's administration, and then I subsequently received teacher candidate consent and parental consent for the middle school students. Zoom was used for synchronous sessions due to transportation constraints. The teacher candidates had access to a computer and an internet connection at home. Each middle school student had been issued a school-owned Chromebook suitable for e-tutoring. Synchronous e-tutoring sessions were held via Zoom on Thursdays from 7–9 pm for fifteen weeks. I monitored the breakout rooms while the groups translanguaged, working collaboratively on assignments.

At the beginning of the semester, the teacher candidates completed a pre-flection tool from Michigan State University's Service-Learning Toolkit (2015) to self-assess their readiness for community engagement. The pre-flection tool can be found in Appendix M at the following link https://communityengagedlearning.msu.edu/upload/toolkits/Service-Learning-Toolkit.pdf. The pre-flection tool included the following evaluation criteria: openness, discovery, curiosity, respect, adaptability, flexibility, and sharing. Course readings were all open access materials, and included theoretical chapters, research-based articles, and practitioner articles. For example, the teacher candidates read Reznicek-Parrado's (2023) research study on peer-to-peer translanguaging academic spaces and reflected on how it related to their e-tutoring experience. They also read theoretical pieces such as Faltis's (2020) chapter on translanguaging in bilingual schooling contexts and reflected on translanguaging as a critical language teaching practice. At the midpoint and end of the semester, I met with each teacher candidate to discuss her performance using the course objectives as benchmarks. At the mid-semester meeting, the teacher candidates created goals for the remainder of the semester, and at the final meeting, we discussed whether they had met them. In lieu of a final exam, they compiled an e-portfolio, which consisted of a tutoring log, the pre-flection self-assessment, reflection papers based on course readings, and a final self-assessment. The teacher candidates reported growth in openness, discovery, curiosity, respect, adaptability, flexibility, and sharing in their final self-assessments.

By design, the e-tutoring sessions were translanguaging spaces (Wei 2011) where everyone was encouraged to use both English and Spanish to arrive at higher understanding of the content. To illustrate, I will describe what happened when a tutee was stuck on an assignment about the continents. The tutee encountered many unfamiliar English words that impeded his ability to complete the assignment. So, the tutor described the unfamiliar English words in Spanish, providing examples to help the tutee understand. Next, the tutor asked the tutee to summarize what he had read orally, encouraging the use of translanguaging. In these situations, Spanish explanations of unknown English words helped the tutees complete their assignments. However, the learning process was not unidirectional. Often, the tutees taught the tutors new words in Spanish or helped them with the pronunciation of Spanish words. During the experience, there were opportunities for everyone to be teachers and learners at various points.

Critical Reflections: Potentials and Challenges

My critical reflection of the e-tutoring experience revealed substantial qualitative and quantitative gains. At the beginning, all tutees had missing assignments that resulted in poor grades. While monitoring the sessions, I often overheard the tutees describe having felt lost in class when they were learning new concepts in English because they could not fully understand their teacher, nor the assignments. By the end of the experience, I noticed the tutees' increase in self-confidence (qualitative gain) as well as a decrease in missing assignments and improvement in course grades (quantitative gains). When the tutees were encouraged to translanguage, they more easily understood the content, gaining self-confidence. Whereas tutees had often shut down while reading a difficult text in English in the past, this newfound self-confidence and support from the tutors helped them complete their assignments.

The teacher candidates also grew throughout the experience. Initially, the teacher candidates had expressed concern about potential communication breakdowns. Each feared that she might not possess the requisite language skills to describe difficult concepts in Spanish. However, as they learned more about translanguaging strategies in weekly readings, they became more comfortable putting them into practice during e-tutoring. In their final reflection papers, the teacher candidates reflected on the obstacles the ESL students faced while trying to learn the same material alongside native English speakers. They were surprised to learn that the tutees only had one ESL class, and the rest of the school day, they were in content area classrooms without ESL support. As language learners themselves, they empathized with the tutees, reflecting on times when they too had felt overwhelmed using a second language. They expressed concern about micro-level issues like the tutees' lack of ESL resources but were proud to have helped them improve their grades and language skills.

The teacher candidates also examined macro-level issues for language learning. For example, they lamented that few university–school partnerships like this one exist in the United States. The teacher candidates expressed their feeling that the US educational system can be unjust toward ESL students, particularly those in low-income areas who often lack necessary support to be successful in school. Each teacher candidate reflected on the merits of translanguaging as a critical approach to developing second language skills and academic content knowledge. Importantly, everyone expressed a commitment to opening up translanguaging spaces (Wei 2011) in their future classrooms as an effort to disrupt a US public education system that they felt perpetuates inequality for English learners.

Although this critical approach to e-tutoring was beneficial for everyone, it was not without challenges. Despite having school-issued Chromebooks, some tutees had weak internet signals at home, which led to connectivity problems. Also, although the tutors always used their video cameras, the public school district could not mandate them for tutees. Therefore, some chose not to turn their cameras on, so we could only hear their voices. The tutors were challenged by not being able to read the tutees' facial expressions. They did their best by asking questions to gauge understanding but tutors sometimes expressed frustration with not being able to see their tutees' faces. While these technology issues could have been mitigated with in-person tutoring, it was not an option due to transportation constraints.

In conclusion, the challenges were worth the growth that everyone experienced. I believe that second language development occurred because e-tutoring was a translanguaging space (Wei 2011) that allowed everyone to use their entire linguistic repertoire. The tutees increased their English skills and demonstrated a more complete understanding of the English language arts, mathematics, science, and social studies concepts they were learning in school which manifested in both quantitative and qualitative gains. As a result, they were able to complete assignments that improved their grades and boosted their self-confidence. The teacher candidates also attained greater self-confidence and developed empathy for their tutees as English learners in an unjust US public education system. I hope this chapter assists teacher educators who want to facilitate a translanguaging stance (Aleksić and García 2022) in teacher candidates and/ or wish to create an e-tutoring partnership like the one described in this chapter.

References

Aleksić, G. and O. García (2022), "Language Beyond Flags: Teachers' Misunderstanding of Translanguaging in Preschools", *International Journal of Bilingual Education and Bilingualism*, 25 (10): 3835–48.

"Facilitate Target Language Use", *American Council for the Teaching of Foreign Languages*. Available online: https://www.actfl.org/resources/guiding-principles-language-learning/target-language (accessed November 11, 2022).

Faltis, C.J. (2020), "Pedagogical Codeswitching and Translanguaging in Bilingual Schooling Contexts: Critical Practices for Bilingual Teacher Education", in J. MacSwan and J. Faltis (eds), *Codeswitching in the Classroom: Critical Perspectives on Teaching, Learning, Policy, and Ideology*, 39–62, New York: Routledge.

Michigan State University (2015), *Service-Learning Toolkit: A Guide for MSU Faculty and Instructors*. Available online: https://communityengagedlearning.msu.edu/upload/toolkits/Service-Learning-Toolkit.pdf (accessed November 16, 2023).

Reznicek-Parrado, L.M. (2023), "Peer-to-Peer Translanguaging Academic Spaces for Belonging: The Case of Spanish as a Heritage Language", *International Journal of Bilingual Education and Bilingualism*, 26 (2): 131–45.

"Service-learning Toolkit: A Guide for MSU Faculty and Instructors", *Michigan State University's Center for Service-Learning and Civic Engagement*. Available online: https://communityengagedlearning.msu.edu/upload/toolkits/Service-Learning-Toolkit.pdf (accessed August 5, 2022).

Torpsten, A.C. (2018), "Translanguaging in a Swedish Multilingual Classroom", *Multicultural Perspectives*, 20 (2): 104–10.

Wei, L. (2011), "Moment Analysis and Translanguaging Space: Discursive Construction of Identities by Multilingual Chinese Youth in Britain", *Journal of Pragmatics*, 43 (5): 1222–35.

Wei, L. and O. García (2022), "Not a First Language but One Repertoire: Translanguaging as a Decolonizing Project", *RELC Journal*, 53 (2): 313–24.

22

Exploring Language, Identity, Power, and Privilege with Secondary-Level EL Teachers: A Critical Language Awareness (CLA) Case Study

Shawna Shapiro

Background

It has long been established that metalinguistic knowledge is an important component of professional development for language teachers (e.g., Andrews 2007). However, in recent years, a number of scholars have called for more critical orientations that take into account the social and political contexts for language use (Alim 2005; García 2017) and that promote plurilingual/translanguaging pedagogies in the classroom (e.g., Goodman and Tastanbek 2021). In essence, we need to equip teachers not just with structural and functional knowledge about language but also with **critical language awareness** (CLA), which Shapiro (2022: 4) defines as a deep understanding of "the intersections of language, identity, power, and privilege" (see also http://clacollective.org/). A CLA approach to language/literacy pedagogy prioritizes three pedagogical goals: (1) self-reflection, (2) social justice, and (3) rhetorical agency (see Figure 22.1). Such an approach is relevant not just to ESOL or other L2 classrooms but also to mainstream classrooms that include English Learners.

This approach is undergirded as well by **six principles**, as illustrated in Figure 22.2. See http://clacollective.org/ for a brief explanation of each principle and Shapiro (2022) for a more in-depth discussion.

But what does it look like to explore intersections among language, identity, power, and privilege in ESOL teacher education? How can teachers be prepared not only to engage in this critical learning for themselves, but also to infuse it into curricula and instruction for English Learners? In this chapter, I present a model for a six-week, online professional development program that responds to these questions. The program included secondary-level English Learner (EL) and English Language Arts (ELA) teachers from two public school districts in the northeastern United States. The districts involved in this program are both located in a midsized refugee resettlement community. English Learners (ELs) comprise 42 percent of the student body in one district and 18 percent in the other. Both districts have been moving toward more

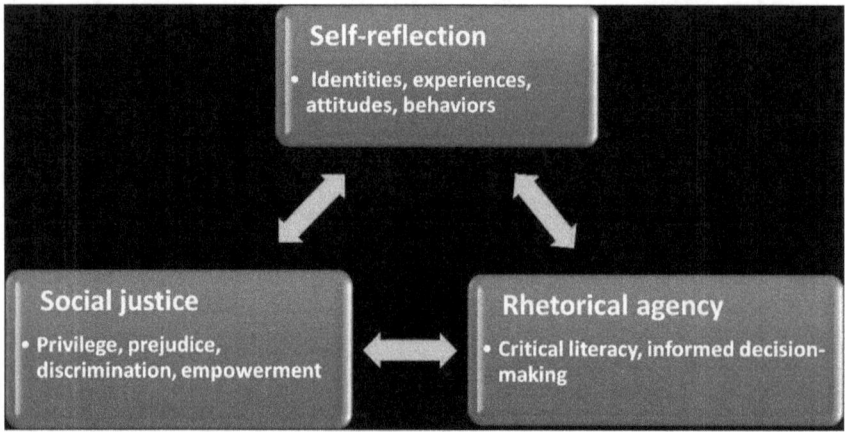

Figure 22.1 Goals for CLA pedagogy. Source: S. Shapiro, *Cultivating Critical Language Awareness in the Writing Classroom* (New York: Routledge, 2022).

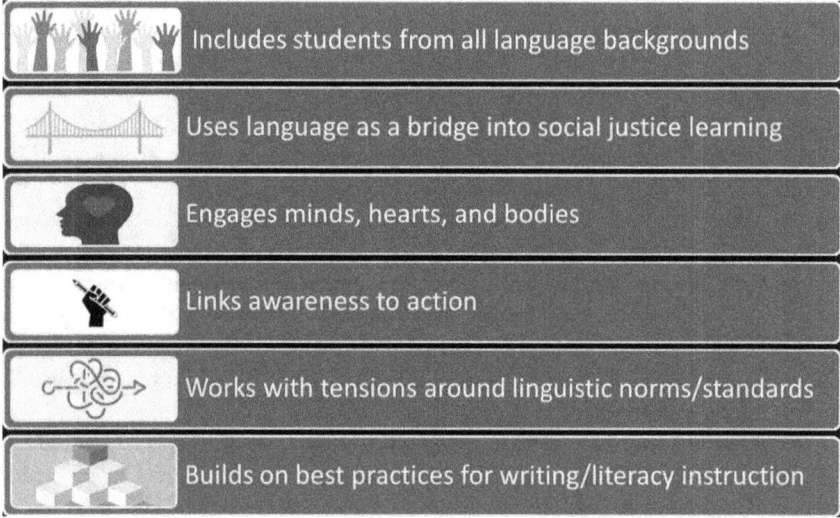

Figure 22.2 Principles for CLA pedagogy. Source: S. Shapiro, *Cultivating Critical Language Awareness in the Writing Classroom* (New York: Routledge, 2022).

equity-based and collaborative models of instruction, in which EL and content area teachers share responsibility for instructional support (e.g., Honigsfeld, Dove, Cohan and Goldman 2021; Shapiro and Ehtesham-Cating 2019). Yet EL teachers rarely have opportunities to engage in sustained professional development and with content area teachers, or with teachers in other districts. This program was designed to fill that gap, building on the equity and inclusion work already taking place in both districts.

Description of the Practice

I designed the "CLA Fellows Program" with input from administrators in both districts. The program took place in January and February 2022, and involved weekly online meetings, plus reading and short tasks to complete between meetings (see overview below). Eleven secondary-level (mostly high school) teachers were selected to be Fellows, via an online application process—five who primarily teach sheltered EL courses and six who primarily teach English language arts (ELA) classes. The primary requirements for selection were that each participant teaches writing/literacy in courses that include ELs (and/or former ELs) and is interested in expanding their teaching repertoire for working with this population. All participants received a pre-print copy of Shapiro's (2022) *Cultivating Critical Language in the Writing Classroom*, which was our primary text. They also received a stipend[1] of $400 and twenty professional learning hours, in recognition of the time spent engaging in meetings, doing assigned readings, and working on a final application assignment.

Each seventy-five-minute session was designed to model pedagogical practices informed by CLA: We opened with a mindfulness practice, followed by a review activity related to the previous session. Then, we discussed highlights from the chapters that had been assigned, engaged in an application or reflection activity (e.g., a "share out" where each teacher provides one connection between a new term/concept and their own curriculum/instruction; an interactive quiz on descriptive vs. prescriptive approaches to language; in-class drafting of prompts for discussion and/or freewriting). Finally, we briefly previewed the topics for the subsequent session. During the final meeting, each participant shared a pedagogical application reflecting their learning, which they later submitted in writing. I used online surveys to collect feedback from participants after the first session and after the conclusion of the program. Table 22.1 presents key topics, readings, and activities from each of our meetings.

Table 22.1 Overview of CLA fellows program

	Foci	**Readings/activities**
Meeting 1	Setting expectations, building community, intro to CLA: 3 goals, 6 principles, key concepts	Chapter 1 of Shapiro (2022). Introductions, personal goals. Reflection on linguistic repertoires and privileges. Discussion of pedagogical quandaries that CLA responds to, and whether they apply to participants.
Meeting 2	Going deeper with CLA concepts and principles (e.g., descriptivism, prescriptivism, indexicality) Introducing the 4 Pathways	Chapter 2 and 3 of Shapiro (2022). Genre play activity (teachers practice explaining CLA in different styles of writing), Terms review (kinesthetic response game), and other concepts review. Discussion about initial reactions to CLA content. Assigned jigsaw chapters for Meeting 3.

	Foci	Readings/activities
Meeting 3	Exploring the 4 CLA Curricular Pathways: Sociolinguistics, Critical Academic Literacies, Media/Discourse Analysis, Communicating Across Difference	Chapters 4–7 of Shapiro (2022) (Jigsaw reading—i.e., each participant read one chapter in-depth and skimmed the others). Jigsaw share (participants shared highlights, responses, and questions for their assigned chapter).
Meeting 4	Connecting CLA to classroom interactions and instruction (facilitating discussion, scaffolding reading, responding to student writing, etc.)	Chapter 9 of Shapiro (2022) "Rose, thorn, bud" applied to CLA. Breakout groups on key questions from chapter. Large group debrief. Practice writing "micro-affirmations."
Meeting 5a (1st half)	Synthesizing and preparing for share-out	Writing "elevator pitch" for CLA. Discussing what to keep, change, and add to the program for future iterations.
Meeting 5b (2nd half)	Sharing and reflecting with administrators	Each participant shared a takeaway or application from the program with administrators from both school districts.

In facilitating this program, I was looking to promote two kinds of learning among participants: The first is a more nuanced and critical orientation toward language—what I call a **CLA mindset**. For example, one participant said in the end-of-program survey that they gained "a solid theoretical framework for discussing power and language." Another reported, "I think it overall just raised my consciousness and capacity to analyze how we employ language in our education system." These comments indicate that teachers gained a deeper understanding of how language use can reflect, exacerbate, and perhaps ameliorate power inequalities—a key insight second language acquisition from CLA scholarship that is sometimes overlooked in discussions of second language acquisition (Garcia 2017; Shapiro 2022).

The second kind of learning involves concrete strategies and resources teachers can incorporate into their instruction—i.e., a **CLA skillset**. One teacher said they "learned about some specific activities and lessons I can directly apply to my teaching practice." Another noted that they came away with "More knowledge and grace about using and teaching academic writing." Several teachers also noted that the program helped to explain and enhance some of the practices the fellows were already using, providing the sort of pedagogical affirmation that is often lacking in educational reform efforts (Eisner 1992).

Perhaps the best indication of teachers' CLA learning is in their final application projects. Below I discuss two examples of how EL teachers working with learners at various English proficiency levels incorporated a CLA mindset and skill set into their existing curricula for language/literacy development.

Logan (a pseudonym, by participant request), who was working primarily with newcomer/beginner students at the high school level, developed an instructional sequence to teach students about the concept of **register**—i.e., language variation by context. The sequence includes activities such as

- Categorizing commonly used expressions as "colloquial/slang" or "formal"
- Providing examples of informal vs. formal register in their L1/heritage languages
- Analyzing written dialogues for linguistic cues indicating register
- Role-playing situations in which different registers are appropriate
- Discussing the effects—negative and positive—of intentionally using the "wrong" register (e.g., public figures who chose to use slang).

Through this sequence, Logan hoped to make beginner students aware of some of the variation within English, so that they might experience more agency as writers and speakers, both at school and beyond.

Another example comes from Sona, who was working that year with upper intermediate and advanced ELs at the middle school level. Sona channeled her CLA learning into the design of a **restorative justice circle** connected to Black History Month. Her plan included the following questions, which she crafted carefully to progress from sharing personal experiences to considering critical questions about language, power, and privilege:

1. When was a time you experienced the power of language? (and/or) When do you remember a word or words that really stuck with you?
2. What's one word you say in your family or your language that means a lot to you?
3. Do you think some people's words have more or less power, depending on who says them?

Although length restrictions limit the extent of detail I can share about other participants' final projects, here is a sampling of curricular goals toward which they applied their CLA mindset and skill set:

- Using language as part of social and emotional (SEL) learning and community-building
- Composing poetry focused on language and identity
- Developing critical media literacy strategies (e.g., checking credibility of sources)
- Gathering more detailed information about students' attitudes toward and use of home/heritage languages at school and in the community
- Analyzing language variation in literature, including multiple dialects, styles, and registers
- Understanding linguistic bias and its impact on marginalized communities
- Complicating assumptions about standard vs. "nonstandard" language
- Examining the implicit "rules" for computer-mediated communication (e.g., texting) and comparing with the explicit conventions of academic writing.

These sorts of projects engage students (and teachers) in exploring intersections among identity, power, and privilege in relation to language. As referenced earlier, such intersections are often overlooked in curricula for second language development, which focus primarily on language structures and functions, with little attention to social and political context. Engaging in these CLA explorations helps to validate students' linguistic repertoires and create space for them to share experiences of linguistic agency and oppression. Moreover, a CLA-oriented curriculum can engage ELs in learning about topics that are generally more prominent in the "mainstream" curriculum, such as media literacy, global citizenship, and antiracism.

Critical Reflections: Potentials and Challenges

Below, I highlight some takeaways for other teacher educators looking to facilitate a similar model. One feature that worked well was that the program was **online.** This was necessary because of the Covid-19 pandemic, but many of the participants noted that they could not have participated in an in-person program because of family responsibilities or other commitments. Participants also very much appreciated the compensation (stipend and licensure hours), and most would not have participated otherwise.

Another agreed-upon strength was that the program included both **EL and ELA teachers**. Although a few participants said they would have liked more time to discuss applications within their respective disciplines, all participants expressed appreciation for the opportunity to interact with colleagues in other departments. The fact that CLA was new to everyone helped to level the playing field. As one EL participant put it, "One of my pedagogical goals has been to work more closely with general education teachers, and this program allowed me to do so in an area which was new to us all." This sort of feedback suggests that programs like this one offer a viable model for promoting collaboration across content areas, which is crucial to improving educational outcomes for ELs (e.g., Honigsfeld, Dove, Cohan and Goldman 2021).

In terms of content, participants appreciated the **accessible style** and many **pedagogical examples** included in the Shapiro (2022) text. Participants also appreciated my attempts to **model best practice** in helping participants engage with and apply their learning from the text, using interactive activities and reflection prompts in each session. The text is quite long, however, and several participants suggested that it would have been helpful to read excerpts from chapters, rather than the entire text. Moreover, although most of the book content was well received by teachers, some EL teachers reported that they would need to adapt the instruction significantly when working with beginner and intermediate learners. Most participants felt that the seventy-five-minute sessions were the right length, but a few would have liked longer sessions. Some participants felt that the duration of the program (six weeks) did not provide as much time as they would have liked to digest and apply what they were learning. However, many also indicated that they would not have been able to commit to a longer program during the regular school year. I hope to pilot a summer iteration of the program eventually, to see whether that might allow for deeper learning and sustained reflection.

Although I have maintained communication informally with several participants, I have not (yet) had an opportunity to conduct follow-up interviews or focus groups to evaluate the program's long-term impact—something I hope to do eventually. I also wish to "scale up" this work in the future, offering online workshops and other events for teachers and teacher educators outside my local community. Readers who are interested in learning more can find information at http://clacollective.org/. This site also has a wealth of materials (syllabi, assignments, readings, etc.) for educators who wish to engage with their students and/or colleagues in deep learning about language, identity, power, and privilege.

Note

1 Although I used mostly personal funds for these stipends, we also received a small grant from the Vermont Humanities Council. Some supplies and logistical support were also provided via an internal grant from Middlebury College's "MiddData" initiative.

References

Alim, H. Samy (2005), "Critical Language Awareness in the United States: Revisiting Issues and Revising Pedagogies in a Resegregated Society", *Educational Researcher*, 34 (7): 24–31.

Andrews, Stephen (2007), *Teacher Language Awareness*, Cambridge: Cambridge University Press.

Eisner, Elliot W. (1992), "Educational Reform and the Ecology of Schooling", *Teachers College Record*, 93 (4): 610–27.

García, Ofelia (2017), "Critical Multilingual Language Awareness and Teacher Education", in Jasone Cenoz, Durk Gorter and Stephen May (eds), *Language Awareness and Multilingualism*, 263–80, New York: Springer.

Goodman, Bridget and Serikbolsyn Tastanbek (2021), "Making the Shift from a Codeswitching to a Translanguaging Lens in English Language Teacher Education", *TESOL Quarterly*, 55 (1): 29–53.

Honigsfeld, Andrea, Maria Dove, Audrey Cohan and Carrie McDermott Goldman (2021), *From Equity Insights to Action: Critical Strategies for Teaching Multilingual Learners*, Thousand Oaks, CA: Corwin Press.

Shapiro, Shawna (2022), *Cultivating Critical Language Awareness in the Writing Classroom*,. New York: Routledge. See also http://clacollective.org/.

Shapiro, Shawna and Miriam Ehtesham-Cating (2019), "From Comfort Zone to Challenge: Toward a Dynamic Model of English Language Teacher Advocacy in Secondary Education", *TESOL Journal*, 10 (4): e488–92.

23

Un-teaching Native Speaker Fallacy: A Practical Application and Discussion

Tan Arda Gedik

Background

Native speaker (NS) fallacy in second language acquisition (SLA) is a condition where NSs are deemed linguistically and qualitatively more superior than L2 speakers. This stems from a decade-long conventional wisdom engendered by generativist linguists without providing much evidence for it (e.g., Bley-Vroman 2009: 179; Chomsky 1975: 11). This wisdom assumes that all NSs uniformly succeed at mastering their L1. Studies show that this may not be the case as print exposure and other individual differences in the cognitive machinery result in different representations and production of the same input (e.g., Dąbrowska 2018, 2019; Kidd et al. 2018). Print exposure is known to foster better language performance as written language exposes speakers to more complex language than spoken modes, which helps with ultimate language attainment of any form (Roland et al. 2007). Similarly, there is fifty years of research emphasizing the importance of individual differences (IDs) in abilities in L1 (e.g., phonological memory) predicting L2 success (Sparks 2022). So far, print exposure seems to be the best predictor of linguistic performance and IDs in comparisons between NSs and NNSs, with high-print-exposure L2 speakers outperforming low-print-exposure L1 speakers (Dąbrowska 2019).

With such evidence, it becomes feasible to deconstruct the fallacy in SLA as most of SLA and teacher training is based on it (Mahboob 2005). This fallacy is known to lead to several problems in non-native (English) speaker teachers (NNESTs) such as being pushed to the periphery, feeling less-than-human, and questioning their legitimacy as teachers (e.g., Phillipson 1992; Selvi 2014). The extent of these problems has been discussed from different perspectives, mainly from social, philosophical, or ethical (e.g., Aneja 2016; Bonfiglio 2013; Selvi 2018). Nevertheless, it has not been much problematized in teacher education or linguistics from a linguistic point of view. Thus, this chapter provides a proposed lesson plan for teachers (and candidates) as to why the assumed NS ideal may not always be the case and what discussions are needed to deconstruct NS in being a language user/teacher.

This lesson plan is intended to be implemented at an undergraduate-level foreign language (especially English) teacher training program as part of a SLA-related course. I believe the lesson plan would be exceptionally useful for a practice-based teacher education program but is applicable to any language teacher education setting. The intended duration of the lesson is sixty minutes and can be used within any course with/out a teaching methodology component. This lesson plan was originally designed for a psycholinguistics course at an undergraduate level in psychology but is applicable to different undergraduate majors, especially language teachers and linguistics. With modifications to the tasks, the target group can also include graduate students.

Description of the Practice

The aim of this lesson plan is to teach teacher candidates and linguists at under(graduate) levels that NSs do not uniformly converge on the same grammar, and times L2 speakers can outperform L1 speakers (e.g., Dąbrowska 2019). This is especially important from an SLA perspective because courses in these programs are still mostly based on the monolingual bias and the premise that NSs reach an idealized end destination in attaining L1, and therefore NSs are inherently linguistically better than NNSs (Mahboob 2005).

In the introduction, the lecturer asks the following discussion questions to engage teacher candidates (TCs). This achieves objective #1 (Discuss the terms NS/NNS and what separates them according to the students):

1. Who is a native speaker?
2. Why/why do we not need the separation?
3. What separates NS/NNSs?

This explores what the TCs think of the topic (that NSs do not exist in their idealized forms and NSs are not necessarily linguistically better than NNSs) and gives the lecturer an overall picture of TCs opinions on the issue. Then, by extending the questions in the continuation, the lecturer aims to gather if the TCs believe L1/L2 speakers differ much in learning language, and if the TCs believe in NS fallacy. By asking about IDs, the lecturer prepares students for a destabilizing of the fallacy in later parts of the lecture (achieves objective #2: Given examples of what IDs in lexicogrammar are). The following questions can be raised for this part:

1. Do you believe L2 learners differ in their linguistic knowledge? How?
2. What about L1 learners? Do you think there are differences? How?
3. Give examples of IDs in lexicogrammatical knowledge from your life (either L1 or L2).
4. Why do you think IDs are important for our NS/NNS dichotomy discussion?

Then, in a short task on an interactive platform (e.g., PollEverywhere), the lecturer asks the TCs if they are aware of any teaching methodology that accommodates such IDs in both L1/L2 learning (achieves objective #3: Discussed how linguistics and teaching methodologies have accommodated IDs). This further sets the scene for a destabilizing of the fallacy. During the lecture, the lecturer presents linguistic discussions of on what grounds linguists proposed NS fallacy and how it does not hold up well against experimental evidence (see Dąbrowska 2016: 70–103 for a discussion of the experimental evidence). The content of the lecture should allow for a discussion of the implications of this line of research to achieve objective #4 (Discussed the implications of usage-based studies and IDs studies by answering at least three questions during the lecture). Possible questions to ask overlap with the ones at the end of the next paragraph.

This is where the destabilizing of the fallacy begins by showing NNESTs that they can also perform at the level of or at times outperform NSs. The TCs are asked to share their personal accounts of experiencing the dichotomy as a TC and how they reacted to it (achieves objective #5: Shared personal stories having experienced the dichotomy). This part of the lecture also includes how culture or socioeconomic status, which has been reported to be tied to ethnicity (e.g., Cross 2018), may play a role in deepening the fallacy by raising the following questions: With so much variation within NSs we need to reflect on: which group do we pick to represent NSs? Are they highly literate speakers? Do they need to come from a certain background (i.e., racial, socioeconomic)? Does the term NS represent all the linguistic and sociocultural variation within NS communities? Or do we pick a certain group as linguists and ignore the consequences of this action? How does basing our discussions in SLA on a monolithic understanding of NS affect L2 speaking communities in the periphery? Does it have oppressionist, colonial, or racist implications? How does this inform our teaching training programs and methodologies? Where do we go from here in teacher training programs?

Such critical questioning will potentially show the TCs that (a) NS fallacy has serious implications that teacher training programs may not discuss, and (b) this fallacy is an idealized illusion that is based on nonempirical claims (e.g., Bley-Vroman 2009). By doing this, the TCs will also realize that being an NNEST does not indicate linguistic subordination by NSs, and brings to the table that race, socioeconomic status, and potentially colonialism are bundled together and result in NS fallacy and its adverse effects (see Gedik and Arpaözü 2022 for a discussion). The performance task has two alternatives, either an in-class debate or a response essay if there is no time. In the debate, the TCs are asked why or why not the dichotomy should be kept and are asked to provide both linguistic and nonlinguistic evidence for their arguments. Similarly, the response essay is the same task but in written format (achieves objective #6: Debated the NS/NNS dichotomy in two groups (for/against) by using linguistic and other extra-linguistic evidence).

Critical Reflections: Potentials and Challenges

Deconstructing the term NS does not deny that a group of people speak a language "natively." What I suggest is the use of L1, L2 … or Lx instead of the term "native speaker," in which L# only suggests the developmental sequence of the learned languages.

Unless the critical questions in this chapter (among many others) are acknowledged in our (applied) linguistics programs, we may be one of the factors powering the dichotomy and its concomitant adverse implications. Thus, our discussions in teacher training programs should acknowledge the importance of these questions and the destabilization of NS fallacy based on both linguistic and nonlinguistic evidence against the convergence hypothesis.

Based on teaching why the term NS is problematic in a psycholinguistics course in Türkiye, I expect TCs and possibly teacher trainers will find this quite shocking. Most of the reactions revolved around struggling to accept that NSs were far from reaching an idealized NS point. The most difficult part to accept was the deterministic nature of the socioeconomic status of a family or person can determine how close this person will be placed to the norm of NS. Some students resisted on the basis of believing that there must be a difference between NSs/NNSs. After all, deconstruction of conventional wisdom is always difficult to accept at first. However, I believe it is this shock value that will empower NNESTCs in reconfiguring their status in the world of ELT as transformative. While the field of ELT in Türkiye has not embraced a critical perspective, in my experience, students are eager to discuss the relevance of critical implications of the fallacy when given the chance. I suggest using anecdotes or real-life examples which explain personal accounts of how this fallacy affects NNEST(s)Cs may be of help in operationalizing the adverse effects of the fallacy on people. A challenge is that this lesson plan is only designed for a single event. As such, it may not be enough to help TCs reconfigure this conventional wisdom and the dichotomies it creates in ELT. A suggestion is using this lesson plan as a springboard to organize events and getting TCs involved to investigate the effects of this fallacy in other subfields of teacher training programs (e.g., material creation, language testing). That way, this deconstruction and its subsequent potential empowerment of TCs may become more realistic. Another challenge is getting familiar with the relevant linguistic literature for educators and TCs, for which I suggest Dąbrowska (2015, 2019), who provides to the point examples of the relevant literature.

References

Aneja, Geeta A. (2016), "(Non)Native Speakered: Rethinking (Non)Nativeness and Teacher Identity in TESOL Teacher Education", *TESOL Quarterly*, 50 (3): 572–96. doi:10.1002/tesq.315.

Bley-Vroman, Robert (2009), "The Evolving Context of the Fundamental Difference Hypothesis", *Studies in Second Language Acquisition*, 31 (2): 175–98. doi:10.1017/S0272263109090275.

Bonfiglio, Thomas Paul (2013), "Inventing the Native Speaker", *Critical Multilingualism Studies*, 1 (2): 29–58.

Chomsky, Noam (1975), *Reflections on Language*, London: Temple Smith London.

Cross, Christina J. (2018) "Extended Family Households among Children in the United States: Differences by Race/Ethnicity and Socio-Economic Status", *Population Studies*, 72 (2): 235–51.

Dąbrowska, Ewa (2015), "Individual Differences in Grammatical Knowledge", in E. Dąbrowska and D. Divjak (eds). *Handbook of Cognitive Linguistics*, 650–68, Berlin/Boston: De Gruyter Mouton.

Dąbrowska, Ewa (2016), "Cognitive Linguistics' Seven Deadly Sins", *Cognitive Linguistics*, 27 (4): 479–91.

Dąbrowska, Ewa (2018), "Experience, Aptitude and Individual Differences in Native Language Ultimate Attainment", *Cognition*, 178 (September): 222–35. doi:10.1016/j.cognition.2018.05.018.

Dąbrowska, Ewa (2019), "Experience, Aptitude, and Individual Differences in Linguistic Attainment: A Comparison of Native and Nonnative Speakers: Experience, Aptitude, and Individual Differences", *Language Learning*, 69 (March): 72–100. doi:10.1111/lang.12323.

Gedik, Tan Arda and Zeynep Arpaözü (2022), "Entangled Humans, Entangled Languages: A Citizen Sociolinguistic Analysis of COVID-19 on Reddit", in Başak Ağın and Şafak Horzum (eds), *Posthuman Pathogenesis*, 167–86, New York: Routledge.

Kidd, Evan, Seamus Donnelly and Morten H. Christiansen (2018), "Individual Differences in Language Acquisition and Processing", *Trends in Cognitive Sciences*, 22 (2): 154–69. doi:10.1016/j.tics.2017.11.006.

Mahboob, Ahmar (2005), "Beyond the Native Speaker in TESOL", *Culture, Context, & Communication*, 30: 60–93.

Phillipson, Robert (1992), "ELT: The Native Speaker's Burden?", *ELT Journal*, 46 (1): 12–8.

Roland, Douglas, Frederic Dick and Jeffrey L. Elman (2007), "Frequency of Basic English Grammatical Structures: A Corpus Analysis", *Journal of Memory and Language*, 57 (3): 348–79. doi:10.1016/j.jml.2007.03.002.

Selvi, Ali Fuad (2014), "Myths and Misconceptions about Nonnative English Speakers in the TESOL (NNEST) Movement", *TESOL Journal*, 5 (3): 573–611. doi:10.1002/tesj.158.

Selvi, Ali Fuad (2018), "Myths and Misconceptions about the NNEST Movement and Research", in John I. Liontas, Tesol International Association and Margo DelliCarpini (eds), *The TESOL Encyclopedia of English Language Teaching*, 1–8, Hoboken, NJ: John Wiley & Sons, Inc. doi:10.1002/9781118784235.eelt0811.

Sparks, Richard L. (2022), "Exploring L1–L2 Relationships: The Impact of Individual Differences". Vol. 155. Bristol: Channel View Publications.

Street, James A and Ewa Dąbrowska (2010), "More Individual Differences in Language Attainment: How Much Do Adult Native Speakers of English Know about Passives and Quantifiers?", *Lingua*, 120 (8): 2080–94.

Appendix

The lesson plan is accessible as a separate document at https://docs.google.com/document/d/1MEoqIjqwgcUK6s7Ay9jIH272dX6M4wgH3Ykwj3hh28Q/edit?usp=sharing.

Part Eight

Teaching Young Language Learners

Teaching English to Young Learners: Critical, Multilingual, and Decolonial Pedagogies

Mario E. López-Gopar, Verónica Rivera Hernández, and Yesenia Bautista Ortiz

Introduction

Teaching English to young learners (TEYL) has been discussed, researched, and theorized for a few decades now. Responding to recent waves of migration into English-speaking countries (e.g., Canada and England) and new educational policies around the world that connect the spread of English and its inclusion into public elementary school curricula with alleged "progress" and "development," different researchers and teacher educators have developed new theories, with the goal of creating more inclusive and multilingual classrooms. The purpose of this chapter is to discuss current issues involving the TEYL, as well as theories including critical, multilingual, and decolonial pedagogies in connection to teacher education. Before addressing these theories, the chapter first discusses three current issues around TEYL across the globe.

Current Issues in Teaching English to Children

Teacher education programs should make pre-service teachers aware of three major issues concerning TEYL: (1) the rapid and neoliberal spread of ELT throughout public elementary schools, (2) the juxtaposition of English with othered languages, and (3) the inclusion of Western ideologies within English textbooks and didactic materials.

The Neoliberal Spread of TEYL in Public Schools

The first issue, regarding the proliferation of ELT in public elementary schools, has been questioned by different researchers. Governments across the globe, along with parents, have adopted neoliberal discourses that allegedly connect English with development, "better" life opportunities, economic success, and modernity (Pennycook 2006). Analyzing educational policies that stipulate the "benefits" of bringing English into public elementary schools around the world, Sayer (2015) has identified multiple neoliberal discourses of economic development, such as the "national development and modernization" of China, the "economic development" of Malaysia, the "internationalization of the Chilean Economy," and the enhancement of "Vietnam's competitive position in the international economic and political arena" (50). Nonetheless, these neoliberal discourses have been problematized. For instance, it has been argued that English has exclusionary effects in most so-called developing countries, such as Mexico (López-Gopar and Sughrua 2014), India (Mohanty 2006), and Indonesia (Lamb 2011). In these countries, it is mostly the upper socioeconomic classes who have more access to English education in costly, well-resourced, and underpopulated private elementary schools or language institutes, in contrast to the lower socioeconomic classes who usually attend free or low-cost, under-resourced, and overpopulated public elementary schools (López-Gopar 2016).

The Juxtaposition of English with Othered Languages

The second major issue, which is the troublesome distinction between English as a "modern" language vis-à-vis othered Indigenous and/or minoritized languages, speaks to social class inequities. Promoting English as the preferable additional language to learn in public elementary schools has resulted in the exclusion of Indigenous and/or minoritized local languages. As a result, the English language, along with its "people," is portrayed as superior, whereas Indigenous and minoritized languages are considered inferior and not worthy to be included in elementary school curricula. This phenomenon has occurred in different Latin American, Asian, and African countries (de Mejía 2011; López-Gopar 2016; Rahman 2010). In the same vein and in terms of social class, it has been argued that minoritized groups suffer "the sinister exclusion of mother tongues," in juxtaposition to the elite groups, which "enjoy the pre-eminence of dominant languages, such as English" (Mohanty 2006: 5). In Colombia, de Mejía (2011) has pointed out that the connection between English and social class has produced elite bilingualism (English/Spanish), which is usually attained by the elite groups who can afford private bilingual schools. She states that other forms of bilingualism (Spanish/Indigenous languages or creoles) are "undervalued and associated with underdevelopment, poverty and backwardness" (7–8).

Western Ideologies in the TEYL Curricula and Instructional Materials

The third major issue involves the ELT curricula, which in most cases are represented by textbooks and materials. These usually are produced by European and North American companies and include ideologies that represent English-speaking countries as the role models to be followed by the rest of the world (Gray 2016). The inclusion of these ideologies results in other cultures being portrayed as inferior vis-à-vis the alleged "modern and desirable behaviour" of Western cultures (McKay and Bokhosrt-Heng 2008: 184). Other researchers have argued that many of these textbooks and materials include racist and classist discourses present in Western societies (Chun 2016; López-Gopar et al. 2009). Most problematic is that English textbooks present a fake, decontextualized reality than the one experienced by children from around the world. For instance, the textbooks typically depict a nuclear family having fun on holidays. This fake reality automatically excludes and/or invisibilizes the children's own reality along with their ways of knowing and being. In order to counteract English's superiority along with the three issues discussed in this section, different theories have been proposed to teach English to young children from a critical, multilingual, and decolonial perspective. In the next section, some of the theories that I consider important for teacher education to include in their language teaching preparation programs are presented.

Theories and Implications for Teaching and Teacher Education

During the last four decades, different theories have emerged to address the teaching of English to young learners, focusing on the knowledge base of their teachers and on teaching strategies. In the 1990s, it was argued that teachers needed the language and competence in primary teaching methodology, as most English teachers were not prepared to deal with young learners (Brumfit 1991). Furthermore, other researchers stressed the importance of patience along with pedagogical preparation to create routines and appropriate learning environments as valued characteristics that teachers of young learners should develop or possess (Scott and Ytreberg 1998; Vale and Feunteun 1995). In the beginning of the twenty-first century, Cameron (2003) identified three major attributes teachers of young children needed: "(a) an understanding of how children think and learn; (b) skills and knowledge in spoken English to conduct whole lessons orally, and to pick up children's interests and use them for language teaching; and (c) to be equipped to teach initial literacy in English" (111). In terms of teaching strategies, other researchers recommended the use of children's literature (Ashworth and Wakefield 2004; Ghosn 2002) and the inclusion of music and games (Khan 1991; Reilly and Ward 1997; Rixon 1991). Even though these theories were important, they focused on "how" to teach English to children, rather than "why" to do so; consequently, they did not address the three issues presented in the previous section.

As previously discussed, learning English has been seen as a "good thing" or a prerequisite to progress, development, and economic success. In the mid-1980s, researchers, such as Auerbach (1986), began to challenge this belief by arguing that English language teachers were not neutrally helping people to communicate; rather, they were maintaining the status quo (e.g., teaching immigrants in the United States how to follow orders in low-paying jobs). Later on, other researchers continued to question the so-called neutrality or modernist ideologies behind the teaching of English (Canagarajah 1999; Crookes and Lehner 1998; Pennycook 2006). Following the work of Paulo Freire, Norton and Toohey (2004) called for the development of critical pedagogies and language learning in order to address the multiple, problematic issues surrounding the teaching of languages in general and English in particular. They stressed the plurality of critical pedagogies as there should not be a single critical language pedagogy because every language educator should develop their own critical pedagogy according to their context and students.

Focusing on the education of young children, critical pedagogues have attempted "to create an equitable educational system and model where all classes, ethnicities, sexual orientations, nationalities, languages, and voices are included" (Christensen and Aldridge 2013: 5). The work of Cummins (1986) with minority children has been rather influential. By analyzing why minority groups had struggled in schools, Cummins (2001) points out that the work of critical pedagogy should focus on the relationships between educators, children, and the children's families. The purpose of establishing collaborative relations of power with the children and their families, Cummins argued, was to challenge deficit perspectives in terms of children's cultural and linguistic background. These relationships also aimed to value the linguistic background of children, by going against the notion of "English-only" classrooms and by incorporating children's minoritized languages into the classroom, which resulted in viewing children as bilingual and/or multilingual (Cummins 2001).

Following this bi/multilingual perspective, the concept of multilingual pedagogies was developed by García with Flores (2012). They state that multilingual pedagogies have two essential principles: "(1) attention to social justice; and (2) attention to social practice" (242). The first principle is important since people are socially situated in different ways. Connecting multilingual pedagogies to critical pedagogies, García and Flores (2012) state, "multilingual pedagogies should always be 'critical' in the sense that they should aim to develop students' critical consciousness in order to transform the conditions that perpetuate human injustice and inequity" (242). Trying to achieve social justice in multilingual pedagogies involves the following:

> Providing equity for the students, their languages, their cultures and their communities. ... Building on the students' linguistic and cultural strengths and developing students' multilingual awareness and tolerance .... Having high expectations and promoting academic rigor .... [and] Becoming advocates of children ... and supporting valid assessments.
>
> (García and Flores 2012: 242, in part referring to Cummins 1986; 2000)

In terms of the second principle that deals with social practice, multilingual pedagogies rely on collaborative social practices while socially constructing language learning. As such, this principle requires the following: "Supporting quality interactions .... Focusing on the practice of disciplinary and academic language .... Building collaborative grouping and cooperative learning .... [and] Focusing on high relevance of lessons and students' maximum identity investment" (García and Flores 2012: 243). Hence, teacher educators must stress the fact that TEYL should go hand in hand with fostering critical multilingual practices that might result in more equitable social relationships.

As previously stated, learning English at a young age goes along with literacy development. Cummins (2001) proposes three important components of language and literacy development in young learners: (1) cognitive processing, (2) language processing, and (3) identity investment. The cognitive-processing component emphasizes the role of background knowledge, its integration with new knowledge, and the metacognitive awareness of the learning process. Failure to tap students' background knowledge and to help students make connections and be metacognitively aware may impact negatively on students' cognitive engagement, language development, and identity investment. Regarding language processing, Cummins (2001) argues that in order for students to develop language and use it critically to fulfill their own purposes, challenge coercive power relations, and negotiate affirming identities, teachers and students must focus on language meaning, language awareness, and language use (see Cummins, 2001, for a more detailed explanation). While Cummins (2001) recognizes that comprehensible input is necessary in language development, critical literacy is a must. Along similar lines, Delpit (1988) argues that critical literacy is essential if students are to unveil how language intersects with power. Regarding identity investment, various researchers have argued that the negotiation of identities is usually forgotten in the educational equation even though it has been widely proven to be an essential factor (Cummins 2001; Denos et al. 2009; McCarty 2002; Norton 2000). They have also pointed out that children and families exert their agency in discursive practices to construct affirming identities or reject imposed identities that position them in certain ways (e.g., being an ESL student, a so-called non-native speaker in need of fixing, or a student who does not meet school expectations). For affirming identities to be established, both teachers and students must recognize each other's affirming identities.

One of the ways students feel that their talents and identities are valued, respected, and affirmed in classrooms is by creating their own texts that reveal their life stories. It is through these "identity texts," which can be written, visual, multimodal, signed or spoken, that students become protagonists, representing and reflecting their identities back to themselves and to a wider audience (Cummins 2004). (For examples of such texts created by both teachers and students, which reflect the struggles, emotions, and dreams of their authors, see Ada and Campoy 2004.) Connecting the notion of affirming identities and the creation of texts to decolonizing theories, López-Gopar (2016) has argued that the primary English language classroom should be regarded "as a space in which all the actors' identities ... are renegotiated in order to value the different ways of being, speaking and knowing ... and to transgress the inferiority imposed by coloniality" (10). Decolonizing texts created by the children should use English in favor of othered languages and their speakers. Furthermore, López-Gopar (2016) has argued that English should go beyond modernist ideologies and problematize the so-called neutral contents and strategies of the language classroom while addressing important and real issues faced by children and families. In decolonizing English-language classrooms, both children and their families are authors of texts and their own histories within their bilingual and multilingual worlds.

Teacher Education Programs and TEYL

Teacher education programs should adopt a critical, decolonial, and multilingual stance should they wish to engage pre-service and in-service teachers in critical approaches in TEYL. Their stance should also be political while acknowledging that most children learning English live in unjust societies where their language, ways of knowing and being have been excluded. Education programs should prepare pre-service teachers to appreciate and foster their multilingual practices. Teacher education programs should be guided by social justice principles through the development of critical awareness about the historical, economic, and social injustices faced by most children around the world. This critical awareness should be the basis to develop critical and decolonial pedagogies whose goal should be the transformation of human injustices and the reaffirmation of children's identities.

As argued in this chapter, the language classroom represents a place where teachers can either continue with this historical exclusion or carve out spaces for children's languages and cultures to flourish. The latter, which is the goal of a critical, multilingual, and decolonial perspective, is certainly not an easy task since most teachers are encouraged to follow monolingual and assimilation-oriented mandates or ideologies. Nonetheless, teachers have the power to challenge these by learning from their students and their families. Finally, it is important to emphasize that teachers must develop their very own critical, multilingual, and decolonial pedagogy according to their contexts and their and their children's material lives.

References

Ada, A. F. and I. Campoy (2004), *Authors in the Classroom: A Transformative Education Process*, London: Pearson.

Ashworth, M. and H. P. Wakefield (2004), *Teaching the World's Children: ESL for Ages Three to Seven*, Toronto: Pippin Publishing Company.

Auerbach, E. (1986), "Competency-Based ESL: One Step Forward or Two Steps Back?", *TESOL Quarterly*, 20 (3): 411–29.

Brumfit, C. (1991), "Introduction: Teaching English to Children", in C. Brumfit, J. Moon and R. Tongue (eds), *Teaching English to Children*, iv–viii, London: Collins ELT.

Cameron, L. (2003), "Challenges for ELT from the Expansion in Teaching Children", *ELT Journal*, 57 (2): 105–13.

Canagarajah, S. (1999), *Resisting Linguistic Imperialism in English Teaching*, Oxford: Oxford University Press.

Christensen, L. M. and J. Aldridge (2013), *Critical Pedagogy for Early Childhood and Elementary Educators*, New York: Springer.

Chun, C. (2016), "Addressing Racialized Multicultural Discourses in an EAP Textbook: Working toward a Critical Pedagogies Approach", *TESOL Quarterly*, 50 (1): 109–31.

Crookes, G. and A. Lehner (1998), "Aspects of Process in an ESL Critical Pedagogy Teacher Education Course", *TESOL Quarterly*, 32 (2): 319–28.

Cummins, J. (1986), "Empowering Minority Students: A Framework for Intervention", *Harvard Educational Review*, 56 (1): 18–36.

Cummins, J. (2000), *Language, Power and Pedagogy: Bilingual Children in the Crossfire*, Clevendon: Multilingual Matters.

Cummins, J. (2001), *Negotiating Identities: Education for Empowerment in a Diverse Society*, 2nd edn, Walnut, CA: California Association for Bilingual Education.

Cummins, J. (2004), "Multiliteracies Pedagogy and the Role of Identity Texts", in K. Leithwood, P. McAdie, N. Bascia and A. Rodigue (eds), *Teaching for Deep Understanding: Towards the Ontario Curriculum That We Need*, 68–74,

Toronto: Ontario Institute for Studies in Education of the University of Toronto and the Elementary Federation of Teachers of Ontario.

de Mejía, A. M. (2011), "The National Bilingual Programme in Colombia: Imposition or Opportunity?", *Apples—Journal of Applied Language Studies*, 5 (3): 7–17.

Delpit, L. D. (1988), "The Silenced Dialogue: Power and Pedagogy in Educating Other People's Children", *Harvard Educational Review*, 58: 280–98.

Denos, C., K. Toohey, K. Neilson and B. Waterstone (2009), *Collaborative Research in Multilingual Classrooms*, Clevendon: Multilingual Matters.

García, O. and N. Flores (2012), "Multilingual Pedagogies", in M. Martin-Jones, A. Blackledge and A. Creese (eds), *The Routledge Handbook of Multilingualism*, 232–46, London and New York: Routledge.

Ghosn, I. K. (2002), "Four Good Reasons to Use Literature in Primary School ELT", *ELT Journal*, 56 (2): 172–9.

Gray, J. (2016), "ELT Materials", in G. Hall (ed.), *The Routledge Handbook of English Language Teaching*, 95–108, London and New York: Routledge.

Khan, J. (1991), "Using Games in Teaching English to Young Learners", in C. Brumfit, J. Moon and R. Tongue (eds), *Teaching English to Children*, 142–57, London: Collins ELT.

Lamb, M. (2011), "A 'Matthew Effect' in English Language Education in the Developing World", in H. Coleman (ed.), *Dreams and Realities: Developing Countries and the English Language*, 186–206, London: British Council.

López Gopar, M. (2016), *Decolonizing Primary English Language Teaching*, Clevendon: Multilingual Matters.

López-Gopar, M. E. and W. Sughrua (2014), "Social Class in English Language Education in Oaxaca, Mexico", *Journal of Language, Identity and Education*, 13: 104–10.

López-Gopar, M. E., O. Núñez Méndez, L. Montes Medina and M. Cantera Martínez (2009), "Inglés Enciclomedia: A Ground-Breaking Program for Young Mexican Children?", *Mextesol Journal*, 33 (1): 67–86.

McCarty, T. (2002), *A Place to be Navajo: Rough Rock and the Struggle for Self-Determination in Indigenous Schooling*, Mahwah, NJ: Lawrence Erlbaum Associates.

McKay, S. L. and W. D. Bokhorst-Heng (2008), *International English in its Sociolinguistic Contexts*, New York: Routledge.

Mohanty, A. (2006), "Multilingualism of the Unequals and Predicaments of Education in India: Mother Tongue or Other Tongue?", in O. García, T. Skutnabb-Kangas and M. E. Torres Guzmán (eds), *Imagining Multilingual Schools*, 262–83, Clevendon: Multilingual Matters.

Norton, B. (2000), *Identity and Language Learning: Gender, Ethnicity and Educational Change*, Harlow: Longman/Pearson Education.

Norton, B. and K. Toohey (eds) (2004), *Critical Pedagogies and Language Learning*, Cambridge: Cambridge University Press.

Pennycook, A. (2006), "The Myth of English as an International Language", in S. Makoni and A. Pennycook (eds), *Disinventing and Reconstituting Languages*, 90–115, Clevendon: Multilingual Matters.

Rahman, T. (2010). "A Multilingual Language-in-Education Policy for Indigenous Minorities in Bangladesh: Challenges and Possibilities", *Current Issues in Language Planning*, 11 (4): 341–59.

Reilly, V. and S. Ward (1997), *Very Young Learners*, Oxford: Oxford University Press.

Rixon, S. (1991), "The Role of Fun and Games Activities in Teaching Young Learners", in C. Brumfit, J. Moon and R. Tongue (eds), *Teaching English to Children*, 18–32, London: Collins ELT.

Sayer, P. (2015). "'More & Earlier': Neoliberalism and Primary English Education in Mexican Public Schools", *L2 Journal*, 7 (3): 40–56.

Scott, W. and L. Ytreberg (1998), *Teaching English to Children*, London: Longman.

Vale, D. and A. Feunteun (1995), *Teaching Children English*, Cambridge: Cambridge University Press.

Suggested Readings and External Links

- Cummins, J. (2021), *Rethinking the Education of Multilingual Learners*, Clevendon: Multilingual Matters. Excellent book that summarizes and discusses Jim Cummins's theories.
- García, O. and J. A. Kleifgen (2018), *Educating Emergent Bilinguals*, New York: Teachers College Press. Excellent practical resource for teachers and administrators about the education of emergent bilinguals.
- The Multiliteracy Project website provides multiple examples of identity texts created by children across Canada. http://www.multiliteracies.ca/.
- The Rethinking Schools website is a great resource that includes articles and books that aim at social justice and education activism. https://rethinkingschools.org/.

Sustainability and Primary Teacher Education in a Swedish Context: From Concept Mapping to Experience Designing

Mai Trang Vu

Background

In contemporary Sweden, within the international discourses of sustainability in response to the climate crises, Education for Sustainable Development (ESD) has been promoted by the government as an integral element of school education (Swedish National Agency for Education/Skolverket 2022) and higher education (Swedish Higher Education Authority UKÄ 2016). However, as found in many countries, the interpretation of ESD in education practices appears vaguely elaborated (UNESCO 2021).

I started working with ESD in Teaching English to young learners (TEYL) Teacher Education after taking a Continuing Professional Development course on ESD. TEYL is part of the four-year Primary Teacher Education Program of 240 credits. On completing a graduation thesis, student teachers are granted master's degree in Primary Education and become teachers for learners grades 4–6 (ages 10–12).

This chapter discusses how ESD was incorporated into the Module *The Language Learner and The Language Teacher* of the TEYL through experiential learning and drama-based instruction. Incorporating ESD into my teaching was also informed by my perspective of English language teaching (ELT) as going beyond being "code-centered, structuralist" to encouraging learners' critical thinking and enabling them to be engaged in social justice (Kramsch 2020). ESD empowers individuals to make responsible decisions and become sustainability citizens, which resonates with this critical view of ELT.

Description of the Practice

The module *The Language Learner and The Language Teacher* is a TEYL methodology course. It was built with the viewpoint seeing ELT professionalism as an amalgam of specialized knowledge and skills with an emphasis on teacher agency (Vu

2016). The module promotes inquiry-based learning, active learning, collaborative learning, and critical-thinking (Vu and Sandström 2019). Its topics include teacher identities, teaching design and delivery, and reflective teaching. The module has various learning and examination forms: lectures, seminars, groupwork, microteaching lab work, role-play, peer observation and feedback, and self-reflection. The ESD integration was conducted based on Backward Design (Wiggins and McTighe 2005)—setting the goals, determining evidence of learning, and selecting teaching activities.

Curriculum Mapping

Curriculum mapping was conducted to identify integration goals. ESD is a framework to empower learners to maintain "environmental integrity, economic viability and a just society"—the three dimensions of the Sustainable Development Goals (UNESCO 2020: 8). ESD objectives fall into three domains: *cognitive*, learners' knowledge and thinking skills to understand the global goals; *socio-emotional*, learners' social skills to collaborate, self-reflect, and self-develop; and *behavioral*, learners' capability to act. ESD organization follows a content/theme-based design, competency-based planning, and suitable pedagogical approaches.

- Key themes (biosphere, society, economy): e.g., climate change, sustainable production and consumption, poverty reduction, social justice.
- Key competencies: systems thinking, anticipatory competency, normative competency, strategic competency, collaborative competency, critical thinking, self-awareness, and problem-solving.
- Pedagogical approaches: learner-centered approach, action-oriented learning, and transformative education.

The curriculum mapping suggested that the module already possesses ESD characteristics. With its existing contents and teaching approaches (described above), the module encourages learner-centered approaches, strategic competency, collaborative competency, critical thinking, self-awareness, and problem-solving. Regarding subject contents, when starting this module, student teachers will have been familiar with concepts including multilingualism and inclusive education (Society dimension) from Module Second Language Acquisition Theories students had earlier. They will have also worked with interactivity and collaborative learning for young learners, individual differences, and learner agency in language acquisition. Thus, the ESD integration can be built on what exists, especially regarding Key competencies and Pedagogical approaches. Key themes, however, can be expanded to topics more pronouncedly connected with biosphere, society, and economy. Meanwhile, the merge between ESD and TEYL needs to stay within the module's scope (including core contents and credits number). Also, the integration needs to benefit both student-teachers and their future English language young learners.

Aim/Goals and Evidence of Learning

The aim of the integration, thus, was identified as four interrelated goals:
(1) Student teachers will expand knowledge and skills related to ESD themes and competences.
(2) They will relate ESD themes and competences to TEYL contents.
(3) Their evidence of learning is demonstrated in all three domains: cognitive, socio-emotional, and behavioral. Student teachers understand ESD and engage with materials via discussions, evaluate and reflect through experiential learning, and apply and act by creating a product (teaching design, reflective report).
(4) The integration follows learner-centered approaches, and aims for action-oriented learning and transformative education.

Teaching and Learning Activities

With these considerations, Drama-based Language Teaching was selected for the integration. Drama-based teaching is an effective method for TEYL (e.g. Bland 2015). The method facilitates holistic language development (Bland 2015). Indeed, learners interact and negotiate for meaning within a context—through which their language develops, while practicing collaborating, empathizing, and multi-sensory learning. Learners also develop critical thinking when taking on perspectives of others. That drama-based activities often have a storyline allows ESD topics to be integrated smoothly. Combining TEYL drama-based teaching and ESD, thus, helps achieve goal (2).

Drama-Based teaching also enables goals (1), (3), (4) to be reached. Within drama-based teaching, role-play was chosen. Role-play is used in higher education as a problem-based learning tool to develop an integrated knowledge foundation, reasoning and problem-solving skills, professional practice skills, and intrinsic motivation (Korin and Wilkerson 2011). Reflective dimensions were added, following experiential learning (Kolb 1984), where concrete experience interacts with conceptual contents and reflections to create new knowledge.

The teaching of this content had originally been a traditional reading seminar with discussions and tasks. With the ESD integration (Appendix 1), student teachers were now asked to focus on environment and design a drama-based activity for young learners (Question 1, Appendix). Videos on these topics were included to raise student teachers' own awareness and provide them with background knowledge (cognitive domain). The videos were also an inspiration and/or materials for student-teachers to design their teaching (behavioral domain). Particular videos (those by Conservation International—Appendix) were selected with an intention to enhance student teachers' own experiences with ESD (socio-emotional domain, and also behavioral domain). The videos are role-play/dramatized themselves—narrated by famous persons playing the roles of Mother Nature, The Wave, Flower, using I, talking to human beings from Nature's viewpoint. The videos, with their strong messages, are quite emotion inducing.

After designing a drama-activity based on theoretical input (the reading), student-teachers were asked to act out, as young learners, their own activity (Question 2, Appendix). This stimulation provides student teachers with another experiential learning opportunity where theories become more concrete (Kolb 1984): student-teachers experience drama-based teaching first-hand. Simultaneously, the act-out allows student teachers to employ young learners' perspectives. This input informs student teachers' analysis later when they put on teacher reflexive lens (Farrell and Jacobs 2020), reflecting on and learning from their own practices (Question 3, Appendix). While part (a) of the question requires student teachers to critically contextualize and apply theories, part (b) facilitates the next level of conceptualization through experimenting and reflecting, thus creating new knowledge (Kolb 1984). Experiencing the design from young learners' perspectives helps student teachers better understand and empathize with their future pupils, while questioning their own beliefs—all can be used to adjust their teaching design. This activity also reinforces student teachers' understanding of learner-centered approach.

Critical Reflections: Potentials and Challenges

Student teachers' evidence of learning (activity design, act-out, analytical reflections) indicates that student teachers were able to design an age-appropriate, interactive drama-based activity with ESD elements (environment/ecology) based on theory. Student teachers could discuss how the activity may benefit their future learners (language development), but also how the assignment itself was educational for themselves (communicating in English in a fun, engaging setting, taking on others' perspectives). Not all groups explicitly emphasized the ESD contents in their reflections, but all expressed that their drama-activity was relevant to young learners, and some groups articulated that ESD should be addressed at school. All groups were able to critically review their design and identify possible adjustments, using insights from the act-out experience.

From the instructor's perspective, two main observations were drawn. When integrating ESD into TEYL, but also into a subject area in general, for a systematic incorporation, rather than a one-off event, changes at the syllabus level, besides the lecture/seminar level, could be considered. The curriculum mapping of this process helped deconstruct ESD and identify common areas and also distinctions between ESD and the subject matter, which in turn assisted the instructor to select the most suitable components for optimal integration (in this case drama-based teaching and experiential learning, but they could be any other suitable contents). Building on what already exists also helped ESD become accessible, rather than completely foreign, so that student teachers are more confident and motivated to use it in their future work. Second, student teachers need more structured input on ESD. Although this ESD incorporation has proved to have achieved its goals, the teaching of ESD on this module remained implicit. ESD principles could be introduced to student-teachers explicitly to minimize the risk of them viewing ESD simply as only including "environment" content. To become independent teachers, student teachers need to understand the pedagogical foundation behind the practices. Aiming for an explicit introduction of ESD could, therefore, be considered in a follow-up course of the program.

References

Bland, J. (2015) (ed.), *Teaching English to Young Learners: Critical Issues in Language Teaching with 3–12 Year Olds*, London: Bloomsbury.
Farrell, T. S. and G. M. Jacobs (2020), *Essentials for Successful English Language Teaching*, London: Bloomsbury.
Kolb, D. A. (1984), *Experiential Learning: Experience as the Source of Learning and Development*, New Jersey: Prentice Hall.
Korin, T. L. and L. Wilkerson (2011), "Bringing Problems to Life Using Videos, Compare/Contrast, and Role-Play", in T. Barrett and S. Moore (eds), *New Approaches to Problem-Based Learning*, 75–86, New York: Routledge.
Kramsch, C. (2020), *Language as Symbolic Power*, Cambridge: Cambridge University Press.
Swedish Higher Education Authority/UKÄ (2016), Vägledning för tematisk utvärdering av hållbar utveckling. [Roadmap for thematic evaluation on sustainable development].
Swedish National Agency for Education/Skolverket (2022), Utbildning viktigt för att nå målen för hållbar utveckling. [Education essential to reach Sustainable Development Goals].
UNESCO (2020), Education for Sustainable Development: A Roadmap. UNESCO.
UNESCO (2021), Getting Every School Climate-Ready: How Countries Are Integrating Climate Change Issues in Education, UNESCO.
Vu, M. T. (2016), "The Kaleidoscope of English Language Teacher Professionalism: A Review Analysis of Traits, Values, and Political Dimensions," *Critical Inquiry in Language Studies*, 13(2): 132–56.
Vu, M. T. and K. Sandström (2019), From a Swedish perspective: Theory + Research + Policy + Practical wisdom + Teacher education = ?, European Conference on Educational Research (ECER) 2019: European Educational Research Association.
Wiggins, G. and J. McTighe (2005), *Understanding by Design*, Alexandria, VA: ASCD.

Appendix

Drama-Based English Language Teaching

Pre-reading
Bland, J. (2015), "Drama with Young Learners", in J. Bland (2015) (ed.), *Teaching English to Young Learners: Critical Issues in Language Teaching with 3–12 Year Olds*. London: Bloomsbury, pp.219–238.

Questions

1. In your group, design one drama-based activity, scripted or unscripted (Bland 2015). Watch the videos for more input.
   Theme: Environmental protection
   Learners: Grade 4–5–6?
   Activity objectives:
   Activity duration:
Describe briefly the activity: Steps + material (multimodal)
2. Act out your drama-based activity (pretending that you are learners of grades 4–6). The purpose of this act-out is for you to experience drama-based teaching and learning, while reflecting on your activity.
3. Then using Bland (2015), write a report (1.5 pages):
(a) How does your activity reflect some characteristics of drama-based (English) teaching? How does the activity facilitate learners' English language development? How is the activity (and its contents) relevant to the L2 English language learners grades 4–6 in Sweden? You may also include some broader social contexts of English Language Teaching in Sweden.
(b) (After the act-out): How did the act-out go? What were your experiences trying the activity? Is there anything you would want to change/add in your design after the act-out to make it even easier for your learners to do the activity?

Videos

- Conservation International (2014). Nature is Speaking—Julia Roberts is Mother Nature. https://www.youtube.com/watch?v=WmVLcj-XKnM
- Conservation International (2021). Nature is Speaking—Jason Momoa is The Wave. https://www.youtube.com/watch?v=GpNeGuP-_Gc
- Conservation International (2014). Nature Is Speaking—Lupita Nyong'o is Flower. https://www.youtube.com/watch?v=0_OxI2JZex4
- WWF International (2018). Plastic Pollution. https://www.youtube.com/watch?v=IA9O9YUbQew
- BBC (2022). Greta Thunberg on how to tackle climate anxiety | The One Show—BBC. https://www.youtube.com/watch?v=pK_nBKtWyvk
- Smile and Learn—English (2020). How to take care of the environment. https://www.youtube.com/watch?v=X2YgM1Zw4_E

Working against the Monolingual Norms of Teaching English as a Foreign Language (TEFL) at the Primary School Level

Hanna Lämsä-Schmidt

Background

This chapter describes a pre-service teacher training seminar at the department of English Language Education in Germany. The seminar was offered for bachelor students of English as a Foreign Language (henceforth EFL) studying to become teachers at the primary school (grades 1–6). Student teachers have gained foundational knowledge of English language education for young learners before this seminar.

Language policies enforced in German schools remain largely monolingual, enforcing the majority language-only use, despite the increasing linguistic diversity (Gogolin 2008). In addition, the language policies of foreign language teaching add another monolingually oriented norm of English-only use (Kerr 2019). This double monolingualism norm (Jørgensen 2008) renders learners' existing knowledge of other languages invisible and unutilized. Considering the increasing number of children that speak a language other than the majority language at home, these policies create unequal language realities in the classroom that may hinder learning. If these monolingual norms remain unquestioned in pre-service teacher training, student teachers carry these monolingual norms further into their own teaching practice, depriving learners of their most important learning resource, their first language.

Learners' heterogeneity, including their linguistic diversity, is represented in its most diverse form at the primary school level in the German context. Furthermore, it is especially relevant to question monolingual norms at this level since at this young age children form their fundamental attitudes toward languages and language learning which they carry on to further learning (Falomir 2015). Fostering open-minded and positive attitudes toward foreign languages and cultures is a central part of the stated objectives of early EFL in Germany (Kultusministerkonferenz 2013).

With the view of schools as cultural arenas, a critical approach can be effective to question the predominant norms and practices and situate them in their historical and sociopolitical context (Pennycook 1990). It encourages teachers to critically reflect on their role in this arena where they possess considerable power and therefore offers a framework for preparing EFL teachers for the increasingly multilingual classroom reality.

Description of the Practice

The present pre-service teacher training seminar sets out to critically reflect on the monolingual norms of language learning and teaching. Moreover, the objective is to familiarize the pre-service teachers with the concepts of multilingualism and multilingual competence (Aronin 2018; Creese 2011; Grosjean 2010 used as readings in the seminar) and finally to plan a microteaching session implementing a multilingual approach.

The seminar begins with a pre-reflection and plenum discussion of the following questions:

1. Does bilingualism affect one's thinking and learning in a negative or a positive way? Why do you think so?
2. Would you consider yourself bilingual? Why (not)? How would you characterize a bilingual person, i.e., who is bilingual?

Own beliefs are then compared to the historical development of attitudes on how bilingualism affects intelligence and cognition (García 2009; Wei 2000, used as readings). This research-based reflection sets the foundations for taking a resource-perspective on multilingualism by questioning the widespread beliefs of detrimental effects of bilingualism. This discussion is then tied to practice by evaluating how one teacher's beliefs may affect the bilingual Tatyana's language learning journey (García 2009: 21–2) in order to raise awareness of the effects of teacher beliefs on children's learning.

The reflection of own language learning experiences and language competences is further supported by three activities: Student teachers draw their own language portrait (Krumm 2013, in Appendix, Part A), map their language learning development by drawing their language learning curve (as in Herdina and Jessner 2002: 124), and reflect on an inter-language comprehension process through an exercise from the Framework of Reference for Pluralistic Approaches (Candelier and Launey 2012; Candelier 2013). These critical reflection rounds dive deep into student teachers' own perception and use of languages as well as their language learning and comprehension processes. Essentially, the follow-up discussions call into question the monolingual nature of additional language learning and make the multilingual reality of these processes transparent. The creation of a language portrait then brings forth the individual emotional side of language learning and provides the first practical multilingual material to be used in an early EFL classroom.

Finally, considerable time is spent on student teachers becoming familiar with alternative, child-appropriate approaches that provide space for learners' multilingualism to be used as a resource when learning foreign languages. After a brief introduction to general guidelines on child-appropriate multilingual pedagogies (Appendix, Part B), in the combined form of presenting and microteaching (Wallace and Bau 2004), students familiarize themselves with one multilingual pedagogical approach and learn to implement it (García and Flores 2015). As appropriate for early EFL classroom, the selection of multilingual approaches lays the focus on receptive competences and interactive, learner-centered methods which require minimal knowledge of the included languages by the teacher. In pairs, student teachers create presentations and plan microteaching sessions for one of the following approaches and methods: A collaborative collection of a multilingual cityscape, more commonly known as linguistic landscapes (Roos and Nicholas 2019); co-storytelling of dual-language books by the teacher and a multilingual parent (Navqi et al. 2013); strategies of pedagogical "translanguaging to teach" (García and Wei 2014a; 2014b); multilingual language awareness strategies in early EFL classroom (as developed by Hopp et al. 2019). As student teachers become familiar with different approaches and discuss their implementation, the challenge of integrating the diversity of learners' languages which the teacher is commonly not familiar with becomes manageable.

Critical Reflections: Potentials and Challenges

Changing pre-service teachers' beliefs toward prevailing monolingual policies remains a challenge, as these beliefs tend to be very individual and heavily based on past experiences gained during own school career. Questioning such beliefs requires furthering their understanding of multilingualism, and reflecting on own language learning experiences and beliefs. While research-based knowledge can bring student teachers further along this learning path, it appeared especially effective to supplement this with practical, real-life examples and the concrete reflection of them. Throughout these processes of reflection, the critical approach provides a lens through which to examine monolingual norms and their alternatives in their cultural, social, and political contexts (Pennycook 1990).

Multilingualism has become a buzzword, which with some teacher students decreases its credibility. Consequently, a few students were rather skeptical of the relevance of the concept for early EFL classrooms. Contextualization of the issues within the monolingual habitus of schools (Gogolin 2008) that connects with student teachers' lived experience, together with realistic teaching material and methods that can counter such issues succeeded in raising awareness of the relevance toward the end of the seminar.

Beyond these challenges, teaching a seminar that implements a critical approach requires the teacher trainer to continuously question their own existing conceptualizations of language, language competence, and language learning. Sociocultural, poststructuralist, and critical theories of language learning can go a long way in deepening one's understanding of the multilingual nature of language learning (Norton 2020). Furthermore, continuous own research on the topic and close contact with real multilingual classrooms are helpful in keeping up with the changing state of the art of research and practice.

References

Aronin, L. (2018), "What Is Multilingualism?", in L. Aronin and D. Singleton (eds), *MM textbooks: Vol. 15. Twelve Lectures on Multilingualism*, 3–34, Bristol: Multilingual Matters.

Candelier, M. (2013), *FREPA: A Framework of Reference for Pluralistic Approaches to Languages and Culture; Competences and Resources*, Strasbourg: Council of Europe Publ. Retrieved from https://carap.ecml.at/Database/tabid/2313/language/en-GB/Default.aspx.

Candelier, M. and M. Launey (2012), *FREPA Exercise: Some Languages of Europe … and Elsewhere*. Retrieved from https://carap.ecml.at/tabid/2313/PublicationID/287/Default.aspx.

Creese, A. (2011), "Pedagogy and Bilingual Pupils in Primary Schools: Certainties from Applied Linguistics", in S. Ellis and E. McCartney (eds), *Applied Linguistics and Primary School Teaching*, 186–98, Cambridge: Cambridge University Press.

Falomir, L. P. (2015), *Multilingualism and Very Young Learners: An Analysis of Pragmatic Awareness and Language Attitudes. Trends in Applied Linguistics: Vol. 12*, Berlin: De Gruyter Mouton.

García, O. (2009), *Bilingual Education in the 21st Century: A Global Perspective*, Oxford: Wiley-Blackwell.

García, O. and L. Wei (2014a), "Translanguaging to Teach", in O. García and L. Wei (eds), *Translanguaging: Language, Bilingualism and Education*, 90–115, Basingstoke, Hampshire: Palgrave Macmillan.

García, O. and L. Wei (2014b), "Translanguaging in Education: Principles, Implications and Challenges", in O. García and L. Wei (eds), *Translanguaging: Language, Bilingualism and Education*, 90–115, Basingstoke, Hampshire: Palgrave Macmillan.

García, O. and N. Flores (2015), "Multilingual Pedagogies", in M. Martin-Jones, A. Blackledge and A. Creese (eds), *Routledge Handbooks in Applied Linguistics. The Routledge Handbook of Multilingualism*, 232–46, Abingdon, Oxon: Routledge.

Gogolin, I. (2008), *Der monolinguale Habitus der multilingualen Schule [The monolingual habitus of the multilingual school]*, Münster, New York, München, Berlin: Waxmann.

Grosjean, F. (2010), *Bilingual: Life and Reality*, Cambridge, MA, London: Harvard University Press.

Herdina, P. and U. Jessner (2002), *A Dynamic Model of Multilingualism: Perspectives of Change in Psycholinguistics*, Clevedon: Multilingual Matters.

Hopp, H., J. Jakisch, S. Sturm, C. Becker and D. Thoma (2019), "Integrating Multilingualism into the Early Foreign Language Classroom: Empirical and Teaching Perspectives", *International Multilingual Research Journal*, 31 (1): 1–17. doi:10.1080/19313152.2019.1669519.

Jørgensen, J. (2008), "Polylingual Languaging around and among Children and Adolescents", *International Journal of Multilingualism*, 5 (3): 161–76. doi:10.1080/14790710802387562.

Kerr, P. (2019), *The Use of L1 in English Language Teaching*, Cambridge Papers in ELT, Cambridge: Cambridge University Press.

Krumm, H.-J. (2013), "Multilingualism and Identity: What Linguistic Biographies of Migrants Can Tell Us", in P. Siemund, I. Gogolin, M. Schulz and J. Davydova (eds), *Hamburg Studies on Linguistic Diversity, 2211-3703: Volume 1. Multilingualism and Language Diversity in Urban Areas: Acquisition, Identities, Space, Education*. Schulz,

Julia Davydova, *University of Hamburg*, 165–76, Amsterdam: John Benjamins Publishing Company.

Kultusministerkonferenz (2013), "Bericht Fremdsprachen in der Grundschule—Sachstand und Konzeptionen 2013: Beschluss der Kultusministerkonferenz vom 17.10.2013" [Report Foreign languages in the primary school—State of affairs and concepts 2013: Resolution from 17.10.2023 by the Standing Conference of the Ministers of Education and Cultural Affairs of the Länder in the Federal Republic of Germany].

Navqi, R., A. McKeough, K. J. Thorne and C. M. Pfitscher (2013), "Fostering Early Literacy Learning Using Dual Language Books: Language as a Cultural Amplifier", in P. Siemund, I. Gogolin, M. Schulz and J. Davydova (eds), *Hamburg Studies on Linguistic Diversity, Volume 1, Multilingualism and Language Diversity in Urban Areas: Acquisition, Identities, Space, Education*, 327–48, Amsterdam: John Benjamins Publishing Company.

Norton, B. (2020), "Identity in Second Language Acquisition", in C. A. Chapelle (ed.), *The Concise Encyclopedia of Applied Linguistics*, 561–7, Hoboken, NJ: Wiley Blackwell.

Pennycook, A. (1990), "Critical Pedagogy and Second Language Acquisition", *System*, 19: 303–14.

Roos, J. and H. Nicholas (2019), "Using Young Learners' Language Environments for EFL Learning", *AILA Review*, 32: 91–111. doi:10.1075/aila.00022.roo.

Ticheloven, A., E. Blom, P. Leseman and S. McMonagle (2019), "Translanguaging Challenges in Multilingual Classrooms: Scholar, Teacher and Student Perspectives", *International Journal of Multilingualism*, 10: 1–24. doi:10.1080/14790718.2019.1686002.

Wallace, M. J. and T.-H. Bau (2004), *Training Foreign Language Teachers, A Reflective Approach*, Cambridge: Cambridge University Press.

Wardman, C., J. Bell and E. Sharp (2012), "Valuing Home Languages", in D. Mallows (ed.), *Innovations Series. Innovations in English Language Teaching for Migrants and Refugees*, 37–48, London: British Council.

Wei, L. (2000), "Changes in Attitudes towards Bilingualism", in L. Wei (ed.), *The Bilingualism Reader*, 18–25, London: Routledge.

Appendix

A. My language portrait

Instructions: Which languages can you understand or speak? Draw the shape of a human body and then color your languages into your body. Use a different color for every language. Before drawing, consider for example what each language means to you, what you use it for etc. You may draw any additional images in the picture you like. At the end, write a brief explanation of why you chose to color the body part with the particular color.
See Krumm (2013) for further examples.

B. Some Guidelines of Multilingual Pedagogy

- Begin slowly with the multilingual methods, as students are most likely not used to such approaches that include the languages other than the majority language

and English. Ease the learners into other languages through multilingual songs, chants, poems, or greetings and explore the languages spoken in the classroom, e.g., through language portraits (Hopp et al. 2019; Ticheloven et al. 2019).
- Students should not be singled out as "experts" of certain languages, but the information of languages spoken by the students should be voluntarily given by the students themselves (Hopp et al. 2019). Low proficiency or the wish to be "part of the group" may lead to feelings of insecurity when it comes to children speaking their home language.
- Group or pair learners into "language buddies" (Wardman, Bell and Sharp 2012) to allow for using their whole linguistic repertoire collaboratively. This allows for comparing words, cognates, and grammatical structures between languages (see Hopp et al. 2019 for examples).

Part Nine

Teaching Culture

27

Teaching Culture for Critical Global Citizenship

Britta Freitag-Hild

Introduction

What role can language and culture pedagogy play in today's globalized world, which is shaken by political, social, and economic conflicts and environmental crises? How can language teachers support learners' development of competences that will enable them to meet the challenges of our times, to act as "critical agents of change" (UN 2015) and shape social and sustainable futures? As I will argue in this chapter, culture pedagogy—if it is conceptualized and enacted in the classroom as a critical approach—can raise language learners' awareness of how individuals and cultures construct meaning through language(s), and develop their skills for reading, decoding, exploring, and negotiating these meanings as well as for participating in cultural discourses. Language teachers therefore need to equip their learners not only with the communicative, but also with cultural competences that will allow them to act as critical "citizens of the world" (Nussbaum 2010) for social change and transformation. For that purpose, culture pedagogy needs to start from a critical reflection of the concept of culture and help learners to develop their awareness of how we all, as language users and as social actors, as language learners, teachers, and teacher educators, take an active part in cultural processes of meaning making. Drawing on Hall's (1997) semiotic and meaning-focused concept of culture, Kramsch's (2006) concept of "symbolic competence," and Hallet's (2002) model of the foreign language classroom as a "hybrid space", this chapter will outline how culture pedagogy can be conceptualized as a "critical" and "transformative" approach, how it can guide language educators' selection of texts and their design of tasks, and how teacher candidates can learn to provide opportunities for language learners to develop the competences they need as critical agents of change.

Key Issues

Moving toward Culture Pedagogy as a Critical and Transformative Approach

The idea that there is a close connection between language and culture has influenced foreign language education ever since Claire Kramsch's (1993) *Context and Culture in Language Teaching*. It is therefore generally acknowledged that the foreign language classroom needs to make culture(s) accessible to language learners in order to help them explore, understand, and negotiate different ways of seeing the world. While language education researchers and teachers usually share this basic assumption, there are diverse approaches in culture pedagogy with different views on "how," "why," and "which" culture(s) should be taught. These approaches often rely on different ideas or concepts of culture (see Risager 2012: 145ff. for a more detailed overview). One of the major lines of development is that from Landeskunde (area studies) to cultural studies and intercultural learning: While the first had been the dominant approach until the 1970s and usually reduced learning about "cultures" to learning facts and figures about the society and history of a specific "country," intercultural approaches developed in the 1990s. They involve learners personally in intercultural dialogue, in exploring and changing diverse perspectives as well as reflecting critically on their own views (cf. Delanoy and Volkmann 2006: 13). Byram's (1997) model, for example, identifies various dimensions (knowledge, skills, attitudes, and critical cultural awareness) for developing "intercultural communicative competence." While his approach is rooted in a nation-based understanding of culture, intercultural approaches aiming for Fremdverstehen (intercultural understanding; see Bredella 2012), instead, operate with subjective, relational categories of "self" and "other," arguing that these are not fixed, but subject to change when entering into a dialogue. Nevertheless, the implied way of thinking in binary oppositions (self/other) in intercultural approaches has been criticized in the past, and resulted in a debate arguing for a critical reflection of the concept of culture. Despite this criticism, the development of (inter-)cultural competence—including the development of attitudes like respect for diversity, empathy, and the ability to change perspectives, as well as knowledge and skills for interaction, for relating, and for interpretation—remains a central objective for foreign language education. Transcultural approaches, however, have also highlighted the internal differentiation, hybridity, and interconnectedness of cultures as features of any culture that need to be reflected in the design of classroom materials and activities (see Freitag-Hild 2010 for a closer discussion).

More recent developments can be traced in attempts to connect culture pedagogy to the aims, principles, and methodologies of global education, education for sustainable development (ESD), and global citizenship education (Lütge 2015; Surkamp 2022). Even though these terms are not synonymous, the approaches share a global perspective and provide new directions for culture pedagogy: they all integrate a focus on glocal issues (e.g., poverty, hunger, access to quality education, gender equality, social inequality, sustainable lifestyles, climate change, human rights, and peace), draw on concepts from peace education, environmental education, ESD and human rights education, and aim at developing young people's sense of global citizenship, of shared responsibility for the planet and people's well-being which enables them to "think globally and act locally" (Cates 2004: 241). According to ESD approaches, participating and transforming our societies, economies, and lifestyles in the direction of sustainable development requires the development of what has been termed "Gestaltungskompetenz" ("shaping" competence): "Those who possess this competence can help, through their active participation in society, to modify and shape the future of society, and to guide its social, economic, technological and ecological changes along the lines of sustainable development" (de Haan 2006: 22).

Developing Critical Cultural Literacy

Empowering younger generations to act as "critical agents of change" (UN 2015) requires transformative approaches and a critical teacher education which helps language teachers become aware of their own role in this context: In order to enable learners to ask critical questions, question established meanings, raise their voice, and participate in cultural processes of social transformation, foreign language teachers need to provide opportunities for learners to

(1) develop competences to access, "read," and understand cultural discourses in a foreign language

First of all, culture pedagogy as a critical approach relies on a semiotic, meaning-focused understanding of culture instead of a nation-based understanding: If "culture is about 'shared meanings'" (Hall 1997: 1) and we use language to produce, share, and exchange meanings in order to make sense of things and "interpret the world in roughly the same ways" (Hall 1997: 1), it follows that foreign language learners need to gain access to this "culture of shared understandings" (Hall 1997: 1). However, it is important to note that these meanings do not unfold to foreign language learners by themselves, just by learning the "new" words of a foreign language. Rather, they need to learn to decode these meanings, which includes "reading" signs, words, or texts within their cultural contexts or "discourses" and understanding what these signs, symbols, or texts may be referring or responding to. This involves learners' exploration of the cultural context by studying further texts, which provide them with the cultural knowledge they need in order to understand cultural connotations, for example (cf. Hallet 2007: 382). In addition, educators also have to account for the fact that "in any culture, there is always a great diversity of meanings about any topic, and more than one way of interpreting or representing it" (Hall 1997: 2). This diversity of meanings can be represented or made accessible in the classroom with the help of an intertextual arrangement (Hallet 2002), in order to avoid reductionist views about culture as fixed or unitary. One of the advantages of an intertextual approach is "the students' opportunity to read, explore, and interpret culture without resorting to some vague encyclopedic knowledge, second-hand information gathered from footnotes and annotations, or background information provided by the teacher or the course book" (Hallet 2007: 387).

(2) develop critical literacy, including language learners' awareness of how language creates meaning, and shapes social relationships and power relations

Secondly, culture also needs be understood "as a process, as a set of practices ... which is concerned with the production and exchange of meanings—the 'giving and taking of meaning'—between the members of a society or group" (Hall 1997: 2). When we interact, we constantly produce and exchange meanings, through the words we choose, the stories we tell about others, the images we choose to represent an event or other people: By choosing one word over another, by selecting or highlighting features or details in a report, by telling a story through a particular perspective, we give meaning to these things and express our view of the world, which may then be taken up, circulated, or contradicted by others (see also Hall 1997: 3ff.). In foreign language education, it is therefore desirable for learners to become competent "readers" as well as critical and active "participants" in these cultural processes of meaning-making, as expressed by Kramsch (2006): "Today it is not sufficient for learners to know how to communicate meanings; they have to understand the practice of meaning making itself" (2006: 251). In line with her concept of symbolic competence, foreign language learners need to learn to read meanings in their (social and historical) contexts in order to understand how the semiotic choice of a speaker positions him or her within these contexts—but they also need to develop the ability to question these meanings or categories in order to resignify or reframe them (see also Freitag-Hild 2022a). If language learners understand how language creates (cultural) meaning, how our words can inspire others or discourage them, how they shape our relationships in local as well as in global contexts, they can also develop a "critical cultural literacy" which enables them to critically reflect their own and other people's use of language, choose their own words responsibly, for respectful and peaceful communication, for a critical evaluation of social injustices, and for developing and communicating visions of inclusive, sustainable communities and futures (see also UNESCO and MGIEP 2017).[1]

(3) actively participate and engage in cultural discourses and processes of transformation

Thirdly, culture pedagogy as a critical approach does not end with learners' access to cultural processes of meaning-making, or with their development of competences for exploring, interpreting, and critically reflecting cultural meanings; it also has to provide opportunities for active participation in cultural discourses and processes of social transformation. The foreign language classroom therefore needs a pedagogical framework and communicative setting which allows learners to act, not only as language learners, but as social actors who are actively involved in processes of meaning-making—not only in, but also beyond the classroom. For this purpose, it is useful to draw on Hallet's (2002) concept of the foreign language classroom as a "hybrid space" (2002: 39ff.), which emerges when texts, voices, or statements from different discursive spheres are introduced into or enter the classroom and are then negotiated by the learners. By responding to these different texts, voices, and ideas and communicating them outside or beyond the classroom, learners themselves enter the cultural discourses and, as "cultural agents" ("(inter-)kulturelle Aktanten," 2002: 34), take part in processes of cultural meaning-making.

Implications for Teaching and Teacher Education

As I have argued, a critical reflection of the concept of culture and of one's own role as an educator within the classroom are central requirements, if culture pedagogy is to be enacted as a critical approach (Freitag-Hild 2022b). The following list of guiding principles can therefore serve as a tool for language teachers and teacher educators alike and provide prompts for the critical reflection and further development of one's own practices in culture pedagogy.

Developing a Sense of Global Citizenship

One of the basic requirements for learners to act as critical agents of change in today's world is developing a sense of global citizenship: As Nussbaum (2010: 80) argues, educators therefore need to cultivate in students the ability to see themselves not only as members of their local and national communities but also as "citizens of the world," as members of a world society. This can be achieved through the use of literary texts, for example, and by reflecting on how one's own actions and decisions (e.g., buying food, drinks, or clothes) in a local context may affect the lives of people elsewhere, by learning about immigration and its history, including colonialism and the global economy, but also by encouraging a "respectful curiosity" to learn more about the lives of people in other parts of the world.

Developing empathy and "narrative imagination": With their focus on lived (or imagined) experiences and individual stories, literary texts can help learners connect to the lives and stories of people across languages, cultures, and religions. As readers of these stories, learners can develop empathy and "narrative imagination," which Nussbaum (2010: 96) describes as "the ability to think what it might be like to be in the shoes of a person different from oneself, to be an intelligent reader of that person's story, and to understand the emotions and wishes and desires that someone so placed might have." In the classroom, educators therefore should make use of narratives' potential to open up different lifeworlds to learners, by reading and discussing characters' lives, their experiences, as well as the learners' reactions, their evaluation, but also a critical reflection of the latter, and by changing perspectives (e.g., through creative writing or drama activities).

Exploring Culture, Engaging with Others and Reflecting One's Own Views

Rather than presenting facts and figures or reducing cultural complexity to annotations in a course book, educators need to find ways to engage learners actively with culture and cultural difference. Learners need to be encouraged to ask questions, voice their difficulties in understanding, enter into a dialogue with others and negotiate different views. Educators should therefore learn to design activities which ask learners to explore cultural issues or the cultural dimensions of a text by themselves, for example, by researching the cultural background. This allows learners a more direct, ethnographic access to culture since they have to search and make sense of connections, correspondences, or discrepancies between different texts, and in this way learn to interpret and construct cultural meanings on their own (Hallet 2007: 385f.). In addition, learners also need to develop an awareness of how their own views or interpretations may be influenced by the "shared meanings" as members of a cultural group.

Becoming critical readers of cultural texts: As has been argued, a critical approach to learning and teaching about culture relies on the development of a critical literacy: For the foreign language classroom, it is desirable to raise learners' awareness of how a specific text creates meaning, how the positionality of a speaker or writer is expressed, and how this text represents a particular view, but never cultural reality as such. While this is an ambitious goal for the foreign language classroom, educators can help to develop this critical literacy by exploring critical questions together with their learners (Janks 2014): Instead of focusing solely on comprehension questions, educators and learners should question the author's views, analyze his or her positionality, raise awareness of the author's choice of words, and examine which voices or perspectives are represented in the text and which are not heard, marginalized, or even silenced. It is therefore also recommended that these skills are modeled and reflected in teacher education contexts.

Representing Culture, Contextualizing Texts, and Reflecting the Representation of Culture

The foreign language classroom usually has to resort to representing culture through text(s) in order to make it accessible to learners. However, because texts are always "partial representations" (Janks 2014), educators have to assess and critically reflect the views or perspectives that are represented through one's own or a course book's text selection or combination. In order to open up culture's complexity, heterogeneity, and internal polyphony, educators need to provide their learners with access to a variety of views and perspectives within a specific cultural discourse, for example. It is to be assumed, therefore, that a given selection of texts may have to be adapted or broadened in order to ensure the inclusion of more recent or diverse perspectives. As has been argued, it will also be necessary for educators to contextualize single texts with the help of an intertextual arrangement (cf. Hallet 2006; 2007 for specific examples). In teacher education contexts, future educators can be encouraged to select or adapt teaching resources and design, test and reflect activities, for example, in micro-teaching sessions.

Designing complex scenarios for participation in cultural discourses: As has been argued, a critical approach to culture pedagogy relies on learners' active participation in cultural discourses and processes of social transformation. Educators therefore need to design complex task-based scenarios with critically informed content (cf. Crookes and Ziegler 2021) which engage learners in relevant cultural discourses, either on a local or on a global level; and they also need to provide tasks and activities which enable learners to act as agents of change, for example, by issuing a statement on how a local problem may be solved, by presenting their visions for a sustainable future, or by engaging with a partner class in a virtual exchange project. Focusing on the linguistic, cultural, and reflective competences needed to accomplish such complex competence tasks (Hallet and Krämer 2012) will also help learners to develop their confidence in their ability to contribute to shaping more just, sustainable, and peaceful societies and communities.

Note

1   The idea that our world is a social construct and that language is the central medium we use to represent and shape the world is also one of the central *tenets* of *Critical Pedagogy*: In Freire's (1970) *Pedagogy of the Oppressed*, learning to "read the word" is seen as an act of empowerment, because it enables learners to "read the world," enter into a dialogue with others and, through active participation, contribute to social change and transformation. Developing "critical literacy" therefore empowers learners to perceive and critically reflect the world around them, to understand how language and power are interconnected, and to actively participate in processes of social change.

References

Bredella, L. (2012), *Narratives und interkulturelles Verstehen: Zur Entwicklung von Empathie-, Urteils-und Kooperationsfähigkeit*, Tübingen: Narr.

Byram, M. (1997), *Teaching and Assessing Intercultural Communicative Competence*, Clevedon: Multilingual Matters.

Cates, K. (2004), "Global Education", in M. Byram (ed.), *Routledge Encyclopedia of Language Teaching and Learning*, 241–3, London/New York: Routledge.

Crookes, G.V. and N. Ziegler (2021), "Critical Language Pedagogy and Task-Based Language Teaching: Reciprocal Relationship and Mutual Benefit", *Education Sciences*, 11 (6): 254.

de Haan, G. (2006), "The BLK '21' Programme in Germany: A 'Gestaltungskompetenz' Based Model for Education for Sustainable Development", *Environmental Education Research*, 12 (1): 19–32.

Delanoy, W. and L. Volkmann (eds) (2006), *Cultural Studies in the EFL Classroom*, Heidelberg: Winter.

Freire, P. (1970), *Pedagogy of the Oppressed*, New York: The Continuum.

Freitag-Hild, B. (2010), *Theorie, Aufgabentypologie und Unterrichtspraxis inter- und transkultureller Literaturdidaktik, British Fictions of Migration im Fremdsprachenunterricht*, Trier: WVT.

Freitag-Hild, B. (2022a), "Ethnografisches Lernen, symbolische Kompetenz und Critical Literacy: Re-framing Visual Representations of People Seeking Refuge", in L. Köning, B. Schädlich, and C. Surkamp (eds), *unterricht_kultur_theorie: Kulturelles Lernen im Fremdsprachenunterricht gemeinsam anders denken*, 299–315, Berlin: J.B. Metzler.

Freitag-Hild, B. (2022b), "Kulturelles Lernen und Bildung für nachhaltige Entwicklung im Fremdsprachenunterricht", in C. Surkamp (ed.), *Bildung für nachhaltige Entwicklung im Englischunterricht. Grundlagen und Unterrichtsbeispiele*, 66–77, Hannover: Kallmeyer in Verbindung mit Klett.

Hall, S. (ed.) (1997), *Representation: Cultural Representations and Signifying Practices*, London, Thousand Oaks, New Delhi: Sage.

Hallet, W. (2002), *Fremdsprachenunterricht als Spiel der Texte und Kulturen: Intertextualität als Paradigma einer kulturwissenschaftlichen Didaktik*, Trier: WVT.

Hallet, W. (2006), "Jazz: Toni Morrison's Novel and the Use of Cultural Studies in the Literary Classroom", in W. Delanoy and L. Volkmann (eds), *Cultural Studies in the EFL Classroom*, 269–91, Heidelberg: Winter.

Hallet, W. (2007), "Close Reading and Wide Reading: Teaching Literature and Cultural History in a Unit on Philip K. Dick's 'Minority Report'". *Amerikastudien/American Studies*, 52 (3): 381–97.
Hallet, W. and U. Krämer (eds) (2012), *Kompetenzaufgaben im Englischunterricht, Grundlagen und Unterrichtsbeispiele*, Seelze: Kallmeyer in Verbindung mit Klett.
Janks, H. (2014), *Doing Critical Literacy*, New York/London: Routledge.
Kramsch, C. (1993), *Context and Culture in Language Teaching*, Oxford: Oxford University Press.
Kramsch, C. (2006), "From Communicative Competence to Symbolic Competence", *The Modern Language Journal*, 90 (2): 249–52.
Lütge, C. (ed.) (2015): *Global Education*, Perspectives for English Language Teaching, Zürich: LIT Verlag.
Nussbaum, M. (2010), *Not for Profit: Why Democracy Needs the Humanities*, Princeton/Oxford: Princeton University Press.
Risager, K. (2012), "Introduction: Intercultural Learning: Raising Cultural Awareness", in M. Eisenmann and T. Summer (eds), *Basic Issues in EFL Teaching and Learning*, 143–55, Heidelberg: Winter.
Surkamp, C. (ed.) (2022), *Bildung für nachhaltige Entwicklung im Englischunterricht, Grundlagen und Unterrichtsbeispiele*, Hannover: Kallmeyer in Verbindung mit Klett.
UNESCO & Mahatma Gandhi Institute of Education for Peace and Sustainable Development (UNESCO MGIEP) (2017), *Textbooks for Sustainable Development: A Guide to Embedding*. Available online: https://unesdoc.unesco.org/ark:/48223/pf0000259932.
United Nations General Assembly (UN) (2015): "Transforming Our World: The 2030 Agenda for Sustainable Development". Available online: https://sustainabledevelopment.un.org/content/documents/21252030%20Agenda%20for%20Sustainable%20Development%20web.pdf.

Using Intercultural Virtual Exchange to Promote Critical Pedagogy Practices of English Language Teachers

Laura Torres-Zúñiga and Sibel Söğüt

Background

The project VALIANT, Virtual Innovation and Support Networks for Teachers, aimed at strengthening teacher training and education by using new technologies (e.g., videoconference, collaborative digital tools) for online collaboration around real-world educational issues (e.g., integrating technology in the foreign language classroom, supporting teachers of Ukrainian refugees, learning during teaching practice).[1] It gathered in-service teachers from all over Europe who responded to different online calls (Autumn 2021, Spring 2022, and Autumn 2022) to participate in virtual exchanges (VEs) that included both other in-service teachers and pre-service teachers and teacher trainers from the universities in the project consortium. The contents and development of the different VEs were varied; our focus in this chapter will be on the VE on "Diversity and Inclusion in our Classrooms," a co-learning experience involving only in-service teachers that was carried out in English in three editions, one after each call from 2021 to 2022.[2] Although registration was open to in-service teachers of all profiles, within the thirty-seven participants there was a predominance of foreign language teachers (51.3 percent in the first two rounds) and teachers of both foreign language and content areas typical of bilingual education based on CLIL such as Social Sciences or Arts (24.3 percent).

Unlike other VEs in the VALIANT project devoted to ELT methods or tools (e.g., gamification, CLIL materials), this VE attempted to raise the participants' critical awareness about the manifold shapes that diversity can take in our classrooms and the contextual factors (social, political, cultural) that may affect the teachers' capacity to address it. This falls in line with the *Profile for Inclusive Teachers* of the European Agency for Development in Special Needs Education, which features criticality within its core value "Valuing Learner Diversity" (2012: 11): criticality is understood here as "the ability to deconstruct educational history to understand current situations and contexts" and the skill of "critically examining one's own beliefs and attitudes and the impact these have on actions," aspects the VE aimed at fostering through its content and tasks.

A third component, "modeling respect in social relationships," was developed by the widely recognized potential of VE/telecollaboration for improving intercultural communicative competence (O'Dowd 2021; Üzüm, Akayoğlu, and Yazan 2020), a further aim of this VE. During a VE, teachers temporarily create an intercultural community of practice "who share a concern […], and who deepen their knowledge and expertise in this area by interacting on an ongoing basis" (Wenger et al., qtd. in Karavas and Papadopoulou 2014: 185). Such interaction entails and promotes a series of intercultural skills such as "interest in discovering other perspectives on interpretation of familiar and unfamiliar phenomena both in one's own and in other cultures and cultural practices," "use in real-time [of] knowledge, skills and attitudes for mediation between interlocutors of one's own and a foreign culture," and what Byram denominates "[c]ritical cultural awareness/political education: An ability to evaluate critically and on the basis of explicit criteria perspectives, practices and products in one's own and other cultures and countries" (1997: 50–3). By taking part in this VE, participants could thus develop their profile as inclusive teachers and improve their intercultural competence as a first step to becoming more reflective practitioners.

Description of the Practice

During the VE, teachers collaborated synchronously and asynchronously for seven weeks (Figure 28.1). With the guidance of several facilitators, they shared five ninety-minute video conferences over Zoom (in weeks 1, 2, 3, 6, and 7) and progressed in groups along a series of tasks available on a Moodle Learning Management System.

The tasks followed O'Dowd and Ware's (2009) Progressive Exchange Model: information exchange, comparisons and analysis, and collaboration. The information exchange consisted of a short video or text on Padlet with the participants' personal introduction and description of their teaching context, including one social issue or problem related to diversity or inclusion of their concern (e.g., integrating immigrant students, teaching students with learning disabilities, motivating hard-to-reach students). The teachers were encouraged to watch/read other participants' presentations so that the first videoconference could be devoted to meeting each other and commenting on the similarities or differences of one's own experience, context, school, etc., with those presented in the introductions. Considering the most repeated topics raised in the presentations, and the results of a survey where more topics were offered for selection (e.g., supporting gifted students or socioeconomically deprived ones), the most relevant thematic blocks were gathered on a Google Jamboard. Teachers then signed up for the topic/s of their interest, forming thus the work groups that would remain stable for the whole VE. Some of these thematic groups created in the two rounds of VEs dealt with topics such as teaching culturally and linguistically

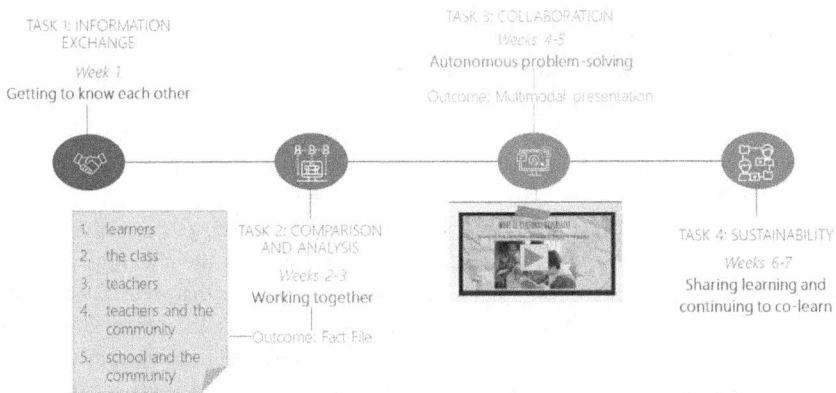

Figure 28.1 Virtual exchange diversity and inclusion in our classrooms—tasks and timeline. Created by the authors.

diverse students, teaching mixed-level classes, motivating hard-to-reach students, or improving students' social relations and good behavior.

The comparison and analysis stage continued the second week, when groups started their co-learning process by distributing roles for group work, deciding their communication channels, and working together on a *fact file* on their selected topic. A fact file or sheet is a concise document (usually one page) containing the main information about a subject; in this case, the facilitators provided each group with a series of questions that could raise their awareness of the needs and responsibilities of all the stakeholders involved in their topic within their different contexts:

1. Learners:
   a. What are the main needs of learners [in relation to your topic]?
   b. Can you give examples of best practice on how to deal with those needs?

2. The class:
   a. What are the perceived threats [caused by your topic] to the learning environment, e.g., to other learners?
   b. Can you give examples of best practice on how to deal with those threats?

3. Teachers:
   a. What are the main needs of teachers?
   b. What are the main responsibilities and/or limitations of teachers for addressing the topic?

4. Teachers and the community:
   a. What are the school guidelines?
   b. Can you give examples of best practice on how to deal with the topic?

5. School and community:
   a. What are the main needs of parents?
   b. Can you give examples of best practice on how to deal with the topic?

Collaboration continued with groups giving feedback on each other's fact files, followed by two weeks of asynchronous work to organize their own workflow in order to turn the fact files into a multimodal presentation with recommendations valid for other teachers that may experience similar problems/issues within their topic. After having reflected on the diverse barriers and leeway in attending to diversity in their settings with the questions above, their focus should now lie on possible solutions that were transversally affordable in different contexts. Sample presentations on YouTube were offered as models, especially those created by groups in previous VE editions, such as Cultural diversity in the classroom: A challenge for teachers, Motivating students in sociocultural diversity, or Teaching mixed-level classrooms (links provided in References).

The last meetings were devoted to sharing and offering feedback on the presentations, evaluating the experience of co-learning as teacher training, and devising ways to create interest groups that could reproduce and sustain the type of community of practice created for this VE.

Critical Reflections: Potentials and Challenges

To provide a comprehensive overview of the affordances and challenges of this virtual co-learning experience, participants shared their perspectives about its advantages and disadvantages on Tricider and Padlet, which are online interactive platforms for collecting and discussing ideas. Also, they completed VALIANT's general surveys (pre- and post-VE) to gain insights into the opportunities and challenges in the project. The qualitative analysis of responses from Tricider and Padlet revealed that the in-service teachers reported an awareness and cognizance of diversity in their VE experiences. Specifically, they emphasized their increased sense of tolerance and flexibility toward each other in the VE, e.g., being more patient when listening to other varieties of English. This correlates with the advancement in intercultural competence revealed by their answers to VALIANT's survey (completed by twenty-two of them before and after the VE): items such as "I change my verbal behavior (e.g., accent, tone) when intercultural interaction requires it" and "I try to look at everybody's side of a disagreement before I make a decision," with the greatest improvement in the post-test survey, show an increased awareness of conflict resolution, negotiation skills, and the Intercultural Communicative Competence (ICC) skills by Byram above.

The teachers also reflected upon professional benefits such as the development of new technological, communicative, and emotional benefits and competences: discovering new online tools, gaining new insights and experiences, and improving their teaching skills. They underlined that the VE experience enabled them to interact with their colleagues and share universal experiences about their concerns and challenges across geographic boundaries, with affective benefits such as feeling supported and sharing common worries and concerns through engagement with peers. On their part, the facilitators also responded to an online survey, in which they highlighted affordances including increased recognition of co-learning among participants with diverse backgrounds, cooperation, interaction, diversity, inclusiveness, and contextual awareness. They emphasized the role of human agency in facilitating the group discussions, enabling active participation, and sustaining the motivation of the teachers during the VE.

Besides these benefits, the multistage, dynamic, cross-cultural, technology-enhanced nature of the VE also offered challenges to both teachers and facilitators. The teachers realized challenges related to diversity, digital divide, and inclusiveness during the VE, like setting too high expectations for their students and forgetting their differences and special needs. They further reflected on realizing their difficulties in leading students to gender equality in their classrooms. As regards their own participation in the VE, they reported experiencing challenges about time management, English language proficiency, local contextual constraints such as lack of access to internet connection, and confusions stemming from the dynamic and interactive nature of group discussions and the idiosyncratic features of group members and their geographical location. The facilitators, for their part, highlighted challenges such as time management, low commitment or even absence of participants during the VE (failure to fulfill the requirements of a module, unwillingness to provide their self-presence in team work, missing videoconferences), sociocultural and work-style differences, and management of group dynamics. Focusing basically on establishing clearer initial procedures, the facilitators noted ways to overcome the aforementioned obstacles, such as helping participants brainstorm rules, devoting more time to prepare group work, engaging the participants actively, and having individual contact with participants.

In conclusion, the proposed VE model on "Diversity and Inclusion in our Classrooms" has transformative potential for teachers and teacher trainers, enhancing their intercultural communicative competence and triggering their awareness about linguistic and cultural diversities through collaborating in videoconferences, co-learning experiences, discussions, and multimodal presentations. This model provides a platform for promoting critical reflection and engagement with ways to make their classroom inclusive, and raising awareness of their contextual variables. Moreover, especially for foreign language teaching where telecollaboration is now a widespread activity thanks to eTwinning (Licht, Pateraki, and Scimeca 2020), this co-learning experience provides language teachers with a first-hand experience of the types of tasks, challenges, and learnings that their own students may undergo in their own VE projects, preparing them to plan and facilitate them better. We suggest that applying critically oriented VEs offers a promising experiential co-learning practice for teachers and trainers to acknowledge, analyze, and support diversity and inclusion in their classes, as well as to develop their intercultural competence and critical awareness.

Notes

1   The research reported in this chapter was supported by the project Virtual Innovation and Support Networks for Teachers (VALIANT) (626134-EPP-1-2020-2-ESEPPKA3-PIPOLICY), funded by Erasmus+ Key Action 3 (EACEA/38/2019): European policy experimentations in the fields of education, training, and youth

led by high-level public authorities. The European Commission's support for the production of this publication does not constitute an endorsement of the contents, which reflect the views only of the authors, and the Commission cannot be held responsible for any use which may be made of the information contained therein.
2   Data refer to the Autumn 2021 and Spring 2022 VEs since at the time of writing this chapter the Autumn 2022 round had not been carried out yet.

References

Byram, M. (1997), *Teaching and Assessing Intercultural Communicative Competence*, Clevedon: Multilingual Matters.

European Agency for Development in Special Needs Education (2012), *Profile of Inclusive Teachers*, Odense, Denmark: European Agency for Development in Special Needs Education.

Karavas, E. and S. Papadopoulou (2014), "Introducing a Paradigm Shift in EFL Continuing Professional Development in Greece: The Development of Online Communities of Practice", in D. Hayes (ed.), *Innovations in the Continuing Professional Development of English Language Teachers*, 179–206, London: British Council.

Licht, A., I. Pateraki and S. Scimeca (2020), *eTwinning Schools: Towards a Shared Leadership Approach—Quantitative and Qualitative Analysis of the eTwinning School Practices*, Brussels: Central Support Service of eTwinning–European Schoolnet.

O'Dowd, R. (2021), "Virtual Exchange: Moving Forward into the Next Decade", *Computer Assisted Language Learning*, 34 (3): 209–24.

O'Dowd, R. and P. Ware (2009), "Critical Issues in Telecollaborative Task Design", *Computer Assisted Language Learning*, 22 (2): 173–88.

Üzüm, B., S. Akayoğlu and B. Yazan (2020), "Using Telecollaboration to Promote Intercultural Competence in Teacher Training Classrooms in Turkey and the USA", *ReCALL*, 32 (2): 162–77.

Links to Sample Presentations

- Cultural diversity in the classroom: A challenge for teachers:
  https://www.youtube.com/watch?v=q1rY0EqNHSw
- Motivating students in sociocultural diversity
  https://www.youtube.com/watch?v=ERrS6qvv_Ms
- Teaching mixed-level classrooms
  https://view.genial.ly/628f0f96d82e5300189cf75e/presentation-teaching-mixed-level-classrooms

Critical Intercultural Education in Moroccan Teacher Education: Practical Insights for Teacher Candidates

Benachour Saidi and Rania Boustar

Background

In Moroccan English language teacher education context, intercultural communication education is often construed in terms of supplying students with sufficient knowledge about the sociocultural and political capital of the "Other," which is usually of the Anglo-sphere (R'boul and Saidi 2023). Equally, the models that are used for the construction and delivery of intercultural knowledge input may remain rather limited to essentialist conceptions of "culture" and the "intercultural," which often ensue in unbalanced perceptions of the Self and the Other. As a result, teacher candidates/students may develop a particular intercultural awareness in which they would aspire to act, behave, and assimilate into Western frames of thinking and culturing (R'boul 2020). Another issue is that, in the process of teaching interculturality, the teaching materials are not usually adapted to reflect the classroom's cultural, linguistic, and epistemic diversity, depth and complexity; additionally, teachers' sense-making of intercultural teaching may stay confined to "Western frameworks of knowledge," which does not necessarily account for non-Western contexts (Aman 2017). These perspectives, if not critically reconsidered within language teacher education, would inhibit the premises of intercultural education, i.e., social justice, cultural diversity, and cross/intercultural understanding.

The "critical approach/turn" of intercultural education as a nuanced reflexivity in language intercultural education is not new, as it has been introduced by some interculturalist scholars (e.g., Dervin 2017). Critical intercultural education is understood here as an educational approach that seeks to reimagine, from critical, decolonial, and social justice lenses, the various educational philosophies and logics that underpin non-Western teachers' thought and praxis of intercultural education. Critical intercultural education endeavors to promote critical and alternative understandings of "culture" and the "intercultural," equal consideration/treatment of cultural differences and social justice in language classroom. At the core of the critical intercultural approach is also the exigency to avert any type of intercultural practices that may reinforce the cultural and linguistic dominance of the mainstream group and possibly obscure forms of exclusion and Othering of non-native English learners. This is particularly indexed in the type of intercultural teaching that tends to foreground and accentuate the lived experiences and perspectives of the dominant (usually Western) groups while overlook and disregard those of the nondominant groups.

The teacher education context where the practical workshop was conducted in the Higher School of Education and Training, affiliated to Mohammed First University (Oujda, Morocco). Students joining this school complete study for a three-year bachelor's degree program in "English Studies" and are trained to work in the educational sector. Teacher candidates who participated in the workshop are mainly first-semester students. The workshop was held in the same school where I work as a Teaching Assistant/Lecturer of English as a foreign language. What prompted the criticality advanced in this practical chapter is a personal observation: I have noticed that a number of students majoring in "English Studies" already came up with taken-for-granted perceptions that situate English language and its associated US and/or UK culture(s) in a categorically superior position. Such assumptions are prevalent and may permeate into and emerge from the way intercultural education is perceived and taught in Moroccan teacher education programs in which, for instance, the intercultural experiences, cultures, and knowledges of the English-West may rather occupy a dominant space in language teacher education given the cultural and linguistic supremacy of the Anglo-West and scant critical engagements with intercultural education in the Global South-Morocco as a case in point. With these insights in mind, the workshop's overall objective was to (a) support teacher candidates to be aware of their positionalities in intercultural knowledge learning and development, (b) develop critically oriented conceptualizations of culture and interculturality, and (c) construct nuanced stances on how to exercise criticality within interculturality in Southern classrooms as prospective teachers.

Description of the Practice

The workshop consisted of three activities with an overall goal of initiating teacher candidates to a set of critical takeaways that foster the best practices of critical intercultural education across various teaching contexts.

Critical Engagements with Culture

The objective of this activity was to enable student teachers to nurture critical and nuanced understandings of the concept "culture" that is quite different from the solid and essentialist renderings that view culture as a nation-sealed unit, representing static traits and behaviors of a given cultural community (Holliday 2022). The aim here was to draw student teachers' attention to how culture is a complex entity that is constantly changing and evolving. Henceforth, by grounding intercultural awareness in the current critical engagements with culture, teacher candidates will not run the risk of breeding unbalanced and biased views about the cultural "Self" and the cultural "Other."

In the first phase, I asked student teachers to generate their own takes on culture and had them to brainstorm ideas about how their own culture influences the way they act, behave, and think in different contexts. The aim was to scrutinize if their views still resonate with the essentialist culture-blocks. They commonly defined culture "as a way of life, set of beliefs, values, traditions and practices that are specific to particular society members"; they mentioned different life aspects, e.g., friendship, work, time … etc., that are culturally bound. Then, I defined culture as an ever-changing entity, not necessarily a fixed device of behaviors, facts, and traits that unify particular group members but as a site for struggle over power and domination (Martin and Nakayama 2010) in which the dominant group's culture often enjoys prominence and visibility while of the nondominant remains marginalized. I explained this point in light of how uncritical and unreflexive intercultural education might reverberate cultural and linguistic hierarchies in language classroom by privileging the perspectives of the dominant groups (e.g., the Anglophone cultures).

In the second phase, through a set of guided questions, I pushed them to reflect on how to teach culture in a way that reflects its complexity and mutability. The rationale here was to help them challenge their potentially ethnocentric and biased views about culture and henceforth intercultural education.

1. Which culture(s) (Local or Western ones) would you consider for emphasizing critical intercultural awareness in language classroom?
2. How would you teach cultural differences (e.g., individualistic vs collectivistic cultures, high context vs low context culture, and mono-chronic vs poly-chronic cultures) in a way that they do not engender polarities and boundaries across cultures and individuals?
3. How would you teach generalizable factual cultural knowledges about countries in way they do not breed prejudices and stereotypes about the cultures at hand?
4. What cultural groups' elements, facts, and aspects would you capitalize on so as to promote global intercultural understandings in language classroom?

These questions prompted an interesting discussion in which student teachers had to verify and rectify their relatively ethnocentric assumptions about culture and its incorporation in an intercultural course. They also got to know that the teaching of culture(s) should encompass not only the dominant (Western) cultures but also local and sub-cultures, i.e., minority group(s), which are often overlooked in interculturality.

Critical Intercultural Teaching Framework

The goal of this activity was to expose student teachers to samples of critical interculturally based tasks that (a) enable them to appreciate their local culture(s), (b) mitigate culture bump while interacting with someone from a different culture, and (c) establish an equitable zone of interculturality inside and outside the classroom. In the first place, teacher candidates were critically engaged with the following statements by questioning and interrogating the embedded stereotypes and prejudices that are often communicated about other cultures through simplistic sayings. The objective was to alert them to the danger of developing stereotypical and essentialist perceptions about other people through a given generable factual knowledges.

1. In Morocco, it is not an appropriate behavior when a guest refuses or belches the offered food.
2. Moroccan students are lazy when it comes to studies and do not meet deadlines.
3. American people are punctual; Moroccans are not; Americans are open-minded and self-reliant; Moroccans are narrow-minded and dependent, etc.
4. Americans eat McDonald's all the time; punctuality and hard work are important values among Americans.
5. Asian people show deference by bowing.

In the second place, I moved to fostering critical intercultural awareness through European democratic culture model (Council of Europe 2018). For language learners to effectively operate in this diverse and globalized society, they need to acquire a set of competences, delineated in the model in terms of values (valuing human rights and cultural diversity), attitudes (openness to and respect for cultural otherness), skills (empathy, flexibility, and adaptability) and knowledge and critical understanding (critical understandings of the cultural Self and the Other). I passed a blank worksheet and asked student teachers to list activities/tasks whereby they promote these competences in language classroom. Figure 29.1 is an illustration of student teachers' product.

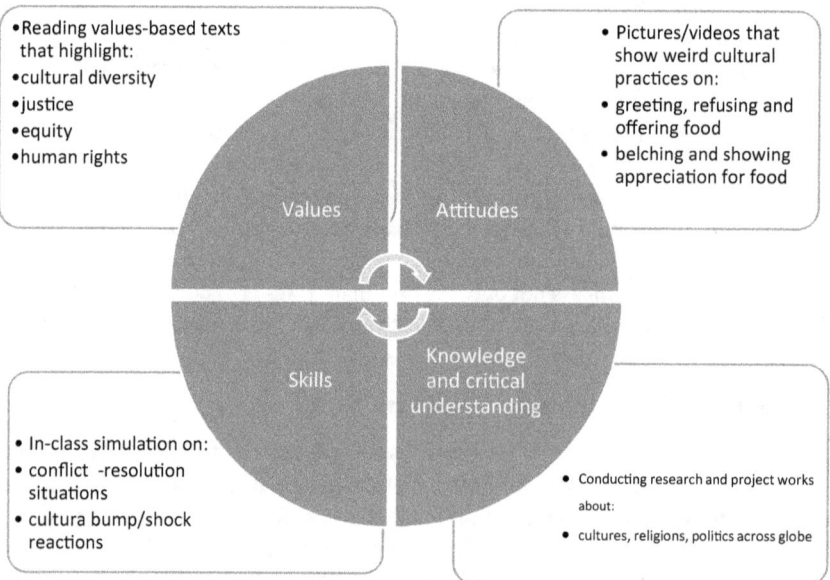

Figure 29.1 An illustration of student teachers' product.

Intercultural Teaching Material Adaptation

The aim of this activity was to assist student teachers to adapt textbooks or materials in a way that reflects interculturality. Student teachers were tasked to make necessary alterations to an assigned material, taken from "Interchange Student Book" (Richards 2015), in terms of pictures, names, conversation protocol, among other things, so as to make it interculturally meaningful. Student teachers actively engaged with the activity and came up with different products. For example, group A changed foreign names mentioned the analyzed coursebook page into local names (e.g., Joshua into Ali and Isabel into Ikram); conversation ethics that attend to local rituals (e.g., Hey, how are you and how is your family? Moroccan cherish the value of family in social interactions); and background picture (e.g., a school yard). On the other hand, group B mixed names and nationalities (e.g., a Moroccan male student, named Omar, is conversing with a Chinese male student called Chang); different greeting styles (e.g., Chinese people usually bow while Moroccan shake hands); background picture (e.g., a hotel); topics to discuss in conversation (e.g., asking about nationalities and languages and avoiding private topics related to income and jobs as they may not be acceptable in both cultures).

Critical Reflections: Potentials and Challenges

The practical activities showcased in this practical chapter offer valuable insights into teaching interculturality from a critical lens. Throughout the workshop, student teachers showed positive attitude toward the activities as they actively interacted with the tasks at hand. They had the chance to revisit their taken-for-granted assumptions about what does it mean to teach interculturality in Southern contexts. Equally, they got to know how to exercise criticality in intercultural education in terms of "culture" and the "intercultural." That was apparent from the products they came up with in the last activity. Therefore, the criticality argued for in this chapter pertains exclusively to decentering the unproblematized assumptions that have long shaped both students' and teachers' understandings of intercultural communication and education. However, despite student teachers' responsiveness to the activities, nuanced and practical applications of critical intercultural education in the Global South need further theoretical and pedagogical re-mapping, especially that English language along with its cultures is increasingly receiving greater privilege and status among Moroccan learners. At stake is also the exigency for intensive reflexive intercultural trainings in both pre-service and in-service teacher education programs. That is why this chapter is an invitation for Southern scholars, educators, and practitioners to contribute with hands-on and innovative intercultural practices that respond to local contexts' complexities and dynamics and that promote social justice and cultural diversity at large.

References

Aman, R. (2017), *Decolonising Intercultural Education: Colonial Differences, the Geopolitics of Knowledge, and InterEpistemic Dialogue*, 1st edn, London: Routledge.

Dervin, F. (2017), *Critical Interculturality: Lectures and Notes. (Post-intercultural Communication and Education)*, London: Cambridge Scholars Publishing.

Holliday, A. (2022), "Searching for a Third-Space Methodology to Contest Essentialist Large Culture Blocks", *Language and Intercultural Communication*, 22 (3): 367–80, doi: 10.1080/14708477.2022.2036180.

Council of Europe (2018). Reference Framework of Competences for Democratic Culture. https://www.coe.int/en/web/campaign-free-to-speak-safe-to-learn/reference-framework-of-competences-for-democratic-culture.

Martin, J. N. and T. K. Nakayama (2010), "Intercultural Communication and Dialectics Revisited", in R. T. Halualani and T. K. Nakayama (eds), *Handbook of Critical Intercultural Communication*, 51–83, Malden, MA: Blackwell.

R'boul, H. (2020), "Re-imagining Intercultural Communication Dynamics in TESOL: Culture/interculturality", *Journal for Multicultural Education*, 14 (2): 177–88.

R'boul, H. and B. Saidi (2023), "Unravelling Intercultural Communication Education in the Periphery: Critical Examination of Interculturality University-Level Courses", *Compare: A Journal of Comparative and International Education*, doi:10.1080/03057925.2023.2179871.

Richards, J. C. (2015), *New Interchange: English for International Communication*, 5th edn, Cambridge: Cambridge University Press.

Immigrant Families and Communities as Agents of Interculturality in Pre-Service Teacher Education

Roxanna Senyshyn

Background

I teach at a branch campus ("the College") of a large public university in the United States. The College is designated as a minority–majority campus with a very diverse (culturally and linguistically) domestic and international student body. The College offers an Elementary and Early Childhood Education undergraduate degree; however, students choosing this major tend to be white/Caucasian, female, and monolingual. At the same time, the College is located near a large and diverse urban school district, where a majority of the teacher candidates complete their teaching practicum. To better prepare the teacher candidates for the multilingual and culturally diverse classrooms, they are encouraged to complete the English as a Second Language (ESL) certification. The ESL certification program encompasses five required courses; all are offered at an upper academic level and include mandated by the state department of education teaching practicum. The course discussed in this chapter is the first course in the sequence, and it is titled, Foundation of Teaching English as a Second Language (referred to in this chapter as the "ESL Foundations course").

I regularly teach the ESL Foundations course in which one of the main objectives is to enhance the knowledge and skills of teacher candidates to work with culturally and linguistically diverse learners, their families, and communities. For that purpose, teacher candidates are required to learn about the complexity of interculturality in education contexts and one's own intercultural development to support the needs of multilingual English Learners (ELs) and their families, who often are immigrants and other newcomers. My pedagogical approach to address these learning goals is to focus on narrative inquiry in the process of (critical) intercultural exchange and communication. The critical approach (e.g., Guilherme 2002; Pennycook 2001) makes issues of social inequality and social transformation central in my work, challenging me as a culture (or interculturality) educator to create a more reflective, proactive, and responsible learners and teachers in their respective communities. Such work in part can be done through narratives, or stories, which are a uniquely human way of understanding the world and therefore are particularly useful for understanding a (cultural) community and its members, as opportunities for intercultural communication increase in a globalized world. In the field of language teacher education, narratives serve as a powerful vehicle for teacher inquiry (e.g., Johnson and Golombek 2011). Storytelling as a teaching tool has been utilized to explore intercultural communication and development (e.g., Byram 1997; Deardorff 2020), counter-storytelling (i.e., Rios Vega 2020), identity exploration and understanding of oneself (e.g., Yazan et al. 2023), and socially just practices (e.g., Penton Herrera and McNair 2021).

Description of the Practice

Considering these scholarly perspectives and the above-stated course goals, teacher candidates in the ESL Foundations course have to complete an inquiry project (see the Appendix for a detailed description) in which they are required to learn about a local immigrant (or refugee) family/community through direct engagement and dialogue. The inquiry project aims to be an exploratory, dialogic, active, and reflective stance toward cultural knowledge and life experiences. Therefore, teacher candidates explore an immigrant community through interpretive and critical perspectives. From the interpretive perspective, culture and intercultural learning and exchange are largely viewed as a way of understanding. This allows for the exploration of many possible ways different cultural communities create understanding with other members but might create misunderstandings when interacting interculturally (Hall et al. 2022). From the critical perspective, the goal is to use knowledge to explore the inequalities and inequities of life (e.g., teacher preparation, bilingual support, availability of assessments in Spanish but not in other languages), how power imbalances are created and maintained (e.g., distribution of financial resources, those in oppressive positions not realizing their oppression), and what can be done about them (e.g., bringing to light the ways groups in power might manipulate things to their advantage) (Hall et al. 2022). Teacher candidates are introduced to these perspectives prior to engaging in the inquiry project. Specifically, the project requires teacher candidates to complete the following:

1. Individually they identify a cultural community (immigrant, refugee, etc.) of interest and make arrangements to engage in a conversation with a family (ideally with young English learners) to discuss language learning, sociocultural adjustment, social capital, funds of knowledge, experiences in the home country(ies), transnational complexities, and family and school engagement experiences;
2. Individually they research credible sources of information (e.g., CultureGrams, National Geographic) about the home country(ies) of the identified family and their local cultural community;
3. Collaboratively they develop conversation/dialogue questions (e.g., about communication challenges in/with school/staff, acculturation and immigrant

experience; lack of socio-cultural capital) to be used when meeting with a family member they identified and secured agreement for a home visit or a phone/video call;
4. Individually they meet up with the family (member) for a conversation/dialogue;
5. Individually they write up the results of the inquiry project, including critical reflection on the experience; and
6. Share the results in class.

For more information about the project and its steps, please see the Appendix.

Critical Reflections: Potentials and Challenges

Overall, this activity is a way for teacher candidates to meaningfully engage with an immigrant family and critically reflect on the intercultural communication and learning experience throughout this project. One of the major benefits of the activity is that it forces teacher candidates to step out of their comfort zone. It also is an eye-opening experience that makes beliefs and attitudes explicit through reflection. For example, a teacher candidate in final reflections on the project stated:

> School administration occasionally assumes that parents of EL students do not care about their child's education. In reality, this is not true at all. The parents of EL students want their children to succeed just as much as any other parent would. A perfect example of this is the mother I interviewed for this assignment. I quickly learned from our interview that one of the main reasons she moved to the United States was to make sure her child would receive a better education and have more opportunities. One note of importance is that the mother is not as involved in her daughter's education as she could be due to her language barrier. This could easily be avoided/remedied by taking the time to get to know the mother and finding an effective way to communicate despite the language barrier.

This project, therefore, provides a context for dialogue about the immigrant experience and gives course participants foundational knowledge and an active experiential stance toward such knowledge through direct intercultural communication that is imperative for navigating interactions in a globalized world, including those in a linguistically diverse classroom and community. Most importantly, this project benefits not only teacher candidates but also validates the experiences of immigrant/newcomer families they visit and interact with, who share stories that otherwise might never be revealed.

Potential challenges when implementing this activity might include the course participants' initial hesitation to complete the project, possibly, due to a lack of experience in interacting with those who come from a cultural and linguistic community different from their own. Other challenges of implementing this project include that teacher candidates might lack confidence in discussing various topics (required by the guidelines; see the Appendix) due to limited knowledge and experience or simply feeling uncomfortable asking questions that might be sensitive (e.g., informant's reasons for leaving home country and coming to the United States, informant's experiences with bias). As an immigrant parent myself, I often share my personal stories of parental engagement to illustrate concepts and provide specific examples of, for example, how privilege or lack of it can impact a child's academic success or social-emotional well-being in a school setting. My own stories contribute to teacher candidates' understanding of interculturality in the education process and support their teacher learning throughout the discussed inquiry project, too.

In conclusion, family and community engagement is an important topic in the ESL Foundations course. Family and community members become essential to cultivating linguistically and culturally responsive spaces for young children. In the United States, early childhood educators and other stakeholders often identify as predominantly monolingual (just as is the case in my own teaching context) and may feel ill-prepared to establish a linguistically and culturally responsive context. In teacher education spaces, engaging teacher candidates in a meaningful interaction with an EL immigrant or refugee or displaced newcomer family allows authentic first-hand learning about family experiences with education, among other important takeaways. Such engagement provides opportunities to hear voices and stories about what it takes to come to the United States; what it takes to learn a new language and integrate into a new community as an adult; what it takes to raise bilingual/multilingual children often without the social/cultural capital; what it is like to engage in child's education; and how teachers can advocate for culturally and linguistically diverse students and their families. Overall, this project serves as an agent of interculturality that takes teacher candidates outside of their comfort zone and effectively enables intercultural dialogue and intercultural learning.

References

Byram, M. (1997), *Teaching and Assessing Intercultural Communicative Competence*, London: Multilingual Matters.
Deardorff, D. (2020), Manual for Developing Intercultural Competences: Story Circles, UNESCO/Routledge. Available online: https://unesdoc.unesco.org/ark:/48223/pf0000370336 (accessed October 20, 2022).
Guilherme, M. (2002), *Critical Citizens for an Intercultural World: Foreign Language Education as Cultural Politics*, London: Multilingual Matters.
Hall, B. J., P. Covarrubias and K. A. Kirschbaum (2022), *Among Cultures: The Challenges of Communication*, New York: Routledge.
Johnson, K. E. and P. R. Golombek (2011), "The Transformative Power of Narrative in Second Language Teacher Education", *TESOL Quarterly*, 45 (3): 486–509.
Pennycook, A. (2001), *Critical Applied Linguistics: A Critical Introduction*, New York: Routledge.
Pentón Herrera, L. J. and R. L. McNair (2021), "Restorative and Community-Building Practices as Social Justice for English Learners", *TESOL Journal*, 12 (1): 1–11.
Ríos Vega, J. A. (2020), "School to Deportation Pipeline: Latino Youth Counter-Storytelling Narratives", *Journal of Latinos and Education*, 22 (1): 1–13.

Yazan, B., L. J. Pentón Herrera and D. Rashed (2023), "Transnational TESOL Practitioners' Identity Tensions: A Collaborative Autoethnography", *TESOL Quarterly*, 57 (1): 140–67.

Appendix

Inquiry Project Description, Components, and Sample Work

The Rationale for the Assignment

Learn about an immigrant community that is of interest to you professionally and/or personally. Meet with an immigrant family that is a part of that community and learn about their cultural background, their experiences in the United States, and the experiences of their child(ren) in primary or secondary educational settings, especially those receiving ESL/English language development support.

Assignment Guidelines

1. Decide what immigrant community or cultural and linguistic group you would like to learn more about. It has to be a country/culture that you are not very familiar with and one that is representative of your current or future EL students' backgrounds. Find an immigrant family that represents that linguistic/cultural group and contact them to set up a meeting to discuss their experiences in the United States and their child(ren)'s experiences in US school(s).
2. Notify me about your plan.
3. Do some preliminary research about the home country(ies), culture(s) and language(s) of the immigrant family. I will provide you with some resources, too (CultureGrams, etc.).
4. Do a home visit or meet with an immigrant family member at a mutually agreed place. In class, we will develop a set of questions to be used during your meeting with the immigrant family. After the meeting, describe your observations and what you learned in a report (see guidelines below).
5. Prepare a two-page resource guide (a variety of useful and credible resources, such as books websites, and articles) that includes an annotated list of five resources about the country, cultures, and languages that are the focus of your inquiry.
6. Keep a log of hours as you work on completing this assignment. It is expected that this assignment requires at least 7–8 hours.
7. Finally, be ready to share the results of this project in class and submit a written report. The presentation will be informal and will be in the form of story-sharing, with the following components: initial reactions, reading sources and meeting family, and final (critical) reflections.

Written Report Guidelines

The report should include the following components:

1. **Five-page double-spaced paper/report** about your experiences and what you have learned from them. It should include a detailed summary of the conversation/discussion with (or a home visit to) the immigrant family and your reflections about the value of this fieldwork experience.
2. **Log of hours** (see below for format) you have put into the assignment. You need to be specific: date/hours/activity.
3. **Two-page** (single-spaced) **annotated resource guide** (five items) that represents the highlights of your investigation about the country and cultural/linguistic group(s) of your inquiry.

Prompt for Developing Conversation Guide and a Sample of Questions Developed by a Group

What would you like to learn by meeting with an immigrant parent/family? What questions would you ask to learn about their experiences and the experiences of their child(ren) in the United States?

Examples of questions developed by a group of students:
- What were some struggles that your family faced?
- What was your initial feeling about a new culture? (Culture shock)
- Did your child introduce any new ideas to adjust to new cultures?
- What are some differences in language learning for parents vs. adults?
- What are some ways you are still involved with your culture?

Suggested Topics/Questions to Explore during the Conversation with the Immigrant Family

1. Thank the informant for finding the time to meet with you. Explain that you would like to learn more about immigrant parents' experience and the experiences of their child/ren.
2. Begin by talking about yourself and how interested you are in understating immigrant experiences. You may point out that your family/ancestors at some point also came to this country as immigrants.
3. Broad topics to be discussed with the informant are the following:

    - Reasons for coming to the United States
    - Maintaining native culture in the United States
    - Expectations regarding schooling
    - Educational experiences in the United States vs. home country
    - Education and support children are getting at school
    - Parental involvement in the education/school
    - Expectations for integrating their culture in the teaching/learning process

- Role of English in interaction with children and experiences of learning English
- Local native culture connections
- Challenges they have experienced and success stories
- Assimilation versus integration into US culture(s)

4. Ask if they have any questions for you.
5. Thank the informant for their time and willingness to share their story.

As soon as your conversation is finished, give yourself time to make notes of your reactions and reflections. Do not try to remember it all later!

Part Ten

Global Englishes

Global Englishes: Pluricentricity of Norms, Benchmarks, Functions, and Contexts

Lili Cavalheiro

Introduction

The widespread use of English across many different domains and contexts has contributed to it becoming an international and global language employed by an array of different users. Its colonial past, along with its close link to more recent economic and cultural globalization, has consequently contributed to it reaching a "glocal" level with distinct "forms, roles, functions, statuses, uses and users" (Selvi and Yazan 2021: 1) worldwide. Most interactions nowadays comprise interlocutors from diverse linguistic and cultural backgrounds with their own Englishes, which requires further reflection when considering not only language, but also the language that is taught/learned.

This has inevitably raised several issues within the "traditional" perspective of English language teaching (ELT) where norms and the idealized monolithic native speaker continue to many of the times be the main input provided and against which learners'/users' proficiency and communicative effectiveness are measured. Since the mid-twentieth century, these issues have been raised and questioned within the fields of World Englishes (WE), English as an International Language (EIL), English as a Lingua Franca (ELF), and more recently, Global Englishes (GE), where English is viewed as being dynamic and flexible, since it is largely used by multicomponent users who acquired it alongside other languages, hence taking advantage of their multilinguistic repertoire. This had an impact not only on ELT, but also on English language teacher education, the latter being the ideal environment to promote innovative approaches where teachers, as agents of change, can critically (re)evaluate their teaching practices. By raising teachers' awareness of the pluricentricity associated with English and its use, a new set of competences are necessary when enhancing learners' mutual understanding, access to other countries/cultures, and self-expression.

Current Issues

The diverse and international use of English worldwide has been the object of study in recent years, with scholars focusing on complicated issues ranging from identity to language use and communication. As a result, several paradigms have emerged with the aim of describing the current sociolinguistic reality of English, namely, WE, EIL, ELF, and GE. Although GE is gaining ground in more recent works, these various notions have all provided an important contribution to the field.

While EIL was first to emerge with Smith's pivotal work in the 1970s and 1980s (Smith 1978; 1983), the WE paradigm quickly became more predominant with Kachru's influential (but also debatable) three concentric circles model (1985) which comprises the Inner, Outer, and Expanding Circles. The Inner Circle encompasses contexts where English is the primary language (e.g., the UK, the United States), whereas the Outer Circle includes postcolonial countries where English has an official status and is used as a common language alongside other local ones (e.g., India, Nigeria). The Expanding Circle, on the other hand, includes countries where English is taught/learned as a foreign language and where it is used as a language for international communication (e.g., China, Portugal). By acknowledging the localization, pluralization, and nativization of English, Kachru's proposal challenged long-standing perceptions regarding such issues as the validity of emergent varieties, the notion of identity, and the monolithic attitudes about the ownership of English. Since then, many WE works have been published that not only establish the legitimization of indigenized varieties of English, but also the study of national, regional, functional, and international Englishes where pragmatic, linguistic, social, and cultural issues are analyzed (e.g., Bolton 2013; Kachru and Smith 2008; Kirkpatrick 2021; Melchers, Shaw and Sundkvist 2019; Nelson, Proshina and Davis 2020; Sadeghpour and Sharifian 2021; Schneider 2020).

Most studies, however, tend to focus on the Inner and Outer Circles, leaving the Expanding Circle most of the time out of the equation as well as the cultural aspects of Englishes (Sharifian and Sadeghpour 2021). These shortcomings have contributed, however, to the emergence of further pluricentric paradigms like EIL and ELF. Smith (1976) already recognized English as an international language that connects countries and, in some cases, even functions as an auxiliary language uniting people within them. Since then, several authors have likewise used the term, such as Seidlhofer (2003), who viewed EIL as promoting the importance of English worldwide as well as its detachment from certain countries/cultures. Sharifian (2013) equally viewed the paradigm as being more inclusive, as it not only incorporated WE but also considered communication across all three of Kachru's circles, investigating both linguistic and cultural features.

Closely linked with this viewpoint is the ELF paradigm, where English is seen as a "common linguistic link and context bringing together individuals from diverse ethnolinguistic backgrounds" (Selvi and Yazan 2021: 1). Dating from the early 2000s (e.g., Jenkins 2005; 2007; Mauranen 2005; Seidlhofer 2001; 2009), ELF adopted a more inclusive approach when compared to WE, since in addition to the indigenous

English language use in the Outer Circle, it also focused on English language use in the Expanding Circle, particularly in international and diverse settings.

Stemming from WE, EIL, and ELF, GE has emerged as a more inclusive paradigm, comprising (non)native Englishes and the communication that takes place between both, as well as establishing the English from the three Kachruvian Circles as legitimate (Jenkins 2011; 2014). It is also seen as including "many peripheral issues associated with the global use of English, such as globalization, linguistic imperialism, education, language policy, and planning" (Galloway and Rose 2015: 224). Therefore, the intention of GE is not to replace these critically oriented paradigms, but rather to consolidate and unite them within this umbrella term (Galloway and Rose 2021; Sadeghpour and D'Angelo 2022; Selvi and Yazan 2021). Matsuda (2019) further reiterates how "different names indicate different intellectual history and affiliation, but they are more similar to each other than different in their assumptions, visions and suggested practice" (146). These research paradigms thus share the fact that they study not only the worldwide spread of English but also, more recently, the pedagogical implications regarding principles and practices in ELT, by raising awareness of a more comprehensive notion of the ownership of English and by questioning the inappropriateness of native norms and native-speaker centered curricula—key issues for language teaching and teacher education. By doing so, ELT may be viewed from a more inclusive perspective, hence contributing to more confident and well-prepared language teachers (especially non-native speakers) as well as more successful and multicompetent learners/users.

Implications for Teaching and Teacher Education

Given the (de)centralization, pluricentricity, and cross-cultural communicative scenarios associated with English, a GE Language Teaching (GELT) approach in ELT seems to respond to today's communicative demands (Fang 2020). Consequently, the traditional ELT paradigm centered on a "fixed" native English culture, along with the notion of Native (Standard) English speakers as being the norm, the target interlocutors, the role models, the "owners" of the language, and the basis for materials, has become largely outdated. Teaching/learning a global language like English nowadays thus requires another set of assumptions in comparison with other foreign languages, as it is necessary to consider the functional, cultural, and linguistic diversity of the language, subsequently requiring teachers to critically reassess and problematize their own pedagogical practices (e.g., Bayyurt and Selvi 2021; Matsuda and Friedrich 2011). Reconceptualizing one's inherent models, targets, principles, and practices, therefore, entails taking a closer look at what presently constitutes ELT, ranging from teaching materials to methodologies and assessment, a difficult task for many (teacher) educators and teacher trainees, since these issues are often underexplored or habitually dealt with at a theoretical level without "research-driven practices for language teachers" (Selvi and Yazan 2021: 3). Teachers and teacher educators may also be unfamiliar with GE or not recognize its importance in both language teaching and teacher education, due to the nonexistence of activities exemplifying the multitude of perspectives on diverse issues of ELT.

In response to this existing gap, Rose and Galloway (2021) propose a GELT framework where a pluricentric approach to language is presented and where six "calls to action" are put forth, highlighting key areas for (teacher) educators or trainees to focus and reflect upon:

1. Increase WE and ELF exposure in language curricula;
2. Emphasize respect for multilingualism in ELT;
3. Raise awareness of Global Englishes in ELT;
4. Raise awareness of ELF strategies in language curricula;
5. Emphasize respect for diverse culture and identity in ELT;
6. Change English teacher hiring practices in the ELT industry.

(Galloway and Rose 2021: 13)

The first call focuses on students coming across a wide range of varieties of English to prepare them for diverse intercultural communicative situations. The second is associated with the heightened recognition of integrating multilingualism, plurilingualism, and translanguaging in ELT pedagogies. The third highlights the importance of a critical approach in ELT, so as to raise a greater understanding of the international/global use of English. The fourth call, similarly to ELF, stresses the importance of students acquiring useful communicative strategies to interact in diverse international contexts. In the fifth, emphasis is placed on the need to recognize and acknowledge cultural diversity, which consequently leads to reassessing what is an "English-speaking" culture. And lastly, the sixth call refers to how native English speakers have held on to the privileged position as the ideal English teacher, dismissing many times qualified non-native English speakers.

In this sense, by encouraging a GE perspective, ELT educators may promote "GE-awareness" or take on a "GE-aware stance" with their learners, as Bayyurt and Selvi (2021) refer to. According to the authors, GELT is not associated with a specific teaching method (e.g., Task-based language teaching, Communicative Language teaching), but with "a set of macro principles transcending into existing methods and serving as a reference point for teachers in critically assessing, revisiting, and redefining their existing practices" (Bayyurt and Selvi 2021: 77). By critically (re)evaluating their teaching practices, teachers may consider the cultural and contextual issues at hand and make informed decisions regarding the teaching/learning goals, methodological decisions, instructional practices, and teaching materials applied in their respective contexts (Bayyurt and Sifakis 2017).

In addition to Rose and Galloway's GELT framework (2021), in recent years other proposals associated with GELT have likewise been put forth for practitioners to critically analyze and reconceptualize long-time established teaching practices. Sifakis and Bayyurt's transformative ELF-aware teacher education model (2015), for instance, is also groundbreaking, as it encompasses three different stages—theory, practice, and evaluation—that lead teachers to actively reflect, reconsider, and reposition themselves as well as their teaching practices. According to the model, teachers begin by becoming familiar with the notion of GE (including WE, EIL, and ELF) and its correlation with ELT, so to afterward distinguish established EFL approaches from a GE perspective.

With this, they may find a way to incorporate a GE approach in their classrooms and develop their own lesson plans by selecting, adapting, and critically developing their own materials and activities. It also allows them to follow students' progress and evaluate how taking a new approach can not only contribute to their own professional development, but also prepare learners for increasingly diverse communicative situations.

The Erasmus+ project English as a Lingua Franca Practices for Inclusive Multilingual Classrooms—ENRICH (2018-1-EL01-KA201-047894) in Europe has followed a similar path through its continuous development course (Sifakis and Kordia 2021), freely available online. Its innovative approach guides (either pre- or in-service level) participants in a way that explains and provides opportunities to reflect on key notions many times underexplored or underdeveloped (e.g., culture in ELT, translanguaging, methods, approaches, assessment), and subsequently, how they may apply this knowledge into their respective ELT contexts.

By bridging the gap between a GE framework and the teaching methodologies already in effect, teachers and teacher educators may take a step forward and critically reflect upon their methods, practices, and teaching materials to make more informed decisions based on their context and learners' needs. More classroom-based research is therefore also called upon (e.g., Galloway and Rose 2021) for teachers and researchers alike to have a better understanding of how GE-aware classrooms are being organized, hence contributing to further change.

References

Bayyurt, Y. and A. F. Selvi (2021), "Language Teaching Methods and Instructional Materials in Global Englishes", in A. F. Selvi and B. Yazan (eds), *Language Teacher Education for Global Englishes. A Practical Resource Book*, 75–81, London and New York: Routledge.

Bayyurt, Y. and N. Sifakis (2017), "Foundations of an EIL-Aware Teacher Education", in A. Matsuda (ed.), *Preparing Teachers to Teach English as an International Language*, 3–18, Bristol: Multilingual Matters.

Bolton, K. (2013), "World Englishes, Globalisation, and Language Worlds", in N. L. Johannesson, G. Melchers and Beyza Björkman (eds), *Of Butterflies and Birds, of Dialects and Genres: Essays in Honour of Philip Shaw*, 227–52, Stockholm: Acta Universitatis Stockholmiensis.

Fang, F. (2020), *Re-Positioning Accent Attitude in the Global Englishes Paradigm: A Critical Phenomenological Case Study in the Chinese Context*, London and New York: Routledge.

Galloway, N. and H. Rose (2015), *Introducing Global Englishes*, London and New York: Routledge.

Galloway, N. and H. Rose (2021), "The Global Spread of English and Global Englishes Language Teaching", in A. F. Selvi and B. Yazan (eds), *Language Teacher Education for Global Englishes. A Practical Resource Book*, 11–19, London and New York: Routledge.

Hall, C. J. and R. Wicaksono (2020), "Changing Englishes: An Online Course for Teachers (v.02.2)". Available Online: www.changingenglishes.online

Jenkins, J. (2005), "Teaching Pronunciation for English as a Lingua Franca: A Sociopolitical Perspective", in C. Gnutzmann and F. Intemann (eds), *The Globalisation of English and the English Language Classroom*, 145–58, Tubingen: Gunter Narr Verlag.

Jenkins, J. (2007), *English as a Lingua Franca: Attitude and Identity*, Oxford: Oxford University Press.
Jenkins, J. (2011), "Accommodating (to) ELF in the International University", *Journal of Pragmatics*, 43: 926–36.
Jenkins, J. (2014), *Global Englishes: A Resource Book for Students*, London and New York: Routledge.
Kachru, B. B. (1985), "Standards, Codification and Sociolinguistic Realism: The English Language in the Outer Circle", in R. Quirk and H. Widdowson (eds), *English in the World: Teaching and Learning the Language and Literatures*, 11–30, Cambridge: Cambridge University Press.
Kachru, Y. and I.E. Smith (2008), *Cultures, Contexts, and World Englishes*, London and New York: Routledge.
Kirkpatrick, A. (2021), *The Routledge Handbook of World Englishes*, London and New York: Routledge.
Matsuda, A. (2019), "World Englishes in English Language Teaching: Kachru's Six Fallacies and the TEIL Paradigm", *World Englishes*, 38: 144–54.
Matsuda, A. and P. Friedrich (2011), "English as an International Language: A Curriculum Blueprint", *World Englishes*, 30: 332–44.
Mauranen, A. (2005), "English as Lingua Franca: An Unknown Language?", in G. Cortese and A. Duszak (eds), *Identity, Community, Discourse. English in Intercultural Settings*, 269–93, Bern: Peter Lang.
Melchers, G., P. Shaw and P. Sundkvist (2019), *World Englishes*, 3rd edn, London and New York: Routledge.
Nelson, C.L., Z.G. Proshina and D. R. Davis (eds) (2020), *The Handbook of World Englishes*, Hong Kong: Wiley Blackwell.
Sadeghpour, M and F. Sharifian (eds) (2021), *Cultural Linguistics and World Englishes*, Singapore: Springer.
Sadeghpour, M. and J. D'Angelo (2022), "World Englishes and 'Global Englishes': Competing or Complementary Paradigms?", *Asian Englishes*, 24 (2): 1–10.
Schneider, E. W. (2020), *English around the World: An Introduction*, 2nd edn, Cambridge: Cambridge University Press.
Seidlhofer, B. (2001), "Closing a Conceptual Gap: The Case for a Description of English as a Lingua Franca", *International Journal of Applied Linguistics*, 11 (2): 133–58.
Seidlhofer, B. (2003), A Concept of International English and Related Issues: From "Real English" to "Realistic English"? Council of Europe. Available online: https://rm.coe.int/a-concept-of-international-english-and-related-issues-from-real-englis/168088782f (accessed February 15, 2023).
Seidlhofer, B. (2009), "Common Ground and Different Realities: World Englishes and English as a Lingua Franca", *World Englishes*, 28 (2): 236–45.
Selvi, A. F. and B. Yazan (eds) (2021), *Language Teacher Education for Global Englishes. A Practical Resource Book*, London and New York: Routledge.
Sharifian, F. (2013), "Globalisation and Developing Metacultural Competence in Learning English as an International Language", *Multilingual Education*, 3 (7): 1–11.
Sharifian, F. and M. Sadeghpour (2021), "World Englishes and Cultural Linguistics: An Overview", in M. Sadeghpour and F. Sharifian (eds), *Cultural Linguistics and World Englishes*, 1–14, Singapore: Springer Nature.
Sifakis, N. and S. Kordia, eds (2021), The ENRICH Continuous Professional Development Course. The ENRICH Project. Available online: http://enrichproject.eu/the-cpd-course (accessed February 10, 2023).

Sifakis, N. and Y. Bayyurt (2015), "Insights from ELF and WE in Teacher Training in Greece and Turkey", *World Englishes*, 34 (3): 471–84.

Smith, L. E. (1976), "English as an International Auxiliary Language", *RELC Journal*, 7 (2): 38–42.

Smith, L. E. (1978), "Some Distinctive Features of EIIL vs. ESOL in English Language Education", The Culture Learning Institute Report, June, 5–7 & 10–11. Also in L. E. Smith (ed.) (1983), *Readings in English as an International Language*, 13–20, Oxford: Pergamon Press.

Smith, L. (1983), *Readings in English as an International Language*, Oxford and New York: Pergamon.

Suggested Readings and External Links

- Galloway, N. and H. Rose (2015), Introducing Global Englishes. Routledge.
  Companion website: https://routledgetextbooks.com/textbooks/9780415835329/
  For each chapter there are: extra activities, PowerPoint slides; reading discussion lessons; debate lessons; extra assignment topics; research tasks; online audiovisual materials; links to speech samples of World Englishes.
- Hall, CJH. and R. Wicaksono (2020), Changing Englishes: An Interactive Course for Teachers (v.02.2)
  Course website: www.changingenglishes.online
  Free online course divided into five main units: Defining English; Using English; Learning English; Teaching English; and Changing English.
- Jenkins, J. (2014). Global Englishes: A Resource Book for Students. Routledge.
  Companion website: https://routledgetextbooks.com/textbooks/9780415638449
  This website provides supplementary resources to develop an understanding of English in the world, namely: exploratory activities to develop readers' critical thinking by questioning and evaluating issues of Global Englishes; flashcards reviewing acronyms, key issues, and definitions; audio files with intercultural exchanges of speakers from diverse lingua-cultural backgrounds.
- Sifakis, N. and S. Kordia, eds (2021). The ENRICH Continuous Professional Development Course. The ENRICH Project.
  Project website: http://enrichproject.eu/the-cpd-course
  This course contains thirty sections grouped into three main categories: Using, Teaching, and Learning English. Each section includes a video lecture, supplementary materials, and activities encouraging reflection and critical thinking concerning one's teaching experience and local requirements. Consult the Handbook as an important companion for the Continuing Professional Development course with indicative responses to the activities: http://enrichproject.eu/handbook.

Raising Pre-Service Teachers' Global Englishes Awareness through a Materials Development Project

Michelle Kunkel and Kenny Harsch

Background

This chapter describes a project from a course titled "Teaching & Materials Development with a Global Englishes Focus," taught at the University of Hawai'i at Mānoa. Each author has taught the course once, with adjustments between Iterations 1 and 2 based on our shared reflections. Thirty-four undergraduates majoring or minoring in Second Language Studies took the course. Although most identified as pre-service teachers, few had formal teaching and contextualized lesson planning experience. Most pre-service teachers seemed open to the critical approach we presented, perhaps because of the nature of our program and frequent exposure to Hawai'i's linguistic diversity.

Rose and Galloway (2019) highlight the compatibility between GE and critical pedagogy. GE recognizes the ideologies surrounding ELT, particularly linguistic imperialism and the alleged superiority and privilege associated with standard language ideology (Lippi-Green 2012), native-speakerism (Holliday 2006), and inner-circle varieties (Kachru 1992) while problematizing these ideologies' influence on ELT. In contrast, a GE approach seeks to eliminate the native/non-native distinction and focus instead on developing successful GE users. Whether L2 or L1 users of Englishes, successful users

1. incorporate interactional strategies to negotiate understanding, navigate communicative conversations, build rapport, and deepen harmony in personal and professional relationships;
2. cooperatively accommodate other interlocutors;
3. continually raise their awareness of varieties of Englishes and appreciation of their validity;
4. develop openness to multiple cultures, perspectives, and ways of expressing ideas; and
5. evolve their sense of ownership and respect of others' ownership of their own Englishes.

In short, underlying GE is the aim to truly level the playing field for Englishes worldwide, something we hoped pre-service teachers would recognize and embrace through our course.

GE proponents acknowledge the scarcity of, and need for, materials exposing learners to a wide array of English[1] users and situations where Englishes are used for meaningful communication (e.g., Matsuda 2012; Rose and Galloway 2019). Published textbooks tend to perpetuate native-speaker norms and Inner Circle varieties (Matsuda 2002; Rose and Syrbe 2018). The above-mentioned literature suggests, at a conceptual level, that GE aims could be integrated into ELT; however, operationalizing and implementing those ideas are rarely addressed. For example, GE scholars hint that the internet contains many examples of varieties of Englishes and users (e.g., Rose et al. 2020), but we are not aware of any one-stop sites for teachers' or learners' access, nor any tasks that focus learners' attention on GE aims while viewing these videos. This gap needs to be filled if we want more teachers to adopt a GE approach.

Our course aimed to address this gap by allowing pre-service teachers to explore the complexities involved in creating materials incorporating a GE focus. In the course, we introduced key concepts underlying GE and GE for language teaching (GELT, Rose and Galloway 2019), discussed how to translate those concepts into GE-focused pedagogy, assessment, and materials, and considered some barriers to GE innovation.

Description of the Practice

What we describe here is a mid-term project that provided pre-service teachers with experience developing materials for exposing learners to different Englishes. Pre-service teachers found samples of users of English varieties worldwide and developed activities to help English learners expand their GE awareness while heightening ownership of their own varieties. Pre-service teachers created materials to expose English learners to Englishes beyond the Inner Circle and provide tasks to help raise learners' awareness about GE aims. Each set of materials included one or more video or audio clips; a cover sheet describing the teaching context, target population, objectives, and student learning outcomes (SLOs); and a worksheet designed for learners. Each worksheet needed to include at least two tasks drawing learners' attention to aspects of the clips that highlight GE aims, plus a reflective task guiding learners to consider what they learned about variation in Englishes and what they could apply to their own uses of Englishes.

We provided a list of potential, but not exhaustive, GE aims (Appendix A[2]), and encouraged pre-service teachers to find clips with examples of successful modeling of one or more of these aims (or failure in one of these areas because both could raise learners' awareness). For the listening tasks, we provided example questions focusing on GE aims (e.g., "How easy is it for you to understand this speaker? (1=very difficult, 5=very easy)" and "What can you do to improve your ability to understand speakers of different English varieties?") along with hints to help pre-service teachers create relevant tasks and questions (e.g., "For publicly available videos, consider using the comments section to draw learners' attention to attitudes toward different Englishes"). Students presented their materials in small groups for feedback from classmates and the instructor, and then revised and submitted their final products. Our presentation guidelines included a suggested process (Appendix B) and guiding questions for peer feedback (Appendix C).

Critical Reflections: Potentials and Challenges

When searching for materials, some pre-service teachers struggled to understand how GE is a critical step away from pervasive ideologies. For instance, one pre-service teacher brought a video of an Australian, an American, and a Brit discussing vocabulary differences despite our requirement that video clips feature varieties beyond the Inner Circle.[3] Some others had difficulty finding examples of real communication and wanted to use "social experiment" videos, which featured pranksters "testing" others' English abilities by pretending not to speak the local language. Such videos, clearly meant for entertainment, did not align with our goal of showcasing authentic communication.

In Iteration 1, Japanese and Korean English users were overrepresented in videos pre-service teachers selected. In Iteration 2, we compiled example videos from around the world and encouraged pre-service teachers to expand the varieties presented in their projects, resulting in broader representation of GE users across Asia, Africa, Europe, and North America.

Some pre-service teachers also struggled to comprehend the expected final product due to their lack of lesson planning and teaching experience, a lack of existing examples, and not experiencing example tasks from a GE learner's perspective. Adapting broad GE aims to measurable SLOs for student tasks was challenging (e.g., How does one measure respect for all varieties of Englishes or ownership of English?), and some pre-service teachers could not conceive how to create tasks or discussion questions focused on the aims of awareness and recognition of the validity of all varieties. Additionally, some pre-service teachers had difficulty paraphrasing GE concepts and aims into learner-friendly language when writing reflection questions, as shown below:

- "What do you notice about how the speaker **initiated and carried out** the conversation? What did they do to **negotiate meaning** or **compensate for uncertainty** while speaking?"
- "How do you think ____ **relates to ownership** of GE?"

These difficulties could be resolved by providing samples of exemplary worksheets, having pre-service teachers complete the tasks as GE learners (a suggestion from one pre-service teacher), or by having pre-service teachers critique micro-teaching recordings from previous semesters.

Despite its challenges, this project helped pre-service teachers develop critical language awareness and positive attitudes toward GELT. In the final course evaluation[4] for Iteration 1, two pre-service teachers mentioned GE's implications for their future practice:

> [W]e looked at GE very critically. We considered who could benefit from it, how to teach it, potential problems teaching and using it, assessment of GE, and we now have easy access to some examples of lesson plans to teach GE.
>
> I think the purpose of gaining this course's content wasn't only to be more knowledgeable, but to help visualize and shape what type of educator we want to become, what content we want to present, and how we can present the content to future students or board of education systems.

Although pre-service teachers understood GE concepts theoretically, some still struggled with letting go of existing ideologies when creating their projects, while others felt challenged by the task of creating lessons with a GE focus, as illustrated in one pre-service teacher's reflection from Iteration 1.

> It was honestly a bit difficult to integrate GE aims into our tasks and activities. We were used to creating lesson plans that did not incorporate these aims, as ... our lesson plans for other classes mainly focused on making sure the students would be able to understand the content and did not find the tasks difficult for their proficiency level ... we were somewhat used to creating plans to teach with more of a native speaker mindset.

Most pre-service teachers acknowledged and accepted the existence of the wide variety of Englishes. Additionally, pre-service teachers who were L2 users realized their English variety's validity, which boosted their confidence and ownership, as one pre-service teacher noted after Iteration 2:

> Learning about the language ideologies have [sic] changed my thoughts on language learning. ... I personally felt stressed when I couldn't pronounce English words correctly or when I couldn't speak English correctly, but I realized that accents or word choices are one of my identities and I don't need to feel stressed about it.

As illustrated above, the course helped pre-service teachers develop critical stances toward native speakerism and standard language ideology. Another student in Iteration 2 problematized standard language ideology in relation to GE, observing:

> Standardization of English ... has been the debated topic of this class for many reasons, including its exclusion for English variation and the fact the "standard" is based around how one country or group of people use English. This class opened my eyes just to how powerful this standard is to the learners of English around the world as these ideologies shape English education.

In Iteration 2, students realized that YouTube comments were useful task content since they revealed attitudes toward standard language ideology. Half of the projects in this Iteration incorporated such comments into their tasks to encourage language learners' engagement in critical dialogue about SLI, native speakerism, and GE. A project exemplifying this is provided in Appendix D.

Overall, this project helped pre-service teachers develop their awareness of GE aims, take critical stances toward ELT ideologies, and consider GELT's role in their future teaching. Given the lack of one-stop sites and example GE-focused tasks, we hope to use these projects in a materials bank that any teacher can access. Providing high-quality tasks rather than full lesson plans may assist teachers who want to incorporate GE into their classes but face contextual constraints. We want to show teachers that even in such circumstances, it is possible to expose learners to the diversity of English norms, uses, and functions in today's world, and thereby, help students develop critical perspectives on their own language use and embrace the validity of their own Englishes.

Notes

1. We use "Englishes" when the word is a noun to emphasize a focus on multiple varieties. However, when used as an adjective, we use "English."
2. Visit this link to view our full appendices: https://go.hawaii.edu/RSk.
3. We did not specify that Inner Circle varieties should be avoided but rather that videos should include at least one non-Inner Circle user whose English was important to the tasks. Appendix D demonstrates how videos featuring Inner Circle users can be used productively.
4. We utilize comments from final course evaluations and reflections because we did not collect feedback directly after the mid-term project.

References

Holliday, A. (2006), "Native-Speakerism", *ELT Journal*, 60 (4): 385–7. doi:10.1093/elt/ccl030.

Kachru, B. B. (1992), *The Other Tongue: English across Cultures*, Urbana-Champaign, IL: University of Illinois Press.

Lippi-Green, R. (2012), *English with an Accent: Language, Ideology, and Discrimination in the United States*, 2nd edn, London: Routledge. doi:10.4324/9780203348802.

Matsuda, A. (2002), "'International Understanding' through Teaching World Englishes", *World Englishes*, 21 (3): 436–40. doi:10.1111/1467-971X.00262.

Matsuda, A. (ed.) (2012), *Principles and Practices of Teaching English as an International Language*, Bristol: Multilingual Matters. doi:10.21832/9781847697042.

Rose, H. and N. Galloway (2019), *Global Englishes for Language Teaching*, Cambridge: Cambridge University Press. doi:10.1017/9781316678343.

Rose, H., and M. Syrbe, A. Montakantiwong and N. Funada (2020), *Global TESOL for the 21st Century: Teaching English in a Changing World*, Bristol, UK: Multilingual Matters. doi:10.21832/9781788928199.

Syrbe, M. and H. Rose (2018), "An Evaluation of the Global Orientation of English Textbooks in Germany", *Innovation in Language Learning and Teaching*, 12 (2): 152–63. doi:10.1080/17501229.2015.1120736.

33

A *Translingual Project* to Explore Multilingual Identity and Challenge Dominant Language Ideologies

Kristina B. Lewis

Background

In this chapter, I describe a project that I assigned in a *Sociolinguistics in Education* course, required for master's students studying TESOL or Intercultural Communication at a large, mid-Atlantic, research-intensive university in the United States. I taught this course online in fall 2020, with class work divided between asynchronous modules and synchronous video-conferencing meetings. Students included both American and international students, primarily from China; they had a range of prior teaching experiences, both in the United States and abroad. While many students aimed to work in language education, others planned to pursue doctorates in applied linguistics or work in adjacent fields, such as international student advising or curriculum development.

The language teacher education program stresses a critical approach to second language development and pedagogy. Within the required Sociolinguistics in Education course, for example, students not only learn about linguistic variation within the global speech community but are expected to reflect and write critically about their own past and future experiences with discourse communities, language varieties, and language ideologies. Both the program and course stress the importance of English as a global language with a range of speakers and diverse norms. For example, we discussed the myth of a neutral standard English language variety that is often taught to language learners and the importance of instead incorporating World Englishes. We also discussed identity from a critical lens, reviewing topics such as the academic discourse socialization of international students and raciolinguistic ideologies (Flores and Rosa 2015; Rosa 2016).

Description of the Practice

One of the culminating projects for the Sociolinguistics in Education course was a *Translingual Project*, which I adapted from Nelson Flores (see Flores and Aneja 2017). This project required students to use translingual rhetorical strategies (Canagarajah 2013a; b) to examine the relationship between language and identity and to challenge dominant language ideologies. The project was open ended, with students allowed to create any form of written or audiovisual text to address this prompt. Students first read Canagarajah (2013a: 50) and reviewed the four translingual macro-strategies that he introduces: envoicing strategies—how "writers mesh semiotic resources for their identities and interests"; recontextualization strategies—which "aim to frame the text according to the desired genre and communicative conventions and establish a suitable footing to negotiate meaning"; interactional strategies—which "facilitate the co-construction of meaning"; and entextualization strategies—how "writers manage text construction to facilitate voice and meaning." We also looked at how others had used translingual strategies, for example in Gloria Anzaldúa's (1987) writing and Jamila Lysicott's (2014) TED talk. Students were encouraged to use any or multiple modalities, such as text, audio, and/or video to convey their intended meanings. Students could incorporate translingual strategies (as described by Canagarajah 2013a) in any way throughout their project, and they wrote a final reflection paper articulating how they did so.

Students completed the *Translingual Project* in four stages:
1. Students wrote a first draft or outline of the project, which they shared with me and a classmate.
2. Students gave each other feedback on their first drafts/outlines, focusing on the author's incorporation of translingual strategies, major messages about language and identity, and attempts to challenge or resist dominant language ideologies. Feedback was either oral or written; students received credit when both partners reported that feedback had been shared.
3. Students met with me for individual conferences to discuss their projects before or after submitting the first draft/outline.
4. Students submitted a final draft of their project, along with a written reflection describing their goals and intentions within the project.

Most aspects of this project were graded for completion (the first draft/outline, peer feedback, instructor conference, and project itself). I used a rubric (Appendix) to assess the written reflection. Students' projects demonstrated a range of engagement with language ideologies, multilingual identity, translingual rhetorical strategies, and creative practices. Final products included analytical and narrative writing, podcasts, videos, and pedagogical artifacts. With permission from the students, the figures in this chapter illustrate some of the *translingual projects* that were created.

Figure 33.1 shows the first page of an Intercultural Communication student's *translingual project*, an extended essay documenting the flooding of the town of Hasankeyf in Batman, a Kurdish-majority town in Türkiye, the sociolinguistic ideologies that position Kurds as languageless (Rosa 2016), and the student's own experiences living and working in Türkiye as an English teacher who married into a Kurdish-speaking family. Visible on this first page are Brooke's engagement with multiple language varieties—English, Turkish, and Kurdish; modes of representation—text, image, and linked video (via the musical notes); and rhetorical genres—analytical writing represented by the citations in her footnotes, narrative and reflective writing in the documentary text, and lyrics in the Kurdish folk song. Through this project, Brooke critiqued an ideology that positions Turkish Kurds as lacking both language

Figure 33.1 Page 1 of Brooke's *Translingual Project*.

Figure 33.2 Screenshot of Shweta's *Translingual Project*.

and a distinct ethnic identity, and she called attention to the value of bilingualism for a minoritized population (Flores, Tseng and Subtirelu 2020).

Figure 33.2 shows a screenshot near the end of a TESOL student's *translingual project*, a video of herself creating original artwork with watercolor paints and colored pencils, with voiceover text conveying a message about the importance of embracing diversity in language and communication. Shweta drew three individuals with separate speech bubbles, each represented by a primary color: red, yellow, and blue—then linked the speech bubbles by mixing the colors. Through this project, she highlighted the fluidity of language and the value of cross-cultural interaction. The final lines of her voiceover, partially shown in Figure 33.2, were, "Every shade is wonderful. Every hue, a blessing." The text and image of Shweta's project critiqued the notion of individuals having singular, static identities and linguistic repertoires. Instead, by mixing the colors, she showed how interactions are always, already drawing across a range of cultural cues and linguistic strategies.

Figure 33.3 shows the final slide of a TESOL student's *translingual project*, a PowerPoint presentation with images and embedded audio clips of an interview she conducted with a German friend who spoke English as an additional language. On this slide, Jessica lists and (in the audio) discusses her "main takeaways" about translingualism from conducting the interview and reflecting on her conversation with her friend about their cultural and linguistic similarities and differences, highlighting in particular the ideas that translingualism is more than simply mixing named language varieties, that meaning is negotiated by all users in an interaction, and that "language and identity are intertwined." Through this project, Jessica developed a better understanding of translanguaging in practice and critiqued the idea that all language users should be expected to use the same "standard" language variety.

A Translingual Project to Explore Multilingual Identity 257

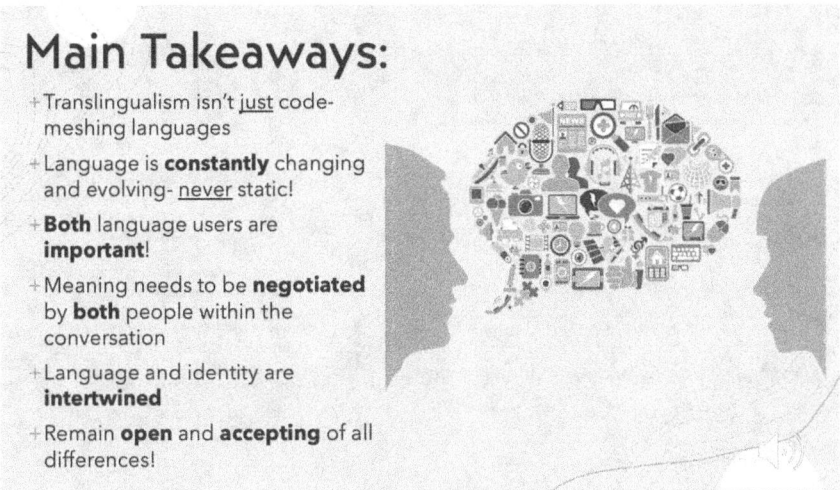

Figure 33.3 Final slide of Jessica's *Translingual Project*.

Figure 33.4 shows two pages of a TESOL student's *translingual project*, a teaching artifact she created to be used with Chinese middle school students learning English as a Foreign Language (EFL). Flora's four-page "'idealized' written diary" draws on her full communicative repertoire: both languages she considered herself fluent in—English and Chinese—and languages she had less knowledge of—Japanese and Korean. These pages also demonstrate her use of other visual modes of representation, such as emojis, brand icons, and illustrations to convey meaning. She created this artifact as a model that could be used to introduce EFL learners to the concepts of translingual writing before asking them to create their own translingual artifacts utilizing their entire communicative repertoires. Flora's project represents the clearest connection to pedagogy, highlighting the critical possibilities of using multilingualism and translingual strategies within a model text for learners of English as a global language.

Critical Reflections: Potentials and Challenges

In asking students to engage in this project, I invited them to try out translingual rhetorical strategies as they reflected on their own identities and experiences with language, culture, and ideology. Their projects were all different, and students were enthusiastic about both the criticality and the creativity that this project facilitated. For most, this project was unlike others they had been asked to complete during their language teacher education coursework—yet, especially with the requirement that they submit a reflection paper describing the intentionality around their rhetorical and ideological strategies, the project was incredibly rigorous.

Asking students—particularly pre-service language teachers—to engage in critical reflection on their own communicative practices and language ideologies is a first step

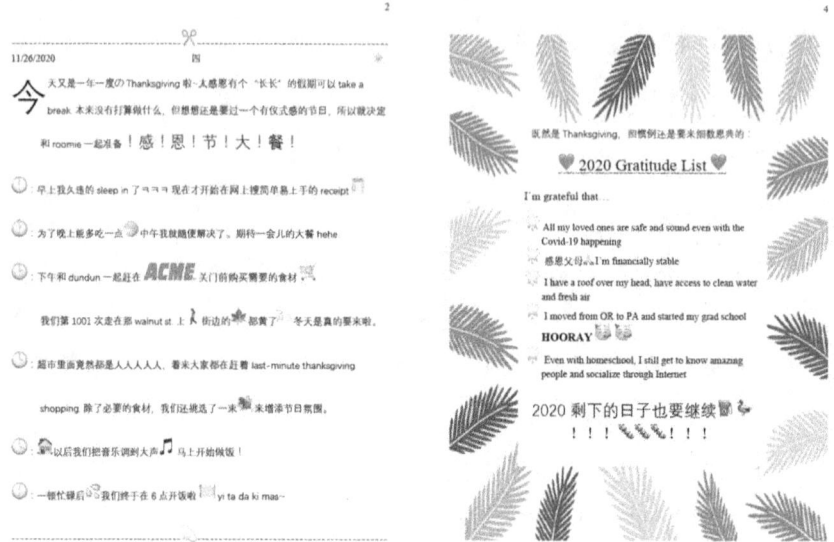

Figure 33.4 Pages 2 and 4 of Flora's *Translingual Project*.

Note: Page 2 is a Thanksgiving day diary entry written from the perspective of a Chinese-dominant multilingual student, whereas page 4 shows a Thanksgiving "Gratitude List" that uses English to represent the influence of living in the United States on an international student.

toward preparing them to engage critically with diverse language varieties and World Englishes, as well as to develop a translingual disposition (Canagarajah 2013b). Just introducing preservice teachers to theory about translanguaging and a multilingual orientation may not be sufficient to prepare them to support multilingual students to engage in such practices within their future classrooms (Barros et al. 2021); this project goes a step further by requiring students to actively engage in the creation of translingual texts and to reflect critically about their own linguistic and cultural identities in relation to circulating language ideologies. As Ponzio (2020: 10) observed, "teacher educators must consider how [teacher candidates] can develop and demonstrate the necessary disposition for translanguaging pedagogy before they enter their field placements." A project such as this one, perhaps especially if students were encouraged or required to create teaching artifacts like Flora chose to or if the reflection included a focus on their future teaching, is an important step—beyond simply responding to theory or course readings—along this path. While I did not conduct research on the effects of this project on students' later orientations to language teaching, Flores and Aneja's (2017) study of a similar project demonstrated that introducing a translingual orientation and asking students to engage with it in this way could lead to them experimenting with a translingual approach to second language teaching. Future research could also observe pre-service teachers' attempts to apply these practices as they begin their language teaching careers.

One challenge of enacting this assignment is the level of support that students need, particularly those who identify as monolingual English speakers (yet even these students draw on a diverse linguistic repertoire in their daily interactions). Developing a translingual orientation toward communication requires one to identify and resist dominant ideologies within English-speaking communities and the field of English language teaching, which have long upheld the ideals of a "standard English" and the norms of an idealized "native speaker" (Holliday 2006; Milroy 2007). In this project, I scaffolded students' engagement with these ideas through course readings and discussions, multiple drafts, and feedback from both peers and instructor. These strategies were successful in preparing students to begin to develop a critical, translingual orientation toward communication and language teaching. For other teacher educators embarking on a project similar to this one, I would encourage flexibility—expect to be surprised by the critical and creative approaches and messages student teachers choose to showcase when given the opportunity.

References

Anzaldúa, G. (1987), *Borderlands, La Frontera: The New Mestiza*, San Francisco: Aunt Lute Book Company.

Barros, S., L. M. Domke, C. Symons and C. Ponzio (2021), "Challenging Monolingual Ways of Looking at Multilingualism: Insights for Curriculum Development in Teacher Preparation", *Journal of Language, Identity & Education*, 20 (4): 239–54.

Canagarajah, A. S. (2013a), "Negotiating Translingual Literacy: An Enactment", *Research in the Teaching of English*, 48 (1): 40–67.

Canagarajah, A. S. (2013b), *Translingual Practice: Global Englishes and Cosmopolitan Relations*, New York: Routledge.

Flores, N. and G. Aneja (2017), "'Why Needs Hiding?' Translingual (Re)orientations in TESOL Teacher Education", *Research in the Teaching of English*, 51: 441–63.

Flores, N. and J. Rosa (2015), "Undoing Appropriateness: Raciolinguistic Ideologies and Language Diversity in Education", *Harvard Educational Review*, 85 (2): 149–71.

Flores, N., A. Tseng and N. Subtirelu (2020), "Bilingualism for All or Just for the Rich and White? Introducing a Raciolinguistic Perspective to Dual Language Education", in N. Flores, A. Tseng and N. Subtirelu (eds), *Bilingualism for All?*, 1–18, Blue Ridge Summit: Multilingual Matters.

Holliday, A. (2006), "Native-Speakerism", *ELT Journal*, 60 (4): 385–7.

Lysicott, J. (2014), 3 Ways to Speak English [TED Talk], TEDSalon NY2014. Available online: https://www.ted.com/talks/jamila_lyiscott_3_ways_to_speak_english (accessed October 1, 2022).

Milroy, J. (2007), "The Ideology of the Standard Language", in C. Llamas, L. Mullany and P. Stockwell (eds), *The Routledge Companion to Sociolinguistics*, 133–9, New York: Routledge.

Ponzio, C. M. (2020), "(Re)Imagining a Translingual Self: Shifting One Monolingual Teacher Candidate's Language Lens", *Linguistics and Education*, 60: 100866.

Rosa, J. D. (2016), "Standardization, Racialization, Languagelessness: Raciolinguistic Ideologies across Communicative Contexts", *Journal of Linguistic Anthropology*, 26 (2): 162–83.

Appendix

Table 33.1 *Translingual Project* written reflection rubric

Criteria	Points
Translingual Strategies—A detailed description of the different translingual strategies (at least 2), examples of their use within the project, and rationale for their use is provided. Discussion uses appropriate terminology from course readings.	15
Major Message—A detailed description of the major message(s) that you hoped to convey in your *translingual project* is provided, with evidence of specific examples from the project.	15
Dominant Language Ideologies—A detailed description is provided of the ways that both the message and the translingual strategies used were meant to challenge dominant language ideologies. Discussion uses appropriate terminology from course readings.	15
Peer Feedback—A detailed description is provided of how and why you chose to incorporate—or not incorporate—peer feedback into your final draft of the project. (Note: You don't have to incorporate your peer's feedback, but you do have to thoughtfully discuss your decision-making.)	15
Total points:	60

Building Global Englishes into a Pre-Service Teacher Education Curriculum

Naashia Mohamed

Background

No other language in the history of the world has ever enjoyed the status of a global language in the way that English does today. With the spread of English across the world, new varieties of the language have emerged. Yet, these varieties have often been excluded and alienated on the belief that they were substandard. In recent years, critical applied linguistic perspectives have started to embrace the diverse ways in which English is used by challenging the Anglocentric interpretation of standard models of language competence (e.g., Kachru and Nelson 2006; Lourdes 2006), while calling for the acceptance and inclusion of varieties of English in language teaching (e.g., Kirkpatrick 2007; Matsuda 2018) and language teacher education (e.g., Rose and Galloway 2019; Selvi and Yazan 2021). The paradigm shift from the traditionally idealized concept of standard English to a pluricentric view where all varieties of English are valued has implications for language teaching and teacher education. This challenges long-held assumptions about the ownership of English and what constitutes good models of language. McKay (2003), for example, suggests that the global nature of English means that it has become "renationalized," and no longer associated with a particular nation. Relatedly, there is a need to move beyond focusing on "native" speakers and adopt inclusive ideologies that validate individuals from various ethnolinguistic backgrounds with multiple forms of competence in English (Mauranen 2012; Ortega 2016).

Language is more than simply a means of expression or communication. The practice of languaging constructs, and is constructed by, the ways we perceive ourselves, our connections to our surroundings, our histories, and our projections about our place in the future (Norton 2013). Given the complex sociocultural and political dimensions of language learning (Duff 2019; Kramsch 2021), and the integral role of sociolinguistic competence in one's ability to use language effectively (Canale and Swain 1980; Littlewood 2011), there is a need for us as educators to refocus our lens to viewing students' linguistic, racial, and cultural diversities not as deficiencies to overcome but as assets, possessing vibrant realities and knowledge useful for teaching and learning (Ladson-Billings 1995; Paris 2012). As Crookes (2013) argues, language teacher education must be built upon awakening teachers' critical consciousness to challenge dominant ideologies in society and work toward achieving social justice.

As a language teacher educator, I aim to raise my students' awareness of these issues and encourage them to engage in critical discussions about the influence of English in our individual lives and in society. I will illustrate how I adopt a critical approach in one of my TESOL (Teaching English to Teachers of Other Languages) teacher education courses. *Contemporary Issues in TESOL* is an undergraduate course that is offered to pre-service teachers as part of the Bachelor of Education in TESOL at the University of Auckland. The topics addressed in this course include examining intercultural citizenship, addressing equity in TESOL, the changing role of the language teacher, and World Englishes, to help empower pre-service teachers to address inequities and critically reflect on their own identities and positioning in society. As most students who undertake the course are from Expanding Circle countries (Kachru 1985) where English is used as an international language, and will go on to work as teachers of English in their home contexts, the critical perspective is important to help them reenvision themselves as legitimate users and future teachers of English.

Description of the Practice

In the module on World Englishes, I aim to first dispel the myth that there is one correct form of English which everyone needs to emulate, by drawing attention to the use of different Englishes in radio and television programs in different parts of world, including English-dominant countries. Some helpful resources for this include the following:

- BBC Sounds website (https://sounds.bl.uk/), particularly the *One Language Many Voices* and *Listening Project* pages.
- Dialects of English Archive (https://www.dialectsarchive.com/).
- World Wide Internet TV (https://wwitv.com/english-news-tv-live/index.html).

My aim in inviting teacher candidates to listen to short segments from these programs is to illustrate that even within English-dominant countries, there are variations of use. In one activity, teacher candidates choose 3–5 recordings on a similar theme (e.g., childhood memories, games, descriptions of a place, etc.) and identify linguistic features that were unusual/unfamiliar. Using their findings as a basis, we discuss the variations in language, and how it affects intelligibility and language attitudes using different prompts (e.g., How much of the recording did you understand? Did you think they spoke good English? What kind of impression did you form of the speaker?). These discussions help to raise awareness of linguistic diversity, develop empathy toward users, and caution against linguistic stereotyping.

On the online discussion forum for the course, I invite teacher candidates to engage in self-reflection by considering:

- Is there an identifiable variety of English associated with your regional context? If so, what are its characteristics?
- How well is this regional variety accepted in the context?
- How important is it for teachers of English to be aware of the features of the regional variety? How can they utilize this knowledge in their teaching?

The most commonly selected varieties are Chinese English, followed closely by New Zealand English. Examples of phonological, grammatical, and lexical differences are noted, and their relative acceptability discussed. In terms of acceptability of varieties, teacher candidates often recount personal experiences, describing their feelings of inadequacy when they feel they are unable to meet societal expectations of emulating a standardized ideal of English.

As a tutorial activity, I assign Amy Tan's essay titled *Mother Tongue* (Tan 2010) as a reading to springboard class discussions in problematizing the supremacy of the "native speaker" ideal and how stereotypes and attitudes impact identities. I ask questions such as: *Why does Tan use the words "broken" and "fractured" to refer to her mother's English? How could her language abilities be framed in more asset-based, identity-affirming ways? How does the author's experiences of using English differently in different contexts relate to your own experiences of language use?*

Following this, they work in small groups to consider ways in which attitudes toward Global Englishes could be changed, and to prepare a mini presentation. *In your groups, consider what you can do to raise awareness of varieties of English and positively influence the views and actions of others (your family and friends, colleagues, community groups). What will be the premise of your argument? What "evidence" can you use to support your argument?*

The lesson ends with an exit card activity where individuals will respond to this prompt in writing: *In no more than two sentences, explain how your learning this week has impacted your understanding of language and language teaching.* A further opportunity to engage in reflection is offered through one of the course assessments where teacher candidates can choose a topic from the syllabus to create a think-aloud and a written reflection, presenting their personal experiences with the topic, both in and out of class, and the importance of the issue in the field of TESOL. This module helps teacher candidates to arrive at the conclusion that rather than being a uniform system of communication, the English language varies in considerable ways. Learning about these variations and their implications sensitizes them to linguistic bias and encourages reflection on attitudes toward linguistic diversity.

Critical Reflections: Potentials and Challenges

One of the biggest achievements of teaching this course is that teacher candidates often report that their initial views about Global Englishes change during the course. After implementing the learning activities, teacher candidates have a more positive attitude about pluricentric English and become more accepting of the varieties associated with their own regions. They recognize that their goal of achieving a "native speaker accent" is an unnecessary one, and they begin to develop pride toward their own varieties. As many of them will go on to become teachers of English, it is promising that their learning positively impacts their identities as language users and encourages the view that Global Englishes have a place in the classroom. Although at this stage they have not begun to teach, this critical lens helps teacher candidates to gain confidence in their own linguistic strengths, and become aware of the important role their future selves can play in empowering language learners to develop a more comprehensive view of English.

These activities provide teacher candidates their first exploration of Global Englishes as a sociolinguistic phenomenon and invite them to critically reflect on their long-held language ideologies. The module is successful in raising critical awareness of the power relations and inequities that relate to language and language varieties. For some teacher candidates, their learning goes beyond awareness raising and extends to becoming advocates of justice, or "moral agents of change" (Kubanyiova and Crookes 2016: 119). For example, one of the suggestions that always come up in the presentations is that hiring policies for English teachers must be reviewed to ensure that "native speakers" are not privileged, and that student assignments for content subjects must not be penalized for language errors. As teacher candidates reevaluate the rigid view that there is one standard way to use English, they recognize monocentric views of English that marginalize the large majority of English speakers can be damaging. Being multilingual speakers of English, this focus on Global Englishes allows teacher candidates to feel pride for their own language accomplishments and patterns of English use and empowers them to take better informed decisions in their own teaching practices in the future.

Of course, not all teacher candidates are fully convinced of the value of Global Englishes. Each year, some continue to make the case that language varieties associated with standardized assessments of English such as IELTS and TOEFL are far superior to others, and that only standardized forms of English are associated with upward mobility in society. Teacher candidates more sympathetic to the idea of Global Englishes are usually quick to counter this by saying that there is much work to be done with regard to equity, suggesting their critical awareness of existing issues.

One of the limitations I acknowledge is that the resources I utilize in introducing the topic are all oral. It would be good to add textual examples of language varieties so that teacher candidates are better able to understand that the diversity extends to written language as well. As the course evolves, I would like to tie in course assessments with Global Englishes and value the use of varieties of English in course work and assessments. However, with an international group of teacher candidates, this can be a challenging endeavor for a single teacher educator.

References

Canale, M. and M. Swain (1980), "Theoretical Bases of Communicative Approaches to Second Language Teaching", *Applied Linguistics*, 1: 1–47.

Crookes, G. (2013), *Critical ELT in Action: Foundations, Promises, Praxis*, New York: Routledge.

Duff, P. (2019), "Social Dimensions and Processes in Second Language Acquisition: Multilingual Socialization in Transnational Contexts", *The Modern Language Journal*, 103 (S1): 6–22.

Kramsch, C. (2021), *Language as Symbolic Power*, Cambridge: Cambridge University Press.

Kachru, B. B. (1985), "Standards, Codification, and Sociolinguistic Realism: The English Language in the Outer Circle", in R. Quirk and H. G. Widdowson (eds), *English in the World: Teaching and Learning the Language and Literatures*, 11–30, Cambridge: Cambridge University Press.

Kachru, Y. and C. L. Nelson (2006), *World Englishes in Asian Contexts*, Aberdeen, Hong Kong: Hong Kong University Press.

Kirkpatrick, A. (2007), *World Englishes: Implications for International Communication and English Language Teaching*, Cambridge: Cambridge University Press.

Kubanyiova, M. and G. Crookes (2016), "Re-envisioning the Roles, Tasks, and Contributions of Language Teachers in the Multilingual Era of Language Education Research and Practice", *The Modern Language Journal*, 100 (S1): 117–32.

Ladson-Billings, G. (1995), "But That's just Good Teaching! The Case for Culturally Relevant Pedagogy", *Theory into Practice*, 34 (3): 159–65.

Littlewood, W. (2011), "Communicative Language Teaching: An Expanding Concept for a Changing World", in E. Hinkel (ed.), *Handbook of Research in Second Language Teaching and Learning: Volume II*, 541–57, New York: Routledge.

Lourdes, M., M. L. S. Bautista and A. B. Gonzalez (2006), "Southeast Asian Englishes", in B. B. Kachru, Y. Kachru and C. L. Nelson (eds), *The Handbook of World Englishes*, 130–44, Malden: Blackwell.

Matsuda, A. (2018), "Is Teaching English as an International Language all About Being Politically Correct?", *RELC Journal*, 49 (1): 24–35.

Mauranen, A. (2012), *Exploring ELF: Academic English Shaped by Non-native Speakers*, Cambridge: Cambridge University Press.

McKay, S. L. (2003), "Toward an Appropriate EIL Pedagogy: Re-examining Common ELT Assumptions", *International Journal of Applied Linguistics*, 13 (1): 1–22.

Monfared, A. (2018), "Ownership of English in the Outer and Expanding Circles: Teachers' Attitudes toward Pronunciation in ESL/EFL Teaching Contexts", *Asian Englishes*, 21 (2): 207–22.

Norton, B. (2013), *Identity and Language Learning: Extending the Conversation*, 2nd edn, Bristol: Multilingual Matters.

Ortega, L. (2016), "Multi-competence in Second Language Acquisition: Inroads into the Mainstream?", in V. Cook and L. Wei (eds), *The Cambridge Handbook of Linguistic Multi-Competence*, Cambridge: Cambridge University Press.

Paris, D. (2012), "Culturally Sustaining Pedagogy: A Needed Change in Stance, Terminology, and Practice", *Educational Researcher*, 41 (3): 93–7.

Rose, H. and N. Galloway (2019), *Global Englishes for Language Teaching*, Cambridge, New York, Melbourne, New Delhi: Cambridge University Press. https://doi.org/10.1017/9781316678343

Selvi, A. F. and B. Yazan (2021), *Language Teacher Education for Global Englishes: A Practical Resource Book,* Abingdon; United Kingdom: Taylor & Francis.

Tan, A. (2010), "Mother Tongue", in M. Ford and J. Ford (eds), *Dreams and Inward Journeys: A Rhetoric and Reader for Writers*, 7th edn, 34–44, New York: Pearson.

Afterword

This is a story shared by an in-service teacher who enrolled in a certificate course for teaching English as an additional language that I recently taught at a Canadian university. I shall call him Eric.

Eric was born in Germany to Chinese parents, both of whom had advanced degrees in higher education. His family moved from Germany to Canada when he was eight years old. With his parents' support, Eric was able to develop his English skills to a level comparable to that of native speakers. Although his parents made sure that Eric would acquire English as quickly as possible, they also supported his maintenance of Chinese and German at home.

However, Eric struggled with his multiple identities that seemed to canceled each other out—he was not Chinese enough for the Chinese immigrants, not perceived as German because of his physical appearance, and not aware enough of Canadian culture to be considered Canadian. Even more devastatingly, his peers in the elementary and high school constantly made jokes about Nazi Germany and called him a Nazi. After years of enduring these jokes, Eric internalized this convoluted identity despite its unreality. He considers this to be an ongoing identity crisis that has persisted even throughout his time in higher education and his teaching career during the last few years.

Eric's story shocked and disturbed me. This feeling was amplified when I went to see a one-person show of *Remnants* (Greenspan 1992) performed by Laen Hershler, our Ph.D student, at a Jewish synagogue. Remnants is based on numerous hours of interviews with Holocaust survivors conducted by Henry Greenspan, an emeritus psychologist, oral historian, and playwright at the University of Michigan. The play revealed multiple forms of harm caused by the Holocaust. Ironically, Nazi as a label linked to the horrific crime against humanity was weaponized by schoolchildren to bully Eric, an immigrant student with multiple cultural and linguistic identities, which ought to be affirmed and celebrated in multicultural Canada. It seems to me that this peculiar way of regarding him as a Nazi was perhaps triggered by his raciolinguistic and intersectional Otherness perceived by his Canadian peers. Being a Chinese immigrant in Canada alone would evoke an image of the Other; a Chinese boy moving from Germany speaking both German and Chinese may have magnified the perceived Otherness assigned to him.

This story made me realize the complexity of identities that are shaped in unexpected ways. It also raises a host of questions: Did Eric's teachers notice the act of bullying among students? What could have been done to stop bullying? What could the teachers do to promote intercultural awareness, critical multiculturalism, and antiracism to affirm students' heritage and identity? How can teachers create a safe, collaborative, and respectful learning space for all students?

Hints for the answers to these questions are offered by this book. Critical and innovative ideas from around the world can provide rich perspectives and resources for implementing critical approaches to language education in contextual ways. Teachers can use inquiry-based and dialogic approaches to raise students' awareness of linguistic, cultural, and racial difference in identities. They can also use multimodal resources, such as picture books, poems, and YouTube videos, and engage students with multimodal hands-on activities, such as creating visual images, videos, and photovoice (e.g., Mambu 2022), which can be used for critical reflections and dialogues. In the case of Eric, a teacher may consider explicitly teach about the Holocaust to raise students' historical consciousness (Stewart and Walker 2017) as well as the past-present continuity of antisemitism and other forms of racism that have led to mass atrocities. In discussing the Holocaust, the teacher will have to establish a safe learning space for students like Eric and others who may potentially be emotionally triggered by these topics.

In fact, a safe space should be secured for students to learn about many of the critical issues, including race, sexual and gender identity, and disability. If only one student is representing a particular minoritized group in a language or teacher education class, the emotional well-being of the learner needs to be safeguarded when discussing issues closely related to the identity of the learner. A tricky problem is that the learner's minoritized status may not always be known to the teacher. Some activities that require students' active participation, such as debating the pros and cons about certain queer issues (e.g., same-sex marriage, transgender bathroom access) can cause distress for learners who are not openly queer (Moore 2021). Similarly, some forms of disability that learners have may be unidentifiable to teachers. It is essential to exercise extra care and reflexivity in teaching about critical and sensitive issues.

A sense of community is also needed for students and teachers who play the role of allies. In fact, anyone can be an ally for peers or learners who have minoritized identities. Some allies may occupy the top of the privilege pyramid, while others may have a certain minoritized identity (e.g., racialized) but not others (e.g., gender, queer, disability). Being an ally requires a great deal of sensitivity, critical reflexivity, and humility. Sister Scholars (2023: 116–17) advise: "Don't speak FOR others (with different identities than your own). Do speak WITH others and learn from them. Do speak ABOUT others (share information, educate). Do speak UP FOR others (advocate, support)." Also, as an ally, you should "educate yourself, question your own assumptions, and listen to others. (But don't ask colleagues [or students] with different identities from yours to educate you; this is exhausting and not their job)." When people are genuinely trying to be allies but failing, they need encouragement and guidance, rather than derision or confrontation.

Back to the class that Eric took, the students seeking a teaching certificate—undergraduate and graduate students as well as in- and pre-service teachers—conducted an individual interview with a nonlanguage specialist about their beliefs and opinions about language acquisition, language teaching, and culture. The interview questions included whether a native speaker is the best language teacher, whether code switching is harmful for language acquisition, and so on. In class, these questions were critically discussed in relation to readings and other materials. Then, students in groups collaboratively created a script for a ten-minute skit with a plot to dramatize the interview responses. A short theoretical analysis also accompanied the script. This culminated with group performances of their skit and presentations of their analysis. The dramatized skit was similar to *Remnants*, in the sense that it was based on interviews. This is aligned in spirit with the methodology of performed ethnography (Goldstein 2001) or research-based theater (Beck et al. 2011). Despite the post-Covid challenges of mental and physical distress experience by many students, the final group performances were fantastic; they demonstrated efforts invested by all members, including the ones who had been struggling. This experience attested to the power of a collaborative and creative learning which can encourage the understanding of scholarly concepts and the exploration of critical perspectives.

This is just one example that can augment the wealth of resources and ideas offered by the authors of this book. The scope of critical English language teacher education is limitless, and educational practices that promote decolonial, anti-oppressive, and justice-oriented values and praxis should continue to be sought. The ultimate purpose is to invite students and teachers to become active agents in constructing a better world.

Ryuko Kubota
University of British Columbia

References

Beck, J. L., G. Belliveau, G. W. Lea and A. Wager (2011), "Delineating a Spectrum of Research-Based Theatre", *Qualitative Inquiry*, 17 (8): 687–700. doi:10.1177/1077800411415498.

Goldstein, T. (2001), "Hong Kong, Canada: Playwriting as Critical Ethnography", *Qualitative Inquiry*, 7 (3): 279–303. doi:10.1177/107780040100700303.

Greenspan, H. (1992), *Remnants*. https://www.henrygreenspan.com/remnants_46018.htm.

Mambu, J. E. (2022), "Co-Constructing a Critical ELT Curriculum: A Case Study in an Indonesian-Based English Language Teacher Education Program", *TESOL Journal*, 13 (3). doi:10.1002/tesj.667 (accessed January 23, 2024).

Moore, A. R. (2021), "A Plea to Stop Debating and Easing Queer Lives in ELT", *ELT Journal*, 75 (3): 361–5. doi:10.1093/elt/ccab029.

Sister Scholars (2023), "Strategies for Sisterhood in the Language Education Academy", *Journal of Language, Identity, and Education*, 22 (2): 105–20. doi:10.1080/15348458.2020.1833725.

Stewart, M. A. and K. Walker (2017), "English as a Second Language and World War II: Possibilities for Language and Historical Learning", *TESOL Journal*, 8 (1): 44–69. doi:10.1002/tesj.262.

List of Contributors

Karen Ashton is Senior Lecturer in Applied Linguistics and Language Education in the School of Humanities, Media and Creative Communication, Massey University, Aotearoa New Zealand. Karen is an experienced languages educator, actively involved in teacher education, both nationally and internationally, supporting teachers to critically reflect on and further develop their teaching practice within their unique teaching contexts. Karen also supports English language teachers through supervision on a wide range of postgraduate research projects. Karen's research interests include teacher training and professional development, language learning pedagogy with a focus on differentiation, diverse learners and learning environments, language policy and assessment.

Netta Avineri, Ph.D., is TESOL/TFL Professor and Intercultural Competence Committee Chair at the Middlebury Institute of International Studies at Monterey. She is Graduate Education and Research Pillar Lead for the Middlebury-wide Kathryn Wasserman Davis Collaborative in Conflict Transformation. Netta is also Lecturer in Critical Service-Learning and Teacher Education at California State University, Monterey Bay. Her research interests include language and social justice, heritage language education, and critical interculturality. She is co-author of *An Introduction to Language and Social Justice: What Is, What Has Been, and What Could Be* (2024) and is Series Editor for the series *Critical Approaches in Applied Linguistics*.

Perla Barbosa is an Assistant Professor in the Secondary and Higher Education and graduate TESOL program at Salem State University, MA, USA. She received her Ph.D. in curriculum and instruction from New Mexico State University and a Master's degree in applied linguistics from UMass Boston. She served as a teacher educator and university supervisor for K-12 public schools in New Mexico, USA, and as an EFL teacher in Brazil. Her research agenda, bonded with her teaching, engages education students from different content areas in dialogue to unpack the political and ideological aspects that underlie multilingual and multicultural education. Dr. Barbosa's research areas include critical pedagogy, critical literacy, and participatory action research.

Clara Vaz Bauler is Associate Professor of TESOL/Bilingual Education at Adelphi University, NY. As a sociolinguist and critical discourse analyst, she is committed to unveiling unjust and often hidden educational practices that propagate language shaming and discrimination. As a teacher educator, she is invested in pedagogical practices that validate and affirm minoritized and racialized multilingual students' knowledge, experiences, and linguistic-semiotic resources. She advocates for the naturalization of multimodality in language teaching and learning spaces via digital media technology.

Rania Boustar is a Ph.D. candidate at Sidi Mohamed Ben Abdellah University and Secondary English Teacher. Her research interests include applied language and culture studies, intercultural pragmatics, teacher education, and intercultural communication. Her most recent published work has appeared in a national magazine on ELT.

Ana Raquel Fialho Ferreira Campos is Professor at the Department of Languages and Literatures and coordinator at the Academic Writing Center at Universidade Estadual do Centro-Oeste, Brazil. Her research interests include language and teacher education and English as a Lingua Franca.

Marcia Regina Pawlas Carazzai is Professor at the Department of Languages and Literatures at Universidade Estadual do Centro-Oeste, Brazil. Her research and teaching focus on language and teacher education, teachers' and learners' identities, and English as a Lingua Franca.

Lili Cavalheiro has a Ph.D. in Applied Linguistics from the University of Lisbon and currently teaches at NOVA University of Lisbon, where she is involved in the Masters in ELT. She is also a researcher at ULICES—University of Lisbon Centre for English Studies and has participated in several European-funded projects (ILTERG, ENRICH, EUREDIE, CIRCE). Her research interests include ELF/EIL/Global Englishes, English Language Teaching, Teacher education, Materials development, and Intercultural communication. She recently edited the volume *Preparing English Language Teachers for Today's Globalized World* (2018) and co-edited *The Handbook to English as a Lingua Franca Practices for Inclusive Multilingual Classrooms* (2021).

John Chi is a Ph.D. student of Applied Linguistics and Language Education in the Department of Teaching and Learning, Policy and Leadership at the University of Maryland. His research focuses primarily on heritage language education, with an emphasis on minority dialect speakers in the context of community-based schools (i.e., after school/weekend programs). He is also interested in the role of race and identity in language education, humanizing pedagogy, teacher preparation for working with multilingual youth, TESOL, and language program evaluation.

Peter I. De Costa is Professor in the Department of Linguistics, Languages & Cultures and the Department of Teacher Education at Michigan State University. His research areas include emotions, identity, ideology, and ethics in educational linguistics. He also studies social (in)justice issues. He is the co-editor of *TESOL Quarterly* (2018–2026) and the President Elect (2023–2024) of the American Association for Applied Linguistics.

Luciana C. de Oliveira, Ph.D., is Associate Dean for Academic Affairs and Graduate Studies in the School of Education and Professor in the Department of Teaching and

Learning at Virginia Commonwealth University, Richmond, VA, USA. Her research focuses on issues related to teaching multilingual learners at the elementary and secondary levels. She served in the presidential line of TESOL International Association (2017–20) and was a member of the Board of Directors (2013–16). She was the first Latina to ever serve as President (2018–19) of TESOL.

Rabia İrem Durmuş is Research Assistant in the Department of English Language Teaching (ELT) in the Faculty of Education at Ondokuz Mayıs University, Türkiye. She received her bachelor's and master's degrees in ELT from Ondokuz Mayıs University and she is now continuing her Ph.D. at the same department. Her research interests include social justice, affective pedagogy, especially, positive psychology in language teaching, and online foreign language education.

Alex Alves Egido is Adjunct Professor at the Federal University of Maranhão (UFMA), Brazil. He holds a Ph.D. and a master's degree in Language Studies from the State University of Londrina (UEL). During his doctoral studies, he was Visiting Scholar at Michigan State University (MSU). He teaches English language disciplines in an undergraduate interdisciplinary teacher education program (UFMA). His main research interests are critical and decolonial language education, ethics in applied linguistics research, Portuguese for Speakers of Other Languages, and qualitative methodology.

Britta Freitag-Hild is Full Professor of English Language Education at the Department of English and American Studies at the University of Potsdam, Germany. She earned her Ph.D. at the Graduate Center for the Study of Culture at the University of Giessen, Germany, in 2009, and her study on British fictions of migration in the EFL classroom was awarded both the Hans-Eberhard-Piepho Prize for Communicative Language Teaching as well as the University of Giessen's prize for the best dissertation within the Faculty of Language, Literature, and Culture in 2010. Her research focuses on literature and culture pedagogy in foreign language education, inter- and transcultural learning, Black and Asian British literature and film, Education for Sustainable Development and global citizenship, as well as teacher education, genre-based approaches, and task-based language learning.

Verónica Rivera Hernández is Lecturer at Universidad Autónoma Benito Juárez de Oaxaca, Mexico. She has an MA in critical language education. Her research focuses on the experiences of migrant students and Indigenous peoples enrolled in higher education programs. She also designs educational materials for local programs.

David Gerlach is Full Professor at the University of Wuppertal, Germany, working in the School of Humanities. He earned his Ph.D. in foreign language research at the University of Marburg in 2013. In his research, he focuses on (English) language teachers and language teacher education/professional development, particularly in the context of inclusive and critical language education. He has also been involved in developing professional development opportunities for future teachers to address diversity and critical literacy. He continues to research basic literacy (in particular reading and writing), learning difficulties (in particular dyslexia), and critical language education.

Tan Arda Gedik is a PhD candidate at Friedrich-Alexander-Universität, Erlangen, Germany and Lecturer at the Department of Psychology at Bilkent University, Ankara, Turkey. He works on the effects of acquiring a writing system on L1 linguistic knowledge. His research interests are usage-based construction grammar, corpus studies, posthumanist applied linguistics as well as second language acquisition, and applied linguistics.

Elizabeth Goulette, Ph.D., is Associate Professor at Madonna University in Michigan, USA, where she serves as Program Director for Spanish and the Master of Arts in Teaching in English as a Second Language. Dr. Goulette is bilingual in English and Spanish and has taught multilingual learners of all ages. Her research interests include heritage language pedagogy and language teacher training.

Jia Gui (Ph.D.) is an adjunct instructor at Clarkson University and affiliated faculty at Virginia Commonwealth University. Her current research interests include the Language-Based Approach to Content Instruction (LACI) and teacher education for multilingual learners.

Natalie Güllü is a Ph.D. candidate and Research Assistant at the University of Wuppertal, Germany. Her research interests focus on critical (antiracist) language teacher education, critical language education, and vocational English teaching.

Özge Güney is an English instructor at Hillsborough Community College, Florida, USA. Her research interests include pre-service teacher education, Global Englishes, multiculturality, critical pedagogies as well as sexual and religious identity in the English classroom.

Graham Hall is Professor of Applied Linguistics/TESOL at Northumbria University, UK. He is the author of *Exploring English Language Teaching: Language in Action* (2011; 2nd edition, 2017), which was the winner of the 2012 British Association for Applied Linguistics (BAAL) book prize. He also edited the *Routledge Handbook of English Language Teaching* (2016), and was editor of *ELT Journal* from 2013–17. His professional interests range from classroom discourse and language teaching methodology to the ways in which English language teachers understand their practice and the role research might play in their professional development.

Kenny Harsch, now retired, worked for twenty-six years in the Department of Second Language Studies (SLS) at the University of Hawai'i at Mānoa. He served as Director of the English Language Institute and as Undergraduate Coordinator & Advisor in SLS. His professional interests include Global Englishes (especially how its concepts can be operationalized in classrooms, including developing a website that provides GE-focused materials and aims to make GE concepts easily understandable to pre- and in-service teachers), and pedagogical approaches to plagiarism and source use in academic writing.

Laura Humes Wahied is an educator who works alongside youth and families in her current role as a public school teacher in the United States. Laura centers equity, identity, culture, and community as core elements of her teaching practice.

Megan Kelley-Petersen is Associate Teaching Professor in the College of Education at the University of Washington, Seattle. As Director of the University-Accelerated Certification for Teachers (U-ACT) Program, an alternative route teacher preparation program, her scholarly research and interests include teacher preparation, equity-centered education, elementary math education, and alternative routes in teacher education.

Ceren Kocaman is a Ph.D. candidate in Applied Linguistics and Lecturer in the Department of English Language Education at the University of Potsdam, Germany. She worked with feminist and LGBTQ+ civil society organizations in Türkiye before she started teaching English in North Cyprus. Her research and teacher education practices draw from these experiences and focus on critical pedagogy, materials development, and language teacher identity and agency in critical English language teacher education settings.

Ryuko Kubota is Professor in the Department of Language and Literacy Education at University of British Columbia, where she teaches applied linguistics and language teacher education. Her research draws on critical approaches to language education, focusing on race, intersectional justice, language ideologies, and critical pedagogies. She is a co-editor of *Race, Culture, and Identities in Second Language: Exploring Critically Engaged Practice* (2009), *Discourses of Identity: Language Learning, Teaching, and Reclamation Perspectives in Japan* (2023). She has also published many journal articles and book chapters.

Michelle Kunkel is a Ph.D. candidate in the Second Language Studies Department at the University of Hawai'i at Mānoa. Her interests include second language teacher education (particularly teacher research and reflective practice), language teacher identity, Global Englishes Language Teaching, sociolinguistics, and second language writing.

Hanna Lämsä-Schmidt holds an M.A. in English Philology from the University of Tampere, Finland, and is currently working as Lecturer at the Department of English Language Education at the University of Potsdam, Germany. She is a Ph.D. candidate at the University of Potsdam and her research focuses on Vygotskyan sociocultural theory and translanguaging with young foreign language learners and heritage language speakers. For her Ph.D. research she was awarded the Junior Researcher LAB (Linguistic Approaches to Bilingualism) award for the most promising Ph.D. project at the EuroSLA conference in 2021.

Sunny Man Chu Lau is Full Professor in the School of Education at Bishop's University, Québec, and Canada Research Chair (Tier 2) in Integrated Plurilingual Teaching and Learning. She specializes in critical literacies, literature and language teaching, and related teacher education. Her research focuses on the use of plurilingual pedagogies to support language and content learning for critical engagements. She co-edited the book volume *Plurilingual Pedagogies: Critical and Creative Endeavors for Equitable Language in Education* (Lau & Van Viegen, 2020) and is a co-editor for *Critical Inquiry for Language Studies*.

Wing Shuen Lau has a Ph.D. in Education from Seattle Pacific University. She holds a Master's degree in Teaching English to Speakers of Other Languages (TESOL) and a Bachelor's in Translation. Her research work has connected perspectives in culturally responsive practice and social-emotional learning. Her recent publication is titled "Empowering English Learners in the Classroom through Culturally Responsive Social-Emotional Teaching Practices" (2022).

Priscila Leal received her Ph.D. in Second Language Studies from the University of Hawaiʻi at Mānoa and a master's degree in Curriculum and Instruction with emphasis in ESL from Arizona State University. She is a teacher educator at the College of Education at the University of Hawaiʻi at Mānoa, and the founder of Aʻo Language Education Consulting. She supervises pre-service teachers and teaches courses in Multilingual Instruction and Assessment, Multicultural Education, among others. Her research explores language teachers' development of critical consciousness and how they become and act as educators for social justice.

Kristina B. Lewis is Assistant Professor of TESOL and Applied Linguistics at Illinois State University. She teaches courses related to TESOL methods, practicum, assessment, and sociolinguistics. Her research focuses on language teacher identity development, particularly within the contexts of language teacher education. She has recently published in *Journal of Pragmatics* and *ELT Journal*.

Gabriella Licata is Postdoctoral Scholar in Spanish Critical Sociolinguistics and Language Education in the Latino and Latin American Research and Studies Center at the University of California Riverside. Gabriella's interests lie at the intersection of linguistics, anthropology, and education, where she uses mixed methodologies to uncover linguistic bias and systemic discrimination.

Angel M. Y. Lin is Professor and Tier 1 Canada Research Chair in Plurilingual & Intercultural Education at Simon Fraser University. Currently, she is also Chair Professor of Language, Literacy and Social Semiotics in Education at the Education University of Hong Kong. Her current research interests include translanguaging and trans-semiotizing (TL-TS), content and language integrated learning (CLIL), languages and literacies in science and mathematics education, critical media literacies, and social semiotics in plurilingual and pluricultural education.

Laura Loder Buechel has been a teacher trainer at the Zurich University of Teacher Education for over twenty years. She holds an undergraduate degree from LaSalle University in Philadelphia, an M.A. from Northern Arizona University and a Ph.D. from the University of Fribourg in Switzerland. She is an editor of *Babylonia*, the Swiss journal of language teaching and learning (https://babylonia.online). You can read more about her work here: https://phzh.ch/personen/laura.loder.

Mario E. López-Gopar (Ph.D., OISE/University of Toronto) is Professor at the Facultad de Idiomas, Universidad Autónoma Benito Juárez de Oaxaca, Mexico. Mario's main research interests are intercultural and multilingual education of Indigenous peoples in Mexico and decolonizing pedagogies for "English" language young learners in Mexico. His articles have appeared in the *Journal of Language Education and Identity, Applied Linguistics, ELT Journal, MEXTESOL Journal,* and the *International Journal of Multilingualism*, among others. He has also published numerous book chapters. His latest books are *Decolonizing Primary English Language Teaching* (2016) and *International Perspectives on Critical Pedagogies in ELT* (2019).

Mareen Lüke works as an educational manager in political education for youth at the educational center HVHS Hustedt. She finished her PhD at the University of Wuppertal with a focus on critical language teacher education funded by a scholarship granted by the Friedrich-Ebert-Stiftung. Her research focuses on L2 reading, language teacher education, critical pedagogy, critical literacy, and the internationalization of language teacher education.

Seyyed-Abdolhamid Mirhosseini is Associate Professor at the University of Hong Kong. His research areas include the sociopolitics of language education, qualitative research methodology, and critical studies of discourse in society. His writing has appeared in journals including *Applied Linguistics; Language, Identity and Education; Critical Inquiry in Language Studies;* and *TESOL Quarterly*. Among other books, he has co-edited *The Sociopolitics of English Language Testing* (2020), and his most recent book is *Doing Qualitative Research in Language Education* (2020). He is currently co-editing a volume on *Critical English Medium Instruction in Higher Education* (forthcoming).

Naashia Mohamed is Senior Lecturer of TESOL at the University of Auckland, New Zealand. Her teaching and research contribute to understanding how school and society can empower racially and linguistically marginalized children, youth, and families to achieve greater social equity. Through her scholarship, Naashia illustrates how home languages serve as powerful resources for students, helping them not only to attain academic success, but to promote second language and literacy development. Her publications critically analyze educational policies and practices in the Maldives and New Zealand contexts to promote those that validate multilingual learners' assets while building on their ethnolinguistic identities.

Hillary Parkhouse, Ph.D., is Associate Professor at the Virginia Commonwealth University School of Education. Her research focuses on how teacher education and professional development can support culturally relevant education and sociopolitical consciousness for teachers and students. She teaches courses on TESOL, curriculum, and teacher education.

Deniz Ortaçtepe Hart is Lecturer in the TESOL programs at the University of Glasgow. Before coming to Glasgow, Dr. Ortaçtepe Hart worked at the University of Leeds (UK), Middlebury Institute of International Studies at Monterey (USA) and Bilkent University (Türkiye). Her research interests are second language socialization, intercultural pragmatics, sociolinguistics, and social justice language education. She has published in *Language Teaching, Intercultural Pragmatics, Teaching and Teacher Education, Journal of Language Identity and Education, System, TESOL Quarterly*, and *Language and Intercultural Communication*. Her book *Social Justice and the Language Classroom: Reflection, Action and Transformation* was published in May 2023.

Yesenia Bautista Ortiz is Lecturer at Universidad Autónoma Benito Juárez de Oaxaca, Mexico. She has an M.A. in critical language education. Her research focuses on the life stories and identity construction of Indigenous peoples and migrant people from Oaxaca. She collaborated in the creation of an educational guide for teachers regarding the needs of transborder students.

Kellie Rolstad is Associate Professor of Applied Linguistics and Language Education at the University of Maryland. Professor Rolstad earned her Ph.D. in Education at UCLA, where she also earned degrees in Linguistics (BA) and Applied Linguistics (MA). Before becoming a professor, she was a bilingual teacher in Los Angeles. Her research interests include the language of schooling, language diversity, translanguaging, alternative learning outcomes, and democratic education, and her work has appeared in the *Bilingual Research Journal, Bilingual Review, Teachers College Record, Hispanic Journal of Behavioral Sciences, Educational Policy, Annual Review of Applied Linguistics, Educational Policy*, and in major edited collections.

Benachour Saidi holds a PhD in cross-disciplinary Intercultural Communication and Relations, Mohammed First University in Morocco. He is a lecturer of English at the Higher School of School of Education and Training. His research examines intercultural communication and education in the Global South, social justice in teacher education, decoloniality and the geo-politics of language education. His works have been published in several reputable peer-reviewed journals, including *British Journal of Educational Studies, International Journal of Intercultural Relation, Compare: A Journal of Comparative and International Education* and *Saudi Journal of Language Studies*.

Ali Fuad Selvi is Assistant Professor of TESOL and Applied Linguistics in the MA TESOL Program at the Department of English at the University of Alabama, USA. His research interests include Global Englishes and its implications for language learning, teaching, teacher education, and language policy/planning; English-medium instruction, issues related to (in)equity, privilege, marginalization, and discrimination in TESOL; and critical English language teacher education. In addition to his scholarship and leadership in these areas, he was recognized as one of TESOL International Association's *30 Up and Coming Leaders* in recognition of his potential to "shape the future of both the association and the profession for years to come."

Roxanna Senyshyn, Ph.D., is Associate Professor of Applied Linguistics and Communication Arts and Sciences at Abington College, Pennsylvania State University. She teaches undergraduate and postgraduate courses in English as a second language education and undergraduate courses in applied linguistics and intercultural communication. Her research interests include three strands. Her current focus is on transformative intercultural learning in pre-service teacher education and the professional development of language teachers throughout their careers. The other strands of her research center on English learners in higher education with an emphasis on second language writing assessment and sociolinguistic integration of international students.

Shawna Shapiro is Professor of Writing and Linguistics at Middlebury College. Her research focuses on college transitions for immigrant and refugee-background students, and on inclusive and innovative approaches to multilingual/L2 writing instruction. She has published in numerous peer-reviewed journals, including *TESOL Quarterly, TESOL Journal,* and *Journal of Language, Identity & Education*. She has published books with TESOL/NAFSA and Multilingual Matters, and her third book, *Cultivating Critical Language Awareness in the Writing Classroom*, was published in 2022. Dr. Shapiro is also involved in several initiatives aimed at promoting educational equity for English Learners in her local community.

Sibel Söğüt holds a Ph.D. degree from Anadolu University and an MA from Anadolu University. She is currently working as Assistant Professor in the English Language Teaching Department at Sinop University, Türkiye. She has participated in research projects funded by the Scientific and Technological Research Council of Turkey and Scientific Research Projects in Higher Education Institutions. She has research interests in pre-service teacher training, language testing, second language writing, data-driven learning, and corpus linguistics.

Yasemin Tezgiden-Cakcak, Ph.D., is a scholar at the Foreign Language Education Department of Middle East Technical University in Ankara, Türkiye. Her research interests include critical pedagogy, L2 teacher education, and critical applied linguistics. She problematized teacher roles, native-speakerism, and mainstream teacher education in her publications. She has authored a book on her own critical teacher education practices in Türkiye titled *Moving beyond Technicism in English Language Teacher Education* (2019). She is one of the associate editors of the book titled *A Language of Freedom and Teacher's Authority: Case Comparisons from Turkey and the United States* (2017).

Laura Torres-Zúñiga holds a Ph.D. in English Studies from the University of Granada, a postgraduate Expert Diploma in Virtual Learning Environments from the University of Malaga and a postgraduate Expert Diploma in University Teaching Methodologies from Universidad Autónoma de Madrid-UAM. She is Assistant Professor at the Department of Philologies and Didactics of UAM, where she teaches English, syllabus design, and children's literature to pre-service teachers of different educational levels. She belongs to the research group Discourse Analysis and Intercultural Communication and her research interests center on contemporary short narrative forms, English language teaching, and active learning methodologies.

Mai Trang Vu is Associate Professor of TESOL Teacher Education, Department of Language Studies, Umeå University, Sweden. Her research interests include teacher education, teacher professionalism, teacher professional development, critical pedagogy, the multilingual classroom, education policy, English as a(n) Second/Foreign/Additional Language.

Adnan Yılmaz is Lecturer and Director of the TESOL programs at the University of Stirling. Before his employment at Stirling, Dr. Yılmaz worked at Sinop University and Dicle University in Türkiye and the University of Arizona in the United States where he also received his doctoral degree. His research interests include language teacher education, intercultural communication, social justice language education, and educational technologies. He has published in *Computers and Education, the Reading Matrix,* and *Contemporary Educational Technology*, along with co-investigating projects on social justice language education.

Index

action research 82, 89, 100–2, 135, 148–51
advocacy 30, 38, 42
   advocacy plan 44, 47
antiracism 71–4, 176, 268 (*see also* textbooks)
assessment
   alternative assessment 117
   assessment literacy 113–15
   critical language assessment 115
   high-stakes testing 116–17
   international testing 116
   measurementism 115
   psychometrics 115
   testing 8, 113–16
   testing industry 116
   washback 116
asset-based approach 29, 141–2, 263

classroom management 79–80, 87–90, 95, 105–8
classroom observation 80–1, 94–5
communicative language teaching 20–1, 242
community 34, 44, 54, 84, 95–6, 141, 143, 155, 161, 166, 175, 219–20, 224, 230, 232, 233, 263, 268
   community agreements 42
content area instruction 142
coursebooks (*see* materials and textbooks)
crip perspective 156, 158, 161
criticality
   critical action 53
   critical awareness 82, 83, 99, 100, 114, 192, 217, 264
   critical consciousness 35, 52, 53, 55, 190, 262
   Critical English Language Teacher Education 23, 52, 82, 99, 269
   critical incident 43, 88
   critical intercultural education 223, 227

Critical Language Awareness (CLA) 27–30, 171–6, 249
critical literacy 191, 211, 214, 215
critical materials analysis development and use 54–6
   operationalizing 4
critical reflection 5, 34, 35, 43, 53, 54, 87, 88, 117, 135, 163, 212–13, 257, 268
critical pedagogy 3, 4, 27, 34, 54–5, 190, 215, 247
culture and culturality (*see also* interculturality)
   cultural awareness 218, 226
   cultural contexts 211
   cultural knowledge 211
   culture pedagogy 209–14

decoloniality 131, 134, 136
dialects 31, 262
diversity
   cultural diversity 220, 222, 226
   linguistic diversity 11, 28, 66, 67, 68, 247, 262, 263
drama-based instruction 197–200

e-tutoring partnership 166–8
Education for Sustainable Development (ESD) 195–9, 210
English as a Lingua Franca (ELF) 5, 116, 239, 240–2
   ELF-aware teacher education 242
English as an International Language (EIL) 116, 239, 240–2
equity 34, 38, 80, 87, 134, 148, 151, 172, 190, 262 (*see also* inequity)
experiential learning 195, 197, 198

family and community engagement 232

Index

gender equality 34, 35, 221
global citizenship 176, 209–15
Global Englishes (GE)
    attitudes toward 249, 263
    GE awareness 242
    GE users 247, 249
    Global Englishes Language Teaching (GELT) 59, 60–2, 239, 241–2, 248, 251
    video materials for GELT 249–51

homophobia 105–8
humanizing pedagogy 27, 83, 115

identity
    learner identity 81, 95, 149, 150, 171, 190–1, 241, 242, 254, 256, 263, 268
    sexual identity 105, 106
    social identity 22
    teacher identity 14, 79, 81, 83, 84, 99, 100, 102, 149, 151, 156, 157, 159, 254
ideologies
    language ideologies 27, 30, 42, 158, 250, 253, 254, 257, 258, 260, 264
    standard language ideology 27, 29, 156, 247, 250
immigrant families 231, 233, 234
inclusion 53, 81, 172, 187, 218, 219, 221
indigenous peoples 72, 73, 134, 135
individual differences 179, 196
inequality 34, 101, 102, 168, 174, 230
    social 3, 5, 101, 210, 229
inequity 27, 33, 148, 190, 230, 262, 264
interculturality 10, 223, 224, 225, 227, 229, 232 (*see also* culture and culturality)
    intercultural communication 10, 230, 231, 253
    intercultural communication education 223
    intercultural communicative competence (ICC) 210, 218, 220, 221
    intercultural education 223–5, 227

language ownership 61, 113, 117
    ownership of English 240, 241, 249, 261
language policing 161
language policy 93–6, 201

language teacher education (LTE)
    critical language teacher education (CLTE) 43, 53, 79, 80, 81, 82, 113, 114, 115, 117, 131, 132, 134, 135, 136
    language teacher education programs (TEP) 5, 13, 28, 29, 30, 51, 52, 53, 65, 79, 105, 108, 155, 158, 187, 191, 192, 227
    located LTE 23
    pre-service teacher education 30, 34
    primary teacher education 195, 201
    social justice language teacher education (SJLTE) 33–4, 38
language teaching methods
    postmethod 19–20, 22–4, 87
    principled eclecticism 22
    principled pragmatism 22
language variation 28, 31, 175
language-based approach to content instruction (LACI) 141–5
LGBTQ+ 34, 53, 105–9, 163
linguistic imperialism 11, 241, 247
linguistic justice 28
linguistic repertoire 67, 165, 168, 173, 176, 239, 259
linguistically responsive teaching 66
literacy instruction 147, 150, 151

materials (*see also* textbooks)
    analysis and development 13, 54–8
    as cultural, ideological, and commercial artifacts 53
    culturally and linguistically responsive (CLR) 66, 67, 68
multilinguality
    multicultural education 65
    multilingual competence 202
    multilingual learners (MLs) 65–9, 141–4
    multilingual pedagogy 205
    multilingualism 28, 134, 144, 159, 202, 203, 242

native speaker (NS)
    as teachers 264, 269
    construct 157, 181, 241, 247, 261, 263

fallacy 179, 180, 181
idealization 116, 239, 259, 263
model 157
native speakerism 115–16, 117, 250
norms 61, 113, 115, 248
needs analysis 89–90
neoliberalism 51, 53, 55, 82–3, 187–8
non-native speaker (NNS)
   as teachers 179, 180, 181, 241, 242
   construct 157, 158, 247

power 19, 22, 24, 27, 33, 34, 38, 41, 74, 82, 83, 99, 101, 211, 215, 230
   coloniality 156
   in critical language teacher education 134
   in discourse 133
   in international testing 116
   in lesson planning 101
   in reflection 101
   in teacher identity 150, 158, 159, 192
practicum 7, 81–3, 94, 99, 101, 102, 135, 229
praxicum 135
praxis 4, 6, 24, 41, 42, 44, 54, 115, 136
praxization 5, 11, 12
print exposure 179
professional
   development 5, 20, 93, 171, 172, 195
   identity (*see* identity)
project-based learning 66

raciolinguistic(s)
   ideologies 155, 158, 159, 253
   perspective 156, 158, 159, 161
racism 71–4, 158 (*see also* antiracism)
reflection
   critical 23, 34, 35, 41, 43, 44, 53, 54, 59, 67, 87, 88, 89, 90, 94, 117, 136, 209, 210, 213, 214, 221, 231, 233
   for-action 88, 89, 90
   implicit 83
   in-action 88, 89, 147, 150
   meta 82
   on-action 88, 89, 198
   pre- 202
   reflective tasks/practices 83, 88, 90, 101–2, 136, 160, 167, 173, 197, 249, 257
   self 27, 30, 31, 34, 42, 81, 82, 83, 84, 103, 114, 149, 151, 159, 171, 191, 201, 202, 210, 225, 242, 258
reflective practitioners 218, 229
reflexivity 198, 223, 268
register 157, 175
restorative justice circle 175

second language acquisition (SLA) 131, 155, 161, 174, 181
second language development 9, 168, 176, 253
semiotic resources 132, 133, 135
social injustice 7, 99, 101, 192, 212
social justice 10, 11, 13, 19, 24, 33–7, 38, 41–4, 107, 108
   eco-social justice 134
   in intercultural education 223
   in literacy instruction 171
   in multilingual pedagogies 190
   in teacher education 134, 136, 147, 192, 262, 264, 269 (*see also* language teacher education)
   in teaching English to young learners 195
   in testing 116
   social and cognitive justice 134
   social justice praxis 6, 41, 43, 44
   social justice-based pedagogies 33
sociocultural
   concerns 114
   context 8, 58
   diversity 220
   theories 203
   variables 106
   variation 203
standard language 27, 28, 30, 116, 155, 256 (*see also* ideologies)
sustainability 195

teacher educators 12–14, 20, 30, 41, 54, 55, 56, 68, 81, 82, 83–4, 114, 135, 136, 145, 176, 190, 243, 258

teacher(s)
  agency 14, 21, 38, 51, 147, 150, 195
  as transformative intellectuals 34, 35, 38, 53, 82, 147
  autonomy 22, 51
  empowerment 21, 22, 44, 52, 152, 182, 262, 264
  English Language Arts (ELA) 171, 173
  in-service 5, 93, 95, 99, 103, 114, 217, 227, 243, 267
  of English Learners (ELs) 171, 172, 174, 176
  pre-service 5, 28–32, 34, 38, 81, 82, 83, 105–8, 123, 125, 159, 202, 203, 217, 247–51
  student teachers 54–5, 81, 126, 195, 197–8, 201, 203, 224, 225, 226, 227
  teacher candidates 53, 68, 71–4, 141, 166–8, 180, 223, 224, 225, 229, 230, 231, 258, 262, 263, 264
  teacher learners 13, 59–62, 66–8

teaching philosophy 83, 88
tension 41–4, 105
textbooks 51, 52, 53, 54, 56, 59–61, 72–4, 101, 121–3, 188, 248 (*see also* materials)
  critical antiracist textbook analysis 72, 74
  critical textbook analysis 71, 72
transknowledging 131, 134, 136
translanguaging 29, 32, 131, 133, 134, 136, 161, 165, 167, 242, 243, 256, 258
  pedagogies 143, 171, 258
  perspectives 156, 159, 161
  spaces 167, 168
  stance 159, 161, 165
translingual strategies 254, 257, 260
trans-semiotizing 131, 132

virtual exchanges (VEs) 217–21

World Englishes (WE) 116, 117, 237, 240, 241, 242, 253, 258, 262

young learners 187, 189, 195–8, 201

www.ingramcontent.com/pod-product-compliance
Lightning Source LLC
Chambersburg PA
CBHW071806300426
44116CB00009B/1214